Images of England through Popul

Also by Keith Gildart

NORTH WALES MINERS: A Fragile Unity, 1945–1996

DICTIONARY OF LABOUR BIOGRAPHY Vol. XI (*co-editor*)

INDUSTRIAL POLITICS AND THE 1926 MINING LOCKOUT: The Struggle for Dignity (*co-editor*)

DICTIONARY OF LABOUR BIOGRAPHY Vol. XII (*co-editor*)

DICTIONARY OF LABOUR BIOGRAPHY Vol. XIII (*co-editor*)

THE COAL INDUSTRY IN VICTORIAN BRITAIN Vol. 6: Industrial Relations and Trade Unionism (*editor*)

Images of England through Popular Music

Class, Youth and Rock 'n' Roll, 1955–1976

Keith Gildart
Reader in Labour and Social History, University of Wolverhampton

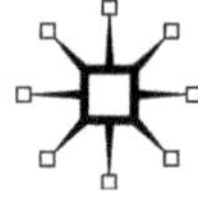

Softcover reprint of the hardcover 1st edition 2013
Corrected Printing 2013

First published 2013 by
PALGRAVE MACMILLAN

Palgrave Macmillan in the UK is an imprint of Macmillan Publishers Limited, registered in England, company number 785998, of Houndmills, Basingstoke, Hampshire RG21 6XS.

Palgrave Macmillan in the US is a division of St Martin's Press LLC, 175 Fifth Avenue, New York, NY 10010.

Palgrave Macmillan is the global academic imprint of the above companies and has companies and representatives throughout the world.

Palgrave® and Macmillan® are registered trademarks in the United States, the United Kingdom, Europe and other countries

ISBN 978-1-349-28582-2 ISBN 978-1-137-38425-6 (eBook)
DOI 10.1007/978-1-137-38425-6

This book is printed on paper suitable for recycling and made from fully managed and sustained forest sources. Logging, pulping and manufacturing processes are expected to conform to the environmental regulations of the country of origin.

A catalogue record for this book is available from the British Library.

A catalog record for this book is available from the Library of Congress.

Contents

Acknowledgements

This book has been a long time in the making. My interest in the continuities and changes in twentieth century working-class culture was initially sparked by research on the politics of trade unionism in the British coal industry. Much of my early work in the field of labour history had an institutional focus on organisations, parties and industrial conflicts. Yet through my involvement in a number of oral history and ethnographic projects in coal mining communities, it was apparent that labour politics and trade unionism represented just one facet of class-consciousness. My interviews, discussions and informal conversations with coal miners and other industrial workers showed that the post-1945 cultural life of the British working-class reflected, reinforced and sometimes challenged occupational, political and social identities. Far from undermining collective identities in working-class localities, aspects of popular culture such as affluence, consumption, music and fashion played an essential role in reinforcing them. This realisation allowed me to move out of an institutional framework and to explore the creation, consumption and absorption of working-class culture. I was especially interested in challenging the notion that a particular type of working-class culture was being diluted by affluence and de-industrialisation in the 1960s. It seemed to me that the arbitrary distinction made by many sociologists, historians and contemporary observers between a pre-war working-class culture of trade unions, working mens' clubs, pubs, brass bands, folk music, dance halls and new forms of youth culture that emerged in the post-war period was problematic. The result of such an excavation of working-class culture, youth identities and popular music is contained in this book.

This work is the outcome of many years of thinking about the relationship between class, youth and popular music. The project has taken me through council estates in North West England, the suburbs of Liverpool and the coffee bars and clubs of Manchester and London. I have spoken to coal miners, factory workers, migrants, American servicemen, Teddy Boys, Mods and glam rockers who allowed me to take them back to their youth of home, workplace, dance hall, record shop, café and concert hall. In particular, I would like to thank Ronnie Carr (the Lemon Drop Kid) for the many hours talking about his exploits in the coal mine, on the dance floor and on the concert stage, while poring over his diaries, photographs, music industry ephemera and for providing the cover photograph of him on stage with the Beat Boys at the Bolton Palais in 1960. Many others such as Mike O'Neil, Terri Quaye, Lloyd Johnson, Jimmy James, Count Prince Miller, Linden Kirby, Eddie Amoo, Richard Barnes and Bill Harry were gracious with their time and must have been exhausted by my enthusiasm, repeated questions, telephone calls and emails. Friends and acquaintances have also been crucial in seeing this book through to publication and have endured many conversations, comments, critiques and rants concerning class, politics, youth culture and the relative merits of obscure songs by Georgie Fame, the Kinks, the Who, Elvis Presley, Solomon Burke and Bruce Springsteen. In no particular order, thanks go to Kevin Jones, Gidon Cohen, Laurence Brown, Matt Worley, Lucy Robinson, Angela Bartie, Andrew Perchard, Ed Amann, Chris Thompson, Barry Pikesley, Dave Metcalfe, Gary Snowden, David Howell, Neville Kirk, Terry Wyke (thanks for the index) Harry Knowles, Stephen Catterall, Russ Taylor, Ben Harker, John Street, Bill Osgerby (and the rest of the Subcultures Network), Hugh Jones (and the rest of the 'secret six'). A very special thanks to all the coal miners of North Wales who had to endure my particular idiosyncrasies in many long shifts underground, on the 'pit-bus' and in the pubs and clubs of Mostyn, Prestatyn and Rhyl.

Two institutions have been crucial in enabling me to carry out research and teach courses on working-class politics, culture and popular music. The University of Wolverhampton has been my academic home since 2004 and has provided generous financial support, a decent working environment and a culture of collegiality that has led to the publication of this book. The fact that the university has managed to do this in a higher education funding regime that favours 'elite' institutions and fails to adequately recognise the work that Wolverhampton has done in attracting working-class and minority students and maintain close links with its local communities is more than admirable. I would like to thank academic staff members who have discussed aspects of my research in the seminar room, coffee bar and pub: Paul Henderson, Simon Constantine, Glyn Hambrook, Mike Cunningham, Chris Norton, Eamonn O' Kane, Martin Durham, Mark Jones, Alan Apperley, Aidan Byrne, John Benson, John Buckley, Laura Ugolini, Mike Dennis, Malcolm Wanklyn, David Hussey, Margaret Ponsonby, and Ros Watkiss. I would also like to thank all the undergraduate and postgraduate students who made a contribution to the two modules in which the ideas for this book were developed. The University of Michigan also provided me with the opportunity to spend six months in Ann Arbor in 2009, where I taught British working-class history to enthusiastic American undergraduates. At Michigan, I was particularly grateful for the support given by Geoff Eley, Kali Israel, Angela Dowdell, the regulars at Ashley's Bar and Grill and Weber's ultra lounge.

Libraries and librarians and archives and archivists have played an essential role in the creation of this book. I would like to thank the staff of the Manchester Central Library, Liverpool Central Library, the British Library, the British Newspaper Library (Colindale), Leigh Library and Wigan Library. Also, the libraries of the following universities: Wolverhampton, Manchester, Manchester Metropolitan, Sussex, Liverpool and Liverpool John Moores. Archives worthy of the highest accolades are the National Archives (London),

Liverpool Record Office, the Peoples' History Museum (Manchester), the Police Museum (Manchester), Mass Observation Archive (Sussex), the North West Film Archive (Manchester), Churchill College (Cambridge) and the Modern Records Centre (Warwick). The archival sources and my attempt to make sense of them have been presented in a range of academic forums. I would like to thank the following institutions for allowing me to present my research to a critical audience: University of Bangor, University of Reading, University of Manchester, University of Salford, University of Texas (Austin), University of Illinois (Chicago) and the State University of New York (Stonybrook).

The material for two chapters has been published in earlier versions as journal articles. Chapter 6 appeared as 'From Dead End Streets to Shangri Las: Negotiating Social Class and Post-War Politics with Ray Davies and the Kinks', *Contemporary British History*, 26, 3 (September 2012) 273–98 (Abingdon: Taylor & Francis), and I acknowledge Taylor and Francis for permission to reprint this material. Chapter 8 appeared as 'The Antithesis of Humankind: Exploring Responses to the Sex Pistols Anarchy Tour 1976', *Cultural and Social History*, 10, 1 (2013) 129–49 (London: Bloomsbury), and I acknowledge Bloomsbury for permission to reprint this material. I would also like to thank the following for permission to reproduce the extracts for the epigraphs that appear in parts 1, 2 and 3 and subsequent material contained in particular chapters: Margareta Berger-Hamerschlag, *Journey Into Fog*, Victor Gollancz, 1955 © Raymond Berger; John Townshend, *The Young Devils*, Chatto and Windus, 1958. Reprinted by permission of The Random House Group; T. R. Fyvel, *The Insecure Offenders*, Random House, 1961. Reprinted by permission of The Random House Group; Sid Chaplin, *The Day of the Sardine*, 1961 © Michael Chaplin; Ray Gosling, *Sum Total*, 1961 © Pomona Books. Extracts from *Jackie* © DC Thomson & Co. Ltd. 2013; extracts from *Mersey Beat* © Bill Harry; extracts from *Daily Mirror* © mirrorpix. Material from Mass Observation reproduced with permission of Curtis Brown Group Ltd, London on behalf of The Trustees of the Mass Observation Archive. Copyright © The Trustees of the Mass Observation Archive. Every effort has been made to trace copyright holders, and the author and publisher will be happy to correct any mistakes or omissions in future editions.

I would also like to thank the anonymous readers and everyone at Palgrave Macmillan for ensuring the smooth publication of the book. It is already causing arguments in the pubs, clubs, record shops and concerts that I frequent. In my view this is how history should be received. Ultimately the book is just my personal attempt to reconstruct a particular period and provide insights and impressions of the relationship between class, popular music and English society. There will be many more histories, but this one, along with its strengths, weaknesses and idiosyncrasies is just mine.

My final thanks must go to my family for living with this book for too long. Class, politics and popular culture have been part of my domestic, occupational and social world since childhood. In my memory, family, community, labour politics, trade unionism and popular music were core components of the working-class milieu in which I was embedded. I would like to thank my parents Brian and Sheila Gildart and my sisters Bev, Lorraine and Gill (gone but never forgotten). Thanks also to Lee, Nicola, Gareth, Jonathan, Leanne and Cousin John (you all know where I am if you need me). My wife Kirsten has had to deal with my trials and tribulations in getting all the research for this project into a finished product, and I will be forever grateful for her patience and understanding. And last, but definitely not least, this book is dedicated to my daughter Ellie Anne Gildart, the light of my life, true inspiration and the ultimate sweet little rock 'n' roller.

Introduction

This book explores the relationship between English working-class youth and popular music between the years 1955 and 1976. It analyses the development of popular music and its reaction to and impact on the economic, social, cultural and political aspects of English society. The text is not a comprehensive history of the music business or an overarching study of youth in the post-war period. The primary aim is to provide a historical reconstruction of the way in which a selection of mostly working-class performers and consumers used popular music to experience, explore and construct notions of continuity and change in English society. The book presents the reader with a selection of episodes, impressions and images of England that capture the importance of popular music in the 'everyday life' of working-class youth. The conception of popular music used is narrowly defined referring to American 'rock 'n' roll' and 'rhythm and blues', which emerged in the early 1950s and the associated sounds that grew out of those genres.[1] Arguments can be made for a more general conceptualisation of 'popular', but the approach taken throughout the text is that American 'rock 'n' roll and 'rhythm and blues' had a more significant social, cultural and political impact on working-class youth than other forms of popular music, in terms of defining aspects of their culture and reflecting, shaping and sometimes challenging a particular sense of individual and collective identity.

The chronological narrative and analytical framework engages with key aspects of English social history such as de-industrialisation, affluence, consumption, working-class identities/experiences and shifting conceptions of locality, race, gender, sexuality and nation. The book explores the ways in which popular music and associated youth subcultures such as Teddy Boys, Mods, Rockers, Skinheads, Glam Rockers and Punks impacted on individual and collective responses to continuities and changes in the realm of leisure activities, personal relationships, politics, social class and ways of reading and understanding England and Englishness. Each of the eight chapters examines the ways in which the creation, performance, consumption and absorption of popular music formed part of a working-class culture that remained a significant feature of English life through to end of the twentieth century.[2]

What follows is a history of post-war England with popular music and youth culture at its centre. First, through a biographical focus on a selection of artists/writers/performers, the book examines the ways in which major emblematic figures in the field of popular music understood and engaged with social change through their personal, musical, geographical and intellectual journeys. Second, the study considers how popular music had a specific impact on English working-class youth through the reinforcement and transformation of particular social identities linked to locality, race, gender, sexuality and nation. Third, there is an emphasis on how popular music was crucial in transforming public spaces in particular localities and defining and constructing new ones through the creation of musical genres, youth subcultures and social scenes. Fourth, the book highlights the experiences of working-class youth in their consumption of popular music through performance, concert attendance and identity construction. The primary argument presented here is that popular music made a significant contribution to the 'everyday life' of English youth and represents an underexplored facet of the resilience of class in the post-war period.

Popular music and youth culture is an area that has remained stubbornly resistant to the focus of academic historians.[3] Straw has argued that it is 'among the most ubiquitous, easily ignored and trivialised of all cultural forms'.[4] Yet throughout the post-war period popular music permeated diverse forms of media and provided a daily soundtrack to a whole generation of English working-class youth in the home, the workplace, coffee bars, pubs, clubs, dance halls and theatres. The last few years have seen a whole array of commercially produced books, articles, magazines, films and television programmes on popular music produced outside of the academy and primarily for the consumption of the general public.[5] Yet the historians' gaze has bypassed the development, impact and experience of popular music on the individual and collective identities of working-class youth.[6] The few who have noted the significance of its arrival in the 1950s have either sought to downplay the claims that have been made for its perceived role in social change or simply made passing reference to it in their more general surveys of the period.[7]

The parameters of the historical debate on the social impact of popular music and youth culture were set by Marwick's extensive examination of the 1960s and the subsequent revisionist critiques of his work.[8] Marwick claimed that the decade was a significant period in unleashing new social and political forces in which popular music played a key role. In contrast, Sandbrook and Fowler point to the continuities in youth culture from the pre-war period and argue that popular music had only a marginal impact on social and political developments. Both positions created 'myths' and 'counter myths', but ultimately fell short of problematising the complex interaction between locality, class, race, gender, sexuality, nationality, creativity and consumption that this book seeks to explore.

The Birmingham Centre for Contemporary Cultural Studies (CCCS)

The CCCS established in 1964 casts a long shadow over much of the literature on popular music and youth culture. The CCCS produced a range of books and articles suggesting that elements of working-class youth culture and popular music could be read as forms of resistance posing a challenge to particular aspects of capitalist society.[9] Richard Hoggart and Stuart Hall laid a methodological foundation for linking developments in popular culture to changing aspects of work, locality and economic transformation. Hoggart's *The Uses of Literacy* (1957) remains the first port of call for scholars in gauging the intellectual reaction to the popular music and youth culture of the 1950s.[10] Famously scathing about the impact of jukeboxes and coffee bars, the book is compelling in its construction of a 'near mythical' working-class culture being swept away by the forces of affluence, consumption and American popular culture.[11] In contrast, Stuart Hall and the Marxist literary theorist Raymond Williams were far more sympathetic to developments in 'popular' forms of consumption and their work on class and culture informs the themes explored in the following chapters. According to Williams, the 'working class does not become bourgeois by owning... new products, any more than the bourgeois ceases to be bourgeois as the objects he owns changes in kind'.[12] This book is deliberately light on theory and concentrates more on reconstructing individual and collective experiences through archival sources, oral testimony, song, performance and concert attendance. Primarily the aim is to historicise the claims made by the CCCS by providing examples of meeting points between class, race, gender and musical genres and their impact on social, political, sexual and national identity.

Much work on youth culture, class and popular music has tended to 'centre' theory at the expense of narrative, empirical detail and the reconstruction of significant episodes, genres and interventions. The organising theoretical concepts applied in this text are applied quite loosely and owe much to the CCCS tradition and a Marxist history that views culture as an important aspect of working-class identity, experience and struggle. Although its meaning, utility and applicability is much contested, Williams's conception of 'structure of feeling' is adopted to highlight aspects of youth culture and suggesting that a sense and experience of class could be felt through both economic and cultural activities. The concept of 'structure of feeling' appears in a number of Williams's writings and is often presented in a complicated and convoluted manner. However, I take its meaning in its most basic form as a way in which the working class experienced economic and social life in cultural terms or, in the words of Williams, 'thought as felt and feeling as thought'.[13] Such a conception of a sense of class perhaps encapsulates the power of music to generate individual and collective responses to the sound, tone and rhythm of particular songs and how they articulated a reinforcement of, or flight from, a feeling of class. Williams's notion of a 'structure of feeling' was concerned mostly with the creation and consumption of particular types of literature, but I would argue that it has some utility when exploring the relationship between working-class performers and consumers of popular music. In the same way that Williams claims that novelists attempted to make sense of a changing England in the nineteenth century, an influential group of emblematic performers in the post-war period also expressed a 'structure of feeling'.[14] This emerged in the form of popular music and youth culture in response to the changes taking place in the industrial sector of the British economy and the pressures brought to bear on working-class communities.

Between 1955 and 1976 popular music provided many working-class youths with a 'structure of feeling' that connected them to a culture that was in decline, but one that continued to leave traces in the individual and collective memory.[15] To many of the performers and consumers examined in the book, class remained important, shaped the way in which they looked at English society and provided both an 'imaginary' and, in many cases, a 'real' experience of collective identity. A sense or feeling of class was both maintained and transformed through involvement in music making, consumption and youth culture. In Williams's view, culture was one dimension of social life where the working-class could make sense of their position in the workplace, community and wider society.[16] To Hoggart, this relationship between identity and culture was beginning to fragment in the middle of the twentieth century. The examination of popular music that follows suggests that such a characterisation of the fragility of class is problematic. For Williams, working-class culture was rooted in and emerged from particular social experiences. The images, impressions and episodes that form the basis of this book shed light on such working-class experiences and how they were lived and expressed through popular music and youth culture.

A seminal text that came out of the CCCS tradition that sought to theorise the relationship between class and youth culture was Dick Hebdige's, *Subculture: The Meaning of Style*.[17] Hebdige saw popular music and the creation of working-class youth subcultures as emerging from the experience of economic instability creating 'symbolic resistance' to the particular contours of capitalist society.[18] Through this framework, he explored the connection between youth subcultures and West Indian migration and how this axis formed the basis of particular youth styles, scenes and sources of identity in the 1960s and 1970s. Yet as with many of the sociological texts of the period, the source base that Hebdige and others utilised was very narrow, rendering much of the work theoretically innovative but empirically weak. Historians can now re-examine some of the periods, genres, and youth subcultures uncovered by the CCCS with the benefit of a much broader range of sources and a critical distance from the then contemporary debates within the discipline of sociology.[19]

The work of the CCCS has been critiqued from a variety of theoretical positions and through the utilisation of more sophisticated social science methodologies. Feminist scholars have argued that the CCCS focus was predominantly on young men and neglected the position of women and their role in the production and consumption of popular music and the creation of subcultures.[20] Others have been critical of the way in which the CCCS utilised a much too narrow focus on particular youth experiences and tended to concentrate on the 'spectacular' and the 'atypical' in order to theoretically embed and reinforce the more mythological aspects of English society in the 1960s and 1970s.[21] More recently there has been a re-appraisal of CCCS methodology leading to a small number of historians re-visiting its initial research questions and assumptions regarding the relationship between class, youth and popular music.[22] This book forms part of such a re-appraisal and suggests that the theoretical framework promoted by the CCCS, although problematic, still has much to offer in terms of providing particular insights into the relationship between popular music, youth culture and social change. The chapters that follow critically engage with the work of the CCCS through detailed empirical studies of particular performers, musical genres, working-class consumers, youth cultures and specific localities.

The marginalisation of popular music in the historiography of post-war England

According to Frith, 'academic historians have not been drawn to the field of 'popular music'.[23] Such marginality can be partly attributed to the overall 'conservatism' of the profession and an orthodoxy suggesting that the role ascribed to popular music and its impact on post-war England owes more to 'myth' than 'reality'. This has been no doubt partly driven by the fact that many academic historians are solidly middle-class and have benefitted from an elitist education that has tended to neglect or belittle aspects of popular culture.[24] Critically acclaimed books on post-war England by Hennessey and Sandbrook[25] bear the stamp of a an Oxbridge view of an embedded cultural hierarchy that is dismissive of the role of youth culture and in the case of the latter an almost sneering condescension towards the seriousness in which some writers 'read' popular music.[26]

Sandbrook's aim in writing his expansive histories of the 1960s and 1970s was to reconstruct 'the lives of the kind of people ... in Aberdare or Welshpool or Wolverhampton ... for whom mention of the sixties might conjure up memories not of ... the Rolling Stones, but of bingo, Blackpool and Berni Inns'.[27] Yet in all these localities in the 1950s/60s/70s large numbers of working-class-youth *were* embracing American rock 'n' roll, 'rhythm and blues' and English pop music.[28] The industrial communities of Northern England and the seaside resorts that relied on their patronage were positively buzzing with new soundscapes, fashions and forms of expression.[29] The old 'industrial world' and its attendant lifestyles were not being completely swept away by affluence and modernity but were affected by American popular culture, new discourses of class identity/anxiety and individual and collective experiences of social change. The embrace and consumption of popular music played an essential role in this process as miners, factory workers and retail employees have attested in diaries, letters, autobiographies, oral testimony and personal recollections presented in this book.[30]

Both Sandbrook and Hennessy fail to fully take account of Hall's claim that popular culture 'yields most when it is seen in relation to a more general…wider history'.[31] Yet in much of their work they seem to prioritise particular social and cultural categories as somehow being more worthy of the historians craft and reduce popular music and its attendant subcultures to the margins. Similarly, Hewison who claims that 'culture…is not merely an expression of personal, collective, or national identity, it *is* that identity' devotes little space to an exploration of popular music.[32] Those like Sandbrook who seek to explode the 'myths' of popular music and youth culture fail to recognise the legitimacy of a multiplicity of sources that suggests that it *did* reflect, inform and shape the experiences of a significant number of working-class youths. Academic historians remain reluctant to recognise the plethora of 'amateur' research projects, autobiographies, reminiscences and the more popular types of regional history.[33] Yet it is in this literary genre where a richness of personal and collective experience of popular culture can be located and critically assessed.[34]

A small number of social historians have made some attempt to map popular music against the broader changes taking place in post-war England, most notably Davis[35], Fowler, [36] Osgerby[37] and Weight.[38] This rather limited historiography presents a survey of the period (Davis), an idiosyncratic critique of Marwick (Fowler), a mapping of the dominant trends in youth culture (Osgerby) and the use of particular songs to illustrate aspects of national identity (Weight). Street's work from a political science perspective has been the most ambitious in its claim that 'pop works by reflecting and shaping the relations within society'.[39] He argues that popular music 'cannot change the world' but it can 'alter the ways in which people experience the world; it can upset old images and provide new ones'.[40] Yet Street remains critical of the view that there is a 'causal relationship between the times and their sounds' and that 'music's politics cannot be read straight from its contexts because music-making is not just journalism with a backbeat. The music is the result of the interplay of commercial, aesthetic, institutional and political processes'.[41] This is an accurate reading of the processes of the production of the music, but in terms of consumption, the reality is more problematic. To many of the consumers examined in this book, popular music provided a 'new' way of seeing the world, a discourse of escape, a political manifesto, and an alternative source for understanding locality, culture and working-class experiences.

Some researchers have attempted to bridge the gap between historical and sociological explorations of popular music and youth culture. Harker, writing from a socialist/radical perspective provided a critique of the 'mythology' of popular music and its impact on society claiming that that 'music didn't threaten capitalism one bit'.[42] His work is both partisan and polemical and he seems to be both a promoter of popular music as a force for social change but also its biggest critic.[43] He claimed that the 'people... have been left out of 'popular' music studies' and that sociologists had 'over-theorised' the subject.[44] This book forms one response to Harker's call to 'bring the people back in', but it departs from his more simplistic views on the production and consumption of popular music. It concurs with the position expressed by Keightley that particular types of popular music created a 'sense of difference, of 'otherness' [which] allowed youth to imagine affinities with cultures of disempowered minorities'.[45] Many of the individuals encountered in the following chapters were introduced to the racism of the American South, the musical culture of the West Indies and the metropolitan sexual milieu of England's major cities through the performance and consumption of particular types of popular music.

Sociological and literary approaches to popular music and youth culture

The dominant works on popular music and youth culture remain tied to the fields of Sociology (Simon Frith) and Literary Criticism (Greil Marcus).[46] Frith is a leading figure in popular music studies with his seminal book *Sound Effects* (1983) representing a foundation text.[47] It is very good on the mechanics of popular music processes and presenting an anatomy of the industry but less convincing on the 'everyday experiences' of working-class consumers. He concludes that 'music doesn't challenge the system but reflects and illuminates it'.[48] Yet, this claim is difficult to substantiate when related to the individual experience of the performers and consumers detailed in the pages that follow. The experiences of particular performers and consumers explored throughout this book suggest that there was a shared perception that a challenge *was* being posed to particular aspects of social and cultural life. Such challenges could take both a formal and informal shape in influencing the way that individuals thought about class, race, gender, sexuality and nation. Through popular music, relationships, emotions, a sense of self, locality and one's place in the world could be confirmed and in some cases renegotiated.

Marcus has produced a broad range of texts on popular music in the United States and on the punk rock genre in England. Some of his work suffers from flights of fancy in terms of historical context and causality, but his conviction and intellectual depth as a proselytiser for popular music has ensured that his insights have reached beyond the academy and have found great success amongst the more 'bookish' public consumers of popular culture. Marcus's most influential work remains *Mystery Train* (1975) in which he attempts to construct 'rock 'n' roll' not as youth culture, or counterculture, but simply as American culture'.[49] Marcus's methodology provides a template for the path followed in this book in placing popular music at the centre of English social history in the post-war period. As the examination of class, youth and nation that follows makes clear, popular music worked in a multiplicity of ways in reflecting, shaping and critiquing notions of England and Englishness through to the late twentieth century.

There is now a canon of non-academic popular music writing that stretches from biographies of Elvis Presley and the Beatles through to edited collections on punk rock.[50] The literature produced outside of the academy consists of impressive material with the most noteworthy being books by Gillett[51] and Savage. Savage's work is empirically robust, methodologically impressive and remains the benchmark of scholarship that links youth, music and popular culture to key aspects of English society in the twentieth century.[52] Although theoretically 'light', it offers far more insight to our understanding of the creation and consumption of popular music than some of the more 'knowingly intellectual' treatments found in the more esoteric sociological literature.[53] Autobiography has also proved to be a fertile ground for the reconstruction of the role of popular music in transforming the identity of the individual and reflecting broader social changes. One notable contribution is Melly's *Revolt into Style* (1971). Melly concluded that 'there must be few people who would disagree that pop culture has profoundly affected the way we live now'.[54] The following chapters seek to complement Melly's observations through a more expansive reading of the working-class performance, consumption and experience of popular music.

England, Englishness, popular music, identity and social change

The framing of popular music and youth culture that follows also draws on developments in film and cinema history. This literature has already made significant advances in mapping changing trends through representations presented on screen against the broader social changes taking place in post-war England. According to Richards, film and television 'functioned as propagators of the national image, both in reflecting widely held views and constructing, extending, interrogating and perpetuating dominant cultural myths'.[55] The examination of popular music and social change in the subsequent chapters borrows from film history the notion of 'contextual cinematic history', in which a particular work is explored within its economic, social and cultural contexts.[56] It also complements recent developments in the study of Englishness and how this concept was both maintained and transformed through the economic, political and social forces that impacted on the country in the aftermath of the Second World War. In the popular music produced between 1955–1976, we find elements of an 'old England' of the Industrial Revolution and the rise of class and a 'new England' of affluence, coffee bars, rhythm and blues clubs and the emergence of youth culture and rock 'n' roll as a transnational phenomenon.

Historians have examined aspects of Englishness through art, literature and film but the material on popular music is sparse.[57] Russell has perhaps been the most ambitious in synthesising music and English national identity, but his work has concentrated mostly on the pre-1950s period.[58] Colls in his book *Identity of England* (2004) has very little on music but does contend that migration and American popular culture were redefining tastes in the 1960s.[59] The most insightful account of the relationship between notions of Englishness and popular music can be found in the work of Cloonan although he tends to concentrate on the so-called 'Brit-Pop' era of the 1990s. The collection of essays edited by Bennett and Stratton are also useful as are the sections in Weight's *Patriots* (2002).[60] Mandler is suspicious of the impact of popular music on national identity claiming that aspects of the 1960s were 'very partial – regionally and class specific, and probably more effective in the imagination than in practice'.[61] Yet to Bracewell, by the 1960s, popular music had become the 'cultural currency of Englishness' and a specific working-class response to particular challenges faced by youth in the post-war period.[62]

Gilroy's characterisation of the link between music and national identity also informs the examination of music, race and class that is explored in a number of chapters. Gilroy's notion of a 'black Atlantic' that transcends 'both the structure of the nation state and the constraints of ethnicity and national particularity' is an aspect of the working-class experience that found its place on the dance floors and theatres of English towns and cities.[63] Yet as is clear from some of the images, episodes and events covered in this book, the nation state and its attendant identity and sense of collective values remained a source that was tapped by musicians, consumers and purveyors of youth culture. Through an exploration of coffee bars, rhythm and blues clubs and connected youth subcultures there is an attempt to reconstruct points of contact between West Indian, African American and white working-class youth.[64] The argument presented here is that for many performers and consumers the nation state remained a point of reference and source of inspiration.

The fragmentary message of popular music in the post-war period ensured that consumers could use it in a number of ways and define their own meanings from the lyrics, style and related subcultural affiliations. As Carey has argued, 'it is precisely being empty of meaning that makes music good ... music leaves listeners free to make up their own meanings as they go along'.[65] The performers and consumers explored in the following pages adopted a range of meanings as way of negotiating their way through the economic, political, social and cultural worlds of post-war England. The complexity of 'meaning' in music has ensured that attempts to map and make sense of the relationship between politics and popular music have been fraught with difficulty. As a result, academic writers have tended to concentrate on examples of the 'explicitly political' in terms of performers, songs, genres and movements. Yet such a focus has tended to conceal more than it has revealed in terms of exploring and explaining the working-class response to popular music and youth culture.

The politics of popular music: class, race, gender and sexuality

The literature on the politics of popular music[66] has tended to operate within an institutional framework of parties, organisations and formal political campaigns.[67] The 'new political history' which has attempted to extend the focus of political affiliations and their relationship to class, locality and community has so far neglected popular music and youth culture. Moreover, there has been a tendency to locate a strict division between the more overtly political forms of music such as folk and the more commercialised popular music, which, according to Black, marked the 'distinction between genuine and phoney socialists'.[68] Yet in a more informal sense rock 'n' roll music did offer a particular type of radicalism to English working-class youth. This might not have led to party activism and political engagement, but at particular moments, which are covered in this book, it clearly had an impact on the thought processes, emotions and sense of self projected by a significant number of young music creators and consumers in the post-war period.

The 'new political history' builds on the work of economic historians such as Benson who examined affluence in relation to a process of weakening class-consciousness.[69] Cashmore writing more specifically on youth culture also claims that particular subcultures were 'classless'.[70] Yet Osgerby has noted that 'classless youth was one of the greatest myths of the post-war era'.[71] What follows in this book is a detailed examination of the complexity of class and how it was confirmed, negotiated and challenged by working-class youth through popular music and specific subcultures. Blackwell and Seabrook alluded to the transformative power of popular music, but merely as providing a 'model for a perpetual escape…from the prism of class'.[72] The subsequent chapters suggest that a 'discourse of escape' was just one facet of the relationship between popular music and working-class youth. Class identity remained a constant in the sense of self, place, and nation and manifested itself in the songs, performances and public discourses of a broad range of working-class musicians and consumers. In essence, affluence did not weaken class-consciousness, but merely moved it in different cultural directions.

The examination of youth and culture explored in the following pages highlights a more complex relationship between politics and popular music that attempts to go beyond the organisational, institutional and formally political. Nehring has argued that consumers 'do not have to be aware, of any express politics for a music or song to be politically effective, particularly in the everyday contexts in which they use music'.[73] To Wicke people use songs in particular ways and 'integrate them into their lives'.[74] Yet he also argues that there is a disconnection between performers and their audience, stressing that 'most rock musicians come from the *petit bourgeois* middle classes and have never experienced the everyday life of working-class teenagers'.[75] This is a partial and problematic view of the class connections and disconnections between performer and consumer. The majority of musicians selected for this book are almost wholly working-class or lower-middle class with wider family networks that offered an entry point into some of the more esoteric dimensions of working-class culture.

A further aspect of this study is to trace the complex relationship between class, race, and ethnicity and how these identities and social categories were reinforced, challenged and transformed through the production, consumption and participation in aspects of popular music and its attendant subcultures.[76] Much sociological work has been done in this area, but it is still relatively neglected by historians.[77] The work of Hebdige, Gilroy and Oliver[78] set the research agenda and continues to provide entry points into further explorations. The book also makes a contribution to the growing literature on gender and masculinity.[79] To Heron in an early intervention on the relative invisibility of women in the study of popular music and youth culture the 'experience was neither examined from a woman's point of view nor looked at in terms of what it meant to be women'.[80] The following chapters reconstruct the lives of working-class women through various newspapers, magazines, documentary sources, songs and oral testimony. More recently, the link between aspects of popular music and in particular the subculture of homosexual lifestyles in London has been explored by biographers and popular historians and this text also builds on such research through an analysis of the sexual and gender politics of popular music and youth culture.[81]

Davey has argued that 'it is our cultural outriders, rather than our politicians, that have been, and remain, more responsive to the challenges of the world in which we now live'.[82] Through the career trajectories of Georgie Fame, the Beatles, Ray Davies, Pete Townshend, Slade, David Bowie and the Sex Pistols, particular images and impressions of England appear that were shared by sections of working-class youth whose attachment to popular music provided them with an oppositional soundscape, a discourse of escape and a mental flight from the drudgery of their workplaces, domestic situations and their place within the constrictions of the English class structure.[83]

The subjects of this book and the consumers who responded to their music and performances provide particular images of England that illustrate the complexity of notions of continuity and change in the lived experiences of working-class youth.

Methodology, scope and structure

Methodologically the book utilises a Thompsonian framework of 'history from below' and Williams' conception of a 'structure of feeling' in examining the ways in which aspects of working-class experiences can be found in particular cultural forms creating what Colls has characterised as an 'oppositional Englishness'.[84] Both Thompson and Williams were clear in their advocacy of the cultural articulation of class in creating and sustaining a collective identity and sense of ones place within economic and social relationships.[85] For many of the musicians and consumers examined in the following chapters, social class remained a firm source of identity. Class often determined musical choices, access to public spaces, leisure venues and meshed with particular youth cultures. Popular music was an important cultural phenomenon that soundtracked the lives of youth in the workplace, the domestic sphere and on the street. Performers, songs and recordings complemented many episodes and experiences of happiness, sadness and reflective contemplation.

As a social history, the book avoids the tendency to fully engage with the kind of theoretical sociology that has informed many studies of popular music and youth culture. Nonetheless, it draws on particular aspects of Marxism in its examination of class and culture. Perhaps its most controversial position is the suggestion that particular performers/artists should be viewed as 'organic intellectuals'. According to the Italian Marxist, Antonio Gramsci, 'organic intellectuals are distinguished less by their profession, which may be any job characteristic of their class, than by their function in directing the ideas and aspirations of the class to which they organically belong'.[86] For Gramsci, such intellectuals had to be rooted in the working-class and be familiar with their habits, customs and traditions. As such, they played a crucial role in both reflecting and shaping aspects of working-class life, culture and politics.[87] This is not to say that the musicians selected for this book fit the template of the archetypal working-class autodidact tradition that produced socialists and associated radicals who created and sustained the British labour movement and dissenting tradition in the nineteenth and twentieth centuries. Moreover, they were never fully able to create a successful counter-hegemony that would challenge the foundations and power structures of contemporary capitalism. They operated outside of institutional frameworks, but their music, image, discourse and performance can be shown to have had a particular impact on the consciousness and experiences of working-class youth in the realm of national identity, class, race and sexuality. Pete Townshend, Ray Davies, David Bowie and John Lydon are perhaps most indicative of a generation of musicians who in the post-war period grappled with the nuances of class, social conventions, contemporary economic problems and attempted through their music and performances to direct working-class youth towards both real and imaginary sites of transgression, escape and social radicalism.

Drawing on a range of primary sources including archival papers, diaries, letters, newspapers and oral testimony, the book is a social history of popular music that seeks to make a sophisticated and nuanced contribution to the still limited literature on post-war youth culture.[88] There is a recognition of Samuel's view that '[h]istory has always been a hybrid form of knowledge, syncretizing past and present, memory and myth, the written record with the spoken word'.[89] In this sense, the book charts things that *did* happen to working-class youth in the post-war period but also, just as importantly, experiences and changes that they felt *had* happened as a result of participation in and exposure to particular aspects of popular music. As such it attempts to forge a path through the mythologies of popular music and youth culture of post-war England and the partial and problematic approaches adopted by historians such as Marwick, Sandbrook and Fowler.

The relationship between the national and the local is also explored in some detail suggesting that particular soundscapes were crucial in determining the development of popular music in a number of English cities and towns. Soundscapes were affected by new technology, mobility, militarism and migration. Picker's work on sound in Victorian England is particularly informative here in stressing the importance of the changing social and cultural meaning of sound. The excavation of the transmission routes of popular music also points to both local peculiarities and national projections and constructions of popular music.[90] Radio, cinema, television, fairgrounds and local musical cultures were all important in the period under scrutiny.[91] Moreover, even in a period of affluence and technological innovation places like fairgrounds, fetes and carnivals continued to provide a space for transgressive forms of popular music such as rock 'n' roll and rhythm and blues. Particular transmission routes had an impact on domestic and public spaces and played a crucial role in the career trajectories of the performers who form the basis of this study.

The book explores the spatial dimension of popular music in the industrial North and London, sharing Bennett's contention that 'music and style highlight rather than obscure localised distinctions between young audiences'.[92] According to Stokes, 'amongst the countless ways in which we 'relocate' ourselves, music undoubtedly has a vital role to play'.[93] This was a process that was certainly true for the subjects that make up the following chapters. Similarly, Chambers has argued that at 'dances, at youth clubs ... in draughty church halls and rural community centres, pop music ... found a privileged space'.[94] Connell and Gibson have also noted how popular music is 'bound-up in our everyday perceptions of place'.[95] They stress that 'place in popular music – nostalgia for lost or distant places, dreams of 'making it' elsewhere... are all part of the ability of music to transport listeners away from their ordinary lives'.[96] The stance adopted in the following chapters is that not only did popular music mentally and physically transport performers and consumers from the drudgery of their everyday lives but provided them with new ways of looking at their position within their own localities in particular and English society more generally.

The geographical trajectory of the book takes us from towns built on coal and cotton such as Leigh and Wigan, the waterfront culture of Liverpool and the urban metropolis of post-war London. Particular urban conurbations became magnets for working-class youth, where they could subvert the social conventions within which they had been centred. Houlbrook's work provides a template here as a way in which the capital provided points of 'incursion into the defining spaces of Britishness'.[97] One interesting aspect of such incursions is the involvement of journeys both individual and musical. English popular music was dependent on the appropriation of a variety of musical genres through both external and internal migration. The link between the Caribbean, Ireland, the United States and the industrial North is crucial in this respect and provides a running theme throughout the following chapters.[98]

The book is divided into three parts, which anchor the chapters in particular aspects of popular music, youth culture and working-class experiences. The chronology captures the arrival of rock 'n' roll in England in 1955 with the release of 'Rock Around the Clock' by Bill Haley and the Comets, Elvis Presley's hit single 'Heartbreak Hotel' in 1956 and the national concert tour of Buddy Holly and the Crickets that followed two years later.[99] To Chambers, and a number of popular music historians 1956 was 'the year when it begins'.[100] Yet as the following chapters highlight, there was no specific year-zero for developments in popular music and youth culture and both were connected to longer term trends. Nonetheless, the symbolism and transformative impact of Bill Haley, Elvis Presley and Buddy Holly on the individual and collective identities of working-class youth *was* significant.

Chapters 1 and 2 explore youth culture and the arrival of American popular music in the northern industrial towns of Leigh and Wigan. They reconstruct the journeys taken by a group of working-class boys in search of metropolitan excitement and possible stardom charting their experiences in local dance halls, coffee bars, pubs and the rhythm and blues clubs of London's Soho. Through a biographical focus on Clive Powell (Georgie Fame) and his contemporaries, they provide an image of a working-class England of coal mines, cotton mills, a vibrant consumer culture and the role of popular music in expanding the mental possibilities of difference and escape. In these towns a traditional working-class culture remained very much in place. Far from diluting a particular sense and lived experience of class, American rock 'n' roll and rhythm and blues proved to be complementary. Fame's career connects with particular aspects of youth culture and bears testimony to the interconnections of class, race and nation and how such concepts were negotiated through popular music. Fame's involvement in music making in the industrial North West, the peculiarly English pop world of the Larry Parnes 'stable of stars', and the subculture of the rhythm and blues clubs of London's West End provides a bridge between different yet complementary forms of popular music and youth culture. His involvement in the 1965 Motown Revue Tour is indicative of the ways white English musicians and working-class youth were engaging with black American culture. The musical worlds and cultures that were traversed by Fame are explored through national and local newspapers, magazines, oral testimony, the records of the Metropolitan Police and London County Council.

Chapter 3 also examines youth culture and popular music in North West England through the city of Liverpool. It contextualises the development of Merseybeat and the career of the Beatles (John Lennon, Paul McCartney, George Harrison, Ringo Starr) from the early years of their personal and musical trajectories from the late 1950s through to the advent of Beatlemania in 1964. There is critical discussion of Beatles scholarship and an emphasis on the relationship between class and race in developing particular aspects of the popular music scene in Liverpool. Of particular interest here are the class dynamics of the group and the way in which the Beatles reflected particular working-class cultures and experiences in 1950s Liverpool. The chapter also contains, through the use of oral testimony, an in-depth examination of the impact of Burtonwood, the American airbase, which was crucial as a transmission route for American rhythm and blues into the city of Liverpool and North West England more generally. The relationship between the local and national is also explored through experiences of consumers of the group's recorded output and live performances and the internationalisation of the Beatles that to some undermined their connection to the city. Using the records of Liverpool City Council, unpublished texts, fanzines, oral testimony and an array of documentary sources, it shifts the focus away from a conventional narrative of a group. The chapter 'centres' the individual Beatles as both reflecting and informing social changes impacting on working-class youth culture in the city of Liverpool in particular and England more generally.

Chapters 4 and 5 consist of a detailed examination of mod culture of the early to mid-1960s. Drawing on previously neglected primary sources and oral testimony, they explore the tensions between class, locality, race and gender implicit in this most mythologised subculture. The focus moves beyond London and also charts the mod experience outside of the capital city. Running parallel to this excavation is an analysis of the music of Pete Townshend and the Who. Townshend was a critically and popularly acclaimed songwriter and performer, but also someone, who as an 'organic intellectual', was keen to both document and attempt to explain the changes that were taking in place in youth culture and English society. From the late 1960s through to the release of the seminal concept album *Quadrophenia* in 1973, Townshend was presenting his own variant of the recent social history of England. The chapter forms a link between the youth culture, popular music and broader social changes of the 1960s to the continuities and ruptures that were a feature of the everyday lives of English working-class youth in the early 1970s.

Chapter 6 navigates the working-class world of Ray Davies and the Kinks through a critical reading of their songs and making the claim that his work should be read alongside the contemporary sociologists of the 1960s who were also trying to make sense of the changing working-class. Davies's background and song writing presents an addition or indeed an alternative to some of the contemporary social investigators of 1950s/60s England. His songs complement the work of social scientists such as Willmott and Young and their research on class, community and suburbia. Unlike many of his musical contemporaries, Davies was a critic of the popular perceptions of 'swinging London', 'affluence' and 'political consensus'. He drew on multiple working-class political identities to negotiate his way through the changing geography and culture of London, in particular, and England, more generally. Particularly noteworthy here is Davies's engagement with slum clearance and the limitations of a particular type of socialist politics that simultaneously liberated and constrained the English working-class. As with the career of Georgie Fame, Ray Davies bridges the world of the working-class of Edwardian Britain with the experiences of youth in 1960s England. The central argument of this section suggests that Davies's songs provide a significant historical source for making sense of economic, political, social and cultural change in post-war England.

Chapter 7 focuses on the development of glam rock and the impact of the image and music of Slade and David Bowie in his guise as Ziggy Stardust between 1972 and 1973. It contrasts the working-class appeal of Slade with the more futuristic and cross-class appeal of Bowie. Bowie's growing popularity led to a number of working-class youths challenging the boundaries of class, masculinity, femininity and sexuality. The fashion and music is contextualised within the development of feminist politics and the growth of campaigns for sexual equality and the challenge to the discrimination of homosexuals in English society. Drawing on a range of primary sources, newspapers, letters, fanzines and oral testimony it goes beyond the more superficial readings of glam rock. As with previous chapters the geographical focus moves beyond London to chart the impact of glam rock on social identities in archetypal working-class communities.

Chapter 8 brings the study to a close with a focus on the Sex Pistols' Anarchy Tour of December 1976. It explores the rise of punk music and its attendant culture and the relationship it had to broader economic, cultural and social developments. Many books and articles have been written on the Sex Pistols and the youth culture that followed in their wake, but none have provided a systematic account of their attempts to reach a larger audience by taking their music and political message across Britain in 1976. There is a detailed analysis of the reaction of the media and national and local politicians to the arrival of the Sex Pistols in particular localities and a critical utilisation of Cohen's 'moral panic' framework. The analysis of a variety of political and social responses suggests that the politics of punk was not easily decoded by particular institutions, organisations and pressure groups. Moreover, the Sex Pistols and their particular form of rhetoric and imagery also pointed to continuities and ruptures that were manifesting themselves in working-class areas of England's towns and cities. The chapter locates the tour in the centre of a growing sense of economic and political crisis offering a critique of the existing literature on both punk and the Sex Pistols.

The book presents an argument that popular music was an important cultural, social and political force in post-war English society. Between 1955 and 1976, popular music provided the soundtrack to millions of working-class lives. It is in this soundtrack where we can locate a particular aspect of Englishness, social change and the resilience of class identities. The images of England that can be accessed through popular music reflect the continuities and change in working-class experiences. By reaching out to a national audience of young consumers, a number of 'organic intellectuals' were able to use music to make sense of England and articulate the feelings and emotions of a section of working-class youth much more successfully than more celebrated figures in the realms of literature, film and politics. In essence, popular music and its associated youth cultures offers a significant entry point into understanding the resilience and complexity of working-class identities and experiences in post-war England.

Part I
Teddy Boy England

I watched their dances... How lifeless and dreary they were in spite of the ear-splitting noise of the boogie-woogie music and the jerking about of their young limbs. (Margareta Berger-Hamerschlag, *Journey into a Fog*, 1955)

Can it happen here – the trouble that goes with rock 'n' roll music in the United States? Over there it has been blamed for starting riots, rape and alcoholism amongst the youngsters... This stimulating rhythm of the coloured people is not new. But it has been taken up commercially and is now becoming the White Man's burden. (*Daily Mirror*, 16 August 1956)

He wore thick crepe shoes that added an inch to his height. Out of these his pink dazzle socks climbed in a brilliant blaze of colour; their glory extinguished by the tight fitting bottoms of his blue jeans. His coat, a black well-cut drape with heavily padded shoulders, was almost knee length, its sombre colour offset by a crimson open-necked shirt. A small religious medallion, purely decorative, hung from a thin silver chain round his white neck. (John Townshend, *The Young Devils*, 1958)

From my distant window I could see the small, dark figures of boys and half-grown youths, drifting off in two and threes and larger groups, and all of them, it seemed to me, wearing the identical Teddy suits... All of them, as if drawn by a magnet, also made off in the same direction, towards the main streets beyond the big railway stations: an untidy area of converging streets and crowded traffic, of shops, cinemas, public houses, and bright lights, aesthetically a God-awful wilderness, but to the boys obviously representing life with a capital L. (T.R. Fyvel, *The Insecure Offenders*, 1961)

> I heard the ships hooting and automatically turned to Thames ... Hamburg...New York, New Orleans...Thinking of those exotic names and comparing them with what was around me made me sick: cobbles smeared with filth...neglected gardens as hardpacked as asphalt; tumbling walls; unwashed curtains x-rayed by naked bulbs, and unwashed kids darting about like rats in the dark. (Sid Chaplin, *The Day of the Sardine*, 1961)

Soundcheck: Buddy Holly and the 'Lemon Drop Kid', Wigan, England, Tuesday 18 March 1958[1]

The 'Lemon Drop Kid' dragged himself out of bed, grabbed his snap-tin and water bottle, stepped out onto the cobbled street, mounted his bike and cycled to Bedford Colliery to begin the usual routine for the morning shift. But this shift would be different. The 'Lemon Drop Kid' knew that the minutes would seem like hours and the hours like days. He just needed to get to the end of the shift, get up the pit and he would then be in the fantasy land of rock 'n' roll and momentary escape. He had been listening to the music for two years in coffee bars, on record players, in pubs and in the dance halls of Manchester, Leigh and Wigan. He was also finding his own technique of guitar playing, fashion style and attitude to life through his embrace of American popular culture in all its forms. But today was different, today seemed more special. For the price of 8s. 6d today would lead him to the presence of the great Buddy Holly and the Crickets at the Wigan Ritz. The theatre had opened in 1938 and was the entertainment mecca of the town. For the last few weeks it not only had been host to the usual Hollywood fare of big screen adventures, romances and formulaic comedies but also a gritty depiction of the London underworld in *The Flesh Is Weak* and its tale of gangsters, prostitution and vulnerable young women. But tonight the stage, the orchestra stalls and the grand circle would all belong to Buddy.

A week earlier, the Ritz had hosted a skiffle music contest in which the 'Lemon Drop Kid' and his group the Dominoes had performed in the style of the ubiquitous Lonnie Donegan. He came away with dreams of recording contracts, concert performances and ultimate stardom. On that night the 'Lemon Drop Kid' had gazed in wonder at the huge stage and the rows of seats that seemed to go on forever. But tonight he would be back in the audience staring in awe at Buddy, and for that moment, the lives of many of the miners and factory workers of Wigan and Leigh would be transformed. As he cycled to the pit the 'Lemon Drop Kid' was already visualising the scene that would unfold later in the day; the shifts ending, young men and women discarding their work clothes and selecting their best suits and dresses and making their way to Wigan town centre by foot, bike, bus and train. All of them off to see a real-life American rock 'n' roll performer in his prime, playing a selection of recent hits that had until now only been heard on jukeboxes, record players and accompanying the thrill rides of the travelling fairs that periodically arrived to add some bright colour to the terraced streets, colliery yards and factory gates.

Like his grandfather, father, brothers, cousins, uncles and mates, the 'Lemon Drop Kid' was steeped in the culture of coal mining and the pit was a constant reference point in conversations about politics, culture and class. For weeks during 'snap time' underground and in the showers, the older miners had been cracking jokes about his obsession with the 'new music' that the *Daily Mail* had earlier described as the 'negro's revenge'.[2] The 'Lemon Drop Kid' had been steadily gaining a reputation as an entertainer, and the year before he had played to local colliers at the opening night of the Leigh Miners Club. He performed on top of the billiard table with no amplification. The club was filled with miners young and old, downing pints of bitter, discussing the tactical intricacies and outcomes of upcoming Rugby League fixtures and marvelling at the exploits of the great Billy Boston. The room was filled with smoke, the smell of spilled bitter and the strong sound of the Lancashire dialect particular to Leigh. When the 'Lemon Drop Kid' went into his routine, he was cheered on by the more inebriated miners, some of them helping with the choruses of the more well-known selections. For Leigh miners, nights in the club really were the good times, and the great lockout of 1926 and the struggles of the 1930s were now a distant memory.

A fellow miner had introduced the 'Lemon Drop Kid' to the music of Buddy. He was not only especially impressed with Buddy's energy and guitar playing but also by the fact his style was not just 'way-out' rock 'n' roll. To the 'Lemon Drop Kid', Buddy's music had something more than all the other rock 'n' rollers and what he heard was a distinct type of melody that was both uplifting and reflective. Today, nothing could shake his excitement or the sense of anticipation of seeing Buddy up-close and personal and hearing the amplified electric tone of the Fender guitar, the crack of the snare drum and thud of the upright bass. The 'Lemon Drop Kid' rushed through the clean lockers, stripped naked and having little time for small talk with some of the miners coming off the night shift he headed for the lamp room and collected his tallies. He snatched at his lamp, attached it to his cap and was first into the cage willing it to descend the shaft at breakneck speed. It was a tough shift at the coal face, hot, sweaty, dusty, and as he loaded the coal onto the conveyor, his head was buzzing with Buddy's renditions of recent hits; 'That'll Be the Day', 'Peggy Sue', 'Oh Boy!', 'Everyday'. No thoughts today of the danger of falling coal or the noxious gasses that had taken the lives of 38 men and boys in the same colliery in 1886. Three years later, the 'Lemon Drop Kid' would also be gassed. He lived to tell the tale and never went down the pit again.

At last the shift was over. He took his last swill of warm water and headed towards pit-bottom. Waiting for the cage, he climbed into an empty coal tub as his dust-covered audience gathered round for his usual rendition of the Bop classic 'Lemon Drop'. Using his shovel as a mock guitar, the 'Lemon Drop Kid' gave his best performance yet. Some miners clapped, others whooped and a few strolled past shaking their heads. Performance over, the 'Lemon Drop Kid' entered the cage with a big grin on his face and pushed the lad in front of him against the back of a burly miner to secure his space before the metal grille was dropped and the onsetter sent his signal to the banksman and the winding house. The cage moved rapidly and silently through the dark shaft into the afternoon light as miners chatted, broke wind, spat out their tobacco and sang songs – old, new and blue. This was it, the final procedure that marked the end of the day shift. Tallies pressed into the hand of the banksman and a sprint back to the lamp room. A quick nod to some mates walking through the lockers on their way to the afternoon shift, a rapid strip peeling the sweat-soaked clothes from his exhausted body and a jolt into the shower. No time for delay now, back washed first by a mate standing under the next shower, eyelashes rubbed clean of the encrusted dust, hair combed just right in the small mirror riveted into the locker. No cup of weak tea in the canteen today, but he did manage to grab a meat pie, which he devoured as he ran through the pit yard. Jumping on his bike, pedalling fast, he was straight home and in mental preparation and anticipation of dreamland.

As usual the smell of cooking food greeted the 'Lemon Drop Kid' as he cycled through the terraces, passing the kids, the matriarchs and the old men sat outside their houses smoking their cigarettes and pipes. He hurriedly parked the bike in its usual spot round the back of the small house. Through the back door, and the 'big dinner' was waiting. The food was eaten at pace and now he was just about ready for the afternoon sleep. It was difficult this time, the concert only hours away, but the 'Lemon Drop Kid' managed to snatch a cat-nap. It was now getting closer. Back out of bed, wash, clean, close shave, and then it was on with the clothes. Perfectly pressed trousers and crisp shirt complementing the killer jacket with the velvet lapels was what was required for both Buddy and the rest of the audience who would be attending. Extra time spent on the hair tonight, and it was off down the street passing the children kicking cans and playing cowboys and Indians. The 'Lemon Drop Kid' didn't normally drink, but he would have a couple tonight. Unlike his mates who would down multiple pints in Plank Lane Catholic Club, it was the music that was the most important thing to him. He had made regular pilgrimages to the coffee bars and dance halls of Manchester sometimes having to walk home and go straight down the pit for the morning shift, but tonight was different, tonight belonged to Buddy.

In the pub with pals, a chat and some banter with the barmaid and then the number 54 bus from Leigh to Wigan with no plan of getting the last one back at half-past-ten. Lots of chatter on the bus, the gossiping housewives, the men complaining about the weather and the government. The drabness of the older men contrasted with the garish colours of the Teddy Boy suits and the dresses of the girls who had gone through the same rigmarole as the 'Lemon Drop Kid'. They too had toiled through a long, slow shift in the cotton mill and the factory but were now dressed to kill and ready to participate in some energetic jiving to the music of Buddy and maybe some necking on the way home.

Leigh to Wigan was only eight miles but tonight the bus was taking an eternity. The 'Lemon Drop Kid' knew that the matinee show was already underway, and he could visualise the excitement in the stalls as Buddy made his pre-show preparations by tuning his guitar and making sure that he looked sharp for the English audience. At last Wigan town centre. The lights of the Ritz with a special glow tonight, the people outside the hall exhibiting a collective energy and excitement that could be particularly felt by the Teddy Boys. The Leigh lads shuffle into the pub for another quick pint. The 'Lemon Drop Kid' couldn't wait any longer and shouted to his fellow miners to 'sup-up and let's get in'. Pulling the ticket out of his jacket he broke into a wry smile at the thought of the view of Buddy he could get from his position in the centre of the tenth row in the stalls. Small talk about how they were dreading the thought of tomorrow's shift ended abruptly when the lights went down.

Ronnie Keene and his Orchestra, billed as 'Britain's New Musical Sensation', were on first playing a selection that included a version of Glenn Miller's recording of 'In The Mood' and 'Blow That Saxophone'.[3] The 'Lemon Drop Kid' was OK with this and had retained a love of the big band sound that had soundtracked his childhood in mining communities in Yorkshire and now Lancashire. Next was Des O'Connor, tonight's compere, comic and link-man. A few words to introduce the Tanner Sisters and the Teddy Boys become a bit more interested now they had a female presence on the stage. The sisters perform a set that includes the Lonnie Donegan hit 'Puttin' on the Style' and a 'Medley of Skiffle'. Then Des is back delivering his 'comedy with the modern style'. The 'Lemon Drop Kid' likes Des and the way in which he combines songs and laughs. Something for the more sedate audience members now with the 'recording star' Gary Miller originally from Blackpool a town that epitomised the hedonism of a generation of Lancashire miners and cotton workers. Miller performs a mixture of 'light pop' and romantic ballads such as 'Story of My Life' and 'Garden of Eden'. The Teddy Boys get a bit restive. During the interval a few of the miners and factory workers charge into the toilets, where they empty bladders, comb hair, and check that they still look good. A few purchase cigarettes, Walls ice creams, toffees and bottles of Schweppes minerals for their girlfriends on the way back.

It's show time again and the moment is getting closer. 'The Lemon Drop Kid' comes out of the Gents and his pace quickens as he walks down the aisle. He can see that the usherette Benny Davies, the character whose effeminacy has made him a local legend is guiding people to their places with a camp delivery of 'come on darling I'll show you to your seat'. Others who subverted the local conventions of masculinity were not treated so lightly. Barry Ince, a fellow music fanatic and friend of the 'Lemon Drop Kid', was later badly beaten outside of a local pub by a group of 'tough' lads.[4] 'The Lemon Drop Kid' laughs as Benny shows him to his seat back in the tenth row. Before he can sit down the lights are dimmed and Ronnie Keene and his Orchestra begin the second half. A bit more Des, a few laughs and then its time.

Buddy Holly and the Crickets had already been rocking English working-class youth in places like the Elephant and Castle, Sheffield, Wolverhampton, Newcastle and Birmingham. The concerts had gone down well with the Teds, the Ton-Up Boys and the young girls with their painted faces. The night before the Wigan appearance Buddy had played his 36th show in seventeen days at the Gaumont Theatre, Doncaster. A little over a week earlier, Buddy's performance at the Bradford Gaumont had been described in negative terms by a local reporter: 'Artistry has been kicked out of the stage door ... At least it would seem so from the fanatical reception given a screeching guitar player ... I would have defied anyone in the audience to tell me what 70 per cent of the words that issued from the lips of this foot-stomping, knee-falling musician'.[5] But the 'Lemon Drop Kid' and the thousands of young men and women who had witnessed Buddy in March '58 understood the words, shook to the beat and for 'one night only', were transported to another place.

Tonight at the Ritz, the transition between acts is quick and smooth and the moment of Buddy's appearance on a Wigan stage draws ever closer. The 'Lemon Drop Kid', the Teddy Boys and the teenage girls leap to their feet as Buddy enters the spotlight. The sound of the sunburst Stratocaster cuts through the theatre complemented by the thunder from the bass and the whip of the snare. As Buddy falls to his knees and the music gets louder, the Teddy Boys and the teenage girls sweep into the aisles and the jiving continues for the rest of the set. For the 'Lemon Drop Kid' this is the moment, this is rock 'n' roll, this is the remedy to the early mornings, the bruises, the black-nails, and the coal dust. Buddy takes a bow, the curtain falls and it's all over. The memory of the performance carries the 'Lemon Drop Kid' and his mates back to Leigh and the reality of the alarm clock, the mine shaft and the coal face. But for that one night they had been somewhere else, a mythical land of diners, exotic cars, sunshine and beautiful girls like 'Peggy Sue'.

1
Coal, Cotton and Rock 'n' Roll in North West England

This chapter examines the experiences of working-class youth in the northern industrial towns of Leigh and Wigan. It highlights the continuities and ruptures in popular culture and Clive Powell's place within an industrial milieu in which rock 'n' roll music played a particular role in both affirming and challenging working-class identities.[1] Here is an image of England that still contained features of the Victorian economy and the social structure it created. Through an exploration of social spaces that were defined by particular soundscapes it explores the role that popular music played in complementing a 'structure of feeling' that connected young men and women to a sense of class, locality and the possibilities of change. The musical journey traversed by Powell and his peers in the coal and cotton industries of North West England sheds light on the complex relationship between class, youth and popular music in the 1950s.

Powell's background and early career is a point of connection between an 'old England' that Hoggart reconstructed in the *Uses of Literacy* (1957) and a much mythologised 'new England' depicted by MacInnes in his novel *Absolute Beginners* (1959).[2] MacInnes had noted a change on the streets of London where 'it *did* look as if some conspiracy was afoot to slay the elder brethren' and the kids were 'spending fortunes on the songs of the Top Twenty'.[3] For northern working-class youth in the 1950s, England was a country of coal mines, cotton mills, smoky pubs and working mens' clubs. Yet the sounds, imagery and style of MacInnes' London began to have some resonance amongst teenagers in Leigh and Wigan and they embraced the coffee bar and jukebox culture that Hoggart had felt was detrimental to their cultural development.[4]

In becoming Georgie Fame in 1959, Powell provided the link between Victorian music hall, the inter-war variety show and the development of a vibrant and challenging popular music that was consumed by working-class youth as a source of enjoyment and as a weapon in attempting to transcend the confining strictures of class, locality, ethnicity, and existing notions of national identity. Powell's geographical and musicological trajectory provides an insight into working-class youth culture and popular music in the industrial north. His career sheds light on the less celebrated foundations of English rock 'n' roll and the experiences of working-class youth through their creation and consumption of popular music. Powell's world was shaped by the cotton mill, the coal mine and a specifically northern working-class culture. Popular music would provide Powell with a means of escape, but he would retain a sense of local and regional identity throughout his subsequent career.

Work, class and popular culture in a northern town

In the 1950s the streets of Leigh and Wigan were still populated by working men and women whose lives were shaped by the factory whistle, the whip of the cable from the colliery head-gear and the culture associated with these particular employment sectors. The lives of young working-class boys and girls were punctuated by the beginning and end of shifts and adults leaving and coming back home each day from the pits and cotton mills. Breakfast, dinner and tea would be accompanied by gossip, banter and tales of workplace peril, conflict and humour. Leigh was also a town that was 'deep red' in politics and steeped in the culture of the Labour Party and industrial trade unionism.[5] The first Labour MP, Harry Twist, a local coal miner and trade union official was elected in 1922, and the seat remained socialist for the rest of the century.[6]

The 1940s represented the last great period of British cotton production. According to Singleton, in 'the summer of 1952, 33 per cent of spinning operatives and 22 per cent of weaving operatives in Lancashire were either unemployed or on short time...But demand picked up in 1953, and more or less full employment was restored'.[7] However, from 1954 onwards foreign competition rapidly diluted Lancashire's export and domestic market. To Fowler, the 'crucial year was 1958, which saw more cotton cloth imported into Britain than was exported, for the first time since the industrial revolution'.[8] Leigh was particularly hard hit with a '63 per cent fall in capacity between 1950 and 1962'.[9] Yet in the early 1960s, there were still visible signs of the importance of cotton to the local economy. Moreover, although some mills had closed they had not been demolished and stood as reminders of an industrial culture that had drawn on the labour of thousands of young men and women since the industrial revolution. In his contemporary description of cotton towns the journalist Geoffrey Moorhouse claimed that you could 'still see women gossiping on street corners...you can still see middle-aged men in mufflers and cloth caps'.[10]

As with the cotton industry, the fortunes of the Lancashire coalfield faced a similar fate. The industry had been contracting since the Second World War; 77 collieries were nationalised, but a wave of closures in the 1960s significantly reduced the number of miners.[11] However, in 1955, there were still

64 collieries in Lancashire with 25 in the Leigh and Wigan area employing over 40,000 men.[12] The miners retained their presence in the town through a network of pubs, clubs, sporting affiliations and political activities. In the small houses of the terraced streets, an oral culture of workplace camaraderie, strikes, good times and bad times retained its ability to instil a feeling of class and place in the collective memory that would be passed down to children and find its way into their sense of self and locality. Coffee bars, record shops and new fashions looked out of place against the backdrop of mill and mine yet in many ways they were complementary. For working-class youth in Leigh and Wigan the past and the present formed part of a 'structure of feeling' that found its way into particular aspects of the creation and consumption of popular music.[13]

The cotton mill and the coal mine formed the basis of the working-class world in which Clive Powell was formed. Powell was born in Leigh on 26 June 1943, to James and Mary Ann Powell neé Gilman.[14] His parents resided at number-five Cotton Street in a small-terraced house that was situated adjacent to the pit-yard of Parsonage Colliery.[15] As a child he would have been familiar with the sounds of industrial machinery and the sight of coal miners arriving for work and departing at the end of their shifts underground. In 1965 he informed *Rave* magazine that where he lived 'was a real Coronation Street[16]. Gas lamps. The lot. We were rough and ready kids'.[17] Elements of the working-class culture that Orwell had documented in the neighbouring town of Wigan in the 1930s were still very much alive although now underpinned by a more affluent workforce and an everyday existence that had been much improved by the creation of the welfare state after the Second World War and the impact that trade unionism had on wages and conditions in the coal and cotton industries.[18]

As was the norm in working-class industrial communities, members of Powell's extended family lived close by, and both adults and children would inhabit a familiar milieu of accepted notions of masculinity, femininity and collective identities that shaped their formative years.[19] Powell's Uncle Jack had a house in the same street, which contained labourers, cotton operatives and coal miners. Like many other working-class inhabitants of the town, James, Powell's father, had a limited choice of employment possibilities due to the economic dominance of coal and textiles. Powell later recalled that '[m]ost of the people [in Leigh] worked in the cotton trade'.[20] Powell attended St. Peter's Junior School and then Windermere Road Secondary Modern.[21] As a child his peer group consisted of the children of cotton workers and coal miners, many of which would spend their working lives in these particular industries.

Eager to pass on his interest in music Powell's father arranged a course of piano lessons for his son. Along with many other working-class families the Powell's had a piano in the parlour. This would form the focus of post-pub performances and special occasions such as weddings, christenings and birthdays.[22] As a precocious seven-year old, Powell soon tired with the rigidity of formal practice and developed his own style of learning. His musical apprenticeship also included singing in the local church choir. As a teenager, Powell spent much of his leisure time playing in a local amateur dance band and attending church, where he was allowed to play the organ, an instrument on which he later excelled. Retaining the link to a local working-class culture that had drawn on religion, drink, and hedonism as a kind of catharsis for dealing with occupational drudgery, bereavement and ill-health, working-class youth in Leigh did not completely reject the culture that had underpinned the leisure time of their parents and grandparents. Powell was one example of this process: 'I'd go to church because... I dig hymns. I'd sing away on my own, trying out little harmonies'.[23] Such a link between popular music and religion has been well-established by historians of popular music in the United States but has not been adequately explored in the English context.[24] Yet the religious contribution to the roots of popular music in Britain highlights the continuities to an earlier working-class milieu of nonconformity, political radicalism and cultural expression.

The English popular music scene in the early 1950s was still dominated by the big band scene, the large music publishers and established impresarios who prepared singers and entertainers for successful careers on stage and screen. Records were released by major companies such as EMI, Decca, Phillips and Pye and reflected the conservatism of the industry in promoting particular genres and artists.[25] The radio delivered the BBC's Light Programme into working-class homes with popular music played on segments such as *Housewives' Choice* and *Two Way Family Favourites*.[26] To Cohn, a perceptive early chronicler of the shifts in popular music and its impact on working-class youth, 'British pop in the fifties was pure farce'.[27] Cohn and other writers have argued that 1956 was a crucial year for transforming popular music in England and its attendant youth culture with a number of chart hits for Bill Haley and Elvis Presley.[28] Yet the notion that there was a sudden revolution in the listening habits of English youth in 1956 is problematic and an examination of the sales charts for that year shows a variety of acts and genres maintaining prominence.[29] Nonetheless, this does not negate the impact that American rock 'n' roll was having on significant numbers of working-class youths.[30]

In 1956 teenagers used rock 'n' roll as a means of differentiation, rebellion and hedonism. The miners of Leigh and Wigan also no doubt identified with the sentiment of songs like Tennessee Ernie Ford's 'Sixteen Tons' and its depiction of a hard shift in an American coal mine and its critique of industrial capitalism. They could then find release and excitement through Bill Haley's 'Rock Around the Clock' and Elvis Presley's 'Heartbreak Hotel' in coffee bars, cinemas and through the soundtracks that accompanied the thrill rides of travelling fairs.[31] Fairs had long been associated with working-class culture, and they became crucial in transmitting popular music to the masses.[32] The Silcock brothers had first provided entertainment to Wigan's miners by erecting games stalls outside of local pits in the years leading up to the Great War. By the late 1950s, bright lights, rock 'n' roll, and images of Americana acted as a magnet to the miners and factory workers of North West England seeking escape from the routine of the working week.[33]

Powell was exposed to the sounds of the fair, the radio and the record collections of his peers at an early age. According to Clayson, he had already 'absorbed a hidden curriculum in his mastery of the harmonica and his ingenuity in making castanets from scraps of old slate', and in 1954 a friend of his sister had introduced him to the techniques of 'boogie-woogie piano'.[34] A few years later, Powell was introduced to the sounds of rock 'n' roll by way of Jerry Lee Lewis, Fats Domino, Chuck Berry and Little Richard, primarily through listening to Radio Luxembourg and friendship with other working-class boys who were absorbing American popular music.[35] In 1956 the impact of rock 'n' roll was visible in the cafés, pubs, dance halls and on the streets of many industrial towns.

Music has always formed a core component of northern English identity, and into the twentieth century, a vibrant network of clubs, pubs, theatres and dance halls provided a space in which the working-class could come together to escape the rigours of the factory, mill and coal mine. According to Russell, music 'provided the region with some of its most potent cultural, symbolic and psychic capital'.[36] In the post-war period, North West England in particular became closely associated with popular music and produced a multiplicity of groups and solo artists. Some performers retained particularly northern traits in terms of accent, style, humour and an identification with the broader working-class that purchased their records and danced to their rhythms.[37] Powell was also notable in this respect and maintained an identification with Leigh and Wigan throughout his subsequent career.

In the 1950s, Leigh's youth culture was well-served by dozens of pubs providing live music and the opening of coffee bars that became spaces where young boys and girls could perfect their style and strut their ambivalence towards particular social conventions. Images of Hollywood could be enjoyed in a range of cinemas including the Palace, Sems, Empire, Regal, New Hippodrome and Bedford.[38] The impact of film on youth had been concerning politicians and a variety of religious and community groups for some time. A paper published by the London County Council argued that 'cinema provides a vivid, glamorous experience unknown to former generations ... cinema-goers of both sexes are regularly shown pictures of alluring ways of life ... which during adolescence may be undermining permanently their sense of values'.[39] Similar concerns also accompanied the arrival of rock 'n' roll and the formation of gangs that were perceived to be aping American outlaw and gangster styles.[40]

New forms of popular culture by no means swept away pre-war working-class entertainment. Traditional variety shows retained their presence in the broader expanse of the town's culture and touring acts continued to play local theatres. Yet even here, African American musical styles were beginning to make inroads through the presentation of particular images and the performance of particular songs. In 1954 the American All Coloured Revue Show visited Wigan. The local press advertised the show with much hyperbole and stereotypically emphasised the exotic nature of the performance: 'As might be expected the accent is on rhythm. Dancing is of a very high order and quite uninhibited, while the music contains all that wonderful improvisation for which coloured people are so justly famous'.[41] Cultural difference could also be experienced first-hand through daily workplace contact with the multiplicity of nationalities that were absorbed into Lancashire mines after the end of the Second World War.[42]

One of the few mixed-race English performers whose career stretched from the big band scene of the 1940s to the rock 'n' roll of the 1950s was Ray Ellington.[43] Ellington was an early symbol of the way in which white working-class youth were exposed to jazz, rock 'n' roll and American rhythm and blues through live performance. Yet his use of humour in his performances gave them a particularly English inflection.[44] There were also many other regionally important figures who were willing to introduce some of the more esoteric aspects of jazz music into their repertoire. Musically enlightened teenagers could now access a much broader range of styles and genres than their parents had been unable to experience owing to a multiplicity of transmission routes that carried new and diverse sounds into the home, the workplace and the public sphere.[45]

Dance halls, Teddy Boys and rock 'n' roll

There was a symbolic shift between 'old' and 'new' forms of popular culture in 1954, when it was announced that Leigh's Theatre Royal had been sold and was to be converted into a dance hall. The theatre had been in existence since the 1880s. In 1955, Harry Boardman, the local Labour MP opened the Casino on Silk Street. Johnny Prior and his orchestra led the opening dance establishing a long-term residency.[46] A year later, the local council responded to the press furore generated by growing concerns around youth culture by deciding to ban *Rock Around the Clock* (1956).[47] This was a rather tame picture even by contemporary standards, but it contained a rock 'n' song by Bill Haley and the Comets. Wigan had already banned it, and Leigh magistrates followed suit by refusing to allow the Palace on Railway Road to screen the film.[48] Many working-class youths avoided the ban by travelling the short journey to Manchester by bus or train.[49] Powell recalled that some of his older school friends came back 'raving about it'.[50] Juvenile disturbances across the country were increasingly given the label of 'Teddy' or 'Ted' and were linked to the Teddy Boy style that had first emerged in London around four years earlier.[51]

Ronnie Carr (the Lemon Drop Kid) recalled that the Teddy Boys suddenly appeared in Leigh hanging outside coffee bars and cutting a dash on the floor of local dance halls.[52] In 1954 and 1955, the local press provided numerous examples of magistrates, local politicians and the police labelling all minor crimes as Teddy Boy inspired.[53] Anxiety around delinquent youth complemented more general concerns about rising crime linked to immorality and violence, which filtered down to the more provincial English towns. Depictions of sex, illegal abortion and illegitimate children found their way onto the pages of the national tabloid press and in local publications. Secrets and lies that once remained firmly locked behind the front doors of the working-class terraces or discussed in hushed tones in the snug of the local pub were now compared to the national scandals that adorned the pages of the *Daily Mirror* and the *Daily Express*. In Leigh, for example, Ethel Shanley was accused of performing abortions with a syringe for the price of £6 and was jailed for two years.[54] For the rest of the decade, images of perceived sexual deviancy challenged the mythological cosy domesticity that had formed the political and cultural rhetoric of post-war England.[55] There was a steady increase in rates of gonorrhoea, and local police forces patrolled public lavatories, parks and cinemas in order to arrest homosexuals.[56] These incursions into the more transgressive aspects of working-class lives created personal dramas that were experienced across the country and not just in metropolitan centres.

By 1956 the Teddy Boy style and subsequent panic over juvenile delinquency now had a rock 'n' roll soundtrack.[57] The Teds had first appeared in London in 1952, adopting a mixture of Edwardian and American fashion styles.[58] From 1956 to the end of the decade, both the national and local press regularly featured stories of Teddy Boy violence and vandalism. The *London Evening Standard* ran a four-part investigation by Robert Edwards into Teddy Boys, interviewing youths, teachers, religious leaders and community activists. The interviews are revealing in terms of the way in which youths saw something transgressive in their style and for their emphasis on the class dimension to Teddy Boy activity. Harry Moore, the superintendent of a London Methodist youth club stressed that Teds were 'remarkably fussy about their appearance'. Edwards added that 'wherever there are poorer homes you will find Teddy Boys'.[59] A teacher from a 'tough North London school' offered a more sober analysis: 'These boys are the Dead End Kids in our society. They have been neglected…their homes are squalid, their education has been poor. Their behaviour is a protest against all that…They cannot create so they destroy'.[60] Yet Teddy Boys were a product of both austerity and affluence. Rationing ended in 1954, and the average weekly wage doubled by 1959.[61]

A feature in the *Sunday Times* on youth in the potteries district of England pointed to the growing affluence of sections of working-class youth. One example was seventeen-year-old Billy who was employed in a slaughterhouse:

'I get five pounds a week clear... In this house we always turn up the wage packet don't we mother? I get twenty-five shillings a week for boppin' an' fags and pictures... I like to go out, have money in my pocket. If I come up on the pools I'd buy about two-dozen shirts, all different colours and about a dozen pairs of jeans'.[62] Journalists like Edwards had noted two types of Teddy Boys that personified a familiar template of working-class respectability and non-respectability. Alec, a sixteen-year-old dockers' son who was employed as a clerk was one example of the non-threatening Ted: 'Alec has never frequented the filthy cafes, thick with decay and dowdy sin, where the worst type of Teddy Boys spend their evenings. The conversation in such cafes hinges monotonously on sex and crime'.[63] *The Times* claimed that the 'teenagers are pathetically class-conscious. It is not a matter of the "toffs" and the workers... It is the distinction between the boy with the GCE and the boy without one, the trade apprentice and the boy labourer, the girl with the short-hand typing and the girl without'.[64] As an illustration, he uses the case of a conversation he had with a garage hand in a dance hall: 'I like her... but she wouldn't look at me. She did two years commercial course after leaving our school. Works in a big office'.[65] This exchange highlights the resilience of class identities in 1950s England, but also its complexities and nuances.

Powell's Leigh was not immune to the heightened concern around issues of youth, sexuality and rock 'n' roll. The local press reported on a so-called 'razor boy' being sentenced to three years for assault. A number of others had clashed at a 'teenage dance' at Astley Unitarian School in 1954.[66] A disturbance involving up to 30 youths on Leigh market was also linked to Teddy Boy violence.[67] The juvenile delinquent was also depicted on cinema screens at each end of the decade in films such as *The Blue Lamp* (1950) and *The Angry Silence* (1960).[68] Leigh now had a number of social spaces that offered working-class youths access to a 'new' discourse and imagery of escape provided by American popular culture. Individuals could spend their money on watching a wave of youth-centred films such as *Blackboard Jungle* (1955) or *Rebel without a Cause* (1955) at Sems cinema, buy the latest recordings from Jimmy's Record Shop or experience live music from performers such as Joe Loss at the Casino or George Melly, Mick Mulligan, Ken Colyer, Chris Barber and Lonnie Donegan at the Co-operative ballroom. The cinema, the record shop, the dance hall and the coffee bar were places were new releases could be heard, singles swapped and nights of dancing and romance planned.

By 1956, Leigh's youth culture was becoming visibly more American. 'Heartbreak Hotel' signified Elvis Presley's arrival when it charted in the spring of that year, offering a more exotic and hyper sexualised image than that proffered by some of the more clean-cut English and American singers. Elvis became an icon for male and female working-class youths across the country. In Birmingham, a respondent to the Mass Observation Project recalled her exposure to the newly crowned king of rock 'n' roll: 'I can't describe the world-shattering experience of hearing Elvis Presley for the first time and knowing the world had changed'.[69]

Political and religious leaders in Leigh began to show some concern for the moral welfare of the town's youth. Miss A. Rigby of a local church-based pressure group told the press that an increase in teenage pregnancy outside of marriage was linked to girls attending public houses and dances. She claimed that many of these girls were underage and made themselves look older through the use of clothing and make-up.[70] Working-class youths were happily spending their increased wages on cultural activities and simultaneously maintaining and subverting existing notions of masculinity and femininity. Many were combining a traditional working-class propensity for maximising their leisure time with a growing interest in American popular culture that was being channelled through a sense of collective identity and generational difference.

Yet according to some writers, this apparent explosion of youth culture in the 1950s has been overplayed. Davies has argued that in Lancashire a clearly defined youth culture consisting of dance halls, cinemas and mobility was already in place by the 1930s.

> The 'dance train' is perhaps the most poignant symbol of the relative privilege of young workers within working class families. Whereas parents, particularly mothers, often went without holidays, living out their lives within the confines of Manchester and Salford, the dance train carried the young and single to Blackpool, to Saturday night dances at the Tower Ballroom.[71]

This argument has some validity, but fails to take account of the sheer scale of affluence, consumerism and the developing multiplicity of the transmissions routes for the channelling of American popular culture that took place in the 1950s. For example, television proved to be a significant catalyst for spreading musical styles, fashions and youth cultures. *Cool for Cats* (1956), *Six-Five Special* (1957) and *Oh Boy!* (1958) brought teen idols and authentic American rock 'n' rollers into the living rooms of working-class youth.[72] This image and style soon found its way onto the dance floors of working-class towns. A reporter for the *Sunday Times* presented a portrait of a typical Saturday night at a dance hall in Staffordshire in 1958.

> Inside many of the girls dance together, and stand between dances still holding hands...The boys stand in groups, side-boarded, tee-shirted, narrow trousered. When they dance, they dance unsmiling, very conscious of their dignity, their style. Some dance 'tough', with a shrugging, jerky movement, more suited really to the boxing ring, others dance 'casual', keeping their own efforts down to a lazy, snake-like minimum, while the girls spin and kick like whipped tops.[73]

By 1958, the popularity of Elvis was confirmed through the screening of *Jailhouse Rock* in a number of provincial cinemas including the Ritz in Wigan.[74] Such cultural representations of youth continued to heighten anxieties around juvenile delinquency and a perceived generation gap opening-up between children and parents.[75] Teddy Boy culture was now cited as a contributing factor to rising crime rates amongst working-class youth in the cotton and coal towns of Lancashire. In Wigan a youth was sent to a remand home for stealing. His father claimed that he did not get along with his parents 'because they did not like him going around in Teddy Boy clothes'.[76] Intergenerational conflict was also noted by MacInnes in *Absolute Beginners*. Although subject to much critique, MacInnes's insight retains some validity and the scenes he depicts of coffee bars and record shops were by 1959 pretty indicative of the average High Street of most British towns.[77]

The proximity of Leigh to the city of Manchester ensured that it was open to a variety of metropolitan influences. Travel to the city by train, bus or car was swift in the 1950s, and youths could take advantage of much broader array of leisure activities and entertainment venues on offer. Mancunian youth were given a taste of American rock 'n' roll in person when Bill Haley toured in 1957 and performed at a local theatre. Manchester also had its own West Indian community in the Moss Side district. This became a focal point for aspiring jazz musicians and white youth who were wanted to experience a touch of the exotic.[78] Moss Side had a number of venues for live jazz including the Reno on Princess Road, the Nile Club and the Western Club.[79] The city's larger fairs and amusement arcades in particular the Belle Vue complex were also magnets for youths from the surrounding towns. Miners and cotton workers from Leigh would visit at the weekends or at the end of the shift where they would hear the sounds of Elvis, Little Richard and the Big Bopper being blasted out on rides such as the Waltzer and the Speedway. Fairs continued to provide a social space for northern working-class youth that contained sexual danger, Americana and exotica through to the 1970s.[80] The conventions of towns such as Leigh and Wigan could be subverted through adolescent sexual activity, rock 'n' roll and contact with social outsiders such as gypsies and itinerant workers.

Technology, music, fashion and film might have been transforming the cultural lives of Leigh's working-class youth, but this took place in the context of familiar experiences of everyday life. Moorhouse claimed that the 'Lancashire paving stones still echo to the clatter of clogs, but more frequently now the mill workers pad along on crêpe soles'.[81] Yet in the more metropolitan districts, class and regional identities were becoming pressured and subject to challenge from within. Mark Abrams in his research on youth in 1960 claimed that 'youths were more likely to vote Tory than Labour, favoured a reduction in class differences and were optimistic about their jobs and futures'.[82] This was patently less true in some of the northern industrial towns such as Leigh and Wigan, but working-class youth did share the longing to escape the workplace and the strictures of the time clock that were being experienced by those in more socially and economically mixed localities. In an article in *Encounter,* Abrams claimed that for 'most boys and girls, going out in the evening is the focal purpose of the day'.[83] This seemed to fit the experience of Powell and his contemporaries, yet they never felt that the culture from which they came actively shunned the music that they were embracing.

Coffee bars, skiffle, youth clubs, class and consumption

For Powell and his friends in Leigh the coffee bar was often the first point of call on a night out to the fair, cinema or dance hall. The first recognisable youth-oriented coffee bar appeared in 1952/3 when the Moka on Frith Street in Soho installed a Gaggia espresso machine.[84] Coffee bars were mostly frequented by youths aged between 15–18 and those slightly older for which the traditional pub offered little excitement. They were also cheaper and represented a social space uninhabited by parents and authority figures.[85] In Leigh, the Espresso Café on Chapel Street was a popular haunt. Ronnie Carr recalled that it was in the coffee bar where style was flaunted and discussions of popular music led to the formation of groups.[86] The coffee bar formed one component of a network of social spaces that included youth clubs, pubs and dance halls leading to the creation of a local milieu in which popular music became enmeshed into an existing sense of individual and collective identity. Carr and his contemporaries retained their sense of belonging to a broader intergenerational occupational identity based on the coal and cotton industries, but popular music and Americana gave them independence and a sense of a world and culture beyond Leigh and Wigan.

The explosion of coffee bars was noted by *Punch* in 1956 when B. A. Young examined the way in which they represented a changing England through the impact of America, Europe and youth affluence. He described the way that coffee bars were colonised by gangs: 'A prevalent Teddy-boy population will tend to turn a coffee bar into a youth club. The boys are very rich, as they often do one job all day and another part-time one in the evenings, chiefly to meet their tailors' and hairdressers' bills'.[87] Two years later, *Punch* again commissioned a piece on coffee bars sending Alex Atkinson into the heart of London's Soho to experience the phenomenon.

> Here the coffee-houses are, first, very cramped; second, so decorated that each has some recognisable, albeit tawdry, foreign aspect …; third, illuminated by the use of as little electric current as may be convenient without rendering the premises entirely pitch dark; and fourth, filled with a hubbub of music so loud and so continuous that a conversation would have little chance of survival…Of the nature of the ladies and gentlemen themselves who frequent these places, it may be said that they are chiefly

> of an age between fourteen and twenty...As to the music which plays without ceasing in these establishments, this is frequently provided by a device known as a 'juke-box'...At other times the music emanates, through loud-speakers, from some dim, hidden recess...where a party of musicians are performing upon stringed instruments, and howling, in a nasal, unmusical fashion difficult to define...These 'numbers', as they are called, had their origin many years ago among primitive peasants and convicted criminals in the United States of America...there was the relentless throb and wail of the music...the resulting bedlam of rattling din crashed and rebounded from every wall...In all my investigations of the night life of London I have observed...I found it infinitely sad.[88]

Concerned members of the public, the police and magistrates viewed coffee bars as places that attracted delinquents and could lead to the corruption of working-class youth. In May 1959, police raided a coffee bar in Bermondsey leading to arrests and a march of up to 80 youths to the local police station in reaction.[89] This act of direct action subverts Hoggart's notion of the typical coffee bar clientele as representing 'a depressing group and one by no means typical of working-class people'.[90] Progressive film-makers were also attempting to present a more measured depiction of working-class youth to counteract the negative portrayal in the press most notably in the documentary by Karel Reisz' *We Are the Lambeth Boys* (1959). Reisz along with a new generation of directors and novelists were keen to present images of England with youth and the working-class at its centre.[91] More populist film-makers exploited youth culture and its attachment to coffee bars, popular music and the Teddy Boy style in films such as *Violent Playground* (1958), *Beat Girl* (1960) and *Wind of Change* (1961).[92]

For many English youths the experience of both recorded and live music in the coffee bar was indeed a transformative experience that is replayed in many biographies, autobiographies, diaries and oral testimonies. Their lives now had a soundtrack that instilled in them a longing for escape from their families, jobs and localities but also an affirmation of a particular sense of self and belonging to their peer group. Both rock 'n' roll and the then current trend for skiffle music also provided opportunities for a career outside the factory, the coal mine and the cotton mill. Skiffle music provided a musical genre for English youth to put their own particular interpretation on the sounds that were emanating from the jukebox. The national embrace of skiffle allowed working-class youth to create their own groups relatively cheaply and to mimic the artists they were listening to on record and watching in local theatres and dance halls.[93]

Skiffle was a distinctly English musical form, albeit one that drew on American folk and blues genres. Chas McDevitt, in his definitive history draws a lineage from musical hall performers such as the ukulele-playing entertainer George Formby through to the popularisers of the form in the

1950s.[94] The simple style of skiffle had been around since the late 1940s but became a national phenomenon in 1956 with the success of Lonnie Donegan and his recording of 'Rock Island Line'.[95] The craze flowered in the burgeoning coffee bar scene of the mid-1950s, as the dance halls were reluctant to dedicate too much space to skiffle music.[96] Skiffle provided one of the main tributaries for the development of English rock 'n' roll. It became a national phenomenon that had wide press coverage, national competitions and a cross-class appeal. By 1961 the movement had fragmented and had been superseded first by rock 'n' roll and then by American rhythm and blues.

As skiffle and rock 'n' roll was forming a specific soundscape amongst working-class youth in Leigh and Wigan, Powell had followed in his father's footsteps, leaving school at 15 and starting work as an apprentice weaver at the Lilford Weaving Mill in 1958.[97] Employment in cotton textiles was now precarious with many mills facing closure, but workers at least now enjoyed an improvement in conditions. By the 1950s, textile workers had gained a ten-day holiday with pay and a 45-hour working week.[98] During their 'wakes weeks', cotton workers would travel to Blackpool, the Isle of Man or the Butlin's holiday camps on the Welsh and English coasts. This vast migration of workers would enable youngsters to meet people with similar interests. Many of the first generation of British rock 'n' roll musicians gained schooling in popular music in the various concert halls at these locations where they were introduced to the big band swing and American vocal style that had been adopted by British performers.

The Buddy Holly Tour stopped at Wigan Ritz in March 1958 and two months later the Jerry Lee Lewis scandal exploded in the press giving rock 'n' roll and its practitioners a subversive edge that made it even more appealing to sections of working-class youth.[99] For Powell, the sounds and images of American rock 'n' roll had a dramatic impact. Powell was caught up in the skiffle craze and at 13 was playing with other like-minded pupils in various musical combinations at Leigh Central Secondary School. Other local musicians that would tread the same path as Powell experienced a similar conversion. Ronnie Carr (the Lemon Drop Kid), the son of a local coal miner, worked underground at Wood End Colliery, Bedford. He regularly performed impromptu musical sessions underground. Along with other Lancashire miners, Carr exhibited a fierce loyalty to his workmates and expressed a proud local identity. The Lancashire Area of the National Union of Mineworkers also personified such characteristics. The General Secretary Edwin Hall[100] commanded respect from all branches and local miners would often rebel against political encroachments from other districts. Although there had been a communist presence in the coalfield, Lancashire remained a pragmatic constituent of the national union.[101]

Both Powell and Carr had fully embraced rock 'n' roll and felt that they could make their own contribution to the youth culture of Leigh and Wigan.

Carr was born in 1935 and from an early age he showed an interest in music and recalls hearing American musicians such as Benny Goodman on the radio. In 1957, he formed his own skiffle group. The Dominoes played in retirement homes, pubs and clubs in Leigh and Wigan. Their musical repertoire was enriched with the arrival of the sounds of Bill Haley and later Elvis Presley. He had met Powell in 1957 when they were both playing in the Foresters' pub in Glazebury.[102] Powell was still in school at this time, but concentrating more on music than his formal studies. His boogie-woogie piano style was now paying him 'ten shillings two nights a week'.[103] Mike O'Neil, from neighbouring Lowton was also a regular at the Foresters'. O'Neil was born in Leigh in 1938. He attended piano lessons from the age of eight at the home of a musician on Cotton Street. He probably passed Powell in the street on his way to lessons. Powell would later play with O'Neil as a duo and as a member of the Satellites. O'Neil had formed a skiffle group, Wabash, with like-minded friends at Lowton Youth Club in 1956 going on to play venues such as the Cross Keys in Ashton-in-Makerfield.[104]

Youth clubs provided a forum for the exchange of records, conversation about popular music, performance and dancing. In 1958 the American writer Clancy Sigal filed a report a two-part feature for a national newspaper that offered an insight to their activities: 'The jive room seems to be growing smaller and hotter. It is 9.45, fifteen minutes to closing time. The atmosphere quickens the spike-heeled girls moving about more freely in quick mincing steps between the groups of restless boys, while couples speedily bob and weave in cha-cha time to "Mister Moonlighter" sung by Fats Domino'.[105] Musicians would exploit the increasing number of pubs, coffee bars, dance halls and youth clubs that were eager to attract working-class youth. Many served their apprenticeships in youth clubs by learning cover versions of popular hits and exchanging ideas with their peers. Such performances would provide useful rehearsal time and space to present 'rough' shows to unfussy audiences.

Between 1956–8, O'Neil played in various guises in the pubs of Leigh, Wigan and surrounding areas. The Globe and the George and Dragon became major venues in Leigh where O'Neil, Powell and Carr would play regular gigs. The Dominoes, including Carr on guitar and Powell on piano were proving a popular draw in the pubs, clubs and dance halls. Their rehearsal base was the Railway public house close to Parsonage Colliery. Some early shows also provided a musical foil for illegal gambling halls. Carr recalled such a premises in Wigan, where the band would play the front room to a small audience, while in an adjacent room people would be playing slot machines.[106] The Dominoes played at various functions throughout 1957 for a fee of £3 10s and moved on to bigger venues such as the Monaco ballroom in nearby Hindley.[107] The lifestyle was far from glamorous with the band consisting of coal miners and cotton operatives who had to work a long arduous shift then cart their instruments by bus or by hitching a ride on wagons delivering soft drinks to the thirsty populace of the industrial towns.

Powell's stepmother was a formidable working-class matriarch and was critical of his new nocturnal habits. He was playing shows late into the night and having to sleep in the outside toilet because she had locked him out.[108] The Dominoes also had to face the wrath of the more serious classical and jazz musicians when playing at particular venues. Carr recalls that the owner of the Leigh Casino would hide the Bechstein grand piano when they were around wanting to avoid Powell 'plonking on it'.[109] Yet the working-class youth of the town were now rocking to a largely American rock 'n' roll soundtrack. At Leigh Casino in 1957, there was a performance by Mike Haslam (the Elvis Presley of Bolton).[110] Each dance hall had its local Jerry Lee Lewis, Buddy Holly and Elvis Presley. At this stage Powell, Carr and others were content to copy the styles of their new American heroes, and it would be some years before this generation of musicians would strive for a more original form of popular music that would be infused with distinctively English inflections.

Abrams claimed that by 1959 teenagers were spending almost half of their money on dance halls, films, magazines and records.[111] Some even resorted to crime to fuel their social lives. A 15-year-old Leigh boy was prosecuted for stealing from a local cotton mill claiming that he was driven to commit the crime because he 'wanted a bit more money to keep with my mates'.[112] Traditional working-class leisure activities such as cinema going were in decline, yet films such as *The Girl Can't Help It* (1956), *Rock Around the Clock* (1956) and *Rock You Sinners* (1958), which featured popular music, provided a magnet to working-class youth.[113] Cinemas had been closing down throughout the decade, and in 1959, Lord Rank announced that many of his would be converted into bowling alleys. The first two to be converted were the Ambassador in Hayes, Middlesex and the Regal in Golders Green.[114] Here was a further example of aspects of Americana jumping from the screen to the English high street. The working-class youth of Leigh and Wigan could spend an afternoon in a coffee bar listening to American rock 'n' roll on the jukebox, play ten-pin bowling at their local alley and then witness the live sounds of American popular music being performed by local musicians in the evening at a dance hall.

Holiday camps and the road to London

The Dominoes began aiming higher than the pub circuit of Leigh and Wigan. They were now commanding £5 10s for performances and were travelling further afield to Cheshire and Derbyshire.[115] Yet they retained their link to the working-class culture that had been enjoyed by their parents. All members of the group were still working and Carr and Powell divided their time between coal mine, cotton mill, concert hall and attending matches involving Wigan rugby league club. They both attended the Rugby Cup Final in May 1959 and witnessed a victory for the team that was being transformed by the sporting prowess of Billy Boston, Eric Ashton, Dave Bolton and Mick Sullivan.[116] Boston had signed for Wigan in 1953 and was already on the way to becoming a legendary figure in the club's history. Powell had himself been a promising Rugby player but was increasingly preoccupied with music.

Mike O'Neil was the first to make the break from the drudgery of his job at the Vulcan works in Newton and aimed to make a career in the music business in London. The catalyst for this was his experience at the Butlin's holiday camp in Pwllheli, North Wales in 1957.[117] Holiday camps in the mid-50s were the testing ground for aspiring British singers and groups. Success in their local, regional and national talent contests would often lead to work in London and recording contracts.[118] Moreover, the camps employed many performers that were already accomplished musicians who had to have the ability to please large audiences who were keen to enjoy a more professional show than they could witness back home in local pubs and dance halls. The fact that musicians were also taken out of their localities by the camps also provided ample opportunities for sexual liaisons and hedonistic behaviour.[119] It was in such locations that working-class youth fell in love, lost their virginity and in some cases contracted sexually transmitted infections.

Carr had been going to Butlin's since 1955 and had witnessed the success of musicians who had come through the contests and were subsequently making good money in London and the provinces. He had won various competitions over the years for his guitar playing, singing and jiving. In 1959, Carr, Powell and a large Leigh contingent arrive at Butlin's. The main draw that week was the resident group Rory Blackwell and the Blackjacks.[120] Two of Blackwell's band members were forced to leave the camp for personal misdemeanours leaving him short of a guitarist and piano player.[121] Carr filled in some nights as did Powell who proved to be an already accomplished piano player and was offered a contract for the rest of the season. Meanwhile, Carr performed with a fellow coal miner Tony Turner, beating Rory Storm and the Hurricanes, with Ringo Starkey on drums in the national talent contest.[122] The success of Carr was helped by the 3000 strong Leigh and Wigan contingent that were at the camp during the coal and cotton 'wakes weeks'.[123] It was here where the Leigh lads sang an alternative version of 'Grand Coulee Dam' exhibiting the resilience of their local identity.[124]

> Wigan have thirteen wonders that the Rugby fans know well
> Eric Ashton and David Bolton I guess you know them well
> But now the greatest wonder in Wigan's Rugby land is good old Billy Boston as he flies down past the stand[125]

Powell now had the chance of joining Blackwell with good pay and career prospects. However, he was still only 16, and his father was both worried and reluctant to let him gamble on a music career. Powell checked the legality of leaving home with the local police. He stayed at home for a week while Carr took his place on Blackwell's band.[126] Powell settled his differences with his family, and Carr records in his diary that he left the Dominoes in July 1959.[127] He told a local reporter that 'with Clive being engaged by Rory Blackwell we've got to look out now for a new pianist but we wish him all the best'.[128] The Dominoes disbanded, and Carr formed the Beat Boys who steadily built a reputation in the region supporting the Beatles and the Rolling Stones when they visited local concert halls in the early 1960s.[129]

Working-class youth culture in Leigh and Wigan continued to develop through the adoption of the latest fashions and the consumption of popular music. The towns also experienced continued outbreaks of youth violence and vandalism that were appearing in some of the bigger cities such as Manchester, London, Liverpool and Birmingham. In March 1959, a scuffle in a Leigh cinema had led to a near-fatal stabbing.[130] In May, Constance Bickmore, a local magistrate, called on the South Lancashire Girl Guide Association to rescue 'Teddy Girl types from insecure lives influenced by commercialism'.[131] In nearby Manchester, a gang of Teddy Boys had pelted Cliff Richard and the Shadows with eggs and tomatoes during a performance.[132] Some were clearly out to make trouble, but others were critical of the inauthentic version of American youth culture and rock 'n' roll that was being offered by the rather tame English performers such as Tommy Steele, Terry Dene and Dickie Valentine.[133] To the more ambitions and adventurous purveyors of popular music, it was the bigger cities of North West England and ultimately London that could get them closer to the real essence of rock 'n' roll, escape, fantasy and social transgression.

The number of social spaces providing a soundscape of rock 'n' roll that were now available to English working-class youth was proliferating through town and country.[134] Young people from Leigh had an array of coffee bars, record shops and clubs in nearby Manchester.[135] As an alternative to live music they could dance to records at the Plaza Hotel Ballroom that were being played by ex-miner Jimmy Savile at his lunch-time specials.[136] According to Haslam there 'was something of a personality cult surrounding him; his followers dressed like him, behaved like him, took his music taste as gospel'.[137] Manchester was also leading the way in witnessing the movement of youths from coffee bars into clubs that specifically catered for their tastes.[138] According to Lawson, by age 17, some wanted to break out of the confines of the coffee bar and sought excitement in clubs like the New Astoria and the Oasis.[139]

The industrial towns of Leigh and Wigan provide a particular image of England in 1960 that was still defined by the Victorian industries of cotton and coal and the working-class culture that had emerged from them. This was a world away from the affluence and social ruptures described by MacInnes in the London of *Absolute Beginners*. Nonetheless, as this exploration of the experiences of working-class youth in these localities has shown, American cinema, rock 'n' roll and the broader youth culture it engendered did have some impact. It did not sweep away an attachment to a particular sense of class, locality and labour politics, but it gave youth a further tool to make sense of their social situation and to both mentally and in some cases physically escape from the boundaries that such a milieu had created. In this way, rock 'n' roll both reaffirmed and challenged a particular 'structure of feeling' that formed part of the shared consciousness of working-class youth in North West England.

The vast majority of working-class music consumers in Leigh and Wigan used popular music as an escape from the drudgery of the workplace and as a soundtrack to love, heartbreak and hedonism. Yet for those like Powell, Carr and O'Neil, this was never going to be enough. Unlike the character in Keith Waterhouse's novel *Billy Liar* (1959), they were unwilling to settle for merely mental escape. For O'Neil, Carr and Powell, the youth club, the pub, the dance hall and the holiday camp would provide a springboard for career advancement and the bright lights of London. This particular network of musicians would leave their mark on the musical history of Leigh and their journeys to the metropolis would connect them to an array of movers and shakers in the entertainment world of the capital. Most notably, in becoming Georgie Fame, Clive Powell's musical journey continued to highlight the working-class origins of English rock 'n' roll, rhythm and blues and its associated youth cultures. His involvement in the London rhythm and blues scene represents a crucial point where English popular music became firmly embedded in the cultures and struggles of African Americans and recent West Indian migrants.

2
Exploring London's Soho and the Flamingo Club with Georgie Fame and the Blue Flames

This chapter examines Clive Powell's geographical and musical trajectory through a period that has been popularly perceived as a crossroads for English popular music between 1959 and 1964.[1] His journey took him from a working-class, industrial Northern England to a perceptibly more cosmopolitan England that by 1964 was shaking to the beats of West Indian ska music, rock 'n' roll and African American rhythm and blues. In this period, London provided social spaces where the boundaries and conventions of class and ethnicity could be temporarily traversed.[2] Popular music played an essential role in this process through the way in which it became embedded in coffee bars, dance halls and clubs. It was in such places where a different England was being imagined on record, stage and dance floor. Powell's engagement with various aspects of the city's youth culture presents a particular image of England that remained rooted in class yet was open to particular incursions into, and transformations of, particular social and cultural milieus.

Powell's career presents a nexus through which aspects of a 'new England' were struggling to emerge. His musical journey across a multiplicity of locales and soundscapes connected him to West Indian migrants, homosexual impresarios, writers, gangsters, United States military personnel and a youth subculture that was influenced by the sounds of 'black America', the styles of Italy and the cinema of the French New Wave.[3] London introduced Powell to the pre-rock 'n' roll culture of the capital's entertainment business that had been built on the 'variety show' and its associated characters and sharp practices. The discovery of his talents at the Two I's coffee bar led him to hit records and wider commercial success as a mainstream pop star. Yet it was Powell's prominence in the burgeoning rhythm and blues scene that confirms his importance in symbolising the connections between class, race, sexuality and youth culture in post-war England.

Northern lads in London

Mike O'Neil caught a train from Leigh to London in 1958 and headed straight for the Two I's coffee bar situated on Old Compton Street in Soho.[4] This venue was a magnet for talent from across the country and became established as a place where careers could be forged and fortunes made. The Two I's was run by Paul Lincoln and Ray Hunter, two Australian wrestlers who installed a jukebox and then extended into the basement to provide a stage for live performances.[5] Here in this one small building was a microcosm of a popular music scene and youth culture that by the late 1950s had appeared on high streets across many of the major towns and cities of England. The Two I's became a mecca for aspiring musicians from across the country seeking an authentic slice of metropolitan youth culture.[6] Working-class men and women frequenting the clubs and coffee bars of Soho would cross paths with migrants, gangsters, homosexuals, prostitutes, pimps, showbiz impresarios, shysters, confidence tricksters, wealthy hedonists and corrupt public servants.[7]

O'Neil was attracted by the music and glamour of London but also wanted to avoid his stint of national service in the armed forces.[8] Unlike many other northern dreamers he had actually made the journey away from the parochialism that to them had been a feature of their lives in the English provinces. In the same year, another aspiring musician, Bruce Welch forged a similar trek from a coal mining community in County Durham and like O'Neil experienced a great sense of exhilaration and liberation. He was shocked by the contrast between the metropolis and North East England. Welch recalled that he 'sometimes saw men kissing each other in secluded doorways in Old Compton Street... [and] there was a thriving rent boy business around Piccadilly'.[9] In the coal mining towns of Lancashire and County Durham homosexuality remained very much in the closet. Yet here in London it was openly expressed, particularly on the streets of Soho and in the variety of coffee bars and clubs that formed the core of the city's youth culture. Elements of the gay subculture of the capital meshed with aspects of youth culture and popular music providing personnel, style, musical genres and completing the matrix of class, race and sexuality that formed the foundation of English rock 'n' roll.[10]

To the many of the northern working-class youths who headed to Soho sex seemed to be everywhere with prostitutes, strippers and transient couples heading in and out of cafés, flats and clubs. Soho was already established in the collective consciousness as a location for hedonism and transgression.[11] In his sensationalist 'indiscreet guide' of the 1940s, Stanley Jackson depicted the district as being awash with music, drugs, criminality and sex: 'You can't move far in Soho at night without seeing the sluts in slacks, wartime hangovers... They all... chew gum and talk a ghastly blend of Brooklyn and Billingsgate'.[12] A report in a tabloid newspaper from 1959 of the last night of an Elephant and Castle pub that was being closed to make way for a junction road was also illustrative of a working-class culture that was being diluted by slum clearance and the emergence of new forms of leisure activities.[13] The pub had opened in 1758 and 'it spanned an era of climbing drink prices, changing songs, entertainment from Marie Lloyd to the telly...They drank the place dry, sang Auld Lang Syne, and, of course Knees Up Mother Brown'.[14] A similar portrait of a culture at the point of transition was later depicted in Michael Orrom's brilliant documentary film *Portrait of Queenie* (1964), which examined the interaction between regular drinkers at the Iron Bridge Tavern, Poplar.

O'Neil was finding some success as a paid musician and revelling in the variety of coffee bars and clubs where he could immerse himself in the sounds of jazz, blues and rock 'n' roll. After exhibiting his piano skills at the Two I's he worked with Clay Nicholls and the Blue Flames.[15] He was then offered a more substantial job playing with Colin Hicks, the brother of Tommy Steele and his band the Cabin Boys.[16] A seven-month tour of Italy gave O'Neil further experience of life as a touring musician and a potential career as a recording artist and pop star.[17] He played in a network of venues across London and became a regular at the Flamingo Club in Wardour Street. The Flamingo featured live jazz through the week and rock 'n' roll on Sunday afternoons. The club had been established in 1952 by Jeff Kruger a jazz aficionado at a cost of £15,000 and had a membership of 17,000.[18] A profile in the *Daily Express* in 1959 claimed that it was 'probably the biggest example of the hard-cash success of the jazz clubs. It is also the prototype for close on 100 other clubs throughout the country in that it has low lights, solid music, but no hard liquor'.[19] O'Neil stood as an exemplar to Powell and others in Leigh who could now point to someone who had gone to London and 'made it'.

Powell followed the path trod by O'Neil in heading for London and the bright lights and swinging sounds of the Two I's. However, he was leaving on a firmer footing than O'Neil having secured his position with Rory Blackwell and the Blackjacks after his performances at Butlin's holiday camp. Powell's father was reluctant to let him leave given his employment in the cotton mill and his youth, but Powell was adamant that the city could lead him out of the life that had been led by his parents and grandparents. He reconstructed the scene in 1965 for *Rave* magazine.

> I went around to the police station and I said, 'I'm sixteen and I've been offered a job working as a musician If I go away can you bring me back? The copper said, 'If you lead a decent life and you're not committing crimes you can stay away as long as you like. All the same, I didn't do it. I said, I'm sorry, Rory, I've decided to swallow it...So Monday comes around and I go back to the factory and find they're all taking sides over the whole business. Some people were saying things like, 'we've heard all about that palaver on t'camp and others were saying. 'This is your chance. You want to get away from it while you're all reet'.[20]

Powell's immediate career opportunities were cut short when the promise of sustained work with Blackwell for the rest of 1959 failed to materialise. He had managed to save £15 but needed more regular work. In an interview for the Radio Luxembourg Annual in 1965, Powell recalled his experiences of his early days in the capital.

> We couldn't get any work and I was staying in a different house every night .... In the mornings we used to take a tube into the West End and hang around the 2 I's coffee bar all day praying someone would turn up and give us a job... Eventually we did find something to do when Rory took the group into a dance hall in Islington. We painted the posters ourselves and stayed for three months. It was a big flop. My daily diet at that time consisted of a sixpenny bag of chips. The owner of the hall let me stay in a room above it, which was the most depressing place imaginable. The furniture added up to a dirty old bed and one chair.[21]

Powell stayed in touch with O'Neil, occasionally slept at his flat in Soho and devoured his collection of jazz records. Like other working and unemployed musicians Powell and O'Neil spent their days listening to the jukebox in the various coffee bars and seeking out recording opportunities and live work. One coffee bar in particular, Act 1/Scene 1, opposite the Two I's became an unofficial talent office for entertainers. Musicians would sit around, nursing cappuccinos, waiting for bookings and contemplating their future.[22] Struggling to survive, Powell found work as a pianist in the Essex Arms in London's dockland where he was also given a room above the pub.[23] His experiences in the working-men's clubs of Leigh and Wigan had provided him with a broad repertoire of songs and stage patter that could be adjusted to particular audiences.

The London that O'Neil and Powell had recently arrived in was now buzzing with a youth culture that was vibrant, colourful and in some cases threatening. Colin MacInnes had attempted to capture the zeitgeist in *Absolute Beginners*: 'you could see everywhere the signs of un-silent teenage revolution... narrow coffee bars and darkened cellars with the kids packed tight'.[24] Yet for all MacInnes's revolutionary rhetoric, the reality was that popular music was still directed by a group of impresarios whose roots stretched back to music hall and variety. Tin Pan Alley (Denmark Street) was a hive of musical activity. The *Daily Express* described the scenes and soundscapes of the engine room of English popular music: 'Up there behind the grimy windows, behind the dirty curtains... There is Johnny Dankworth[25] on the top floor. Underneath there is Regent Sound... this is the street where love is manufactured, sweated and pounded on honky-tonk pianos into crotchets and quavers'.[26] The reporter acknowledged that consumers also played a role in generating product, and it was the 'teenager' who represented the most powerful force in Tin Pan Alley.

> He operates mainly behind the scenes. He spends £300,000 a day – in cash. His support automatically ensures a well-nigh permanent place on the hit parade, TV appearances by the dozen, and probably a five-figure salary before you are 21. His death ear is the kiss of death. The identity of this all-powerful music arbiter. The teenager, that body of 7,500,000 pairs of ears and eyes who now hold almost complete control of the record industry.[27]

Powell, O'Neil and other working-class lads realised that the social conventions of the industrial towns from which they came did not adequately prepare them for the brutal world of music business capitalism. The impresarios who hovered around the coffee bars and clubs of Soho were primarily driven by the profit motive and 'bottom-lines'. Larry Parnes was a key-player on the teenage entertainment scene. He had developed a stable of stars and given England its very own Elvis Presley through the figure of Tommy Steele. Parnes saw rock 'n' roll as a first step to a conventional show business career. He spent much of his time trawling the coffee bars for new talent and found Marty Wilde, Billy Fury, Dickie Pride, Vince Eager, Duffy Power, Joe Brown and Johnny Gentle.[28] All his charges were under 20, and he moulded their image to fit the provincial sensibilities of English youth primarily in the form of pubescent working-class girls.[29] In an interview with the national press, Parnes outlined his relationship with his performers: 'Let's say Marty [Wilde] grossed £26,000 last year. Well, I get 30 per cent commission and another 10 per cent goes to the booker, so that's £10,400 off right away. Backing group gets £6,600, road manager £1,500, travel and accommodation £4,000 a year. Keeping his wife and his flat £1,500. He ends up with £2000 – and that's before tax'.[30] Parnes was also another crucial link between the world of London's homosexual subculture and the masculine working-class world from which many of his performers emerged. Similarly, Joe Meek, the talented but troubled record producer who was plagued by his inability to adequately deal with his homosexuality and his obsession with the supernatural was indicative of the particular types encountered by working-class youths from Northern England on arrival in London.[31] Carr recalled that when the Beat Boys recorded their debut single in Meek's studio the producer had only just met the group and 'he was already trying to tap me up'.[32]

Another important figure in spotting young working-class talent was Lionel Bart, the son of a Jewish East End tailor and already an accomplished songwriter. He was influenced by music hall and understood the values and culture of the working-class through his membership of the Communist Party. Bart worked closely with Parnes and provided his stable of stars with their early hits.[33] Like Parnes he was homosexual, and they both frequented the network of gay clubs around London and the coffee bars of Soho.[34] According to Mort, the Two I's itself 'attracted some younger queer men'.[35] Parnes and Bart also attended La Caverne, a late-night drinking club in Soho.

Napier-Bell claims that 'Parnes's technique of titillating his own sexual tastes by cleaning-up working-class boys and sending them out to sing [became] the template of all gay managers'.[36] The way that Parnes reinvented acts was a reflection of class identities that were still encoded in the fabric of post-war England. To Napier-Bell, 'class distinction was deeply ingrained in the record business. Companies were controlled and run by people from middle-class backgrounds, mostly from public schools'.[37] This provides a crucial insight into the way in which class underpinned relationships in the entertainment industry and how many of the working-class youths who forged careers in this sector of the economy faced a similar process of exploitation that they had experienced in the factory, mine and mill.

Beneath the likes of Parnes and Bart was a sub-stratum of grasping impresarios and their charges. These figures had long been visible figures around Denmark Street. Jackson's 'indiscreet guide' provides a portrait.

> Here is 'ham' in 57 varieties; tired acts in long overcoats, nicotine stained fingers and phoney American accents; the acts that are 'resting'; the acrobats, midgets, vents, conjurers, tap dancers, cross-talk comedians with faded routines; the tenors striking John Barrymore poses and flashing old press cuttings; the song-and-dance teams that slew Wigan six months ago. The aura of provincial 'digs' clings to them but the patter is desperately bright and confident'.[38]

After the initial burst of American rock 'n' roll in the form of Elvis Presley, Jerry Lee Lewis, Little Richard and Buddy Holly, the English popular music scene seemed stagnant and constrained by the conservatism of the power brokers in the industry. In 1959, the *New Musical Express* declared that rock 'n' roll was 'being absorbed into the mainstream of Tin Pan Alley's output'.[39] The influence of the music business over young people was debated in the House of Commons amid growing calls to deal with the way that unscrupulous individuals were manipulating teenage consumption. England had its very own version of the 'payola scandal' that had rocked the popular music business in the United States. The Labour MP Roy Mason claimed that 'teenagers were being swindled by an unruly alliance behind the plugging of songs – DJs, producers of record programmes'.[40] The *Daily Express* picked up the story and named the DJs in the pay of the record companies. 'Pete Murray – BBC DJ and in pay of Decca, Jack Jackson – ditto, Jack Good – EMI Luxembourg DJ and TV Producer; Sam Costa – BBC DJ EMI, DJ for Luxembourg; Peter West – BBC Compere of Housewife's Choice – EMI DJ; Tony Hall – BBC Jazz Compere Decca DJ; David Gell – BBC DJ Luxembourg DJ for Phillips; Kent Walton – TV compere TOP rank DJ; David Jacobs BBC DJ – Luxembourg DJ for Pye.[41]

Throughout 1959 Powell was still seeking elevation into a regular well-paying route into the music business. His break came when Parnes sought out Powell on the advice of Bart.[42] He had encountered Powell in a Soho club amongst a group of musicians looking for work. He attended a performance of Rory Blackwell and recommended that Parnes should set-up an audition for the pianist. Powell also stayed with Bart for a few days where he put on a display of his skills with renditions of Jerry Lee Lewis classics.[43] In October, Bart arranged for Powell to audition for Parnes at the Lewisham Gaumont during the Marty Wilde Show. He performed Jerry Lee Lewis's 'High School Confidential' and was hired as a backing musician for Parnes's 'stable of stars'.[44] Powell's first tour was with Marty Wilde's Big Beat Show where he used the stage name of Wells. Ronnie Carr caught his performance at the Liverpool Empire as part of a Leigh delegation that included Powell's family and friends.[45] Many of these concerts were not the innocent gatherings of smitten youths depicted in newsreels and cinematic representations. Violence often broke out during and after performances with a heavy police presence at many venues. When the show arrived at the Leeds Empire a fight broke out in the galley and a 17-year-old Barry Cattle was stabbed in the back.[46] Concerns around youth violence revolved around the anti-Americanism of the more Conservative tabloids. There were attacks in newspapers such as the *Daily Mail* and the *Daily Express* on the impact of American films and the showing of westerns on television.[47]

As with other members of Parnes's stable of stars Clive Powell was advised to change his name to Georgie Fame. Parnes reasoned that Powell sounded like George Formby and was going to be famous, so Georgie Fame was the result. Fame provided piano to the live performances of Billy Fury, Marty Wilde, Dickie Pride and others, but his musical education was transformed by his tour with Eddie Cochran and Gene Vincent in 1960. In becoming Georgie Fame, Powell had traversed the crossroads that led him to performing with American rock 'n' roll stars and embracing American rhythm and blues. Here was a clear example of a 'historic encounter' between a working-class textile worker from North West England and the sounds of black America that would influence the development of popular music and youth subculture for the rest of the century.

Class, race and rhythm 'n' blues

The Cochran/Vincent tour that started at the Ipswich Granada on 24 January 1960 was a seminal event.[48] The music performed at these shows brought American rhythm and blues to a mass audience. When the tour reached the Liverpool Empire between 14 March and 19 March, John Lennon and Paul McCartney were in the audience.[49] At Cardiff Gaumont on 26 February, a young singer from a South Wales mining village, Tom Jones, was in attendance. The tour provided a bridge between the 1950s and the 1960s with the pioneers of American rock 'n' roll passing the baton to a new generation of English musicians that would gain significant success through performing rhythm and blues numbers. The typical running order for the show was Billy Raymond, Tony Sheridan and Joe Brown. After the interval, Fame (now dubbed the new singing pianist) performed 'High School Confidential' followed by sets from Cochran and Vincent.[50] Vincent's image fed into the style adopted by motorcycle gangs that had emerged in the 1950s providing a rebellious image for Ton-Up Boys and Rockers across England.[51]

Cochran's life was ended in a fatal car crash on 17 April after the last show of the run at Bristol Hippodrome. He had introduced Fame to the groundbreaking music of Ray Charles during the tour. Charles was the key figure in the development of American rhythm and blues and the creation of soul music. This proved to be a revelation to Fame providing the bridge from rock 'n' roll into rhythm and blues and soul. He continued to work with Vincent and made his recording debut providing piano backing when he recorded 'Pistol Packin Mama' and other songs at Abbey Road studios in the spring.[52] In May he teamed with his Mike O'Neil as part of Parnes's International Rock Show also featuring Vincent. O Neil' was now finding success as a composer writing songs for Colin Hicks but also through his involvement in Nero and the Gladiators.[53] Their first single 'Entry of the Gladiators', was based on a tune that had been used by Leigh Rugby League Club as a pre-match introduction and reached number 37 in the charts in 1961.[54]

The problem for Fame and other musicians was that at the end of tours they had to face many weeks without an income. In the summer of 1960, he accompanied Nero and the Gladiators in a summer season at Blackpool's Queen's Theatre with George Formby topping the bill.[55] This represented a bizarre meeting of worlds combining variety with elements of Soho bohemianism and English pop. After a further spell out of work, Fame became a member of Billy Fury's Blue Flames in 1961. Fury was perhaps the closest thing that England had to Elvis in the late 1950s.[56] Ronald Wycherley (Fury) was born in Liverpool in 1940 to working-class parents and had previously been a deckhand on the Mersey ferries.[57] Working his way through skiffle and rock 'n' roll styles, he was discovered by Parnes and groomed for stardom. He had a hit in 1959 with 'Maybe Tomorrow'. A year later he recorded *The Sound of Fury*, a long-playing slice of English rock 'n' roll written by Fury. Lyrically the album was formulaic, but it nonetheless represented a break in the tradition of artists recording songs written by others and selected by their management team. Class impacted on Fury's personality and how he viewed himself in the world of show business. He was riddled with insecurity about his humble origins and rarely spoke on stage in order to hide his Liverpool accent.[58] Through working with Fury, Fame made his broadcasting debut, appearing on the radio programme Jazz Club and on television in the BBC's children's programme *Crackerjack*.

Fame spent the summer and autumn of 1961 playing piano with Fury but felt frustration by performing the same songs each night. He had now embraced rhythm and blues and wanted to express himself through the sounds and styles of 'black America'. The absorption of rhythm and blues by a number of aspiring musicians was creating a dividing line between English pop and a more serious push toward authenticity by the emerging 'beat group' scene in London, Liverpool, Manchester and Birmingham.[59] Tensions between Fury, Parnes and the Blue Flames became strained, and during a 'soundcheck' at the Paris Olympia in February 1962, the group were asked to leave the tour.[60] Fame now had no money and no work. He found himself back in London with nowhere to live until O'Neil provided a sleeping space in his Soho flat. Fame had travelled back to Leigh for Christmas 1961 in the back of Nero and the Gladiators' touring van and returned to London the day after Boxing Day.[61] In Leigh, Fame's parents were concerned about his lack of progress. In 1965, he told the *New Musical Express* that he had 'two years just leaping around London getting nowhere and finding that the pavements weren't gold'.[62] Yet it was in Soho where Fame immersed himself in the multiplicity of sounds and cultures that were transforming youth culture in the capital.

To Fame, O'Neil and other young working-class migrants to the city, Soho was both an imaginary dreamscape and also a reality in which classes, races and divergent sexualities created an alternative urban counter-culture. It was a centre of bohemianism and youth culture and popular music continued to transform its character.[63] The district attracted writers, actors, painters, musicians and a whole array of marginal characters that had attached themselves to its night-time economy.[64]

During the war and after, Spivs would trade their wares in various pubs and cafés taking advantage of the new thirst for consumer goods.[65] The Spiv provided a role model for the youth subcultures and styles that were to appear in the 1950s and 1960s.[66] In his 'indiscreet guide' to the Soho, Jackson provided a portrait.

> They are the men who have no fixed occupation and live on their wits ... Your Spiv is always a snappy dresser. His jacket is a long bum-warmer, hand stitched, with the lapels generously wide ... His collar-attached shirts are pseudo-American ... You see him in suburban dance halls doing fancy steps ... and talking big about his West End pals.[67]

According to George Melly, Soho 'was perhaps the only area in London where the rules didn't apply ... tolerance its password, where bad behaviour was cherished'.[68] The draw of the Soho coffee bars and clubs created a melting pot of classes, races, ethnicities and sexualities. There was also a long-standing drug trade initially based around opium, but during the war, it became an area that was popular for those seeking marijuana cigarettes in the form of 'reefers' 'priced at five shilling each'.[69] The drug problem in Soho and other less desirable parts of English cities was causing some concern in the national and local press. The jazz clubs of London had long been spaces for recreational drug use, but of greater concern were the legal highs that were being taken by musicians and others in the form of pep pills. O'Neil recalls that Preludin was widely available from chemists and was a staple on the jazz scene from the late 1950s.[70] In January 1960, the *Daily Express* reported that musicians and fashion models were widely using amphetamine pills.[71] It claimed that a doctor had accused Johanna Ehrenstrasser, Miss Europe of 1958 of drug abuse.[72] After a debate in the House of Commons, the sale of Preludin was banned, but this did not stop its proliferation in the rhythm and blues clubs.[73] The seamy side of Soho formed regular reports in the newspapers and also reached cinema screens in the form of *Peeping Tom* (1960), a ground-breaking horror film set against contemporary murders and concerns with vice.[74] The depiction of sex on the screen was critiqued in the context of disquiet over perceived youth promiscuity. In 1959 and throughout the following decade doctors expressed concern at the rising rates of venereal disease amongst young boys and girls with the highest rise in the 18–19 age groups.[75]

The connection between class, race, popular music and youth culture posed a challenge to particular perceptions, social norms and identities. Racial mixing in London and other cities had periodically led to violence and fed the rhetoric of the dangers of immigration.[76] During the war there had been outbreaks of violence between London's West Indian population and white American servicemen. Yet West Indian clubs proved popular with white working-class youths. The Caribbean on Denmark Street had been opened in 1944 and along with Frisco's had a large multiracial membership. The more conservative journalists and local politicians of the 1940s were critical of the potential of racial mixing. This was often based around conceptions of female identity and the view that white girls could be corrupted by West Indian men. Jackson's 'indiscreet guide' reflects such concerns in his account of 'negro clubs'.

> Here the emphasis is on women and "boogie woogie". Several of the women are local tarts, black and white, but there are always white women of a different class in these places ... It gives you a shock, at first to see quite an attractive woman of this type gushing over a big ugly negro ... He stares at her moodily, leads her to the dance floor and lazily slips his dark hand inside her dress. She has a look of ecstasy on her face that is quite repulsive ... It is only when you have patronised these clubs for a while that you begin to feel pity and not contempt for these nymphomaniacs.[77]

This passage illuminates the stereotypical view of West Indian men that was being constructed and promoted in post-war England. Between the wars, London's black population had been concentrated in Brixton, Notting Hill and in a small network of streets around Tottenham Court Road, but by 1954 they had fanned out to Soho. This was period of overt racial prejudice with a social survey showing that 'most British people would not be quite unwilling for a black man to enter their homes, nor would they wish to work with one as a colleague'.[78] In 1956 West Indian migration to England reached a peak coinciding with the arrival of rock 'n' roll. Yet over the next two years, they faced overt discrimination in public spaces that were shaking to the sounds of rock 'n' roll. In 1958 the Mecca chain of ballrooms ruled that 'coloured men would not be admitted without their own partners on rock 'n' roll nights'.[79] Yet in the coffee bars and night clubs of Soho a number of white working-class youths were connecting with West Indians. An article published in *Encounter* in 1956 is illustrative.

> The Grenada is favoured by negroes, which makes it exotic right off... Behind the bar is an alcove with pin-ball games, two drape-suited negro youths clicking at the machines and a stagey sign warning 'hemp pedlars' to peddle their wares elsewhere. After paying 2s 6d you can go downstairs to the basement dance-room, a dark, cold place... In the far corner a five-piece jazz band plays music which has a hypnotic quality of always sounding the same... Across the room, a girl... clung tenderly to the shoulder of a West Indian... On the floor a negro youth, wearing a long, square-shouldered jacket... jitterbugged with a hefty, trousered, crew-cut white girl. With empty faces and blind eyes, they played their interminable shuffling and jerking game of crack the whip.[80]

The experience of West Indians in London was also depicted in Sam Selvon's novel *The Lonely Londoners* (1956). The central character is acutely aware of the capital's animosity: 'Nobody in London does really accept you. They tolerate you, yes, but you can't go in their house and eat or sit down and talk'.[81] Yet it was in the local dance halls that West Indians could relive memories of home and experience the sounds, smells and tastes of the Caribbean. A West Indian character in Colin MacInnes's novel, *City of Spades* (1957) is indicative of familiar experiences: 'For the very moment I walked down the carpet stair, I could see, I could hear, I could smell the overflowing joys of all my people far below, and when I first got a spectacle of the crowded ballroom, oh, what a sight to make me glad'.[82] The alienation experienced by West Indian migrants was reinforced by outbreaks of racist violence in Nottingham and London in 1958 in which Teddy Boys were implicated. Yet Pilkington has suggested that the racial attacks were perpetrated by a much broader demographic than the press claimed.[83] As a result of the racial discrimination, West Indian musicians started to record their own visions of England through songs such as 'Carnival Boycott' by the Sparrow Caribbean Allstars.[84] In *Absolute Beginners*, MacInnes acknowledges the racial tension and links this to England's retreat from empire: 'In the history books they tell us the English race has spread itself all over the damn world... Yet when a few hundred thousand come and settle among our fifty millions, we just can't take it'.[85]

English working-class youth were drawn to the sounds and style of West Indian migrants in what Gilroy has characterised as an 'historic encounter'.[86] Some Teddy Boys might have exhibited racist attitudes, but others were captivated by the music and style of West Indians in Soho, Notting Hill and Brixton, where they would visit basement clubs and shebeens.[87] Between 1955–58, Patterson noted in her sociological research in Brixton that off the main shopping streets 'apart from some shopping housewives and a posse of teddy boys in tight jeans outside the billiards hall, almost everybody in sight had a coloured skin'.[88] A depiction of interracial relationships and the tensions they created was also dramatised in Roy Ward Baker's film *Flame in the Streets* (1961).[89]

By 1960 a clear point of contact between white working-class youth and African American culture was provided by jazz music. There was a thriving jazz scene in Soho in the 1950s around venues such as, Ronnie Scott's, Ken Colyer's, the Establishment, the 100 club, the Marquee, and the Flamingo. Entry prices varied from five to ten shillings with only Ronnie Scott's serving alcohol. These clubs formed the basis of the jazz subculture.[90] Young jazz enthusiasts stood out from the crowd in terms of their style, demeanour and language. According to Jackson, they all wore 'violet cravats tied in a big, floppy knot...belted jackets, dark flannel trousers and suede shoes...their hair strays wildly over eyes that seem glazed by this strange musical dream'.[91] The girls wore skirts, black stockings, polo neck jumpers and ponytails.

In January 1959, over 2000 youths had gathered at Euston Station to welcome the George Lewis Jazz band, around 20 of them clambered onto the roof of a workshop for a better view, which collapsed leaving many injured.[92] In July 1960, violence had marred a jazz festival held in the grounds of Palace House, the home of Lord Montagu of Beaulieu. Fires were started, BBC scaffolding wrecked and policemen attacked.[93] Jazz went mainstream with the popularity of 'trad' through artists such as Acker Bilk and Kenny Ball. Yet according to Gorman, by 1959, 'there was a growing split between the existential beatnik look...and the cool, sharp and almost anonymous "modernist" style prevalent among less educated youth'.[94] This group formed the foundation of the mod subculture that appeared on the streets of London in 1962.[95]

Jazz enabled youths to temporarily transcend the barriers of class and locality. A respondent to the Mass Observation Project recalled the diversity of the London scene: 'A mutual interest attracted little groups from all levels of society...I soon became part of a crowd that included a failed medical student from Edinburgh, a budding journalist from Manchester, a black docker scouser and a bricklayer from Newcastle'.[96] Yet it was the rock 'n' roll and jazz divide that became the marker of social class. The jazz musician Tubby Hayes was particularly critical of rock 'n' roll. He told the music press that he 'tried not to listen to it...it's a row...it's bad for youngsters to be brought up on this kind of music'.[97]

Fame at the Flamingo

Fame continued to move between the jazz clubs and cafés of Soho and Ladbroke Grove, gaining a musical education and an empathy with the struggles of West Indian migrants in England and the fight for civil rights in the United States. In March 1962, O'Neil introduced Fame to Rik Gunnell, who ran the Flamingo Club with his brother Johnny, who was looking for a band to play the 'twist sessions'.[98] At this time the Flamingo was still a jazz club and the grand piano remained off-limits to musicians like Fame.[99] The club was a microcosm of the how England was undergoing a process of change in terms of migrant experiences and what Marwick described as the 'knitting together of English youth subcultures'.[100] American rhythm and blues came to the Flamingo through visiting GI's with ska and calypso being provided by West Indians. Homosexuals who frequented the club exhibited a sharp fashion style that was later to be adopted by sections of the mod movement. The underbelly of Soho also gathered at the club including gangsters, strippers, prostitutes and petty criminals.

Fame had been attending the club with O'Neil for some time and had played at various sessions backing Earl Watson before establishing his own act as Georgie Fame and the Blue Flames in the spring of 1962. He endeavoured to introduce elements of African American and West Indian music into his own repertoire. His embrace of these musical genres also led to the Blue Flames becoming a multiracial group. The percussionist Speedy Acquaye provided a distinctive beat to the sound. Acquaye was born in Ghana and after migrating to England found work as a machine operator before trying his hand in the entertainment business as fire-eater, dancer, actor and drummer.[101] He was already established on the jazz scene through work with Ronnie Scott and Tubby Hayes.[102] Fame attracted a positive response from the discerning mixed-race audience with Acquaye providing him with an entry point into the more esoteric cultures of London's African community. From one night a week his run was extended to the 'all night' Friday shows and Mondays and Saturdays. Fame was initially paid four pounds for the all-nighter and up to three pounds for the others enabling him to rent his own flat.[103] Fame had now ditched his piano and bought himself a Hammond organ costing £825.[104] This marked his transition from Lancashire's Jerry Lee Lewis to the Flamingo's Booker T. Jones.[105]

The African American GIs, Africans and West Indians who formed Fame's network of friends and acquaintances provided him with recordings by the likes of Mose Allison, Oscar Brown Jr, Booker T. and Jimmy Smith.[106] Both Geno Washington and Count Suckle were also regular figures at the Flamingo. Washington had come to Britain in 1962 with the US airforce and would later be managed by Gunnell.[107] Suckle had been a key figure in promoting ska music through his sound system and had an extensive record collection that proved an attractive draw to visiting black GIs at his

Cue club.[108] Suckle also had access to rare records that the more discerning Soho musicians craved. Fame recalled that Suckle 'had this guy in Memphis who sent him all the new American soul records and he also had a Jamaican connection'.[109] Terri Quaye, a black female musician, occasionally joined the Blue Flames on stage strengthening the multiracial dimension of the performance.[110] Unlike other acts on the burgeoning rhythm and blues scene, such as the Rolling Stones, Georgie Fame and the Blue Flames not only embraced African American and West Indian music but also promoted a multicultural and multiracial image through the groups personnel and the kind of venues they were booked to play.

At the Flamingo, Fame played two sets a night at 1.30 and 4.30 before resting in his flat that had been owned by the notorious Peter Rachman.[111] He would average ten shows a week where, according to Leigh, 'amphetamine' and 'good African weed' eased the way'.[112] A number of guests would often join the sessions including Elkie Brooks, also down from Manchester, Chris Farlowe and Rico Rodriguez the West Indian trombonist.[113] *Disc Weekly* described the scene on a typical night: 'The club is really one huge room downstairs in the basement of an old building. It is exceptionally dark and crowded...There are two bandstands with a balcony round them and the club's only decoration is five rows of cinema seats in front of the stand. There is a bar and a hot dog stand'.[114] No alcohol was served but Geno Washington recalled that 'the kids would sneak in a small bottle of Scotch or bourbon and then order...a cola and fill it up with booze'.[115]

According to Farren, 'the big Friday all-nighter featured ... the coolest dancers in town, but a whole rainbow of footpads, cut-purses, plausible thieves, serial rapists and knife-wielding rip-off artists'.[116] Johnny Edgecombe,[117] the sometime jazz promoter and Soho shyster recalled his period of selling drugs at the Flamingo: 'I now devoted my time to selling dope. My main customers were the black GIs...they felt comfortable in clubs like, the 'All Nighter'.[118] He regularly met Christine Keeler there and in October 1962 was involved in a fight with Lucky Gordon.[119] According to Fame, Lucky Gordon's brother, 'Psycho', occasionally performed with the Blue Flames.[120] In June 1963, Cassius Clay, in London to fight Henry Cooper, visited the club when Fame was performing. He had apparently asked his guides for the night where 'the brothers hang out'.[121] Ronnie Carr and other members of his group the Beat Boys made the trip from Leigh to London to watch Fame in action and were also mesmerised by the sight and sounds of Soho.[122] Back in Leigh the local press made reference to 'the boy with the Ray Charles sound'.[123]

Fame's three-year residency at the Flamingo between 1962 and 1965 was responsible for the dissemination of rhythm and blues music across the capital. Due to the success of the 'all-nighter' other jazz clubs such as Ronnie Scott's and the Marquee started to introduce a rhythm and blues programme. Fame and the band continued to play multiple shows in London and surrounding regions. In any one week in 1963 they would play the Scene Club, the Roaring 20s, the Studio, Klooks Kleek, Eel Pie Island and the Chicksands and Alconbury US military bases.[124] Fame later recalled the atmosphere when performing at the bases: 'No stiff British seating rows. There were tables, a bar, imported local women, some wives, and a jukebox'.[125] A number of specialist record shops in London, such as Plane Tone Records, that were black owned were also disseminating the sounds of the West Indies and Black America. In 1963, the Island label was established by Chris Blackwell leading to the release of a multiplicity of Jamaican singles and albums.[126]

Chris Roberts, in the *Melody Maker* was already noting Fame's place in the seismic changes taking place in popular music and youth culture: 'If anyone ever writes a history of the beat boom gripping Britain at the moment, let's hope they mention the long-forgotten name of Clive Powell'.[127] The draw of rhythm and blues and its white English variant 'beat music' was creating a stir in the music press with competing views stressing that it was the next big thing or merely just a passing fad. One contributor to the *Melody Maker* felt that it would be a short-lived trend that was already 'cracking under the weight of numerous talentless groups'.[128] Yet youths *were* moving away from the jazz clubs. Kook's Kleek decided to drop jazz claiming that they could not 'give tickets away'.[129] In 1965 *Melody Maker* reported the further demise of jazz; 'ousted from London's West End by the forces of pop, folk and R&B, jazz today is moving into a scene once the domain of darts throwers, ha'penny shovers and crisp eaters'.[130] In contrast, the Flamingo was now a magnet for what would later become the aristocracy of British popular music, including members of the Beatles and the Rolling Stones.

Fame's residency at the 'all-nighter' was captured on 25 September 1963, with the recording of *Georgie Fame and the Blue Flames Live at the Flamingo*. The album represents a typical night at the club with the group running through a selection of songs by James Brown, Smokey Robinson and Barrett Strong. Rik Gunnell can be heard encouraging the punters to buy soft drinks and hot dogs – the rather official, conservative-sounding English voice masking the drinking, drug-taking and social transgressions that were taking place to the pulsating soundtrack. Tommy Thomas, who had replaced Speedy Acquaye on percussion, and the Jamaican, Eddie Thornton, on trumpet consolidated the multiracial nature of the group. Thomas was the son of a Nigerian sailor who had been playing clubs and nightspots in the capital since 1953 and had played in a variety of venues operated by Gunnell.[131] Fame was now managed by Gunnell with Andrew Loog Oldham and Pete Meaden responsible for public relations.[132] The 'rhythm and blues' explosion was in full swing with the *Melody Maker* claiming that 'there were 300 groups across the country and 300,000 people in a 40-mile radius of central London paying to hear R+B every week'.[133] Fame fulfilled a gruelling regime combining his Flamingo residency with appearances around the rest of the country where he could command up to £50 per show. The multiracial nature of the group was reflecting and influencing the social and cultural networks developing on the dance floor between working-class white youths, West Indians and African Americans.[134]

Fashion was also becoming as important as the music in signifying cultural transfer between England, America and the West Indies. Fame recalled that the band 'used to dress like GIs ... it was like being American. The West Indians, they wanted to be Yankees as well so we would call them Bermuda Yankee or Jamaica Yankee'.[135] At other times the group would take to the stage in silver-grey jackets, dark grey trousers and light-blue shirts.[136] Fame's link to ska music was cemented when he opened the Roaring Twenties club that was being run by Count Suckle for a predominantly West Indian clientele. It was here that Fame met Prince Buster and other West Indian musicians. In 1963 Fame and the Blue Flames had also provided backing for Derrick Morgan's single 'Telephone'.[137]

The Flamingo soon attracted the attention of senior US military personnel at Chicksands in Cambridgeshire and the Metropolitan Police. Violence involving GI's in 1964 led to them being prohibited from attending by the military authorities. As a result Fame was no longer invited to the US bases. He felt that racism was at work here and that the response was primarily motivated to curtail the leisure activities of African American servicemen.[138] This is reflected in the press coverage and police response to the growth of rhythm and blues clubs like the Flamingo. From 1964 the London County Council (LCC) and the Metropolitan Police had been monitoring the club scene and later set up a working party on West End 'jazz and dance clubs'.[139] Similar initiatives were also developed to curtail the popularity of clubs in Manchester.[140] The press continued to make a link between rhythm and blues clubs, drug use and immorality. In February 1964, *New Society* ran a feature claiming that the use of amphetamine in the rhythm and blues clubs was widespread: 'I myself recently saw a boy of 15 years who had been the round of the Soho and other clubs in London and described taking purple hearts'.[141] The *British Medical Journal* was also caught up in the furore over 'pep pills' claiming that 'despite precautions against theft there seems no doubt that many of the tablets reaching the public in the streets of Soho and elsewhere are stolen, presumably from warehouses, hospitals and pharmacists'.[142] The Metropolitan Police had for some time been making arrests in Soho related to drugs. A report from June 1964 on the dance clubs stated that 'amongst the large number of teenage persons attracted to these premises there is a ready market for stimulants of the drinamyl tablet type and ... Indian Hemp'.[143]

The issue of race and the corruption of youth were of particular concern regarding the Flamingo because of its mixed clientele of Black Americans, West Indians, white working-class youths and members of the criminal underworld. The LCC working party gathered evidence from the police, social workers, teenagers and concerned members of the public. A number of references were made to the Flamingo as a place 'where young girls go and get drugs and meet coloured men'. A connection was also made to social class: 'The temptation is particularly strong for young people from poor or unexciting backgrounds'.[144] Connell claimed that 'the clubs concerned are sometimes frequented by homosexuals, prostitutes and individuals addicted to morphia, heroin etc., and the possibility of contamination is definitely present'.[145] The LCC working party heard the story of a girl who had been taken into care and claimed that the Flamingo was populated by prostitutes and that there was 'a great deal of "necking" especially with coloured people'.[146] It was also noted that Rik Gunnell, the owner of the club, had been found guilty of various charges relating to running unlicensed premises.[147]

Fame at last

Fame released a further album, *Fame at Last* in October 1964, reaching No. 15 on the charts. In December he gained a number 1 single with 'Yeh, Yeh'. The success of the single led to a headlining 20-date tour supported by Elkie Brooks and Zoot Money and his Big Roll Band. The *New Musical Express* noted that 'Georgie may sing in a Negro way, but he still retains a touch of *Coronation Street* in his speaking voice'.[148] Fame's 'northerness' would often come through in interviews with the music press, where he claimed that his favourite food was meat and potato pie, which formed the staple diet of the population of Leigh and Wigan.[149] Parnes was still hoping to cash in on this combination of English northern charm and rhythm and blues in telling Fame's life story on screen. Gunnell wanted the picture to break the mould and was determined that it would 'be a good film and not just a vehicle for pop songs', but the film never materialised.[150]

James Powell was still working night shift in the cotton mill when his son was top of the charts. After recording a *Top of the Pops* in Manchester, Fame travelled to Leigh to visit his parents and was interviewed by the local press. He pointed to his attachment to the town: 'It's a great world in Leigh...I wouldn't advise young people who are happy living and working in the town to break away. I suppose I was a black sheep when I left at 16'.[151] Throughout 1964, Fame would return to Manchester to play numerous shows at the Twisted Wheel, North West England's very own version of the Flamingo Club.[152]

Fame's musical journey from playing to the miners and mill workers of Leigh and Wigan through to his embrace of rhythm and blues and ska music was completed by his contribution to the Tamla Motown tour of Britain in March 1965. The tour represented a 'coming of age' for Fame and acceptance amongst African American performers that he was an authentic rhythm and blues artist.[153] He returned to Lancashire when the tour stopped at the Wigan ABC and the Manchester Odeon, where he was cheered on by Ronnie Carr and other friends who had made the journey from Leigh. The running order of the Motown shows was Earl Van Dyke followed by Stevie Wonder, The Supremes, Martha and the Vandellas, Fame and then the headline act Smokey Robinson and the Miracles.[154] Each artist would play for around 20 minutes while the others watched from the wings. Fame claimed that the tour had been his 'greatest experience' since he started 'in the business'.[155]

The Motown Tour was a disaster in terms of ticket sales, especially at shows outside of London. In Bristol, the promoter had to give away one thousand tickets to the local black population.[156] The *New Musical Express* claimed it 'a flop' which 'left behind a trail of near-empty theatres halfway across the country'.[157] Yet it was the tour's symbolism, impact and legacy that were important. Concerts might have been sparsely attended but to the more discerning purveyors of the American soul music who witnessed the performances it proved to be a moment of epiphany in presenting an image of England where class and racial boundaries could be temporarily transcended. The mixed audiences were symbolic of the way in which elements of English youth culture was laying the foundation of a more egalitarian and liberal society.

The interconnections between white working-class youth, American rhythm and blues and West Indian migration provides an image of England in which popular music and was both reflecting and shaping the continuities and changes that defined aspects of its culture. Fame, Carr, O'Neil and others transposed aspects of a traditional working-class culture into a shared identity with the struggles and experiences of African American and West Indian youth. Fame's background in Leigh had endowed in him an acute awareness of a working-class culture that was disappearing in some parts of the country, but remained relatively potent in the industrial north. The development of English popular music and its connected youth culture owed as much to the agency of northern working-class migrants as it did to middle-class consumers, music impresarios, and entrepreneurs of the capital city.

3
Liverpool, the Beatles and the Cultural Politics of Class, Race and Place

The Beatles hang heavy over social and cultural histories of post-war England. The vast literature on this most influential and celebrated of groups covers every aspect of the lives and career trajectories of John Lennon, Paul McCartney, George Harrison and Ringo Starr.[1] These musicians emerge from various genres of writing as totemic figures whose impact went beyond performance, recording and the post-war culture of celebrity. The Beatles 'industry' has produced a multiplicity of biographies, autobiographies, magazine articles, films and documentaries.[2] This is complemented by a significant heritage industry that has led to the protection of Beatle homes, the creation of museums, the erection of statues, and the naming of Liverpool's airport.[3] This chapter examines the origins of rhythm and blues music in Liverpool in the 1950s and ends with the Beatles 'leaving' of the city after the civic reception held in their honour in July 1964. The formative years of the Beatles and the social and cultural milieu from which they emerged are symbolic of the connections between class, race, ethnicity, locality, popular music and youth culture in post-war England.[4]

In recent years, historians have sought to confirm the impact of the Beatles on social change or to strip them of their role in reflecting, creating and sustaining new forms of youth culture.[5] Marwick is generally sympathetic to an interpretation that sees the Beatles as central to the process of 'cultural revolution' in England. He describes such developments as informing 'a participatory and uninhibited popular culture...which in effect became a kind of universal language'.[6] Similarly, MacDonald connects the arrival of the Beatles with seismic changes in English social and political identities claiming that '[l]ong-standing class barriers collapsed overnight'.[7] Sandbrook presents a critique of such claims and questions the belief that affluence and youth culture in the 1960s were of great importance. He challenges much of the mythology of the Beatles' relationship to shifting class identities stressing that 'in most communities class boundaries still seemed as strong as ever'.[8] More controversially he claims that 'the stark truth is that had it not been for the sheer coincidence of the Beatles encounters with Brian Epstein and George Martin, they would surely have remained just another...unsuccessful skiffle band'.[9] This characterisation patently fails to take account of the implicit talent of the group as live performers and in the case of Lennon and McCartney, two of the greatest songwriters of the twentieth century.

Sandbrook suggests that 'the sixties are best understood not as a dramatic turning point...but rather as a stage in a long evolution'.[10] This has some merit, but the decade provides historians with new forms of youth culture and rhythm and blues music as a way of exploring continuities and changes in working-class perceptions of economic change, politics and notions of national identity. The prominence of popular music in the lives of young people was measured in a 1961 Gallup Poll, which showed that 64 per cent of them spent their spare time listening to records.[11] Sandbrook fails to locate the experience of rock 'n' roll outside of government records and the policies of political parties.[12] The impact of popular music was felt in abundance in the coffee bars, clubs, dance halls and bedrooms of English working-class youth particularly in the city of Liverpool.

Fowler also presents a revisionist critique of the Beatles suggesting that 'in effect, they were family entertainment, rather than at the cutting edge of youth culture'.[13] Wald has shown a little more sophistication in his particular brand of revisionism and claims that the 'Beatles...led the audience off the dance floor, separating rock from its rhythm and cultural roots'.[14] Such critical approaches have sought to undermine the more traditional characterisations of the group promoted by writers such as Gillett who claimed that 'in the years around 1962, Britain served the useful function of re-establishing popular music as a medium for personal expression rather than as the raw material for mass-produced entertainment'.[15] Most recently, Brocken has produced a cultural history of Liverpool that pushes the Beatles to the periphery of the city's musical development.[16] Yet their power to attract the interest of historians, musicologists, sociologists and cultural theorists remains potent.[17]

The Liverpool of the Beatles presents us with a microcosm of some of the broader currents in English society that were simultaneously confirming and transforming the lives of working-class youth. In terms of the sheer numbers involved in music making and the contribution made by working-class youth, Liverpool stands out in comparison to the surrounding towns and cities of North West England. Bill Harry, a contemporary of John Lennon and noted Beatles historian, has calculated that between '1958 and 1964 there were probably around 500 different bands in the Merseyside area'.[18] Contemporary perceptions of locality, class, sexuality, religion, ethnicity, race, gender, globalisation, politics and consumerism were all points of contention in the England of the Beatles. What follows is an attempt to excavate the processes that led to the manifestation of a local, national and international cultural phenomenon that became known as Beatlemania and how working-class youth and local socialist politicians responded to its emergence in the early 1960s.

Sea, ships, sailors and Liverpool exceptionalism

Recent developments in research on regionalism have led to the emergence of a significant historical literature on northern identity.[19] Yet the city of Liverpool has posed problems for historians and has been characterised as atypical in terms of its place in conceptions of Englishness. Du Noyer has suggested that as 'far as Scousers are concerned, Liverpool is not a provincial city, but the Capital of itself'.[20] Belchem has claimed that 'Liverpool's apartness... has been upheld (and inflated) in self-referential myth'.[21] Irrespective of the mythology of an identity sometimes described as 'Merseypride' inhabitants of the city *did* see themselves as different from their contemporaries in neighbouring towns and cities.[22] In his tour of England in the early 1960s, the journalist Geoffrey Moorhouse noted that 'Liverpool maintains a queer, rather sinister, hold over its people'.[23] This affiliation to place and locality shaped the attitudes of local performers and consumers of popular music. According to Russell, the hold of the city had a particular resonance with the Beatles 'making them the first major pop group to make their local identity and cultural background a part of their success'.[24] The post-war soundscape of the city and its class, racial and ethnic identities were crucial to this process of maintaining a local inflection in Liverpool's popular music scene.

Liverpool's existence as a port had a significant impact on the politics and culture of the city. The diverse population contained English, Irish, Welsh, African, West Indian, Jewish and Chinese inhabitants ensuring that a variety of cultural activities and practices were a feature of 'everyday life'.[25] Liverpool's working-class created a popular culture that could be found in the home, street, pub, club, concert hall and football stadium.[26] Yet politically the city had been a strong bastion of Toryism, which cut across class identities. The strength of Protestantism and the nature of the maritime economy and its culture of casual labour no doubt weakened the Labour Party and socialist politics in its formative years.[27] Ricky Tomlinson who formed a skiffle band in the late 1950s recalls fights in working-class areas between Protestants and Catholics and the anti-socialism of his Tory-voting father.[28] Bill Harry also witnessed sectarian demonstrations and street violence throughout the same period.[29] Historians of the city have neglected to explore the importance of popular music in challenging the social, religious and political divisions that were a feature of Liverpool life. With the advent of rock 'n' roll a generation of working-class youths saw commercial opportunity, physical and mental escape, and the possibility that music could play a role in dispensing with the prejudices of the past and present.

Russell claims that 'music has ... power to evoke an almost tangible sense of time and place' and was 'a vital element in the construction of social identities'.[30] Yet some writers have questioned the link between popular music and the expression of local particularities. To Sandbrook, the 'amateur beat boom of the early sixties was more a product of national teenage affluence ... There was nothing unique about the Liverpool beat circuit'.[31] But Liverpool *was* different. Musicians across North West England in the early 1960s were aware of the sheer scale of the number and quality of the groups in the city.[32] The social and cultural roots of the Beatles created a local music scene in which structural factors intertwined with human agency to produce an incendiary combination of popular music that both reflected and shaped aspects of the city's identity.

Water, ships, sailors and migrants created the Liverpool of the Beatles. Lane provides an illustration: 'In Liverpool the sea cannot be avoided. All the arterial roads to the city converge on the river at the Pier Head ... Standing outside the Town Hall and looking down Water Street at high tide, inward and outbound ships move across the frame made by the Cunard and Liver Buildings'.[33] Cohen claims that 'the wealth of music-making partly reflected an influx of foreign cultures and influences entering Liverpool through its port'.[34] To Du Noyer, the waterfront formed part of the collective consciousness of the city's working class: 'the sea and the docks determined every aspect of life. In terraced houses ... you could always spot a mantelpiece or cabinet full of global paraphernalia; keepsakes from the Orient, souvenirs of Panama, knick-knacks from Newfoundland'.[35] Such interiors formed spaces where music came through the radio or from the songs sung by families and friends at parties and post-pub gatherings. Such imagery and sounds remained lodged in the memory of the city's working-class youth and in the case of the Beatles found its way into their live performances and recording sessions. This was particularly the case in the later recording career of the Beatles and most notably on *Sgt Pepper's Lonely Hearts Club Band* (1967) and the *White Album* (1968), where they drew on a diverse range of lyrical styles, images, instruments and musical genres.[36]

Yet the waterfront that underpins the historiography of the Beatles has also led to the consolidation of particular myths that present the maritime economy as being the major transmission route of rhythm and blues into the city. The relationship between sea and soundscape has led to the so-called 'Cunard Yank theory', in which sailors working for Cunard and other shipping companies are seen as the major conduit for American popular culture in the 1940s and 1950s. Lane's characterisation of this process is indicative: 'For the vast bulk of the British population, American culture was transmitted through the cinema, but in Liverpool's docklands there was a long-standing direct link through the seamen who had deserted, worked ashore on the waterfront in New York or Boston and then taken jobs on American ships which traded back to Liverpool'.[37] Spitz gives some credence to the theory claiming that Eric Griffiths, a local sailor and musician would bring rock 'n' roll records into the city and swap them with others.[38] McCartney also sees the port as crucial: 'There were always sailors coming in with records from America, blues records from New Orleans'.[39] Norman also recreated a scene of the city responding to imported records: 'Rhythm and blues ... sung by still obscure names ... pounded through the terraced back streets each Saturday night as the newly returned mariners got ready to the hit the town'.[40]

The 'Cunard Yank' theory as a concept did not just emerge after the demise of the Beatles in the 1970s. In the early 1960s, local creators and consumers of popular music were keen to make sense of what was happening in their city. In the pages of *Mersey Beat* in 1963, the 'Cunard Yank' theory was discussed and there was agreement that there was some truth in the link between sailors and popular music.[41] Yet Clayson and Leigh in their debunking of the theory claim that most of the significant records performed by beat groups were widely available in England by the mid-1950s.[42] Similarly, Sam Leach, a local concert promoter notes that many of the musicians in the city in the late 1950s were on mailing lists of the major record companies.[43] Similarly, Harry argues that by 1960, 'Liverpool youth could obtain a variety of recordings from local record shops and the docks were already in decline with Cunard moving their operations to Southampton'.[44] Moreover, a study of the Beatles set-list in the early 1960s 'proves that every song they played was available on record in Britain through the normal channels'.[45] Yet to McManus, the theory *is* applicable to the introduction of country western music into the city.[46] According to Harry, Liverpool had the largest country and western scene in Europe. The cowboy was a regular feature of cinema programmes in the 1950s and singers would imitate particular stars in clubs such as the Black Cat and Wells Fargo.[47] The outlaw image was also one that filtered into the style of Teddy Boys in the city and throughout England.

For Harry, it was the cosmopolitan nature of Liverpool and its distinct cultural composition that was responsible for the development of rhythm and blues in the city.[48] Yet more generally, it is undeniable that the port and its ships were crucial in creating a particular Liverpudlian soundscape, political identity, sense of place and difference. Liverpool youths could ponder an alternative society/lifestyle by gazing out to sea and across the Atlantic. Rock 'n' roll and rhythm and blues music was the perfect soundtrack for such escapism with its discourse of the different, exotic and transcendent. The pubs and clubs of Liverpool also provided an interface for sailors, migrants and dockers to spin tales of foreign shores and maritime adventures. This milieu was documented in the documentary *Beat City* (1963), which sought to understand the beat group phenomenon. The film contrasts both the Liverpool of a poverty stricken working-class and a vibrant musical culture enmeshed in a network of pubs, clubs, cafés and dance halls.[49]

A vast array of musical genres could be heard in the domestic and public spheres of post-war Liverpool. In the 1950s working-class children would be exposed to folk, country and western, rock 'n' roll, calypso, American show tunes, sectarian religious street songs and the terrace chants of Anfield and Goodison Park. The complex mixture of classes, ethnic groups, religious affiliations and community identities also imposed their own particular traditions and interpretations on to the popular culture of the city. In the case of the Beatles and other groups associated with the 'beat scene', West Indian and African American music played a crucial role that has still to be adequately explored by social historians.

Race, Americana and rhythm and blues

Liverpool's culture was infused with a variety of religious, ethnic and racial identities. Since the nineteenth century, the Welsh and Irish had flocked to the city creating a social mix that was articulated through the local peculiarities of particular streets and communities.[50] Such identities underpinned by religion and class were reinforced through sectarianism, political activism and football. The construction of a 'Scouse' identity had only a partial impact on such divisions and sectarianism and political factionalism remained a feature of Liverpool life into the post-war period.[51] Moreover, the dominant sense of 'Scouse' excluded the small but significant African, West Indian, Chinese and Jewish sections of the city's population.[52] Yet through popular music the city's white working-class youth gained an appreciation of minority cultures and some empathy with the experiences of West Indian migrants and the African American struggle for civil rights.[53] This was especially the case with the Beatles. According to MacDonald the 'influence on them of black singers, instrumentalists, songwriters, and producers was, as they never failed to admit in their interviews, fundamental to their early career'.[54]

African Americans had been based in Liverpool during the war at Maghull, Aintree and Huyton.[55] Tensions between the white working-class and African and West Indian minorities manifested themselves in overt racism and violence. The city's African and West Indian population in 1950s was mostly concentrated in Liverpool 8.[56] In 1953, there were clashes between West Indians and white American soldiers in a dance hall leading to the implementation of a colour bar.[57] Yet by the end of the decade, such exclusion was being challenged through popular music.[58] Local musicians would freely mix across the 'colour line' in the clubs and coffee bars of Liverpool 8. Ricky Tomlinson recalled in his memoir that his father was known as 'Black Dick... because of his dark skin'[59] and that his next door neighbour was West Indian. Moreover, as with Moss Side in Manchester and Soho in London, Liverpool's West Indian and African enclaves acted as a magnet to working-class youth who wanted to transcend the conventions of their homes, streets and workplaces. The Rialto ballroom in Toxteth was a key venue and hosted a range of beat groups and dances. Some mixed race marriages occurred as a result of such encounters. In 1959, the *Daily Express* carried out an investigation into these relationships. The reporter noted that he had met 'in Liverpool an American negro who married his Welsh wife 12 years ago'.[60]

Liverpool in the 1960s also provides an image of England that stands in stark contrast to those depicting working-class affluence. In 1961 Robin Guthrie visited boys clubs and filed a report for *New Society* in which he documented the continued existence of poverty, class and racial inequality: 'Walk down Upper Parliament Street at night: Indians, West Indians, English, Irish, Chinese and other nationalities move up and down... it looks as though the life of the streets outside has simply moved within four walls; boys move around without apparent restraint, coming to the counter for a table-tennis ball or a Coca-Cola, or playing billiards, or watching TV; or they just stand and talk and scuffle'.[61]

To Harry, Liverpool 8 and the Upper Parliament Street area was a sort of 'miniature Harlem'. Here was a real-life 'black presence' in the city that could be consumed by working-class youth accompanied by a soundtrack of jazz, blues and calypso.[62] One local group were the Roadrunners who played a set of Chicago blues and between 1962 and 1963 supported the Beatles at a number of venues. Harry claimed that he had later heard George Harrison state that the 'Rolling Stones are good – almost as good as the Roadrunners'.[63] There were a number of other black artists in Liverpool who had been playing since the 1950s including Sugar Dean, Steve Aldo and Derry Wilkie. Wilkie's band the Seniors were very popular in the city and the surrounding towns and were the first group to take advantage of the Hamburg link in 1960 which proved to be an apprentice scheme for a generation of English performers.[64] While in Hamburg, Wilkie crossed paths with Ray Charles cementing the link between the 'beat group' scene in England with American rhythm and blues and soul music.[65]

Liverpool also had a long-standing African community that had settled in the city through employment on ships. In the 1950s, social scientists linked the more overcrowded and less desirable parts of the city to rising levels of crime and social dislocation. Writing in 1954, Mays claimed that 'juvenile delinquency is in the... over-crowded areas where the population is of a mixed race origin, and where exceptional degrees of poverty and casual employment are found'.[66] He also noted that 'there can be no doubt that a colour bar does exist at employment level... [but] no indication of colour bar between local children'.[67] Owing to this generational shift in attitudes a number of West Indians were able to make a significant contribution to the development of the city's soundscape. Harold Phillips (Lord Woodbine)[68] arrived in 1948, a year of racial violence in the city that saw individuals attacked and businesses vandalised.[69] By the late 1950s, he was a singer, barman, club owner and founder of the All-Steel Caribbean Band. The

Beatles played his New Colony Club and once provided the soundtrack for a Mancunian stripper at his New Cabaret Artists Club.[70] In his survey of colour prejudice in Liverpool also published in 1954, Richmond mentions some of the less salubrious places where racial minorities gathered: 'There are several other cafes and clubs ... which cater primarily for coloured colonials ... There are two private clubs ... Both have a small band and dance floor'.[71] Such places offered white-working youth a sense of excitement, adventure and transgression where they could get a taste of the exotic and the dangerous. The sights, sounds, styles and discourse experienced in these venues left a mark on working-class youths who went on to embrace American rhythm and blues and West Indian ska music.[72]

The subtle connections between class, race, geography and music are difficult to unravel, but the fact that working-class youth was increasingly affluent, mobile and adventurous meant that they had the means and desire to spend more time out of the home and to seek out a broader variety of musical genres. Liverpool had a thriving coffee bar scene through which working-class youths could access the latest American and Caribbean sounds. Afternoons, evenings and weekends were spent in a dreamscape of cokes, coffee and rock 'n' roll. As Norman illustrates: 'whole days could be spent, over one cold coffee cup, looking through the window steam at passing Chinese, West Indians, East Indians ... going to and from the nearby unemployment office'. [73] In 1962, *Mersey Beat* described the Jacaranda as the 'only Boy meets Girl Coffee Bar in England that has dancing to the Royal Caribbean Steel Band'.[74]

The arrival of rhythm and blues in Liverpool was also attributable to the presence of the United States Air Force (USAF) at nearby Burtonwood. The site had been developed in 1932, and by the outbreak of war, it was the biggest airbase in Europe. Its geographical position, situated 15 miles between the cities of Manchester and Liverpool, ensured that it would have a long-standing impact on the cultural transmission of American music, literature and film on the region's youth. A steady stream of American stars performed at the base in the 1940s, including James Cagney, Bing Crosby and Bob Hope. Female dancing troupes from New York and other cities were regular performers accompanied by accomplished dance bands. By 1949, 'the base had five chapels, six theatres, a service club, and NCO club and an officer's club'.[75] The reach of the base was crucial in connecting working-class youth in Liverpool, Manchester, Leigh, Wigan, St Helens and the surrounding towns to American youth culture. A small number of Burtonwood personnel also lived in a satellite camp in Lowton close to Leigh.[76] Mike O'Neil recalls that kids would visit the camp and were given Coca-Cola and recordings by American artists such as Tommy Dorsey and Benny Goodman.[77] American sounds were also finding their way into the homes of the Liverpool working-class through American Forces Network radio.

By 1957, Burtonwood was the biggest USAF base outside of the United States with over 5500 servicemen and their families stationed across its sprawling site. The Skyline Service Club held regular parties and dances proving a magnet for young working-class girls from across North West England in search of real-life American glamour.[78] The attraction of American men and American culture was linked to local perceptions of Hollywood that had been gleaned from magazine covers and the cinema screen. Film and music offered a discourse and imagery of fantasy and escape to both men and women.[79] For some, the arrival of Americans made fantasy a reality with local girls forging relationships and finding marriage partners. The liaisons between English girls and visiting Americans became part of the collective memory of those who lived close to US bases. Gardiner provides many examples of this process through novels, rhymes, films and jokes: 'Have you heard about the utility knickers? One Yank and they're off!'[80] In *Coronation Street*, Elsie Tanner had a reputation as a 'good-time' girl who had a relationship with an American based at Burtonwood.[81] The transgressive opportunities offered by the base were no doubt the subject of many conversations, gossip and pub discourses.

The contrast between working-class life in the prosperous regions of the United States and the poverty still in existence in England was noted by a number of servicemen. Jack McMichael arrived at Burtonwood in 1951 and remembers that 'times were bad and most people you met on the street looked very sad'.[82] Ed Floyd was stationed there between 1955 and 1957 and recalls listening to rock 'n' roll. Max Stucky from West Virginia performed at the base and in surrounding towns such as Blackpool and Southport.[83] Phil Kroper arrived in Liverpool from New Orleans on Christmas Eve 1951. He attended Reese's Ballroom where a dance to a five-piece band was taking place. It was here that he met his English girlfriend Hilda and they married in 1952.

> My first impression of Liverpool was the lasting devastation from the war, both in property damage from the war and the rationing of food and goods ... The music played at the base club was more popular music of the 50s in contrast to the ballrooms in Liverpool where they played Big Band dance music.[84]

Jeanette Land recalls attending dances at nearby USAF Sealand.

> Dances were held on Thursday and Sunday nights. Invitations were sent to ... large companies in the area, Lever Brothers, Littlewoods etc. The GI buses would pick up young ladies ... and deliver us to the base ... We danced in the service club/NCO club to the very latest recorded music from America ... We could always count on a parcel of tinned goodies when they came to the house to visit. Many times we would ride the ferry and go to Liverpool from the Wirral ... Our very favourite hang-out was New Brighton, dancing at the Tower Ballroom ... The GIs were very well paid which would bother the English boys.[85]

The pubs, cafés and dance halls acted as a magnet for American servicemen. Mays claimed that such places of disrepute and the flamboyance of Americans posed a threat to Liverpool's youth. He noted that the 'proximity of Lime Street is a further source of moral danger... Not only do a few girls develop the "pick-up" habit but even infants find it profitable to hang around milk bars and public houses there, begging coppers from American servicemen'.[86]

Burtonwood formed part of a network of pubs, clubs, dancehalls and coffee bars where young working-class men and women were exposed to new sounds, styles and attitudes. The cultural politics of such a milieu hinged on existing class identities and a new set of generational attitudes that sought to challenge particular aspects of social life in Liverpool. Maureen Nolan and Roma Singleton recalled the transformative nature of the period: 'It gave us tolerance for new ideas, and brought us a step nearer to equality of rights, removing many prejudices of sexual, racial and moral origin'.[87]

Yet continuing racial tensions in Liverpool in the 1950s–60s are revealed through the experiences of Eddie Amoo and the Chants, a talented vocal group who formed a close relationship with the Beatles. Amoo was born in 1944 to mixed parentage. His father had been an African sailor and his mother was white. Growing up in Liverpool 8 in the 1950s, Amoo recalls playing with Irish, Welsh, African, West Indian and mixed-race children. He claims that racism was much more apparent when he moved to a more affluent area of the city. Popular music provided him with a sense of identity and place that would find its way into his writing and performances. Burtonwood was also critical to Amoo's musical education. He recalls African Americans from the base visiting Liverpool 8, drinking in the bars and attending dances. The calypso and jazz he had heard as a child was now complemented by Doo-Wop and rhythm and blues.[88] The Chants were also receiving records from white working-class youths who were interested in rhythm and blues. Harry recalls loaning the group 'albums of the Miracles and the Marvellettes which they literally wore out'.[89] This was indicative of the way in which black youth in Liverpool and in other English cities were gaining a musical education from each other, but also from their white working-class peers in the a quest to embrace the more esoteric dimensions of jazz, blues and rock 'n' roll.

The Chants found a safe social and cultural space in Stanley House, a community centre on Upper Parliament Street. In 1964, Amoo told *Mersey Beat* that 'we were all interested in singing so they used to let us practice... The members of the club used to come around and watch us and give us encouragement'.[90] One of the few night clubs that provided another haven for Amoo and his contemporaries was the Mardi Gras Club, which hosted live performances by visiting jazz and rhythm and blues acts.[91] Geno Washington arrived in the UK in 1961 with the USAF and performed at the club in the years that followed.[92] Harry claims that the 'Upper Parliament

Street scene' provided a much broader musical education for white working-class performers who until the late 1950s had been largely confined to the less cosmopolitan districts of the city.[93]

Coffee bars were also crucial meeting points for white working-class youths, ethnic minorities and members of the urban underworld. Allan Williams, owner of the Jacaranda provides an illustration: 'Artists, musicians, pimps, beggars, ordinary layabouts and all the rag-tag-and-bobtail of Liverpool 8 soon made it their headquarters…It was unlicensed, but people brought in liquor and spiked their soft drinks'.[94] It was this contact with race that was crucial for the development of popular music in the city in particular and England more generally. According to Gilroy the 'black forms in which Britain's young people took pleasure during the 1950s and 1960s were not innocent. They were already articulated by political language, symbols and meanings given by the struggle of social movements for emancipation and equality'.[95] This process was crucial in Liverpool, Manchester, Birmingham and London, eventually filtering through to the consciousness of the more discerning working-class consumer of popular music in the provinces.

Popular culture, class and the Liverpool 'beat boom'

The Liverpool of the Beatles was marked by continuities in class identities but ruptures in particular political affiliations. In 1963, Dennis Chapman, a lecturer at the University of Liverpool had noticed that the city's youth were simultaneously apolitical and obsessed by pop music: 'The young men and young women I have talked with see society as arbitrary, irrational, and often malevolent, and see little possibility of changing it…In all this there is a strong element of romantic sexual love, the poetry of which is found in the lyrics of the Top Ten'.[96] Yet contemporary observers such as Chapman were too quick in dismissing the more complex aspects of listening to popular music and how it reaffirmed a particular 'structure of feeling' in elements of the city's working-class youth. The consumption and creation of popular music in Liverpool offered both an affirmation and temporary escape from the rigidities of class. For Harry, science fiction comics and popular music presented an alternate universe to the reality of poverty, deprivation and domestic squalor.[97]

The ethnic and racial mix of the city played a role in introducing listeners and performers to a variety of musical traditions, styles and social identities which provided a soundtrack to work, home and leisure. Belchem claims that what 'made Liverpool different was…the disproportionate Celtic presence'.[98] The port again was crucial here as a reception for Irish migrants. Many of them settled in the dockside area maintaining particular traditions and cultures. Religious and political sectarianism had been a feature of the city's culture since the nineteenth century and was a determining force in restricting the growth of an effective working-class politics through the

Labour Party and other socialist organisations.[99] The link between Ireland and Liverpool formed a core component of the city's soundscape. Du Noyer notes that the 'Irish shaped many facets of the scouse character ... but their greatest contribution was the view of music as one of life's necessities'.[100]

The pub was also important in reinforcing a collective identity that was expressed through song, conversation and a particular discourse that drew on the collective memory of the city's migrant groups.[101] In the 1950s, sectarianism was still a feature of the city's politics and the street life of particular districts and Harry recalls avoiding particular locations because of their anti-Catholicism. Yet the multiplicity of music venues and coffee bars attracted him to various parts of the city and the wider environs of Merseyside. On his travels he kept a series of red notebooks that documented the various groups, the songs performed and the particular characteristics of performers.[102] To Harry the live music geography of the city was creating a particular soundscape and communal space that was easily accessible and seemed to temporarily dissolve particular social and cultural barriers that had been a feature of pre-war Liverpool. By 1960 the new cultural spaces provided by coffee bars, music venues and record shops were presenting youth with a variety of images and sounds that added colour, excitement and vibrancy to everyday life. Maureen Nolan and Roma Singleton recalled that 'record stores ... were another good place to hang out ... You could in fact, stand there all day listening'.[103] The record shop was also a place where boys and girls could meet with a common purpose of consuming music. The development of rock 'n' roll and rhythm and blues music in Liverpool became a repository of excitement, romance, heartbreak and a personal and collective expression of masculinity and femininity.

Liverpool's working-class youth culture revolved around popular music, football and cinema. In her social investigation of the city in 1955, Kerr found that in one the most deprived areas 'children visit the cinema very frequently ... they use the dance halls ... to pick up girls and dancing is generally an excuse ... for petting on the way home'.[104] Boys also adorned themselves in the Teddy boy style. One of Kerr's subjects is illustrative: 'Robert, aged 16, has now become a Teddy Boy and has landed his parents in debt for Teddy Boy suits bought. His father has threatened to put the next pair of "drain-pipes" on the fire'.[105] She was also surprised by the way in which young men were becoming obsessed with their appearance: 'many of the boys are rather effeminate looking ... fussily clean, keen on hair-do's and deceptively gentle in manner ... always combing their hair'.[106] A year later Abrams noted that 'typical boys' spent their time 'playing the pin tables, sitting and smoking in cafes over tepid cokes ... or taking a girl out to a dance or the pictures'.[107] Cinemas provided a space where youth could seek solace, escape and visions of an alternative future. Colin Fletcher recalled local youths going to see *Rock Around the Clock* in 1956: 'Gangs filed in and filled up row after row ... When the music started it was infectious ... Soon couples were in the aisles copying the jiving on the screen'.[108]

Yet working-class youths were also still embedded in the street life and neighbour networks that had been a feature of pre-war Liverpool. Harry recalls the continued existence of pianos in working-class households and pub singing sessions well into the 1960s.[109]

Class has been the source of much debate in the historiography of the Beatles. The group have been largely viewed as working-class, especially by American writers, with others seeking to emphasise the suburban middle-class background of John Lennon.[110] According to Riley, 'Ringo's...upbringing can be called poor, the other Beatles were solidly middle-class grammar-school types'.[111] Brocken claims that 'Lennon would not have fared well in the boondocks (e.g., Toxteth, Scotland Road, Everton Valley, Garston, Dock Road) of the city where actual bodily harm, gangland brawls, and juvenile delinquency were far more prevalent'.[112] Yet this characterisation seems to simplify the workings of class in the 1960s. Popular music breached the barriers of class but did not undermine its foundations. Working-class and middle-class identities remained a feature of the beat scene, but they became more subtle and complex. Such identities were both challenged and reinforced in the dance halls, clubs and coffee bars of the city.[113]

According to Harry, Beatles scholarship has presented an erroneous interpretation of the class basis of beat music in Liverpool. He claims that the art school has taken priority over the factory and the waterfront.[114] He argues that the city's 'beat scene' in terms of both performers and consumers was 'ninety-nine per-cent working-class kids' and an overwhelmingly 'working-class movement'.[115] The art school dimension was minimal with only Harry, John Lennon and Stu Sutcliffe coming from such an educational background.[116] The live music scene and the tributaries that led to a burgeoning rhythm and blues movement emerged from the social clubs that were linked to particular factories and waterfront industries that were willing to promote rock 'n' roll and rhythm and blues shows. This process again highlights the link between a pre-war working-class culture and popular music making in the industrial north in the 1950s.

Lennon's class identity was complex and rooted in a variety of social and domestic milieus. His father Alf was a merchant seaman, an occupation that linked his son to the world of adventure, popular music and escapism. Lennon attended Quarry Bank School, which to Norman was 'the Eton of the Labour Party owing to the number of socialist alumni including future Members of Parliament including Bill Rodgers and Peter Shore'.[117] The complexity of class identity and how this impinged on Lennon's sense of self is best understood through the two most important women in his teenage years; his mother, Julia and his Aunt Mimi. These characters/types symbolised both class distancing and embrace in 1950s England. Julia worked as a cinema usherette in a period when American film offered an optimistic, multicoloured visual alternative to the drudgery of everyday life for the city's working-class through what Norman has referred to as 'a life of glamour by proxy'.[118] Julia was a free spirited 'good-time girl', living in a council house with a love of Elvis and rock 'n' roll music whereas Mimi was a Lancashire matriarch with delusions of grandeur. Such a contrast was indicative of the experience of many working-class families that had strained relations based on marital infidelity, social climbing and networks of gossip that fuelled slights, feuds and tensions that could last years. In such contexts working-class youths found solace in the bedroom, the coffee bar, the dance hall and in the fantasy worlds of American popular music.

Lennon's ambiguous position within the class structure of Liverpool was familiar to a generation of working and lower middle-class children who experienced social mobility through education, but retained an affiliation to aspects of working-class culture.[119] His rebelliousness was rooted in his negative reaction to formal schooling and the class nature of the English education system.[120] Lennon fitted the archetype of MacInnes's 'absolute beginner'.[121] At Liverpool College of Art, he adopted a range of personas: Teddy Boy, Beatnik, tortured artist, rebellious rock 'n' roller. According to Spitz, Lennon 'disliked jazz almost as much as he hated jazz fans'.[122] The division between rock 'n' roll and jazz was demarcated along class lines in Liverpool and other English towns and cities.[123] Some writers have tended to focus on Lennon's art school experiences as his entry point into the more esoteric elements of American rock 'n' roll. Frith and Horne claim that 'art school...inflected pop music with bohemian dreams'.[124] Yet they underestimate the resilience of class and locality in the roots of English popular music. Lennon personified the complexity of class identity with his bridging of both working and middle-class cultures. In an unpublished interview from 1969 he stressed that he was 'always torn between being a teddy boy and an art student'.[125] Like Hoggart's 'scholarship boys', Lennon and his working-class contemporaries retained a sense of class that could be both a burden and a liberation.[126]

McCartney's background and upbringing also highlights the subtleties of class identity in Liverpool. His father Jim was a cotton salesman who saw the possibility of social mobility through location, education and occupation. He encouraged his son to develop his academic skills and like Lennon he passed the 11-plus examination and gained entry to grammar school.[127] Both Lennon and McCartney had the benefit of standing outside of the Liverpool working-class in terms of social position and education, but they were able to draw on particular social identities through family members and the broader culture of the city. Biographers have focused on McCartney as being more attuned to the importance of social climbing and career development than the rest of the Beatles. According to Spitz, the Beatles manager Brian Epstein provided the perfect role model: 'He was so widely travelled and cultured...That made all the difference to Paul'.[128] The tensions of class, authenticity, stardom and recognition were a constant source of tension between Lennon and McCartney in their formative years and throughout their subsequent career.

Harrison and Starr can be more firmly located in Liverpool's working-class milieu. Harrison's father had been a steward on the Cunard liners and later a bus driver and trade union activist.[129] Harrison also passed the 11-plus, but unlike McCartney his family were less actively socially and culturally mobile.[130] Starr was born in the Dingle, an impoverished section of the city. His father worked in a commercial bakery. His stepfather, Harry Graves, was a painter at the Burtonwood airbase. In a 1964 interview, Ringo recalled his formative years: 'When I was sixteen…we'd have a few laughs with the rival gangs…then I got the drums…we stopped going out and hanging around corners every night'.[131] To Brocken, the fact that the Beatles could avoid conventional work patterns gave them 'more time during the day to "research" into American music'.[132] McCartney later stated that '[b]eing in a band meant you had the chance of avoiding a boring job'.[133] Such opportunities could provide a physical flight from class, but the mental connections remained important and aided the Beatles in developing a mass following that cut across social boundaries.

Mersey Beat, entrepreneurship and social change

By the late 1950s Liverpool's industrial and working-class heritage was being diluted by economic change and slum clearance. Kynaston notes that '1956 saw both the closure of the Overland Railway (known locally as the dockers' umbrella), and the opening of the Creswell Mount…the city's first multi-story dwelling block'.[134] This 'new' working-class, detached from traditional communities, was seen by some as being ripe for cultural corruption. In 1962, the headmaster of a private school in Birkenhead attacked aspects of youth culture: 'Teenagers today are becoming sloppy, untidy, Americanised, and show little taste when choosing clothes…which I consider suitable for only those with only fourth-rate minds'.[135] Yet working-class youth in Liverpool were finding an ability to respond to such attacks through different forms of media, which enabled them to present a collective voice of protest. The most successful of these initiatives was *Mersey Beat*.

The development of a particular musical identity in the city was dependent on grass-roots proselytising and Bill Harry was a key figure in this process. He realised that the local press was not covering the groups, venues and the general explosion of youth culture in the city, so he developed his own strategy to link-up the various scenes, styles and genres.[136] He imagined a musical map of Liverpool and this represented his 'policeman's beat' from which he would cull reports, stories and analyses of the popular music scene.[137] Here was an example of a desire to express the importance of popular music in the everyday life of the city's working-class. In a response to the attacks on 'teenagers' in one issue of *Mersey Beat*, Bernard Falk emphasised the generational conflict that was finding its voice in and through popular music: 'I am becoming fed up with these pompous, high-minded, overgrown cabbages, spouting their outdated Victorian views all over the place'.[138] Rhythm and blues provided an antidote to the conservatism gauged by Falk and other music consumers in the city. All four Beatles stressed its transformative impact.[139] There was radicalism in the cultural politics of the Beatles that related to what working-class youth experienced in their heads, but also in the ways in which their embrace of the group provided new perspectives on everyday life regarding class, race and place.[140]

The beat scene in Liverpool also owed much to the entrepreneurialism of promoters, club owners and small businessmen. Harry views the role of Brian Kelly, Charlie McBain, Ray McFall and others as being crucial in providing space, time, energy and entrepreneurial spirit in creating opportunities for young musicians to hone their craft.[141] In an article in *Mersey Beat* in 1964, local promoter Alan Williams claimed that '[y]ears ago in Liverpool the dancing scene was controlled by promoters who...would not entertain the youngsters who wanted to jive. Fortunately, a number of young promoters came along...and the scene developed from there'.[142] Joe Flannery was another notable beat music entrepreneur. He moved away from his greengrocery business in order to try his hand at music promotion. In an interview with the *Daily Express,* he informed readers that 'when the rest of Britain slowed down the tempo Liverpool stuck to the Rock, adding to it the Irish, Welsh, and coloured influences of this polyglot city. Clubs flourished. Local idols gained fantastic followings'.[143]

Beatles manager Brian Epstein had his own particular experiences of entrepreneurship, exclusion, alienation, transgression and class anxiety.[144] Born to middle-class Jewish parents he moved from a flirtation with acting to work in the family business at the North End Music Stores (NEMS).[145] In the figure of Epstein, we have a repository for the contradictions of Liverpool and indeed the England of the early 1960s – a socialist businessman, repressed homosexual and a figure who was simultaneously attracted and repelled by the nuances of class. According to one biographer, 'the archetypal pop star's manager in the mid-1960s was not renowned for ethics, manners, honesty, taste or style...Epstein was utterly different'.[146] Unlike Parnes and his ilk he was a far less cynical operator and could see in the Beatles an opportunity to do something more than just prepare them for a career in light entertainment. Epstein's lifestyle also sheds light on the homosexual subculture of England's metropolitan centres. In Liverpool gay men socialised in venues such as the Magic Clock, the Spinning Wheel and the Old Dive.[147] Brocken has noted that the Beatles narrative has tended to underplay the importance of gay subcultures on the development of beat groups in the city.[148] Epstein's background was extremely comfortable, but he had an affinity with the less blessed communities of Liverpool. Coleman claims that Epstein 'was a socialist at heart, and could never vote anything other than Labour'.[149] This was no doubt linked to the problems that he could see Liverpool's working-class having to deal with on a daily basis. Epstein's social position added to the subtle yet notable class identities and tensions that were contained within the Beatles and their wider entourage.

Contemporary observers and participants in the Liverpool music scene were interested in trying to make sense of the origins of the Beatles and the 'beat phenomenon' and whether this was related to the economic and social changes taking place in the city. In a report in *New Society* in February 1964, ex-gang member Colin Fletcher claimed that beat music had provided a flight from juvenile delinquency: 'Out of the unemployment, the endless two-up-and-two-downs with tin baths in the cobbled yards ... the beat invaded the gangs and changed them beyond all recognition'.[150] In the same article he noted that '[i]n the Park Gang there was the boy who played a good harmonica; the one who was adept at a rhythm with knitting needles on a lamp post'.[151] The music of Buddy Holly and the hit single 'That'll Be the Day' had a particular impact on Fletcher and his peers: 'Ten members of the Park Gang bought this record'.[152]

Class was again important in contributing to the shifting musical genres of particular clubs in the city. By 1963, jazz clubs that had attracted a predominantly middle-class crowd were superseded by a more working-class rhythm and blues scene.[153] George Melly witnessed the transformation of the Cavern Club.

> ... we noticed that the management was no longer hiring a local jazz band to play during our interval. Instead we returned from the pub to find the small stage cluttered with amplification ... there were these young men with electric guitars playing and shouting the modern Negro urban blues at what seemed to us a quite unnecessary volume.[154]

Performers and consumers of popular music in Liverpool also retained a strong sense of civic identity. By January 1964, *Mersey Beat* had become a national publication with thousands of readers spawning a number of regional imitators, but Harry wanted to retain its local focus. In one editorial, the sense of the neglect of music scenes outside of the capital was palpable: 'London – You've ignored the North long enough'. Harry claimed that 'National seems to stand for 'London' and the rest of Britain is treated in a minor fashion – shrugged off with small columns on 'Around the Provinces' and 'Up North'.[155] Letters from readers also reveal criticisms of the London-centric entertainment industry. A letter from K. Knight of Childwall is illustrative: 'For years the cream of our musical talent have trod the long road to London, never, in some cases to return'.[156] The letters suggest that although popular music and developments in youth culture had particular national characteristics, local peculiarities continued to be a feature of the beat scene in Liverpool. The magazine contained editorials, news items, classifieds, profiles of entertainers/managers, film/record reviews and reader's letters. Yet it also aimed to retain a link to the broader working-class culture of the city and contained features on working mens' clubs and the more traditional type of entertainer.

Mersey Beat was also more than just a publication focusing on popular music. The paper covered political issues that were particularly pertinent to youth.[157] An article on 'The New Town Blues' highlighted the sense of dislocation that emerged as a result of slum clearance. Falk claimed that youth on the Woodchurch Estate in Birkenhead 'had no facilities for engaging themselves unless they make a half-an-hour bus journey to the town centre...we city dwellers can realise how fed up we would feel if we could never get to the theatre, cinema, rock club or bowling centre'.[158] Unemployment was also a growing problem for working-class teenagers in Liverpool and other industrial districts. Consumerism may have been symbolising a break with aspects of traditional working-class life, but the industries that could provide adequate levels of disposable income were slowly declining. Factory closures in South Wales, Lancashire, Yorkshire and the North East were indicative of what would become long-term trends. In March 1963, the national press reported that 800 girls had been made redundant from the Liverpool Littlewoods Pools offices with many in tears as they left at the end of the shift.[159] Also, over 3000 pupils due to leave school in December 1963 were asked to return to ease the shortage of vacancies. The city had started the New Year of 1963 with 36,000 unemployed.[160] At the peak of Beatlemania in 1964, Moorhouse also highlighted the continuing problems of poverty, violence and crime in the city: 'Vandalism in various forms seems to flourish here more vigorously than anywhere with the possible exception of Glasgow...The most noticeable thing about Liverpool, though, is its air of tension. It is a place where you half-expect street fighting to break out at any minute'.[161] This contrasts with Melly's recollections of the period in which 'you could sense behind the words and music, the emergence of a new spirit; post-war, clever, non-conformist, and above all cool'.[162]

The reach of *Mersey Beat* spread from Liverpool across the North West, nationwide and was soon receiving letters from France, Germany and the United States. Liverpool youths dreaming of fame and fortune would write to Harry asking for advice on how to make it in the business. In a number of replies one can sense the difficulty of musicians finding a voice and an audience in an increasingly crowded local market. In one reply, Harry states that 'a group must be good musically to get anywhere. Discerning audiences on Merseyside will not tolerate musicians who can't play their instruments'.[163] An interview with Manchester band the Dakotas also points to the a-typicality of Liverpool in terms of the music performed: 'In Manchester and in other parts of the country, the audience seem only interested in top-twenty numbers...Yet on Merseyside...groups pick the best numbers and are closer to the American music'.[164] Nottingham rocker Shane Fenton was 'amazed to find that Merseysiders are still enthusiastic about such stars as Jerry Lee Lewis and Little Richard'.[165] In his article 'Is Liverpool a Frontier for Rock?'

Maurice Woolf claimed that 'Liverpool was the first centre in Britain to show mass interest in rock guitar playing – years before solid bodies, amps and reverb and tremolo were thought of. I know this to be so because I had the job of selling guitars all over the North'.[166] The technical superiority of the Liverpool groups was also noted by Ronnie Carr and other musicians from the wider North West.[167]

The national profile of *Mersey Beat* attracted negative views from some local readers. There was criticism from female contributors who felt that it had started to copy the national magazines through the inclusion of glamour models. A letter from Sheila Darley of Bootle is illustrative.

> Oh Mr Bill Harry, shame on you.
> What is the 'Mersey Beat coming to?
> Once I could read it on train or bus
> Without fear of causing a bother or fuss
> But not anymore!
> Each page has a pin-up – a glamorous figure.
> So all the boys turn to each other and snigger.
> While the poor girls don't know what to think.
> And look at the floor.
>
> I remember that just a few months ago
> A survey told a tale of woe.
> A lot of male readers appear to have gone.
> And we girls outnumber them two against one.
> Did you feel sore?
>
> To get the boys back you feel strongly compelled.
> And from then on their interest just had to be held.
> So now there's bikinis and gay bathing suits.
> With necklines more plunging than steep water-chutes.
> Should keep to the shore.
>
> It's not that we're jealous – we're just plain annoyed.
> And feel sore that the space could be better employed.
> And if your male readers want this kind of fun they've got the wrong paper.[168]

The letter subverts the notion that young women were primarily passive consumers of popular music.[169] Yet many young girls *were* finding a connection with the music of the Beatles just through the sheer pleasure of the listening experience. In a letter to the Lord Mayor of Liverpool from 'Elaine Waring and the Gang', the effect on schooling is noted: 'I take my transistor [sic] radio to school with me and if the Fab Four's records come on we cry because we can't dance'.[170] Pat Delaney, a supervisor at the Cavern Club was sure that the Beatles success was linked to the strong bond that they formed with local youth. He claimed that the 'youngsters who watch them see themselves up there – the Beatles have the ability to set off the spark in them. They are a symbol of their own desires'.[171] This was clearly the experience of young women like Maureen Nolan and Roma Singleton: 'we swarmed down Mount Pleasant, aware that we were at the hub of something exciting... and Liverpool... was at the front of this heady cultural thrust'.[172]

Socialist politics, popular music and the 'leaving' of Liverpool

On 3 August 1963, the Beatles made their final appearance at the Cavern Club.[173] Hall and Pannell writing a year later claimed that 'the Beatles belong to Liverpool in a way in which Cliff Richard never belonged anywhere'.[174] This certainly seemed to be the case when gauging the response of local fans to the fact that the Beatles were now national and international celebrities.[175] The city that they left behind remained plagued by the some of the problems that it had experienced in the 1930s. Moorhouse penned the following description: 'Life, with a perennially high unemployment rate, is infinitely more precarious... It is also, marginally perhaps, more brutish. Liverpool is about the only English provincial city where if you walk alone after midnight... you stand a fair chance of ending up in the gutter with your wallet missing'.[176] Guthrie writing in 1966 also provided a portrait of the less salubrious parts of the city: 'Plunging streets of slums, bombed sites, rubble, pubs, dirt and kids – you either live on where you were born or you get a good job and move out. The houses are condemned, and everybody knows everybody else – there are no newcomers'.[177]

Interviews in *Beat City* (1963) explore a post-Beatles Liverpool in which an air of sadness pervades their local fans.[178] Contributors to *Mersey Beat* also concurred claiming that the Beatles no longer belonged to the city. Lin and Pam 'two ex-Beatle fans' penned a letter which was indicative of such feeling claiming that 'they were Liverpool incarnate – but alas, no longer... They are not our Beatles'.[179] Harry also felt that the camaraderie that had existed between the Liverpool groups suffered with the national profile of the Beatles and petty jealousies and fractious relationships were the result.[180] Yet in many ways the Beatles would never leave Liverpool and the impact of the group continued to be maintained as part of the collective memory and the cultural geography of the city.

One aspect of the development of beat groups in Liverpool that has been marginalised in existing accounts is that role that local socialist politicians played in promoting the Beatles and linking them to a sense of civic pride and a collective working-class identity. The Chants had already become very close to Bessie Braddock[181], the working-class matriarch and formidable Labour MP whose very presence and personality on the national political stage reflected the various identities of the city.[182] The Chants were based in her constituency, Liverpool Exchange. She was the first successful Labour candidate to win the seat and the first woman in the city to win the constituency in a general election.[183] Braddock was an unlikely figure in seeing the potential of popular music for transforming the fortunes of working-class districts and offering an opportunity for political advantage and propaganda. This strategy would be taken up later by Harold Wilson in his attempt to woo the youth vote for Labour in the 1964 General Election.[184] The Cavern Club was in her constituency, and she realised that media attention could be used to generate awareness of the economic and social problems that still blighted parts of Liverpool.

Given the increasing social prominence of popular music in general and the Beatles in particular, reporters were keen to gauge the views of politicians on their particular tastes. In 1963, the *Daily Express* carried out a survey of leading MPs in both the Conservative and Labour parties. The Prime Minister, Harold Macmillan, claimed that he had 'no views on, nor interest in popular music'. Harold Wilson the leader of the Labour Party said that he had 'always liked popular music' and was 'familiar with all the Top Ten'. Julian Amery, Minister of Aviation, was 'not interested in pops' and George Brown, the Deputy Leader of the Labour Party didn't listen to popular music because 'it all sounds the same'. Geoffrey Rippon the Minister of Transport preferred musical comedy and 'did not dance'. Similarly, George Strauss, the Shadow Transport Minister told the reporter, 'I very seldom dance and can't twist'. Frederick Willey, the Shadow Education Minster claimed that his favourite record was the Beatles 'From Me To You'.[185]

Some Labour Party politicians felt that youth was becoming detached from an earlier working-class culture. A party press release in 1964 claimed that 'youth is one of the main victims of private affluence and public squalor…in a I'm Alright Jack, bingo, betting shop Britain, moral standards have fallen and a sense of true priorities has been weakened'.[186] The resilience of aspects of class in English society was something that was also noted by foreign observers. Katherine Oettinger, a visiting American writer who was examining English youth and youth services presented a particular portrait: 'The class consciousness of the older generation, I was told, has almost vanished among the young…class consciousness has not so much disappeared as changed into consciousness of strata based on educational achievement'.[187] The Communist Party held discussions on the impact of popular music and youth culture on British society.[188] The Beatles appeared on the cover of the *Daily Worker* generating a mixed response from party members. Writing in *Music and Life*, the newsletter of the Communist Music Group in 1964, John Evans was generally positive about the way in which the group challenged the hegemony of the United States in the field of popular music: 'We in the working class movement have long deplored the swamping of our native culture by American pop art…we should welcome something home-grown rather than damn it out of hand'.[189]

Socialists in Liverpool felt that the city could gain much through harnessing youth culture and popular music for a greater good. Eric Heffer, a Labour councillor elected in 1960 and future left-wing Labour MP for Walton was an important promoter of the Beatles and saw a clear connection between the city's youth culture and an existing working-class consciousness. In the 1964 general election campaign, Heffer would 'sing snatches of Beatles songs such as 'If There's Anything That You Want' from [the] platform'.[190] He claimed that 'they made a powerful contribution to Labour's victory without recognizing it'.[191] Yet this is difficult to substantiate. However, Labour did make significant gains in the city in subsequent general elections. In 1950, the Conservatives held five out of nine seats but with Labour's victory in the 1964 election Labour held seven out of nine.[192] To Heffer, the 'Liverpool beat scene was fundamentally working-class... Working people appeared to be coming into their own at last. It was their youth who were... playing and recording the music you could hear in every pub and club... They asserted working-class values'.[193] Heffer floated the idea of a civic reception for the Beatles in a letter to the Lord Mayor.[194]

> For some time now, I, no doubt like every citizen in Liverpool, have followed the career of the 'Beatles' with particular interest... They are... wonderful ambassadors for our city... their successful visit to Paris, and their forthcoming trip to the United States, are all achievements which have helped to put Liverpool on the map... as a city we should do something to honour them.[195]

This was taken up by the Mayor of Liverpool Alderman John McMillan and then by Alderman Louis Caplan who replaced McMillan on 10 July 1964. Epstein agreed to the offer, and it was decided that the event would coincide with the northern premier of the Beatles film *A Hard Day's Night* (1964). Once the civic reception became public knowledge the Lord Mayor's office received numerous letters of support and a few that were critical. Ernest Hayes a 70-year-old former shipping employee expressed utter disdain for the group: 'There are other industries for which the city is renowned... Their vocation is not important to Liverpool... Fortunately they will, by their own mode of life, not last very long'.[196] Yet others were realising that popular music and youth culture were presenting evidence of a transnational identity that could transcend local peculiarities and tensions between nation states. Ray McFall of the Cavern Club organised a trip to Hamburg that would see Liverpool teenagers meeting their German counterparts. In a letter to the Lord Mayor, he stated that the purpose was 'to promote goodwill between the young people of both cities who ... have been brought closer together ... by groups of young Liverpool rock 'n' roll musicians... I would also venture to suggest that this will be a contribution however humble towards improving Anglo German relations'.[197] The mayor was in agreement and sent a message of goodwill to the people of Hamburg: 'In recent times the virility of seaports such as Liverpool and Hamburg have found expression in the 'Beat' type of music...during the last few years groups of young Liverpool...musicians have visited Hamburg. I feel confident that these visits will result in the formation of friendships amongst members of the younger generation'.[198] Requests also came into the mayor's office from the United States, Canada and Eastern Europe supporting the official recognition of the Beatles. In response to a letter from a Polish youth, it was agreed that Beatles records would be sent to the author.[199]

The attitudes of Braddock, Heffer and other labour movement activists in relation to the Beatles offers a counterpoint to the traditional characterisations of socialist attitudes to popular music. MacDonald has argued that: 'In the fifties, the people's music was an ideological fiction whereby left-wing artists set a supposedly authentic 'roots' music of the common man against the allegedly artificial products of the capitalist music industry'.[200] Yet in Liverpool the popular music scene was having a psychological, social and political impact on working-class youth and socialists responded accordingly. The national and local press were also reporting how particular workplaces were now moving to the sound of popular music. In one instance when 'a foreman shut off the radio in the middle of a Beatles record at a textile mill in Lancashire, 200 girls went out on strike'.[201] The experiences of working-class youth in Liverpool through their embrace of the Beatles would soon be shared by millions of others in England, Europe and the United States.

The Beatles contributed a multiracial soundtrack to a 'structure of feeling' that both confirmed and challenged a particular sense of class and place. The continuities and changes in the experiences of the everyday lives of the city's youth offer a particular example of the interplay between class, race and ethnicity in creating a popular music scene that had a national and international impact. The sea, migration, the American airbase at Burtonwood all created a cultural matrix where classes, races, ethnicities and nationalities came together through an embrace of English, American and West Indian popular music. The beat scene had a significant social impact. Rhythm and blues was now a central part of the city's soundscape offering opportunities for working-class musicians to pursue alternative careers or providing a temporary escape from the strictures of class and the restrictions of monotonous shift work. Yet it also had direct political consequences with socialists like Braddock and Heffer claiming that beat music was a working-class phenomenon that could make a contribution to a progressive programme of social change that they hoped would be implemented by the Labour Party.

Between January 1962 and July 1964 the Beatles had developed from a local Liverpool beat group into a global cultural phenomenon.[202] To MacDonald, the 'Beatles acted as a major conduit of black energy, style and feeling into white culture'.[203] The music was '[f]ast-moving and devolved, the pop culture of the Sixties was intrinsically democratic. Its meaning grounded more in feeling than sense, it represented an upsurge of working-class expression'.[204] As such the Beatles and the popular music scene in Liverpool provide a particular image of England that contained both poverty and affluence, the resilience of class identities and new discourses and soundscapes that seemingly promised transformation, transgression and liberation.

Part II
Mod England

Modern clubs, such as the Flamingo in the West End or the Acton Bop Club in the suburbs, have publicly recruited mainly from the dance halls ... if jazz clubs can steer a middle course between the two undesirable extremes of hooliganism and academicism, they do nothing but good. (*Times Educational Supplement*, 20 January 1956)

The Teddy suit has gone, and given way to the Italian thing. The aggression has moved into arrogance. (Ray Gosling, *Sum Total*, 1962)

[T]he use of 'purple hearts' and the Margate disturbances. It would be absurd to place the blame for these on pop music but it can be blamed to a certain extent. For it reflected the get-rich-quick character of capitalism. (*Music and Life: Newsletter of the Communist Music Group*, 1964)

Mods were trying to be a little bit New York ... correct and cool ... Saturday night at the Flamingo ... clubs were the bedrock ... people were finding their own space. (Terri Quaye, Jazz Musician)

The Modernist thing started in 1959 ... stopped in 1966 ... I was a Mod because I wanted to express myself as an individual through clothes, that's what it was all about. (Lloyd Johnson, Original Mod)

4
My Generation: Pete Townshend, the Who and English Mods

Mods are part of the iconic imagery of 1960s England. They exhibited an air of sophistication, upward mobility and generational antagonism that to some symbolised broader economic and cultural changes. The first Mods appeared in London in the late 1950s, and by 1964, they had become a national phenomenon with a distinctive identity based on fashion, music, mobility and attitude. The historiography of Mod is extremely limited, but there is a significant non-academic literature that has created a mosaic of Mod lifestyles in London.[1] This chapter examines Mods through the music of Pete Townshend and the Who.[2] Townshend and the Mods present a particular image of England, where the relationship between white working-class youth, black America and West Indian migrants was indicative of a country that was becoming more cosmopolitan, affluent and multicultural, yet remained divided by social class.[3]

Pete Townshend was a writer and performer who was not content writing pop songs but also wanted to provide narratives and analyses of youth culture and how it posed a challenge to the social conventions of English society.[4] Doggett argues that Townshend was different from other performers of the 1960s in that he saw his 'role not to provide false hope but to reflect the negativity felt by "the kids"'.[5] For Townshend, 'popular music had a serious purpose' and that was 'to defy post-war depression'.[6] Like many of his musical contemporaries, he was aware of the English social structure and his position within it that defined him as middle-class. Townshend expressed his feelings to the *New Musical Express* stressing that 'class, the attributes and consciousness... has always been something that has evaded me'.[7] Yet like Lennon he was connected to the working-class through friendship, popular music, geographical proximity and a fascination with its youth culture.[8]

Townshend's parents were musicians and his father traversed the country as a member of the popular dance band the Squadronnaires.[9] As a child in the mid-1950s, Townshend visited provincial theatres and holiday camps where a pre-war working-class culture now mixed with the contemporary sounds of rock 'n' roll. It was on the Isle of Man in 1957 where he attended a screening of *Rock Around the Clock* (1956) and 'nothing would ever be quite the same'.[10] He followed what would become a fairly typical route into a music career and shared with his contemporaries a transformative experience of American rhythm and blues music.[11] He was a member of a skiffle band before establishing a successful recording and performing career as a member of the Who along with Roger Daltrey, John Entwistle and Keith Moon.[12] Through his involvement in art school, the music industry and the cosmopolitan culture of London, Townshend would connect with a variety of characters that epitomised the British class system.[13] According to Davey, Townshend was a member of the Campaign for Nuclear Disarmament and the Young Communist League and had played banjo as part of one of the Aldermaston marches against nuclear weapons.[14] Denselow also claims that Townshend had also discussed politics with veteran leftists who were on the trad-jazz scene.[15] Yet ultimately, he was more interested in youth culture as a political form of expression that operated outside *of* and could not be defined *by* particular ideological and organisational structures.

The Mod subculture to which Townshend attempted to become a spokesman was political in the sense that it posed a challenge to particular social boundaries that were a feature of 1960s England. Mod was an identity, subculture and movement that seemingly aimed to transcend class but in many ways was an expression of its resilience. The network of clubs, performers and consumers that created Mod exhibited a sense of style and hedonism that had been a feature of pre-war working-class culture and had produced a particular critique of authority and convention.[16] Townshend's history of Mod contained on the album *Quadrophenia* (1973) was based on events surrounding a concert by the Who at Brighton Aquarium on 29 March 1964, where he had witnessed the energy, excitement and violence of working-class youths who had embraced the culture as a source of collective identity.[17] The album was written and recorded in a period of industrial militancy in England that had not been witnessed since the general strike of 1926. Along with the novels and films of the English 'new-wave', it is a classic slice of 'social realism', social history and cultural commentary. The narrative documents the frustrations of a working-class youth, his connection and distance from the social milieu in which he was raised and ultimately his attempt to transcend the conventions of his home, workplace and locality through becoming a Mod.[18]

Townshend wanted to articulate the feelings and emotions of working-class youth through song and performance, and as a result his work with the Who was far more ambitious than the Beatles and the Rolling Stones in attempting to make sense of post-war England. According to Denselow, 'Townshend believed in his audiences, believed it was they and not the performers who were the real sixties idealists'.[19] Songs such as 'I Can't Explain', 'Anyway, Anyhow, Anywhere', and 'My Generation', which charted in 1965, became Mod anthems providing a soundtrack for a working-class youth who expressed an inarticulate, but keenly felt, sense of liberation and transgression in the coffee bar, dance hall, provincial theatre and coastal resort.[20] Mods present a particular image of England where some things changed and others remained the same. Yet within this image we see challenges to the boundaries of class, social convention and numerous examples of 'historic encounters' between white working-class youth, West Indian migrants and the sounds and struggles of black America.[21]

The tributaries of English Mod

There are a variety of interpretations in terms of locating the origins of Mod. As with many aspects of youth culture characterisations and definitions have been underpinned by claims of originality, authenticity and specificity.[22] According to Elms, the excavation of the first Mod 'has become a Holy Grail of youth culture archaeology'.[23] There is some disagreement in the literature in terms of the exact periodisation, but in general, the primary sources suggest that as a recognisable and sizeable youth culture it can be located in the years 1959–66, where it had developed from being the preserve of purveyors of modern jazz music to becoming a source of identity amongst a significant number of working-class youths.[24]

The tributaries of Mod can be found in the changing musical, social, sexual and racial geographies of London in the 1950s. To Du Noyer, Mod was 'a very London cult' with 'roots in post-war jazz and, arguably in a much older tradition of aspirational cockney dandies'.[25] Rawlings also locates Mods in the jazz clubs of Soho in the mid-1950s where they developed a style and musical affiliation that set themselves apart from the followers of 'trad Jazz'.[26] Hewitt has emphasised the importance of jazz musicians such as Ronnie Scott, Pete King and others first congregating in Club 11 in the late 1940s who attempted to replicate the playing and fashion styles of Charlie Parker and Miles Davies.[27] Gorman connects Mod to the beatnik culture of the 1950s noting that by 1959 'there was a growing split between the arty existential/beatnik look associated with art colleges and the cool, sharp and almost androgynous "Modernist" style prevalent among less educated youth'.[28] Barnes claims that the look was developed by middle-class Jewish youths from the Stamford Hill district of the capital who had some connection to the tailoring trades of the city.[29] To Melly, the original Mods were 'young working-class boys ... totally devoted to clothes'.[30] Burton claims that Mod was part of the fabric of the gay subculture of London's night clubs. He remembered that teenage homosexuals and Mods shopped in the same boutiques and listened to the same music.[31] Hebdige sees the Mods as 'the first in a long line of working-class youth cultures which grew up around the West Indians, responded positively to their presence and sought to emulate their style'.[32] Yet to Fowler, Mod 'was essentially no different from those lifestyles of interwar teenage consumers … who visited … dance halls as habitually during the 1930s as Mods visited dance halls … in the 1960s'.[33]

MacInnes was one of first contemporary writers to capture the essence of Mod in *Absolute Beginners* (1959): 'College-boy smooth crop hair with burned-in parting, neat white Italian rounded-collared shirt, short Roman jacket *very* tailored … no turn-up narrow trousers with … pointed-toe shoes'.[34] In an article for *Universities and Left Review* in the same year Stuart Hall also provided a profile.

> Here are the very smart, sophisticated young men and women of the metropolitan jazz clubs, the Flamingo devotees … Suits are … severely cut and narrow on the Italian pattern. Haircuts are 'Modern' – a brisk, flat-topped French version of the now-juvenile American crew-cut, Modestly called 'college style'. Shirts are either white stiff or solid colour close-knit wool in the Continental manner. Jeans are de rigueur … American, striped narrowly or black or khaki. The girls are short-skirted … pin-pointed on stiletto heels, with set hair and Paris-boutique dead-pan make-up and mascara … an acquired taste for the Modern Jazz Quartet … Their attitude to adults is less resentful than scornful. Adults are simply 'square'. Mugs. They are not 'with it' … Office-boys – even van-boys – by day, they are record-sleeve boys by night.[35]

In 1960 the *Daily Express* in its report of the trial of nineteen-year-old Michael Dowdall, who was subsequently imprisoned for the murder of a prostitute, also provided an insight into the early years of Mod culture through the testimony of Cindy Rankles.

> It was in the Two I's coffee bar that I first met Irish Mick. He was one of our crowd … we called ourselves the Modernists because all the fellows dress Modern Italian and the girls wear short jackets. We have our own pass sign and a dance called the square … The sign is made by looping our right forefinger in the air and we say, 'he's bold'. This means the fellow you are talking about is one of us.[36]

Morse in her study of English youth in 1960 presents another image of Mod style. Here was recognition that Mod had emerged out of the jazz clubs and was now attracting the attentions of working-class teenagers. In her description of a typical coffee bar she writes that 'many of the boys wear smart Italian suits'.[37] Laurie also noted the popularity of the image describing Mods as 'immaculately dressed fourteen-year-old boys looking … like account executives'.[38] Yet the publication that initially brought Mod to the masses was an article that appeared in *Town* magazine in September 1962, which included photographs and interviews with youths from Stamford Hill, London.[39] One was Mark Feld who would later find fame through glam rock as Marc

Bolan.[40] Feld was from a working-class household and as a child had been attracted to both the Teddy Boy and Modernist styles of the late 1950s. He was a prime example of a teenager who traversed London's cultural geography and connected with individuals from a range of social classes with a penchant for social and sexual transgression.[41] To Bolan's biographer, Feld 'wanted to be recognised by his peers, but didn't want to be perceived as a part of a group'.[42] Barnes claims that through the article 'all the individual and diverse elements finally fused into the overall Mod style'.[43] Yet as the participants in the *Town* article made clear, this did not indicate a more general transformation of earlier youth styles. Feld and the others noted the number of Teddy Boys that were still a feature of the pubs, clubs and cinema queues of early 1960s England. Nonetheless, in the wake of the magazine's publication the number of Mods defined by fashion, musical affiliation and particular social attitudes multiplied across London.

A number of individuals were responsible for the commercialisation of Mod and taking it out of London and into the provinces. A combination of scene setters, musicians, fashion designers, entrepreneurs, retailers and disc-jockeys in English towns and cities between 1962–5 took Mod culture into the home, coffee bar and dance hall. Pete Meaden even attempted to develop a philosophy of Mod as a 'way of life' that would directly appeal to working-class youth. He was employed as a publicist in the music industry and frequented the Scene Club and other centres of London's Mod subculture.[44] Oldham recalls forging a friendship with Meaden through absorbing the fashions worn by American jazz musicians on their album covers and buying similar garments from Austin's on Shaftesbury Avenue.[45] At this stage of its development Mod was more about clothes than music. The emphasis was on looking cool and standing out from the crowd. Yet Meaden felt that the creation of a pop group that could reflect the vibrancy of the Mod milieu would give the scene more coherence. He later told the *New Musical Express* that he 'saw the potential in Modism' and that he was 'thinking about revolutions'.[46]

Meaden acted as Townshend's guide to the Mod subculture and in particular the nuances of its style, discourse and soundscapes.[47] The Who became a vehicle for the popularisation of Mod. The group started as the Detours in 1962 and had played a variety of venues including the Jewish Club in Ealing and the American Servicemen's' Club in Marble March.[48] They changed their name to the Who in February 1964 and after connecting with Meaden in the summer became the High Numbers.[49] Meaden took the group on a tour of all the Mod clubs of London. Moon was already familiar with places like the Flamingo and had performed with Georgie Fame and the Blue Flames.[50] Jack Lyons witnessed the spectacle of the High Numbers during their residency at the Railway Hotel in Harrow and felt that here was a group that seemed to be speaking directly to him and his working-class friends.[51] Mim Scala remembers it 'as a madhouse with hundreds of Vespa scooters outside'.[52] Meaden also got the group a residency at the Scene Club from 5 August to the 2 September.[53] In Blackpool on 23 September the High Numbers supported the Beatles and the Kinks at the Opera House the only time that three of the key groups of the 1960s would share a stage together. The arrival of the High Numbers symbolised the way in which Mod was expanding from its exclusive connection to the world of Modern jazz and the rhythm and blues scene. Recent adopters of the subculture sought English groups who could speak to them directly through image, recordings and performance.

Local Mods flocked to the High Numbers and the following expanded once they established a residency at the Marquee reverting to their previous name of the Who in November 1964.[54] The songs they covered were symbolic of the way in which white working-class youth were absorbing the sounds of black America. The Who performed a range of Motown and rhythm and blues songs in an attempt to both reflect and shape the sonic features of the Mod subculture.[55] In order to tightly bind the group to Mods, the group's new managers Kit Lambert and Chris Stamp created the 100 Faces who became regulars at shows.[56] The management team of Lambert and Stamp was indicative of the way in which particular individuals were crossing class boundaries through engagement with London's youth culture. Kit Lambert, the son of the composer Constant Lambert, had attended private school and Trinity College Oxford and retained particular elements of his upper-class upbringing.[57] In contrast, Chris Stamp was the son of tugboat captain from the East End of London who had left school and found work on the fringes of the film industry.[58] Lambert, Stamp, Townshend, Entwistle, Daltrey and Moon were representative of the social structure of England in the 1960s and each of them brought something specific to the image and appeal of the Who.

In 1965, the group expanded their appeal beyond London attracting working-class Mods to their performances in places like Margate, Manchester, Sheffield, Newcastle and Liverpool.[59] Along with the Who, groups such as the Kinks, the Small Faces, the Creation and the rhythm and blues scene that had attracted singers and musicians, such as Rod Stewart, all played their part in selling Mod to the masses.[60] Like Townshend, Stewart had experienced music as a cultural and political force, taking part in particular campaigns and espousing left-wing rhetoric.[61] He attended the Aldermaston marches in 1961, '62 and '63 and was arrested for public order offences during demonstrations in Trafalgar Square and Whitehall.[62] Yet unlike Townshend, Stewart had firmer roots in the working-class. His father was a newsagent and a staunch Labour Party supporter.[63] The national profile of Mod was aided by the appearance of its style and advocates on television. The prime vehicle here was *Ready Steady Go!*, which was first broadcast in the summer of 1963. This featured a number of African American performers alongside the more successful English beat groups.[64] The influential presenter, Cathy McGowan wore the latest fashion styles, and Mods could be seen in the studio giving provincial teenagers a glimpse of dances that had been the preserve of London clubs.[65]

John 'Moke' Rowley was an example of many of the less celebrated purveyors and popularisers of Mod culture.[66] He had grown up in London's East End and from an early age was interested in fashion. In 1963, he travelled across Europe where he watched French films, perused magazines and adopted styles that he'd seen on page and screen and introduced them into the Mod scene.[67] Another was Guy Stevens who became resident DJ at the Scene Club in 1963, where his esoteric mix of American rhythm and blues and English beat music attracted Mods from across London and the rest of England.[68] His enthusiasm was picked up by Roger Eagle who had visited the club and went on to establish his own credentials as a promoter of American soul music in Manchester.[69] In Sheffield, Terry Thornton established the Club 60 and the Esquire as a centre for rhythm and blues and a repository of Mod styles and sounds.[70] In Newcastle, Mike Jeffery opened several clubs 'including the Downbeat, the Marimba, and most famously the A 'Gogo' that was a major Mod haunt in the city.[71] At the Ship and Rainbow in Wolverhampton, Ray Hill established Sunday as a soul night attracting Mods from across the West Midlands.[72]

The amalgamation of particular fashion trends and musical genres was indicative of the role of working-class youth in attempting to traverse existing social and cultural boundaries. In this sense, Mod was much more significant than earlier forms of youth culture. Townshend was acutely aware of this and through his work with the Who was able to articulate the frustrations of his core audience. The disparate elements of the Mod subculture and the collective identity they created present a particular image of England that both reflected and shaped the way in which popular music and youth culture were challenging existing notions of class, race, gender and nation.

Mod fashion, identity and class

Paytress claims that for Mods the emphasis on style was a 'symbolic refusal of their class position'.[73] Yet Mod fashion can also be read not just as repudiation of class but a restatement of its resilience.[74] Mods like the Spivs, Teddy Boys and dandies that were a feature of working-class communities in the 1940s and 50s continued to live, work and socialise in environments bounded by class. The wearing of suit for weekends in the pub remained a feature of working-class dress into the 1960s. Items of Mod fashion continued to carry the marks of class; the heavy parka, denim jeans, work boots. The Fred Perry tennis shirt might have suggested an embrace of middle-class leisure, but Perry himself was the son of a working-class socialist politician from Stockport who remained critical of the more conservative aspects of English society.[75]

The link between the worlds of class, fashion, music and Mod culture was perhaps best epitomised by John Stephen the self-styled 'King of

Carnaby Street' who by the mid-1960s had opened a number of boutiques that became synonymous with Mod and the notion of 'swinging Britain'.[76] Stephen had been raised in Glasgow in a tough industrial district of the city. He was one of many working-class teenagers who were attracted to the youth culture and greater employment prospects offered by London. Stephen's sense of style and his incursions into a range of class, sexual and cultural milieus ensured that his clothes and the consumers that wore them exhibited elements of American, French, Italian and English couture.[77] His obituary noted that he 'was the first to mass-market what had been a transgressive gay style to straight lads'.[78] Burton recalled that working-class homosexuals and straight Mods 'looked much alike' 'as their clothes came from the same shops'.[79] Much to the annoyance of the original Mods Carnaby Street acted as a magnet to young working-class boys and girls in London and beyond as a centre for this more mass-produced and populist version of Mod culture.[80]

Stephen cemented the link between fashion, music and Mod culture by playing records in his shops.[81] Reed claims that 'Stephen, while having no direct affiliation with Mod…subscribed to their ethic of placing clothes first…as a way of dissolving associations with class'.[82] Yet as Marwick argues, youth culture remained 'affected by class'.[83] In northern England, miners, factory workers, shop assistants and office girls might have been buying more clothes and adopting all the accoutrements of the Mod lifestyle, but their everyday lives continued to be punctuated by the factory whistle, time clock and the nuance of social division. Nonetheless, they could recreate their own Soho and Carnaby Street when sitting in coffee bars on a Saturday afternoon, attending a rhythm and blues club in cities like Manchester, Sheffield and Newcastle or just through listening to records, reading magazines and imagining the escape and excitement of a mythical London in their bedrooms.

Stephen's shops such as 'His Clothes', 'Paul's Boutique' and 'Domino Male' acted as exemplary beacons to entrepreneurs and retailers in the provinces who sought to create their own version of his empire on their own high streets. For example, in Newcastle, the Marcus Price clothes shop 'dressed the Mods'.[84] The fact that Mod style had to be constantly changing suited the entrepreneurial zeal of younger fashion designers and retailers. In particular clubs, coffee bars and dance halls, the type of suit, shirt, shoes and casual wear worn by Mods was in a state of constant flux. In 1964, the *Mod's Monthly* claimed that 'dressmakers…were turning out almost one new dress a week designed by a Mod'.[85] In his survey of East End working-class youth in the same year, Willmott noted that 'clothing shops…emphasise Modernity – 'Hippy Hippy Hipsters' on a pair of blu slacks. Others stress the international inspiration – 'Wrangler Super Denim'…'Preferred by Champion Cowboys' on a display of jeans'.[86] Hierarchies based on the adornment of particular garments in local 'scenes' determined who were the 'Faces', 'Numbers' and 'Tickets'.[87] In the *Mod's Monthly*, McGowan tried to explain the Mod language to a reporter by defining the difference between 'first, second and third class tickets'.[88] The Beatles and the Rolling Stones were not recognised as style icons by the more discerning Mods. The editor of the *Mod's Monthly* claimed that 'Mod Or Not? I say "NO!"...fashionwise they are OUT! Well and truly out! They simply aren't there. All of them wear the clothes they like, which marks them as stylists and individualists rather than straightforward Mods'.[89]

Townshend's relationship to Mod differed from that of the Beatles and the Rolling Stones who said little about the subculture. The emphasis on style that was crucial to Mod identity filtered into the themes of Townshend's song writing. Meaden had already given the High Numbers 'I'm the Face/Zoot Suit' (1964) and Townshend continued the theme with 'Substitute' (1966) and later in songs such as 'Cut My Hair', 'I'm One', 'I've Had Enough', and 'Sea and Sand' from *Quadrophenia* (1973). Particular items of clothing worn by the group in live performance and publicity shots also experimented with symbols of national identity such as the Union Jack and English military regalia. Mod fashion more generally was based on Italian designs, the clothes of French film stars and American casual wear.[90] Hebdige characterised Mod style as an amalgam of particular images such as the Italian Mafia member, the Brooklyn Sharp Kid, the British Spiv and the Jamaican Hustler.[91]

In his survey of the development of Mod, Hewitt argued that they 'chose not to dress in opposition to society, they chose to infiltrate'.[92] Yet such experimentation in style *did* have a more radical impact than he suggests. The adoption and creation of particular styles led to an inversion of existing notions of masculinity and femininity. Townshend claimed that Mod meant 'that being macho was no longer the only measure of manhood'.[93] Young working-class male adherents of Mod applied eye-liner and experimented with the length and cut of their hair. Don Hughes became a Mod in 1963 despite 'the nasty school rumours that it was 'full of queers'.[94] Similarly, young girls cropped their hair and wore trousers, shirts and casual jackets. A feature in the *Mod's Monthly* in 1964 claimed that 'trousers and waistcoats have been "stolen" from the boys and taken over by the girls'.[95] Linda Clarke from Middlesex informed the magazine that Mods in Harefield were 'wearing some very unusual clothes'.[96]

In 1964, local versions of Mod London perhaps consisting of a couple of boutiques and coffee bars became features of high streets across England. The *Mod's Monthly* noted that 'the real ultra-Mods have their own shops'.[97] Letters to the magazine highlighted the changing trends of particular locales. Joanne Dowman informed readers that in Nottingham 'the latest rage...for boys and girls are paisley shirts'.[98] In her regular column McGowan surveyed the local particularities of the Mod scene: 'Mods in Glasgow might be wearing for the first time that those in Cardiff buried weeks ago...clubs in central London spark off the crazes and they are caught on to sometime in the next few weeks...in the suburbs'.[99] Vicki Wickham, the producer of *Ready Steady Go!* told the *Mod's Monthly* that she would 'try to spend at least two evenings a week going around the clubs to see what...fashions are happening there'. She claimed that it was the Scene Club that 'sparked off the current American craze, with its blue jeans, white sneakers and T-shirts and it was the Disc at Peckham that...saw Anoraks worn with pants by both boys and girls'.[100]

Peter Laccohee, a Mod and trainee journalist from a family of dockers in the East End expressed the importance of clothes in a contemporary interview with Hamblett and Deverson: 'To us clothes are a status symbol and they must always be immaculate. If we couldn't afford...them we would stay in for a couple of weeks until we had the money to buy them'.[101] Clothes as a mark of attractiveness and danger had already been noted by social investigators in the late 1950s. Spencer, Tuxford and Dennis in their research into youth on new housing estates provide an illustration: 'When Desiree describes new boy friends the question always is 'what are his trousers like?'.[102] The American writer Tom Wolfe noted the obsession with style in his characterisation of the Mod club Tiles on London's Oxford Street. He describes one of the attendees, Larry Lynch, as a 'working-class boy...he left school at 15 ... has been having his suits custom-made since he was 12 at a place called Jackson's'.[103] Lloyd Johnson, a Mod from Hastings, was a regular at Tiles lunch-time sessions, but avoided the venue in the evenings as it attracted a rougher element and was symbolic of the way in which the subculture was becoming more commercial, populist and prone to violence.[104]

The divisions within Mod culture were soon apparent as the style and identity attracted increasing numbers of working-class youth. According to Reed, Mod groups in London were defined by their locality and dress 'with the Shepherd's Bush contingent preferring to dress in three-button tonic Italian suits...while the prominent East End fashionistas...wore period revival or customised clothes'.[105] Willmott's study of East End boys in 1964 revealed a growing style consciousness that set them apart from their peers: 'In clothes, shoes and hairstyles they looked almost indistinguishable from boys of similar ages in Plymouth or Wolverhampton, Newcastle or Glasgow, except that the East Enders...are...trend-setters rather than followers'.[106] Johnson recalled Mods in his local youth club wearing pin-stripe suits and winkle pickers. He developed an interest in the look, which was further sparked by attending a concert in Croydon and witnessing the existence of another small group of youths who referred to themselves as Mods.[107] Similarly, Linden Kirby claims that the first thing that attracted him to Mods were the stylish nylon macs. The older Mods tended to have better clothes and he recalls one group, the Chiswick Four Faces who may have worked for John Stephen who were the real trend-setters. Yet ultimately, for Kirby, the pursuit of Mod purity became both ridiculous and exhausting.[108]

Rave magazine noted rising and falling fads on the fashion scene: 'Moving out Fast are Tom Jones bows, large handbags, Cleopatra sandals, Grandma shoes and jerkin jackets for boys'.[109] Hall had earlier claimed that Mods knew 'that the teenage market is a racket, but...seem culturally exploited rather than socially deprived'.[110] Yet this was a simplistic view and Mods themselves had been instrumental in creating such a culture that gave their lives more meaning and substance. Moreover, Mod journeys through the social geography of London in search of exclusive items of clothing had enabled them to participate in a form of cultural tourism that provided opportunities to observe and challenge class, but ultimately they remained bounded by its rigidities.

Mod music and London's rhythm 'n' blues clubs as sites of transgression

Laurie had noted the connection between music and youth identity in his book *The Teenage Revolution* (1966): 'Music is the pulse and flow of teenage life...Teenagers meet at concerts, talk about their stars, copy the singers' clothes, spend money on records'.[111] Once Mod had emerged from its origins in the jazz clubs of London and became a national phenomenon it formed an indelible link to American rhythm and blues music and its English variant in the form of groups like the Who, the Kinks, the Small Faces, the Action, the Birds and the Creation.[112] Cities and towns across England also produced their own particular versions of these groups who would cover songs by African American performers and copy the style and moves of Townshend and his contemporaries. Townshend had closely monitored the audience in places like the Scene Club noting that Mod 'had become more than a look. It had become a voice, and the Who was its main outlet'[113].

There was a distinct difference between the Mods of 1959, 1962 and 1964. There had been a fairly rapid shift from modern jazz to American rhythm and blues to the distinct sound of English beat groups. According to Bacon in his history of live music in London, the earliest rhythm and blues club was at St Mary's Hall, Putney established in September 1960.[114] He sees 1963 as the key year in 'which R&B spread through London's clubs'.[115] Bill Carey of the National Jazz Federation told *Melody Maker* that 'R&B is what jazzmen call rock 'n' roll and the rockers call jazz'.[116] Many on the jazz scene were critical of the spread of rhythm and blues as a passing fad, while others were realistic in their view that it would have sustained popularity. The editor of *Jazz News* noted that 'we hear of clubs well away from London trying tentative R&B nights with obvious success. That the cornier trad scene is bleeding to death there seems little doubt'.[117] The Crawdaddy, Eel Pie Island, the 100 Club, the Marquee and most notably the Flamingo with Georgie Fame and the Blue Flames at the helm were all now pulsating to the sounds of American rhythm and blues.[118] The Roaring Twenties, a club that catered primarily to West Indians was also a key catalyst for the developing Mod affiliation with ska music.[119] Such a transition brought more working-class youths into the jazz clubs that were now responding to the clamour for rhythm and blues. This music provided a Mod soundscape that largely excluded the more commercial recordings of the Beatles and the Rolling Stones.[120]

Mark Burns writing in the *Mod's Monthly* assessed the musical affiliations of the capital's Mods: 'I talked with some of London's Mods, and they all had different opinions. Many of them voted for The Yardbirds, others for the new group, The Teatime Four. Some were all for The High Numbers'.[121] For Marks, the network of Soho clubs connected Mods to the music of 'Motown (from Detroit)...Stax and Volt (Memphis) and Atlantic (New York).[122] These cities provided Mods with mythical symbols of America and its youth culture. Jamaican Ska music released on the Bluebeat label was also purchased in great numbers by Mods and complemented the racial dimension of their sonic consumption.[123] He claims that 'as early as 1963 some 15,000 records entering Britain from Jamaica each month'.[124] Marks goes on to stress that the 'gradual appropriation of soul music into the Mod world took place...at the intersections of three different but not necessarily mutually exclusive groups: Mods, West Indians, and the homosexual community'.[125] The rhythm and blues clubs were crucial in this process.

Fowler's view that Mods were too young to attend 'discos' does not reveal the extent of teenage entry into the subculture of London's rhythm and blues clubs.[126] As Peter Shertser, a Mod from Ilford, told Jonathan Green: 'in the days of going to the Flamingo...we used to get taken by guys of seventeen and eighteen in their cars'.[127] Similarly, Maldwyn Thomas started attending the Scene at age fourteen.[128] According to Rawlings, Mods 'would go the club on weekends, pick-up dance and clothes tips and hopefully score drugs'.[129] Yet class remained a restrictive factor in living the Mod lifestyle. The arrival of working-class youths into the clubs led to the shattering of the elitist veneer of the original Mods. The 'all-nighter' at the Flamingo Club under the guiding hand of Rik Gunnell was a venue where the number of young Mods increased between 1962 and 1963. Gunnell had an illustrious background as a boxer, Smithfield bookie, club bouncer, promoter and Georgie Fame's manager. In the 1950s, he had been involved with jazz clubs such as the 2-Way, the Blue Room and Club M.[130] In 1964, *Rave* magazine claimed that the Flamingo was one of 'the Mod centres in London'.[131]

The clubs provided a space for transgressing the boundaries of class, race and sexuality. Terri Quaye claims that the 'Mods were open racially' and would access the broader parameters of African American and West Indian culture through the network of parties that were organised from meetings in clubs like the Flamingo: 'People would use business cards (bus tickets) with the name and date of the party. One party then led to another extending the network of friends, acquaintances and hangers-on'.[132] Georgie Fame provided the bridge between jazz and rhythm and blues over which Mods flowed. He claimed that there was a fairly rapid change in the clientele of the Flamingo as 'all the white kids who had been scared to come before heard about it, and next week, the place was packed with Mods'.[133] To Quaye, London's Mod clubs were the bedrock of England's shift to a more multiracial society.[134] Kirby also claims that such clubs gave an opportunity for West Indian and English white youth to meet on equal terms through a shared love of music, style and image.[135]

Similarly, at the Scene Club, Guy Stevens exploited his expansive collection of soul records providing Mods with a multicultural musical education.[136] The Scene had witnessed the convulsions in British popular music and youth cultures as it had formerly been the Club Eleven, Cy Laurie's Jazz Club and the Piccadilly Jazz Club.[137] According to *Rave* magazine the club was 'strictly way-out Mod' with 'the shake', 'the monkey' and 'the hitch-hiker' the most popular dances.[138] Linden Kirby was a regular attendee at the Scene and was arrested one night for being underage. As a 16-year-old, he was incarcerated in West End Central and returned to his parents a day later.[139] Burton recalled the similarities that existed between the Mods of the Scene Club and the gay teenagers attending the Le Duce Club and that 'both came from the same working class – South and East London'.[140] Oldham also remembers the Scene Club as being 'a loud smoky haven for the disenfranchised working-class'.[141]

The Discotheque club with its interior of 'car radiators, headlamps and metal twisted into weird shapes' was frequented by Mods and also attracted studio dancers from *Ready Steady Go!*.[142] Don Hughes once entered the club after being refused entry to the Flamingo and discovered that it was 'a pill-popper and rent boy paradise'.[143] The Last Chance was a less exclusive Mod club that had all night sessions on Saturday and was deigned to look like a western saloon 'complete with swing doors'.[144] A diary entry from Willmott's research on working-class youth in Bethnal Green is indicative of the centrality of London's clubs to their leisure and cultural activities: 'Friday 8pm. Went round to my mate Steve... had a few drinks in the Green Man and went up the West End at 11pm. We went to the Flamingo. We got talking to three girls there, had a few dances with them and Steve went off with one of the girls'.[145] Another youth wrote a letter to the *Mod's Monthly* to 'sing the praises of The Crawdaddy Club and their resident group, The Yardbirds.[146] This Richmond club is the gathering place for the most way-out Mods in South England and the queues outside the club every Sunday night are nothing short of mammoth'.[147] The Marquee Club and Eel Pie Island Hotel were also part of the geography of Mod, and by 1964 the *Mod's Monthly* claimed that even 'many local Palais are "going Mod" because of the wave of popularity of groups in the rhythm and blues field'.[148] Linden Kirby's week would be punctuated by visits to different clubs: 'Saturday at the Scene, Sunday at the Crawdaddy, Monday at the Palais'.[149] In his account of youth published a year later, Laurie also presented a picture of a typical Sunday morning in the vicinity of the Mod clubs.

> It was 4.50 a.m. on a summer Sunday in a deep court off Great Windmill Street… All round the walls of this black funnel, there were Mods… refreshed by the drizzle after dancing all night in the Scene… All the clubs were chucking out at 5.30 – the Discotheque, the Marquee, the Whiskey a Go-Go and the Scene. For an hour or so the plexus of London was their private patch, before they caught the first tubes home to Putney and Mill Hill.[150]

The amount of young working-class Mods on the streets in the early hours attracted the attention of the national press and the Metropolitan Police. In May 1964 the *Daily Mirror* reported that over 200 youths were involved in disturbances at Waterloo Station.[151] A Metropolitan Police report from June is also illustrative of criminal activities associated with the Mod scene. Arrests for the first six months of 1964 in the Wardour Street vicinity included the following: insulting behaviour (14), drunkenness (31) and possession of purple hearts (20).[152] The Metropolitan Police and the London County Council (LCC) were concerned at the proliferation of clubs and their ability to attract working-class youth. As many operated as members clubs proprietors could play a game of cat and mouse with the police and the licensing authorities. The LCC took action against those that failed to show that they were 'bona fide clubs'. This could be done if there was evidence that they were contravening legislation referring to unlicensed public performance, dancing, drinking or in terms of the building legislation on fire escapes.[153] The LCC had already successfully prosecuted a number of jazz clubs in the 1950s. In 1957, Cy Laurie's jazz club had been prosecuted for unlicensed music and dancing. In 1961 Gunnell had been fined for similar contraventions. In 1963, the Scene Club was prosecuted with Ronan O'Rahilly fined £10 as was La Discotheque. In early 1964 Gunnell was again prosecuted this time with a fine of £50.[154] Yet, as Chief Superintendent J. Starritt stressed, prosecution under existing legislation was difficult as the 'offence is not easily proved from casual observation'. Moreover, he claimed that as they were unlicensed 'they are free of all the normal forms of supervision e.g. the police have no right of entry'.[155] Another way that the police could intervene was through the Children and Young Persons Act of 1933. Juveniles in the care system when found in West End clubs were taken to 'West End Central Station as a place of safety'.[156] Such paternalistic moves by local politicians and the police were evidence of the growing popularity of rhythm and blues clubs and the associated Mod subculture.

The ability of working-class youths to participate in the 'all-night' club scene was fuelled by the use of amphetamine and the Scene Club was a cockpit of drug dealing. Shapiro has noted that in the 1950s the authorities were already alarmed about the use of amphetamine in the vice trade.[157] In 1955, the tabloid press ran a series of features on the drug-taking habits of suburban housewives and youths: 'Miss B took PEP PILLS so that she could be the life and soul of the party, dance till three in the morning and keep lively until the last guest had gone. "You can meet her type in any night club on any night of the week"'.[158] The more hysterical press coverage pointed to a supposed link between amphetamine and insanity.[159] By early 1964, some politicians and social commentators were calling for government legislation to stem the tide of drug abuse. In a front page feature the *Daily Mirror* claimed that 'vast quantities of...pep pills are peddled in clubs and cafés throughout the country to young people who take them "for kicks"'.[160] Willmott interviewed a 'working class rebel' in his exploration of youth in London's East End who gave his take on drug taking: 'he and his friends regularly take Purple Hearts... "It may seem sinful to some people. But we're just young people who like to enjoy ourselves and forget the Bomb"'.[161]

In an article for *New Society*, P. H. Connell assessed the current trend for 'pep pills'. He noted that the most popular were 'amphetamine (Benzedrine), dexamphetamine (Dexedrine), methylamphetamine (Methedrine) and phenmetrazinc (Preludin)'. They were often 'combined with barbiturates' as was 'done in the case of Drinamyl (the purple heart tablets which are really blue but shaped like a heart).[162] He claimed that he had seen 'a boy of 15 years who had been the round of the Soho and other clubs...and described taking purple hearts'.[163] Tony Williams, a 'rocker' told Hamblett and Deverson that he 'started taking Purple Hearts six months ago'.[164] Scala recalled that 'methedrine was common as an all-night boost; cocaine, Dexedrine, Benzedrine, Purple Hearts and Black Bombers were all taken to keep us going through the long weekends'.[165] Similarly, Barnes claims that there 'were small clubs and cafés set-up exclusively for pill-popping...you could get tea 'with' or 'without'. 'Without' was 5d and 'with' was 2/5d'.[166] Each club had one or more amphetamine sellers. At the Flamingo, a character called 'Pete the Pill' was a particular type.[167] John Pidgeon recalled his nights at the club: 'From midnight to six we dance and fidget and talk nonsense, start to feel not so great, swallow more pills and feel great again'.[168] According to Shapiro, the Marquee was also 'a pill palace, catering for a younger Mod set'.[169] As a 16-year-old youth Linden Kirby would take amphetamine that he purchased in Richmond in order to stay awake all night in the La Discotheque.[170] Hughes recalled that the coffee bars around Wardour Street, such as the Bamboo and the Moka, were also centres of amphetamine sales.[171]

The use of amphetamine amongst teenagers and its coverage in the media generated heightened concern from politicians. A meeting between representatives of the LCC and the Home Secretary to discuss the problems of West End clubs in September 1964 revealed the scale of the problem. The minutes note that the clubs 'represented a magnet attracting young people to Soho; the youngsters wandered about the streets...took "purple hearts"...There was an element of moral danger'.[172] The Metropolitan Police and the LCC were particularly concerned with the clubs acting as a conduit for vunerable teenagers and the criminal underworld:

> A girl...talked of having visited clubs called 'The Discotheque', 'The Scene', 'Coco's Club' and the 'Heaven and Hell Club' where purple hearts were obtained...A boy who had homosexual tendencies had frequented clubs...Reference has been heard amongst teenagers to a club called 'The Flamingo' where young girls go and can get drugs and meet coloured men...'The Scene' has been described by a young man as the 'Mods' stronghold where the boys wore perfume and the girls after-shave lotion.[173]

The LCC also noted the link between drug distribution and the attraction of the clubs to runaways. The Coco Club in Goodge Street was 'a recognised haunt of the "Mystery" girls who have run away from home...The girls become addicted to drugs and are then used by peddlers to carry the drugs for them in their handbags'.[174] The attraction of working-class youth to drugs was conditioned by the inability to purchase drinks in pubs and the unattractiveness of what such spaces offered.[175] Linden Kirby remembers a number of hot dog stands around the West End where amphetamines could be purchased on the way to the clubs.[176] Mods, drugs and rhythm and blues music also became a feature of the English coastal resorts.[177] In March 1964, there were over one hundred arrests in Clacton for public order offences.[178] Townshend later claimed that in places 'like the Aquarium at Brighton...pep pills...were openly for sale'.[179]

Mod clubs were spaces where working-class youth could mix with a variety of characters that were features of the night-time economy of London's underworld. The 'moral dangers' that more conservative commentators attributed to racial mixing and illicit drug use were in fact symbolic of the way in which youths were attempting to challenge existing social identities. On the dance floors of the Mod clubs and through the soundscape of West Indian ska and American rhythm and blues, they could temporarily transgress the boundaries of class, race and sexuality. Townshend was acutely aware of this feature of the Mod subculture and it became a theme of his song writing through to the early 1970s.

Townshend as cultural commentator, organic intellectual and social historian

According to Marwick, 1963 had witnessed a 'knitting together' of youth subcultures that led to 'definite, and highly liberating, patterns of behaviour' that 'were now beginning to influence the wider culture'.[180] Townshend and the Who were central to this process. They gave Mods an outlet for their sense of alienation, angst and discontentment with particular elements of their everyday lives. Townshend was an 'organic intellectual' who viewed popular music as a transformative aspect of youth culture. He claimed that popular music 'clicks your social conscience – makes you think about the world, makes you think about life'.[181] Moreover he viewed popular music as forming a particular response to the limitations of the post-war consensus with the Who seeking to 'articulate the joy and rage of a generation struggling for life and freedom'.[182]

Three hit singles by The Who, which all made the Top Ten between 1964–5, encapsulated the feelings of the individual Mod. Following a musical template laid down by The Kinks in 'You Really Got Me' (1964), The Who's 'I Can't Explain', released in January 1965, provided Mods with a statement that signalled their dislocation from the conventions of English society. To Townshend, Mods were saying to him that 'we need you to say what we are unable to say'.[183] This was followed by 'Anyway, Anyhow, Anywhere' released in May in which the subject of the song presents an ill-defined but effective attack on authority, rules and social boundaries. Here was the voice of an 'angry young man' accompanied by the screaming feedback of an electric guitar. Five months later, Townshend and the Who fired another salvo with the anthemic 'My Generation'. Cohen described 'My Generation' as 'Townshend's battle hymn of unresolved and irresolvable tensions, which, more than any other song, was the sound of Brighton, Margate and Clacton'.[184] Such towns became locations where the collective identity and force of Mod was most apparent. 'My Generation' was a symbolic of the way in which sections of working-class youth were using youth culture and popular music as a source of oppositional identity.[185]

After a further batch of successful singles and two albums *My Generation* (1965) and *A Quick One* (1966), the scope of Townshend's song writing became more ambitious.[186] *The Who Sell Out* (1967) was a pivotal recording drawing on aspects of youth culture and consumerism more generally.[187] The album was partly a celebration of 'pirate radio' that had helped to spread the sound of Mod culture across England before its activities were curtailed by government legislation.[188] Some of the songs take the form of commercials advertising products aimed at teenagers such as deodorant and acne cream. Here was an example of Townshend documenting the times he was living through as an acute observer of the nuances of the individual and collective experience of working-class youth. The release of 'Dogs' a year later emphasised Townshend's awareness of the resilience of a pre-war working-class culture. Partly sung in a mock cockney accent, the song contains references to greyhound racing, beer, gambling and the consumption of pies.

In 1969, The Who released their 'rock opera' *Tommy*.[189] Across four sides of vinyl, Townshend engages with aspects of 1960s counter-culture through the 'messiah figure' of Tommy. The interventions of Kit Lambert during the writing of the piece ensured that it was imbued with aspects of both high and low culture.[190] Symbols of Englishness and particular 'types' punctuate the narrative with references to the Great War, school bullies, prostitutes, perverted uncles, amusement arcades and holiday camps.[191] Although often seen as overblown and ambitious, to Townshend *Tommy* 'owed more to British music hall than to grand opera'.[192] Two years later, the abandoned 'Lifehouse' project led to the release of *Who's Next* (1971) with the centre-piece song 'Won't Get Fooled Again' forming a critique of the idealism and limitations of English counter-cultural politics and the revolutionary left.[193] Yet it was *Quadrophenia* (1973) that most accurately captured the Mod phenomenon and the ways in which it reflected aspects of English society in 1964/5.

To Marsh, *Quadrophenia* 'is a marvellous piece of social criticism, trying to place the public and private history of the 1960s into a context from which something more productive can be built'.[194] To Davey, it 'is an audit of the successes and failure of the 1960s, the illusions of its youth cultures, and the failure of political projects to connect with popular aspirations' and 'provided a bleaker but more telling account of the sixties than cultural studies would soon produce'.[195] Yet the album was also relevant to the England of 1972–3 when industrial militancy, economic and political instability and concerns around youth delinquency were a feature of everyday life. Townshend himself claimed that in preparation for *Quadrophenia* he 'needed to look at the people I was writing about. This was almost Socialist writing for me'.[196] The album was accompanied by an essay setting out the narrative and an extensive book of photographs commissioned by Townshend capturing working-class aspects of the Mod subculture.[197] Many of the youths used for the photography were from the working-class streets of Battersea, where the Who recorded the album.[198] The photos depict a working-class black and white world of domestic drudgery, egg and chip dinners, coffee bars, dirty occupations, youth vandalism, rhythm and blues clubs, alienation, cheap pornography, the English seaside, class divisions, deference and the centrality of popular music in teenage life.

Quadrophenia charts the experiences of Jimmy, a working-class Mod, in the home, workplace, club and coffee bar, but it is also a comment on the experiences and problems that youth faced more generally in post-war England. Jimmy's father is a 'socialist' and 'war veteran' who espoused the pragmatism of English Labourism. Mod's relationship to aspects of working-class politics, identity and experiences is explored most directly in 'The Dirty Jobs', where Jimmy confronts his fellow workers by critiquing their industrial and political Moderation.[199] Townshend's Mod is not the sophisticated, metropolitan mould-breaker of MacInnes's *Absolute Beginners*, but a young working-class 'dustman' who is disdainful of the way in which older trade unionists have been moderated by a particular form of Labour socialism. In 'Helpless Dancer', Townshend exposes the inequality, racism and poverty that remained a feature of English society. In essence, *Quadrophenia* presents a more nuanced and sophisticated analysis of Mod and 'swinging London' than exists in some of the more superficial narratives of the period. The album is a compelling slice of social history that can be usefully read alongside the sociological and historical explorations of youth in post-war England.

Some historians have simplistically characterised Mod as a largely apolitical subculture or as symbolic of the capitalist and individualist leanings of working-class youth.[200] Yet the as this chapter has shown, the social, cultural and political aspects of Mod culture were more complex and far-reaching. The England that Mods experienced in the home, workplace and on the street formed part of a 'structure of feeling' that provided a collective sense of belonging to 'a scene' and a 'distance' from the more conservative social and cultural norms that continued to pervade aspects of English life. Mod culture and the fashions and soundscapes that it embraced provide a particular image of an England, where existing conceptions of class, race, and sexuality were subject to a series of challenges that largely took place in the dance hall, coffee bar and rhythm and blues club. Yet both inside and outside of the capital city Mod culture did not completely dissolve social differences, but it did inject youth culture with a sense of excitement, escape and the possibility of an England in which class and racial inequality could be pushed to the margins.

5
Mods over England: Local Experiences and Social Control

In 1964, Mod was a significant component of English working-class youth culture.[1] As revealed in the previous chapter, the spread and popularity of Mod music, image and style were dependent on television, musicians, radio, records and the proselytising zeal of promoters, managers, publishers and designers. According to Fowler, 'it is not clear how many people were Mods ... and if there was a Mod lifestyle before television invented one'.[2] Yet the emergence of Mod across England was not wholly generated by the media and in 1964–5, new elements of the subculture were being formulated in a multiplicity of bedrooms, youth clubs, coffee bars and dance halls. To Nelson, the new wave of Mod identity led to the erosion of the individuality that had been a characteristic of pioneer Modernists.[3] Similarly, Hewitt and Hellier claim the original Mod finished in 1963.[4] Yet the more populist version of Mod that had left behind the exclusiveness of London's jazz clubs arguably had a greater impact in terms of both reflecting and shaping social change in English society.

Mod in the provinces was not nearly as exclusive or esoteric as its London variant, and it contained a 'do-it-yourself' ethos that enabled less affluent youth to participate in their own version of the movement. Working-class Mods across England were unable to purchase some of the more excusive clothes of Carnaby Street, but through American rhythm and blues music and its English variant, they nonetheless identified with the multiracial and sexually transgressive aspects of the subculture. Groups like the Who, the Kinks and the Small Faces performed multiple concerts in cities and towns across industrial England and played an essential role in selling Mod to working-class youth.[5] The national dimension of Mod and its perceived link to delinquency, violence, drug abuse and social transgression generated particular responses from local government, national politicians and more progressive bodies who felt that the media had exaggerated its more negative aspects.[6]

The *Mod's Monthly*, *Fabulous*, *Rave* and the construction of Mod culture

Cohen noted that by 1964 'there were at least six magazines appealing mainly to Mods ... when ... whole schools and even whole ... housing estates were talked of as having "gone Mod"'.[7] The *Mod's Monthly*, *Fabulous* and *Rave* are valuable sources for tracing the experiences of working-class youth and their embrace of particular aspects of Mod culture across England. The publication of the first issue of the *Mod's Monthly* in September 1964 was indicative of the journey that Mod had made from London to the provinces. Edited by Mark Burns the first issue attracted readers by claiming that they would find 'the new hairstyles, the new dances, new Mod records'.[8] The magazine was published on a commercial basis to exploit the current trend in youth culture and offers a detailed insight into the experiences of Mods across England. Each issue illustrates the similarities, differences and complexity of Mod identity in a variety of urban and rural locations. The *Mod's Monthly* opens a window on an England where working-class youths were challenging and in some cases subverting social conventions and existing conceptions of masculinity, femininity and national identity.

The *Mod's Monthly* was instrumental in attempting to give some coherence to Mod culture. From the pages of the magazine, we can detect the way in which youths across the country were grappling with the meaning of the Mod lifestyle. There are a number of articles in each issue that attempt to construct a typology of what was and what was not Mod. Labels such as 'Faces, Tickets, and Numbers' are introduced to describe the sense of hierarchy that had been a feature of the original scene in London, and the quest for a working definition of Mod reappeared in subsequent issues. In August 1964, an editorial claimed that 'Mods run in an age group between 14 to 22'. Margaret Connor from Jarrow was intrigued by the age profile: 'I would be interested to know the average ages of Mods in other towns. One problem my friend and I have ... is that, tho' there are many Mods, their average age is about 16 or 17; which makes it awkward when we two ancient 18-year-olds go dancing, as we invariably find ourselves dancing with boys younger than us'.[9] The construction of Mod was a two-way process with contributors periodically challenging *Mod Monthly*'s definitions of the trend.

Letters to the magazine informed youths across England of what was happening in local scenes and played its part in the creation of social networks. It noted that 'Mods get together with other Mods. Mods from Manchester and the North and the Midlands regularly come to London to the Scene, Beat City and other clubs in London, and find that being Mods helps break the ice'.[10] Rosemary Fearon of Banbury describes the opening of a new club called 'The Gaff' that had 800 members and hosted performances by the Alex Harvey Soul Band, the Animals and Georgie Fame and the Blue Flames.[11] Readers also sent in details of new dance crazes specific to their localities. Ruth Thompson from Manchester described 'the Dodo' with its complex moves and shapes.[12] The sense that 'northern' England was 'different' found its way into discussions of Mod culture. A letter from Dave Ulting of Orpington, Kent, who became a Mod in 1962, claimed that there couldn't really be any northern Mods.

> I cannot see how you can talk of 'Mods' in the north. I live 13 miles from the West End and have great difficulty in staying Modern ... There cannot be degrees of Modernism; you're either a Mod or you aren't and I'm afraid the further you go from London, the more difficult it becomes.[13]

Mods from the provinces responded in defence of their participation in the scene. A letter from Scottish Mods warned the editor that the magazine must change or no one would buy it north of the border: 'Believe it or not but there is a country just past Carlisle and it is called Scotland. It has around six million people and lots of Mods'.[14] Wendy Deans commenting on Mod fashion in Scotland claimed that 'white nylons are rather common in Edinburgh and the best Mods don't wear them'.[15] Judith Collier-Roberts from Cardiff said that Mods in Wales were still a distinct minority: 'Mods are few and far between in Wales and we are very much behind the times as far as Mod trends are concerned. I am considered something of an oddity'.[16] In Blackpool the Mod hangouts were the Roaring Twenties coffee bar on King Street and the Golden Nugget in Cookson Street.[17] Diane and Anne from the West Midlands emphasised the vibrancy of Mod in Birmingham: 'there are quite a few Mods who live up here, and they go to the West End, Locarno, Whiskey A Go Go ... Mods exist in Birmingham too'.[18] Gillian Harwood from Northampton also presented a portrait of her local scene.

> This is what Northampton Mods are wearing: – *Hair* Very, very short. *Clothes.* The French look is in, flowered jackets and black or white skirts, stack heeled shoes, light stockings, short sleeved sweaters, jeans or slacks, long waistcoats, sneakers. We girls are very fond of creating our own styles ... I think our Mods are *very* Mod because when I'm reading the letters in your great magazine I see that Mods in other towns are wearing things which went out long ago.[19]

Sylvia Connolly and Sue Dugdale from Preston highlight the mobility of Mods and how they were connected by a growing number of rhythm and blues clubs that catered to their particular musical tastes.

> Mods stick together in the same places i.e. The Presto Bar at Top Park. From there we travel out to clubs all over the North West e.g. The Kubi Club (Rochdale), The Cubic (Birkenhead), The Twisted Wheel (Manchester),

> The Iron Door (Liverpool) and The Caves and The Cedarwood (Preston). We travel round in vans, and Saturday night is the most hectic night of the week ... We Mods do exist in the North and set our own fashions.[20]

Margaret Connor noted the difference between London Mods and those in the provinces: 'I recently went to Manchester, where I saw and met many Mods who all wore completely different clothes to each other. The same thing doesn't happen so much in London, because the groups are split by Stylists, Mids and other extremist groups.'[21] The exclusivity and perceived authenticity of the London scene was something that troubled some contributors such as T. Price from Pontnewydd, Wales: 'some of the writers are too big-headed and seem to think anything tat is not Mod ... I think I'll go right on being fashionable ... with my long skirt, Tom Jones hair, white socks and stockings, low heeled shoes, high waists, less make up'.[22] Similarly, Chris Gretorex from Sheffield was left confused as to whether she was a Mod or not.

> I thought I was a Mod till I read it but now I am wondering, together with my friend Jill, just what we are ... She has long straight light brown hair and hardly wears any make-up ... and digs The Rolling Stones, Muddy Waters, and Sonny Boy Williamson. Now me ... I wear either a long skirt with a frilly blouse or bell bottom jeans with a blue blouse and yellow waistcoat (my dad's).[23]

Another forum for all things Mod was *Rave* magazine, which was first published in February 1964. As with the *Mod's Monthly,* it attempted to define Mod and invited readers to see where they fitted into particular gradations of Mod identity.

> There are half-a-dozen ways of being a Mod. ... FACES – You set the trends in every-thing ... dances, talk, gear, the lot. If people don't follow you, you're not a Face. CASUALISTS – You were one of the original Mods, but you got tired of being copied by all the others. INDIVIDUALISTS – You thought you were being stamped into styles that changed too quickly and cost too much. You avoid being copied. STYLISTS – You like slightly more formal clothes, matching perfection, balanced accessories. MIDS – You don't want to be classed as anything. You're middle of the road and not all of your money is spent on gear. TICKETS – Anything a Face does, you follow. You have to be way up front ... regardless.[24]

This description of Mod was accompanied by a number of letters explaining the financial burden of being Mod and discontentment with its national profile. Dave Martin from Tottenham claimed that 'being Mod costs too much. I get £6 a week and I spend £2 5s of it on clothes'.[25] In contrast, Harry Matthews from Pimlico argued that 'Being a Mod is a frame of mind. You can't just buy it off some geezer in a shop'.[26] Barry Condon, a decorator from Wandsworth stressed that he was 'Individualist now. That's what Mods were supposed to be before, but I didn't like being pushed into gear I couldn't afford'.[27] Similarly, Margaret McFayden, a typist from Chelsea 'stopped being a Mod two months ago because it was getting played out ... a lot of little kids in mass-produced gear'.[28] Mick Taylor, a tailor's cutter from Stepney also bemoaned the commercialisation of Mod:

> Before, tailors used to invent the styles and everyone bought them. Now we invent them and the tailors are going out of their way trying to keep up. I started wearing crepe nylon cycling jumpers because they were cool ... All the tickets wanted to know where I got it – but if I told them they'd all be down the shop tomorrow.[29]

Pete Townshend noted that the 'Mod era that was – say, a year ago – is dead. Those were the days when about every four days a different look would be in'.[30] The authenticity of the new wave of Mods also generated comment in the popular press. A letter printed in the *Daily Mirror* from Pam and Jacky in Battersea is illustrative: 'We have always classed ourselves as Mods but now strange creatures seem to have taken over from us. In a well-known dance hall last week, we saw boys in kilts, wearing eye make-up, dancing with girls in trousers'.[31]

Fabulous was another magazine that catered for working-class youth drawn to Mod. Each issue contained pictures and interviews with the current stars of popular music. It also noted the changing culture of London's clubs. An issue from June 1964 claimed that 'a year ago, The Flamingo, in Wardour Street, was a mecca for Modern jazz addicts: today the jazz murals on the walls shake to American style blues'.[32] The publication and national distribution of Mod literature in 1964–5 both reflected and shaped Mod culture in the capital and across the English regions. The contributions from readers show that although Mod had particular national characteristics it also contained local peculiarities that were conditioned by economic, social and cultural factors.

Mods in London, the coastal resorts and the industrial north

Although London has been noted as the centre of changing trends in youth culture other English cities and towns were instrumental in generating their own scenes.[33] Mods were frequenting coffee bars, dance halls and clubs in some of the bigger English cities and coastal resorts around the same time that Mod was becoming more prominent in London. The holiday camp and the annual working-class excursions to Brighton, Southend and Clacton were crucial in this process. For many young people, this was one of the few occasions where they would come into contact with their peers from other cities and towns. One original Mod, Lloyd Johnson, claims that there were Modernists in Hastings as early as 1959.[34]

London Mods were seemingly more affluent and mobile than their counterparts across the country with access to the clubs of Soho and the south coast resorts. Willmott's work on working-class youth from the East End provides an insight into the Bethnal Green Mods: 'there were those who went by scooter ... 'to the coast' – Southend, Margate, Brighton, Hastings or Clacton ... Some went dancing at the Tottenham 'Royal' and the West End jazz clubs'.[35] Yet many Mods were confined to their specific districts either through lack of funds to travel or through embracing a localism that gave them a sense of security. Poorer youths found mobility difficult and Willmott claimed that amongst his group 'only one in ten had a scooter'.[36] Mods entering their late teens were also keen to differentiate themselves from teenagers who had recently embraced the style. Their ability to do this increased on entering the paid workforce. An 18-year-old told Willmott, 'I go to the jazz clubs up the West End. The youth clubs are too dull. You get too many young Mods there. To my mind it's a drag'.[37]

In 1964, sections of working-class youth in London were increasingly embracing elements of Mod culture. In her work on youth clubs in South East England, Blandy noticed the way in which some were defining themselves as Mods: 'In the place of the departed seniors came new members, nearly all sixteen year old Mod types'.[38] Melly claims that Shepherd's Bush was 'the main launching-pad for the blast-off stage in the Mod explosion'.[39] In London, the scene was divided by territory, local loyalties and animosities. Jack Lyons recalled that the 'Goldhawk Social Club ... was the ... power base, for the Who ... Mods from Tottenham and the East End wouldn't go'.[40] This is confirmed by Hughes in his memoir of the period: 'Neither The Who or ... the High Numbers, ever played in Hounslow ... Hounslow Mods didn't make a habit of venturing into the Goldhawk Road area despite only being a bus ride away. The reason? Good old-fashioned turf wars'.[41] Large groups of London Mods would ride in groups on scooters to the coastal resorts and the more popular clubs, yet locality remained a defining identity expressed by the 'tell-tale fly screen, or the slogan on the back of a parka, indicating their home turf'.[42]

Rave magazine revealed the extent that Mod had moved beyond London in its guide to the how youths could 'HAVE A REAL SWINGING RAVE!' when they were on holiday. In Blackpool, Mods could congregate at the Top Ten coffee Bar in Dickson Road and buy the latest fashions at Corley's in Birley Street.[43] David Helliwell depicted the Mod scene in Lancashire's pre-eminent resort: 'Most nights I just rot away in coffee bars with my friends, talking about girls and cars'.[44] In Bournemouth, Le Discque-A-Go-Go in Holdenhurst Road was 'the place'. Williams and Hopkins "21" Shop on Christchurch Road was also 'worth a look for light-wear holiday casuals'. In Brighton, Mods could listen to Modern jazz at the Ship Inn on Lewis Road.

Rhythm and blues could be heard at the Scene Club and the Florida Rooms at the Aquarium. Shopping was provided by the Fab Gear Store situated at Brunswick Place and Western Road. In Jersey the variety of entertainment was more limited with the West Park Pavilion being the centre of 'the beat scene'. In Scarborough the Olympia and the Belle Vue club catered for 'beat fans'. In Torquay the Empire and the 400 ballroom had live music along with the town hall. 'Zenith's in Victoria Parade was 'reckoned to be the exclusive "Face" store in town'. In Newquay, Cornwall, 'His Casuals' provided style 'for the local "Faces"'. North of the border in Ayr, teenagers could attend the Pavilion, 'Bonny Jones' and the Blue Grotto.[45]

Outside of London, networks of Mods were brought together through the attraction of particular clubs and performers and seemed to be more united than their southern counterparts. Terry Thornton of Sheffield's Esquire Club would organise coach trips to events at other venues such as Manchester's Twisted Wheel connecting groups of Mods in Lancashire and Yorkshire.[46] Some even made a regular pilgrimage to Mod clubs in London. Brian Rae travelled from Warrington in North West England and experienced the sensory overload of the youth culture of the West End 'watching streams of suit-wearing young Mods coming off trains and buses and frequenting the all-night clubs and café bars'.[47] In Hastings, Lloyd Johnson spent his time in the two main Mod coffee bars. He had developed a sense of Mod because of the youth networks that developed between the capital city and coastal resorts. London youths would holiday and work in Hastings and regale local kids with tales of fashion boutiques, music clubs and the latest trends.[48]

In May 1964, *Rave* magazine provided a national map of Mod clubs.[49] This geography of the Mod movement provides a fascinating insight into the features of local music scenes that underpinned Mod culture. The Cave in Glasgow was 'a conventional Mod club' 'Under a railway tunnel, through a dark, damp alley'. Birmingham had the Morgue club in the King's Head Hotel in Bearwood with 'dim lighting and white coffins on the walls ... sometimes frightening to the newcomer'. In Wolverhampton the Milano coffee bar was the place for Black Country Mods. In Liverpool, Mods attended the Mardi Gras in Mount Pleasant where they danced the 'whack, stomp, shake, hitchhiker and the monkey'.[50] Stoke-on-Trent had 'The Place' and Leeds 'The Three Coins'. The Plebeians Jazz Club in Halifax was also an important centre for Yorkshire Mods.[51] In Bradford the Continental Coffee Bar was a Mod venue as was the Bell Hall in Warrington.[52]

Manchester had a thriving Mod scene based around a cluster of coffee bars and nightclubs in the city centre, most notably the Oasis on Lloyd Street, the Bodega and the Twisted Wheel on Brazenose Street.[53] The Twisted Wheel was a northern version of the Flamingo; with its first all-nighter organised in September 1963, it subsequently attracted a roster of American and English rhythm and blues performers.[54] Georgie Fame and the Blue Flames again provided a key link here between northern working-class youth, the Soho

Mod scene and the sounds of West Indian Ska and black America. According to Rylatt and Scott, the Mod scene in Manchester was very small until the Twisted Wheel became its promoter.[55] The Mod weekend would follow a particular format.

> Saturday afternoons were spent cruising around Manchester on chromed Lambrettas ... before meeting up at the Cona ... or the Mogambo. Early on Saturday night the Mod crowd would head down to the Jungfrau where, like the Cona, there was lots of space to park the scooters. At about 11.00 pm, it was time to make the short trip down Deansgate to Brazenose Street, ready for the Wheel Allnighter.[56]

The Mod scene in Newcastle was also a significant aspect of the city's youth culture. A local entrepreneur was crucial for providing a Mod focal point. Mike Jeffrey was the key figure in developing clubs such as the Downbeat, the Marimba, and the A'Go Go.[57] Tony Groves recalled that 'we were all Mods, buying our clothes from City Stylish or Marcus Price ... Most of us had accounts at John Temple the Tailors'.[58] On Saturday afternoons, Mods would congregate in the centre of the city to display their latest styles and discuss popular music. In Sheffield, it was the Esquire Club where Mods flocked to hear rhythm and blues and in Liverpool, it was the Mardi Gras and the Sink Club. In the cities of the industrial north the hard graft in the coal mine, factory and mill could be temporarily forgotten through the adornment of a smart suit, the playing of the latest record by the Who, the Kinks and the Small Faces and the chance to try out some new dance moves and attract potential partners in the smoky rooms of the Mod clubs.

Mods, violence, juvenile delinquency and social class

The historiography of Mod has tended to overly focus on the seaside disturbances of 1964.[59] Yet violence between Mods and Rockers had been developing since 1962.[60] Nell Dunn's novel *Up the Junction* has a number of scenes involving Rockers: 'We were in a transport café on an arterial road. A gang of boys came in with eagles on their backs ... One of them wore a shirt spotted with blood, his hand wrapped in a blood-soaked towel'.[61] Yet it is clear that the violence between Mods and Rockers was exaggerated by the press, and both Lloyd Johnson and Linden Kirby refute the notion that violence was endemic between the two groups. Johnson claims that in Hastings Mods and Rockers often attended the same shows.[62] Kirby recalls that much of the violence was based on territory that drew on the traditions of gangs that had always existed in parts of London. Moreover, gangs of working-class Mods often fought with each other. Kirby's group of West London Mods were reluctant to go to venues in the East End given the reputation of their counterparts in that particular district of the capital.[63]

As with the Teddy Boys of the 1950s, newspapers were keen to link numerous forms of juvenile delinquency to Mods and Rockers.[64] A concert by the Rolling Stones in Rochdale in April 1964 was claimed to have been abandoned because of fighting between Mods and Rockers.[65] Yet it is the scenes from selected coastal resorts in 1964 that are etched in the collective memory of Mod. The episodes occurred between Easter and August in Clacton, Brighton, Margate, Bournemouth, Hastings and Great Yarmouth.[66] The *Mod's Monthly* argued that 'of all the photographs of Mods in national newspapers hardly one was a Mod!'[67] Yet it is undeniable that some Mods and rockers were taking their conflicting and oppositional identities seriously. Robert Matthews, a 17-year-old youth from Basildon was jailed for assaulting a Mod in September 1963. According to the *Daily Mirror*, Matthews told police that 'I'm a Rocker, He's a Mod. I lost my temper and hit him'.[68]

Interviews conducted by the press during the events at Clacton also highlight the dislocation of some working-class youths from the drudgery of their daily lives. One respondent, 20-year-old Mick, a docker from Canning Town was indicative: 'You've got to get away from the monotony. I leave my house at 7.30 every morning and I'm at work in five minutes – that's how much I live on top of it. And it's the same thing day in, day out'.[69] Tony Williams, a Rocker, told Hamblett and Deverson that at Clacton he 'kicked in a few scooters and caused a disturbance ... larking around'.[70] Moreover, although the scale of the events was exaggerated, police records from the period show that the numbers of young people travelling to the resort had been significantly increasing. The Chief Superintendent of the Essex Constabulary noted that over 'the three holiday weekends in 1963, Easter, Whitsun and August, several hundred youngsters between 16 and 20 ... came into the resort on scooters, in cars and by train, and it was noticed during that year that the numbers were slowly building up'.[71] In preparation for the following year the numbers of officers on duty were increased, and reinforcements from neighbouring divisions were drafted.

The police reports of the Easter weekend in Clacton provide a more nuanced and less sensationalised characterisation of the situation than what was provided by the press. The Chief Superintendent's memorandum stressed that there was 'no suggestion at all of any kind of "gang warfare", although from time to time there were comments regarding "Mods" and "Rockers"'.[72] By Saturday 'it was estimated that about 800 males and 300/400 females were in the area ... Throughout the day reports of damage and disturbances ... were reported'.[73] The police were clear in their assessment that reporters had created a sense of crisis: 'It was apparent that during the afternoon of Sunday the national press had received some inkling of the difficulties that had been experienced in Clacton and they started to arrive in force'.[74] Nonetheless, there were 76 arrests compared to 27 in 1963. The majority of those arrested were aged between 16 and 18. Some of those arrested were in possession of purple hearts but 'there was little sign of drinking'.[75] The crimes reported were merely examples of anti-social behaviour as opposed to the rioting described in sections of the press. Two examples from the Essex police records are fairly indicative.

> Women shop-keeper was in her small sweet shop when a group of youths went in and asked her if she sold cigarettes. On being told she did, they shouted, 'You can stick them up your arse', and left the shop. Shop-keeper was extremely upset. Twelve youths went into a café for breakfast. During the course of the meal had to be admonished by the proprietor for using bad language. When they left they jostled and confused the waitresses and it was found that four meals were not paid for.[76]

The Chief Superintendent's memorandum also provides an insight into the resilience of class in 1960s England and the way in which sections of youth were labelled and stigmatised. According to the document, both 'males and females appeared to be the lowest type of undesirable, ill-disciplined teenager with little or no respect for the police or the comfort or property of other persons'.[77] The Chief Superintendent rejected claims that Clacton did not offer enough cultural attractions to the youths who had travelled to the town: 'They are merely idle, dirty persons who would probably not be allowed into any civilised gathering'.[78]

In the days after the scenes in Margate others pointed to the negative role of the press. The local mayor, Reginald Freebairn-Smith claimed that '[t]hese louts have too much publicity ... I admit the newspapers did not bring them down. But they gave them the publicity they expected'.[79] A criminologist concurred claiming that 'the disturbances and general punch-ups at Clacton ought to have occupied no more than a few lines in a local paper'.[80] The *Daily Mirror* responded with a front page editorial extolling the virtues of the press in reporting unsavoury incidents: 'It is not our function to hush things up because they happen to offend, scandalise, shock, disturb, or otherwise needle the individuals concerned or any other pressure group'.[81] A reader replied calling for a sense of perspective: 'For goodness sake let us keep a sense of proportion over these Mods and Rockers. The number of people involved is small, and would be smaller if crowds of innocent bystanders did not directly or indirectly encourage these young men by treating them as a Bank Holiday spectacle'.[82]

The literature on the events of Clacton and other resorts in 1964 has largely concentrated on male youths and neglected the gender aspects of the events.[83] Pamela James writing in the *Daily Mirror* was keen to speak to the young girls that had travelled to Margate.

> I spoke to two 18-year olds, Pam and Mary – 'just call us Mod Birds' – down on the sands when the fighting stopped. Over the blare of the transistor tuned to Radio Caroline they shouted; 'Listen – it gives you a kick, a thrill.

> It makes you feel all funny inside. You get butterflies in your stomach and you want the boys to go on and on'. Pam and Mary travelled from Ealing on Saturday to join the boys ... Both the girls, dressed in the latest Mod style – initialled sweaters, straight skirts and sneakers – had Purple Heart pills, brought in Soho. 'You've to got to be ready to stay up all night when you know this sort of thing is going on ... You've got to get your kicks somehow. You've got to make up for all that boring time you're going to spend at work next week'.[84]

The paper also attempted to go 'inside the mind of a Mod' through a Marjorie Proops interview with Teresa Gordon. Like other Mods Gordon places great stress on authenticity and differentiation: 'A State is a person who thinks he (or she) is a Mod ... but they don't really know what a Mod is'.[85] Yet under the veneer of rebelliousness there was a longing for security. When questioned about drugs she goes on to say that 'I have never taken any ... They say girls who take them won't be able to have any babies ... I want to get married sometime and have babies'.[86] A number of young girls were arrested for the disturbances. Patricia Curtis, a 21-year-old mother of two, was jailed for three months for trouble at Bournemouth along with Jean Evans and Jill Robbins for affray.[87]

In preparation for the August bank holiday, riot police were flown to Hastings by the Royal Air Force from Northolt Airport.[88] Again, there were many arrests and the body of 14-year-old James Smart was found on the shore after consuming alcohol, amphetamine and then drowning.[89] The press gave much prominence to the distribution of amphetamine amongst Mods. In a report on youths prosecuted in the magistrates' court at Clacton a reporter claimed that '[o]ne of them openly displayed a handful of Purple Hearts wrapped in a newspaper: "Ninepence each, if you want one", he said. "I buy them for twopence. Good business, eh!"'.[90] Similar scenes were evident in Brighton. Rocker Peter Welsh later recalled that 'when we got down to Brighton we found two to three thousand Mods charging about shouting, 'kill the grease! Kill the grease! It was unnerving'.[91] Steve Mann went to Brighton and 'threw a few deckchairs through various peoples' windows'.[92] Yet other Mods such as Linden Kirby have little recollection of any significant violence.[93]

The aftermath of the events attracted journalist, politicians, doctors and social scientists in attempting to make sense of the Mod/Rocker clashes. Justice Lawton a high court judge claimed that unless sentences for those involved were not more draconian 'there was a danger that the police would take the law into their own hands'.[94] According to the *Daily Mirror*, Reverend Bill Shergold of the '59 Club' of motorcyclists attempted to gain a slot on *Ready Steady Go!* to call a truce in the violence but his request was refused.[95] The paper also claimed that even the Pope was aware of the youth clashes referring to 'the unhappy faces of Teddy Boys and of Mods and Rockers' in a speech to the Italian Rover Scouts in Rome.[96] The seaside disturbances also left a mark on the consciousness of Pete Townshend. In an interview with the *New Musical Express* in 1973, he recalled scenes he had witnessed: 'I saw about two thousand Mod kids, and there were three rockers against a wall. They'd obviously just come into it thinking that that they were going to party and they really were scared as hell, as the Mods were just throwing bottles at them'.[97]

The most insightful analysis of the coastal disturbances came from *New Society* and its survey of 44 youths who had been prosecuted for public order offences.[98] Barker dispelled some of the myths that the clashes had been orchestrated and connected: 'Only four of the Margate group had also been at Clacton. One had been at Brighton'.[99] He also pointed out that the view that hordes of Mods and Rockers had arrived in Margate on motor cycle and scooter owed more to hyperbole than reality: 'only seven went by bike or scooter'.[100] Yet the interviews of Hamblett and Deverson suggest that some youths revelled in the violence. John Braden, an 18-year-old from London told them: 'I joined in a few of the fights ... the beach was like a battlefield ... I felt great, part of something important instead of just being something they look down or because you haven't passed a GCE'.[101] There were also some real casualties as the seaside clashes were copied on a micro scale across England. George Monk, a 21-year-old youth was caught in a melee between Mods and Rockers at a dance in Grays and was stabbed to death.[102] Blandy noted that in the summer of 1964 violence increased in the vicinity of her youth club in South East England: 'Inter-club fights became uncomfortably prevalent; gang warfare spread from district to district'.[103] Willmott claimed that 'one in ten' of his Bethnal Green boys 'seemed to accept or approve of the fighting'.[104] In Nottingham, there were over 30 arrests after Mods and Rockers clashed in the city centre. The press also noted violence in Coventry and police being deployed to break up crowds in Whitburn, County Durham.[105] Melly claims that a rougher element had created a very different kind of Mod that was 'urban working class ... quite sinister ... dark glasses, Nero hair-cuts, Chelsea boots, polo-necked sweaters ... gleaming scooters'.[106] The antipathy shown to working-class northerners and their embrace of Mod culture was articulated by magistrates. In sentencing 18-year-old Robert McKenzie to six months in a detention centre for theft from a Hastings seafront souvenir shop, A.G. Coote referred to him as '[o]ne of the drifting scum from Liverpool'. He went on to say that 'Mods and Rockers were one problem ... Now we have another ... Young people who came from the North, neither looking for work, nor intending to find it'.[107]

Mods travelled to the coastal resorts in 1965, but there were less arrests and the whole media circus began to dissipate.[108] Yet tensions between Mods and Rockers continued. Hughes's account of Hounslow and the way in which particular social spaces were defined as 'Mod' or 'Rocker' is indicative: 'The Egg Nest Café and Wimpy Bar were both havens for Mods. Out of bounds completely were the Happy Talk Coffee Bar and the Cecil Road Youth Club ... They were strictly Rocker'.[109] In the East End of London, Peter Welsh recalled the division in Leyton Baths Dancehall: 'A system of segregation developed ... We covered the front near the stage and the Mods hung in the dark of the rear of the hall. There used to be a lot of fighting, sometimes with knives and people would stumble out of the baths cut and bleeding'.[110] Reed also claims that Carnaby Street on Saturdays became a 'mini-war zone with violent run-ins between Mods and Rockers'.[111] A year later, Glasgow was still experiencing violence with the Blue Angels Rockers from Maryhill attacking 'Fleet's Scooter Squad, which they broke up by knocking Mods off their scooters with chains'.[112] As a result of the 1964 disturbances a range of political, social and cultural responses were initiated in an attempt to curtail juvenile delinquency and the attractions of Mod culture.

State intervention, community activism and social control: the Portobello Project and the 'policing' of Mod England

In examining the social and political responses to the Mod phenomenon, historians have tended to concentrate on the interventions of politicians through parliamentary debate and government legislation.[113] Yet there were a number of local initiatives that dealt with Mod culture and juvenile delinquency through undercover surveillance carried out by the police forces in London, Manchester and Sheffield and more progressive interventions that were developed by community organisations. Although both approaches differed in terms of causes, consequences and cures, they nonetheless shared a sense that economic and social change had played a role in the seaside disturbances in particular and more generally in the way in which working-class youths were adopting subcultural identities.

The National Association of Youth Clubs (NAYC) was one organisation concerned with rising levels of delinquency. It sent observers from Northamptonshire to Brighton, which they described as a 'Mod town' in 1964 and produced a detailed report. They claimed that 'Rockers turned up throughout the two days, and this caused running fights. There were several ugly scenes, including hooliganism in the main shopping street'.[114] Yet a conflicting section of the report suggests that the violence had been exaggerated.

> On Sunday and Monday a very large crowd of Mods gathered on a small beach area. Here the situation was very much like Trafalgar Square on Guy Fawkes night or New Year's Eve – much larking about, throwing clothes and screaming girls into the sea; leaps from the pier with umbrellas aloft; tipping policemen's helmets – general larks.[115]

The NAYC was particularly concerned about the future of the minority who were involved in criminality and were prosecuted as a result of their actions.

The subsequent report emphasised the problems of working-class youth who had been largely excluded from the 'affluent society' and remained plagued by the existence of social inequality: 'this minority constituted a much more difficult problem, which needs to be tackled at source. The source is a long way from the beaches; in the neighbourhoods, council estates and metropolitan boroughs, from which the fighters come'.[116] H. Haywood the NAYC Education Officer argued that greater provision for youths would have gone some way to minimising disruption: 'The conclusion of the observers ... is that some kind of entertainment on the beach ... would absorb a good deal of interest'.[117] The report concluded that 'most of the boys and girls on the loose in Brighton were looking for excitement ... not for violence'.[118]

The most innovative intervention into Mod culture was the Portobello Project that ran from early 1963 until December 1964. The initiative was developed by the Notting Hill Social Council (NHSC), which had been established in 1960. The NHSC brought together religious, political and community groups in the aftermath of the 1958 riots in an attempt to highlight the problems of inadequate housing, poverty, racism and crime. The aim of the Portobello Project was to improve social provision for 'unattached' local youths in Notting Hill, Hammersmith and Paddington by establishing a youth club and coffee bar. A youth leader 'was to have a roving commission to seek out the youngsters in the cafes, pubs, dance halls'. This progressive move by the NHSC was developed so that working-class youth could 'discover their real needs as seen by themselves, [and] the coffee bar/club was to be an incidental tool'.[119]

The opposition and obstruction that the NHSC faced from the Metropolitan Police highlighted the racism and conservatism that remained a feature of law enforcement in the capital through to the late twentieth century. From the outset, the police hampered the establishment of the coffee bar/youth club by insisting on 'membership, certain hours [and] they objected to West Indians whom they called Spades'.[120] Reports and documents compiled by the youth workers attached to the project illuminate the lifestyles of local Mods.

> We call them the Rhythm and Blues group because of their current addiction to music ... Amphetamine pills are used by most of the group to keep them going throughout the weekend ... Even for the young and healthy seven or eight hours dancing in a hot, smoky, steamy atmosphere, is a marathon session and it is not surprising that they welcome some artificial stimulants to keep up with the pace-setters.[121]

One youth worker, Ian Guild, shared an interest in rhythm and blues music with Mods attending the club and between April 1963 and January 1964 and spent many evenings with them in cafés and night clubs.

> I followed them locally and up the West End ... They used the outer (suburban) beat clubs till 10 or 11, then went to the West End all-night sessions which led to Sunday mornings ... Goldhawk beat clubs and cafes in Shepherd's Bush were pick-up points for drugs.[122]

Guild noticed a distinct pattern to the behaviour of the Mods: 'Monday night is record night at the Hammersmith Palais, and Friday and Saturday are spent either at the Goldhawk Beat Club or up at the West End, usually in Wardour Street at the Discotheque, Flamingo, or round the corner at the Scene'.[123] He felt that many youths in the district had been excluded from the perceived affluence of the period: 'There is a minority (of the unattached) ... whose situation, particularly when related to the enhanced opportunities for contemporary youth is particularly tragic'.[124] He goes on to make a connection between bad housing, the pre-existence of criminal networks and a culture of violence affecting a minority of the locales youth. Guild also recorded 'a scene involving a number of the causalities of the Mod clubs': 'On Monday morning 6th February I was concerned at the condition of one of the lads who had arrived from the West End ... it was obvious that he had taken a large quantity of pills very quickly ... he had been seen at the Flamingo being violently sick'.[125] He noted that drug abuse was particularly endemic amongst the 'rhythm and blues group': 'some are on them throughout the week ... Behaviour is occasionally completely frenzied'.[126]

The Flamingo was always keen to stress its law abiding credentials as a serious live entertainment venue. In a report by journalist Brian Boss for the *Daily Mirror*, the club is depicted as a place where music was the key attraction. A notice above the reception stressed that '[a]ny person suspected of consuming or selling 'reefer' cigarettes or narcotics of any kind on the premises will be pointed out to police officers and prosecuted'.[127] Within the confines of clubs like the Flamingo, violence was controlled and sporadic. One art student told Hamblett and Deverson that 'bright spotlights suddenly come down and four or five enormous muscle men come from nowhere and sort it out'.[128] Georgie Fame later recalled that there 'were terrific fights between the US airmen and Africans and the West Indians'.[129]

The LCC viewed clubs like the Flamingo as places where rebellion could be engendered: 'An inspector of child care with a great deal of experience with adolescents knows of several who are or had been in care who have drifted into clubs ... where the restrictions of ordinary life which they find irksome do not exist'.[130] They concluded that the clubs were a dangerous environment for the vulnerable teenager: 'Excitement is readily available ... it requires a strong character ... to avoid contamination once the young person has entered the "club world"'.[131] Such interventions into Mod clubs owed much to racial stereotyping and an aversion to the aspects of Mod culture that were posing a challenge to what the police perceived to be social norms. The reports by youth workers compiled for the Portobello Project expressed such concerns with police attitudes to West Indian youth.

> There is also some evidence that police attitudes to us are affected by the fact that we have a strong West Indian and coloured element in our clientele. There have been continuous attempts to suggest that [fighting between gangs] were the work of 'Spades' (the term is theirs not mine), although there was only one coloured boy involved in all these incidents.[132]

As a result of the research engendered by the Portobello Project, the NHSC devised a plan to place large groups of youths in seaside resorts, such as Brighton, and then attempt to divert them into more constructive types of social activity, but the Metropolitan Police felt this was inadvisable. There was also some concern that that project was part of a wider political movement. In correspondence, the police referred to Reverend David Mason who was a leading figure in the project as 'sincere' but had 'colleagues associated with C.N.D. & Left Wing Groups'.[133] The report of the Portobello Project also revealed the tense atmosphere between the police and working-class youth in the district: 'Relationships between Police and youngsters are uniformly bad in this area ... I am aware of a number of cases of chivvying and provocation of youngsters by policeman on the streets'.[134]

In order to enforce some form of social control over Mod culture, the police also worked undercover in order to dismantle the coffee bar scene and the distribution of amphetamine. Surveillance of the Metropolitan Police of West End clubs in 1964 revealed concerns around juvenile drug abuse. The Children's Department of the LCC referred to the Bamboo Club in which runaway girls were found: 'A child care officer (special duties) has been there several times ... He has seen young people there with glazed expressions presumably under the influence of drugs'.[135] The police description of the El Rio Club in Notting Hill is also illustrative. The club was 'run by Indians ... Heroin and hemp were said to be available and coloured men were associating with young white girls'.[136] The Blue Room café in Elephant and Castle was raided in June 1965 leading to arrest of five men and four girls.[137]

The police and the courts also cracked down more firmly on youth violence with harsh sentences passed down to those responsible. One example of this was the prosecution of those involved in the so-called 'Battle of Mare Street' in London involving Christopher 'Beard' Pegley and Peter 'Buttons' Welsh. Welsh had been involved in Mod and Rocker clashes in the East End since 1961.[138] The fighting had involved blades, wooden staves and firearms with Welsh being hospitalised with a shot gun blast. A number of Mods and Rockers were sent to detention centres at the end of the trial.[139] Welsh recalled that in youth prisons identities were maintained 'with the negroes and the Mods grouping together'.[140]

Clubs in Sheffield, Manchester and other towns and cities outside London were also targeted by the police. In August 1963, Sheffield's Esquire Club was raided.[141] In Manchester, police established a self-styled 'Mod Squad' that worked undercover and provided evidence that led to the closure of a number of coffee bars.[142] In September 1963, the Sovereign Club was targeted as a venue where purple hearts were being sold.[143] In his report of 1965, the chief constable presented his view of the coffee bar scene: 'The more deplorable of these clubs attracted individuals of exaggerated dress and deportment, commonly known as Mods, rockers or beatniks'.[144] According to police files, the Twisted Wheel was 'well known to the Drugs Dept as being a place where the more dangerous types of drugs such as morphine, heroin and cannabis can be obtained'. In December 1964, three men from Liverpool were arrested for being 'in possession of a cigarette containing hemp'.[145]

Manchester police used both male and female officers to infiltrate the clubs to monitor drug distribution, illegal drinking and prostitution. One female police officer visited the Jungfrau Coffee Club in June 1964 and described the scene: 'The club was dimly lit and the dance floor was crowded with young couples ... A number of girls appeared very young and three we questioned were only 14 years of age'.[146] The police were concerned that young runaways were using the clubs for accommodation and then were influenced by a range of undesirable characters.[147] The case of two missing girls aged 16 and 17 from Staffordshire who had run away after being dismissed by their employers for attending a 'Beat Show' were just one example of the clientele that the undercover police came across in their trawl of the clubs.[148] The surveillance of coffee bars and clubs led to the passing of legislation at Westminster that seriously curtailed the night-time economy of the city in general and Mod culture in particular.[149] In Manchester as in London, there was clearly a racialised aspect to the policing of Mod clubs. In November 1964, the Beat Club in New Cannon Street had been taken over by a proprietor, who according to the police reports was 'a man of colour'. It was renamed the New Cosmopolitan and 'older women and many coloured men were frequenting the club'. The report states that 'two coloured men were arrested for conspiring to procure a 16 yr old to become a prostitute'.[150]

Some commentators also claimed that Mod clubs could lead to delinquent behaviour and deviant practices. In *New Society*, Connell stressed that they were 'sometimes frequented by homosexuals, prostitutes, and individuals addicted to morphine, heroin etc, and the possibility of contagion is definitely present'.[151] Ultimately, the attraction of youth to rhythm and blues clubs introduced working-class youth to a 'real' yet 'mythical' world in which they could mix with a range of different races, sexualities, cultures and temporarily transgress the boundaries of their homes, workplaces and communities.

The class, sexual and racial dimensions of English Mod culture

By 1964 Mod had become a national phenomenon. Alex Macguire writing in *New Society* claimed that the Mods and Rockers were far more numerous than the earlier youth subcultures. In his technical school 'over half the boys between the ages of 13 and 18 identify themselves in some way with these groupings' and in 'Secondary Modern schools the involvement is said to be even more evident'.[152]

Moreover, he argued that the 'cult of "individualism in unity" can hardly be a creation entirely of the advertising and merchandising world'.[153] Mod emerged and spread as a result of number of economic and social factors and depended on media promotion, but individual musicians and local trend-setters also played a crucial role.[154] The vibrancy of the culture suggested growing affluence, but its impact on class identity was marginal. Yet Mod culture proved much more significant in reflecting and shaping challenges to popular conceptions of gender, sexuality and race.

According to Barker in his survey of the Margate offenders the 'typical Rocker had an unskilled manual job; the typical Mod was a semi-skilled manual worker'.[155] Lloyd Johnson was an early Mod from a working-class background whose mother was a machinist and his father worked for the Post Office. He failed the 11-plus and felt that one way he could express himself was through 'clothes and dancing'.[156] Hughes remembered that by the mid-1960s class remained a central aspect of Mod culture: 'Hounslow was far more working class than its immediate neighbours'.[157] Linden Kirby from Chiswick was another working-class Mod. The son of a builder, he failed the 11-plus. All the Mods Kirby knew were solidly working-class.[158]

To contemporary observers such as Hamblett and Deverson, northern youth was 'moving rapidly from the dark, satanic mills of the greedy past ... towards the new egalitarian society struggling hard to establish itself in the most class-conscious country in the world'.[159] Yet northern Mods never really left the industrial working-class culture from which they had emerged. According to Rylatt and Scott the 'Teeside scene was very working class; apprentices from British Steel, turners, electricians and welders'.[160] In the cities of Manchester, Sheffield, Liverpool and the surrounding towns, working-class Mods proliferated. The youth attending Blandy's youth clubs in the mid-1960s were also indicative of the nuances of class and how it permeated Mod sensibility. Her Mods were not 'switched-on ... sophisticated and sexy ... they lacked that little extra essential something'.[161]

Class might have remained fixed for many Mods, but conceptions of masculinity and femininity were less stable. Young working-class girls used Mod as a process of transgressing gender boundaries in terms of style, leisure and consumption. They had already been purchasing scooters since the late 1950s. A newspaper feature in April 1960 claimed that what 'was once the exclusive sport of young men is now the pastime of the smart young girl'.[162] Mod also offered the opportunity for middle-class girls to defy the conventions of respectability. One respondent to Hamblett and Deverson's survey claimed that being 'middle class is the most degrading thing in youth. You'd do anything rather than be thought conventional'.[163] Blandy was scathing in her assessment of working-class Mods in her youth club: 'Some of our

Mods ... were decidedly grotty ... More and more of these little Moddy birds now joined the Club ... Once inside they sat round like zombies, occasionally getting up to indulge in some lackadaisical twisting'.[164]

Female Mods showed initiative and enterprise by making their own clothes.[165] According to Kirby, the East End Mod girls wore amazing long suede coats owing to the links they had to workers in the leather tanneries.[166] Contributors to the *Mod's Monthly* made reference to the way in which they and their boyfriends were breaking social taboos. A letter from Stephanie Brown of Leeds is illustrative: 'My boy wears his hair very long eight inches below his collar ... His face is lightly made up and finished with a nice shade of lipstick. Nail lacquer of the same colour completes the effect'.[167] The LCC claimed that that London's Scene Club was 'described by a young man as a Mod club 'where the boys wore perfume and the girls after-shave lotion'.[168] Other sources suggest that Mods often frequented ladies hairdressing salons.[169] Laurie noted a geographical aspect to the femininity of Mod with those from the south 'experimenting widely with feminine trappings'.[170]

Mod culture also posed a challenge the existing boundaries of sexual identities. The Kandy Club in Gerrard Street, London attracted working-class Mods and elements of London's gay subculture. According to the LCC, 'there were 99 men there, mostly known homosexuals and four women known to be lesbians'.[171] David Holbourne, a 19-year-old Mod interviewed by Hamblett and Deverson expressed his openness on sexual transgression: 'No one says anything about queers anymore ... It's funny, I'm not queer, but I must have some queer feelings and I think everyone has although they won't admit it even to themselves'.[172] Hughes also enjoyed the sexual ambiguity of Mod culture stressing that it 'kept everyone guessing'.[173] He claims that it was hard to distinguish Mods from the rent-boys who congregated around particular locations in the West End.[174] Townshend also recalled male prostitution outside of the Scene Club where 'young Mod faces used to rent themselves out'.[175] Burton's description of the Le Duce Club is also indicative of the overlapping world of working-class heterosexual Mods and homosexuals: 'All around the dancers, boys with boys, girls with girls, boys with girls and boys and girls alone – pill happy, dancing, forgetting the awful drabness of everyday living'.[176] Yet he also stressed that both gay youth and Mods remained distanced by class with 'the middle and upper classes ... viewed as passports to pleasures otherwise unaffordable'.[177]

Mod also reflected the way in which African American and West Indian popular music was challenging particular racial stereotypes. In 1964–5 England could not be described as a multicultural society, but the seeds of its development were being planted in clubs like the Flamingo and the Roaring Twenties. McKay has argued that jazz as a soundtrack 'accompanied, articulated, facilitated ... the construction of post-imperial identities'.[178] This process became much more apparent through the network of Mod clubs that were established across England. One respondent to the Hamblett and

Deverson survey claimed that he was 'hero-worshipping the spades taking 'hashish and hemp' doing the 'shake and hitchhiker to fast numbers ... because the Spades do it'.[179]

Racial mixing at the Flamingo raised some concern for the LCC and the Metropolitan Police. The LCC claimed that a person 'who has been there has said ... there is a great deal of "necking" especially with coloured people. In this atmosphere any young person is obviously in serious moral danger'.[180] Yet to some working-class teenagers, such clubs were a vehicle for politicisation and liberation. One female Mod told Hamblett and Deverson that 'teenagers ... have an absolute obsessional hatred of colour and race prejudice'.[181] The West Indian singer Jimmy James who arrived in England in 1964 recalled the way in which audiences at his shows with his group the Vagabonds moved from 'predominantly black to increasingly multi-racial'. He claimed that 'Mods at the Flamingo and the Marquee were changing everything'.[182] Yet according to Terri Quaye outside London other parts of England were slower in adopting more enlightened attitudes to race: 'Safe place was Newcastle ... La Dolce Vita nightclub ... Manchester lots of different clubs was ok ... Liverpool was ok ... port towns ... white audiences ... they were fine ... horror upon horror is Leeds ... It was so racist ... Bath was a nightmare'.[183]

The height of Mod culture was over by 1966. Yet in the early years of the decade it presented a particular image of England bounded by both continuity and change. This England retained many features of the pre-war period in terms of class divisions and social inequalities. Yet such boundaries defined by, race, gender and sexuality were being challenged in the bedrooms, coffee bars, music clubs and boutiques of London and the provinces. Popular music played a crucial role in this process by providing a daily soundtrack to the experiences of working-class youths and introducing Mods to imaginary worlds where race, sex and gender were more ambiguous. The sounds of American soul, West Indian Ska and English beat provided a soundscape of excitement, hedonism, transgression, radicalism and in some cases liberation.

6
Class, Nation and Social Change in the Kinks' England

Ray Davies was one of a small group of 'organic intellectuals' who emerged in the 1960s seeking to explore class, nation and social change through popular music. Like Lennon and Townshend, he saw music as a way of reflecting and shaping the experiences of working-class youth and their adaptation to particular features of post-war English society. As a member of the Kinks, he traversed the country performing concerts to enthusiastic audiences and gained a particularly strong following in the industrial north.[1] Davies went on to write hundreds of songs for the Kinks that transcended the simplistic subject matter of much of the popular music of the 1960s. Such recordings emphasised the importance of culture in creating and affirming social identities and can be firmly located in a 'structure of feeling' that remained part of the individual and collective consciousness of the English working-class.

As an examination of continuity and change in the post-war period, Davies's work presents a particularly insightful image of England and experiences in the home, the workplace, the street and in the spaces defined by new forms of youth culture. His songs can be read alongside contemporary sixties analyses and polemics such as Michael Shanks' *The Stagnant Society* (1961), Anthony Sampson's *Anatomy of Britain* (1962) and Arthur Koestler's *Suicide of a Nation* (1963)[2]. These texts were popular state-of-the-nation addresses that emphasised the notion that England had entered a period of decline. Yet arguably, the songs of Davies provide a much richer and personalised account of the limitations of post-war political change than that provided by journalists and conventional commentators. His work bears similarities to the intervention of the CCCS and its claim that working-class youth culture represented a form of 'symbolic resistance to existing social and political orthodoxies'.[3]

The tension between class, locality, nation and social change in 1960s England finds dramatic resonance in the music of the Kinks. An examination of Davies's work highlights the fact that while many cultural figures were extolling the virtues of 'affluence' and 'modernity', a small number of working-class 'organic intellectuals' were deconstructing the 'myth' of the sixties and exposing the limitations of both Labour and Conservative politics through popular music. Kinks' records are an example of the way in which elements of youth culture and popular music were exposing fault lines in the notion of political 'consensus' and presenting an alternative image of England to that provided by contemporary politicians, social elites and more conventional commentators.[4]

In the 1960s, class identities were being confirmed, challenged and redefined through particular forms of popular music. The Kinks as a group were notable for retaining such a sense of 'class' in their music, imagery and public discourse.[5] Yet like Lennon and Townshend, Davies was suspicious of the organisational forms of working-class radicalism and their apparent inability to harness the energy of youth culture. The ambiguity of Davies's politics, which at various times ranged from patriotic, socialist, conservative and, in some cases, all three, was rooted in a particular strand of English working-class identity that was underpinned by a loose attachment to the Labour Party and a strong connection to locality and community. In an interview for the *New Musical Express*, in 1979, Davies stressed that he was a socialist: 'I was brought up to think that way, and then I had success and made a lie of what I was ... but I didn't become a capitalist'.[6]

The changes wrought by the policies of both Labour and Conservative governments between 1945 and 1974 became the subject of Davies's musings on British society.[7] His observations and critiques were based on a negotiation between class and politics that were not rigidly attached to a particular socialist ideology but were nonetheless conscious of social division. As with the later punk movement, Davies utilised a language of class to attack particular government policies on slum clearance, poverty and the welfare state.[8] The Kinks articulated a critique of post-war politics that to them seemed to be transforming the working-class world from which they had emerged. Their songs found resonance in the consciousness of working-class youth by presenting them with a realistic portrait of the times they were living through.

Davies's songs written between 1965 and 1971 tell the story of a working class still clinging to particular features of its pre-war existence. The benchmark for this kind of exploration was set by Hoggart's *The Uses of Literacy* (1957) and the subsequent work of the CCCS.[9] Hoggart's elegiac text opens a window on a working-class world that was retaining particular traditions in the face of the development of mass entertainments. Like Hoggart, the Kinks experienced in the working-class a 'local, personal, and communal way of life'.[10] The group were at the forefront of not just popular music but of a contemporary critical movement of academics, novelists and film-makers that were seeking to illuminate, define and reconstruct the class aspects of English society in the 1960s. The fact that the Kinks had both commercial and critical success and were linked to aspects of youth culture more generally ensured that their music reached beyond the bedrooms of teenagers, coffee bars and concert halls.

England, popular music, social class and the world of the Kinks

The negative view of popular music and youth culture in Hoggart's *Uses of Literacy* has been noted by a number of writers. He was critical of the fact that there was 'practically no writing of songs by members of the working-classes'.[11] Yet this was to soon change in dramatic fashion with the advent of beat groups such as the Beatles, the Kinks and the Who. Unlike the Beatles, the class credentials of the Kinks were less ambiguous with all members coming from typical low-income backgrounds in London.[12] Davies shared Hoggart's awareness of the cultural dangers that accompanied social change, and more than any of his popular music contemporaries he aimed to preserve aspects of working-class culture through his songs. Moreover, along with film-makers like Karel Reisz, Tony Richardson, John Schlesinger and Lindsay Anderson[13], Davies developed what Samuel later refereed to as a 'new social basis for narrative'.[14] Such narratives created an image of England that remained marked by class differences and inequality.

Dave Davies has stressed that part of the appeal of the Kinks was that they were able 'to communicate the struggle of the working man trying to survive in a greedy and purely materialistic society'.[15] Ray Davies developed an acute sense of English types and scenes in communicating the working-class experience to a broader audience. His critical defence of Englishness shares similarities to Orwell's patriotic socialism expounded in *The Lion and the Unicorn* (1941).[16] Orwell had noted the diversity that both created and sustained English patriotism and a collective identity that was underpinned by class. He evoked images of the 'clatter of clogs in the Lancashire mill towns, the to-and-fro of the lorries on the Great North Road, the queues outside the Labour exchanges, the rattle of pintables in the Soho pub'.[17] Davies produced similar vignettes that epitomised the ebb and flow of English society. In general, his songs were driven by pessimism that was uneasy with the economic changes of the 1960s and the way that they were transforming the everyday lives of the working-class and the 'community' that had emerged from their struggles in the pre-war period.

Like much of Orwell's writing on England, Kinks songs are underpinned by nostalgia, patriotism and class. Krause sees Davies as being part of the English romantic art tradition.[18] Cloonan has noted the articulation of an 'ambivalent Englishness' that is a 'preoccupation' rather than a celebration.[19] Baxter-Moore has viewed the Kinks constructing an Englishness that was 'caught between tradition and modernity and competing senses of class and nation'.[20] However, the tendency to emphasise ambiguity underplays a unity in the world view of Davies. His pronouncements through song were fairly indicative of a particular strand of English working-class experiences. This world was earlier explored by Orwell in *The Road to Wigan Pier* (1937).[21] Orwell's politics have been excavated by many writers leading to a variety of characterisations of him as a 'moralist', 'non-ideological socialist' and 'patriotic democrat.[22] Davies's politics can be deconstructed in the same way revealing a 'small c conservative', 'nostalgic patriot' and 'small state socialist'. Such personas inhabit the narrative of Kinks songs giving space to pride in class and locality but also a resignation that somehow things are always getting worse.

In *The Uses of Literacy*, Hoggart claimed that the 'old forms of class culture are in danger of being replaced by a poorer kind of classless...culture'.[23] Davies shared Hoggart's concern with the emasculation of a particular working-class culture. On later reflection he saw the 1960s as 'a carrot held up to youth to distract us so that we would not rebel against the ruling classes'.[24] He was aware of the limitations of the rhetoric of 'progressive politics' claiming that 'the ideas about uniting in a classless society went out of the window and everybody reverted to type'.[25] Davies's working-class is one that can be found in the autobiographical section of *The Uses of Literacy* and not in the 'affluence' and 'mass entertainments' of the second half. According to Hoggart, the 'more we look at working-class life, the more we try to reach the core of working-class attitudes, the more surely does it appear that the core is a sense of the personal, the concrete, the local'.[26] This core was inhabited by Davies and continued to inform his song writing into the 1970s.

The Kinks were products of a London working-class that both embraced and resisted change in the post-war period. The Labour-voting Davies family led by Fred and Anne included six girls and two boys. They were typical of the working-class milieu that could be found in various parts of London in the 1940s. The family moved from the urban centre of the city to Fortis Green close to Muswell Hill as part of the exodus of people forced away by slum clearance. Ray and Dave's extended family provided them with a range of working-class characters that would populate their songs. According to Rogan, Davies would hang around outside of the local pub frequented by his father, a local character and womaniser, 'listening to half-drunken sing songs'.[27] Davies would return to the working-class community and the pub on many occasions as a framing device for his songs. Nell Dunn had also noted the centrality of the pub in *Up the Junction* (1963), her novel based on observation of the Battersea working class: 'The piano bangs out and the singer holds a pint of cold beer in one hand and the mike in the other...The air is thick with smoke and beer'.[28] In Willmott's 1964 study of the East End, these elements of pre-war society were still in place: 'Mothers and their married daughters go shopping together...the old choruses are sung in the pubs on Saturday night'.[29] Hoggart also noted the resilience of the 'old tunes' in northern clubs where people performed 'songs their grandparents sang'.[30] The club scene of industrial England with its 'blue comedians', crooners and home-grown rock 'n' rollers remained a feature of the cultural life of the working class into the 1970s and was recreated in the television studio in the form of the *Wheeltappers' and Shunters' Social Club,* which was broadcast by Granada between 1974 and 1977.[31]

In the Davies household, popular tunes, American standards and music hall ditties would vie for space with the working-class oeuvre of Gracie Fields and George Formby.[32] Communal singing would be accompanied by joke telling, impromptu sketches and recreations of particular scenes from adolescence. The Davies family experienced the displacement of many who were transported to the New Towns of Harlow, Hemel Hempstead and Stevenage between 1946 and 1950.[33] Culturally, working-class families attempted to maintain links with the streets they had left behind through particular forms of popular culture such as the pub, football, parties and drunken singing session around the piano. The domestic scene had a lasting impact on Davies as it did on many other working-class children. His extended family included industrial workers, spivs, matriarchs and pub entertainers.

Davies did not share the social and educational mobility of some of his popular music contemporaries. Unlike Lennon, McCartney and Townshend, he failed the grammar school entrance examination and his experience of failure mirrored that of thousands of working-class children. Such failure often reinforced a sense of class that remained resistant to the economic and cultural changes of the 1950s. This bred resentment amongst some working-class youths who were aware of the debilitating effects of class. Davies fits the typology of Willmott's 'working class rebel', which he saw as a particular type in traditional working-class communities'.[34] Such rebels missed the chance of grammar school and its attendant social mobility. Davies carried the scars of his educational experiences with him into his career as a songwriter and remained a critic of the class discrimination that underpinned the English education system and maintained the country's structural inequalities.

In the 1960s, popular music was the latest manifestation of a working-class autodidact tradition that had created a generation of socialists, writers and performers. Davies was aware of the way in which working-class culture was being transmitted into mainstream culture through literature and film. Davies' brother Dave had purchased a copy of Sillitoe's *Saturday Night and Sunday Morning* (1958) and passed it on to Ray.[35] For Davies, popular culture in the form of pulp fiction, rock 'n' roll, and the 'b-movie' was both a discourse of escape and call to action. To Hoggart this was 'a passive visual taking-on of bad mass-art geared to a very low mental age'.[36] Yet the Kinks worked against the apocalyptic vision prophesised by Hoggart. Davies never became disconnected from an earlier working-class culture and spent the rest of his career in the Kinks trying to reconstruct it through song. The message/observation of the Kinks formed a working-class discourse that was not rigidly attached to a particular socialist ideology, but was nonetheless conscious of social division and difference. The songs composed by Davies between 1965 and 1971 provide an alternative take on post-war England to the characterisation provided by the more conventional texts produced by sociologists and historians.[37]

Respected men, good times, urban danger and gender politics

The Kinks went beyond their contemporaries like the Beatles and the Rolling Stones in attempting to make sense of what was going on around them and giving the listener insights into the lives of others and how they were affected by social change. 'A Well Respected Man' recorded in August 1965,[38] presents an image of the upper-middle-class conservative and the world he inhabits. The character could be a 'Sir Humphrey' type civil servant respected by his peers and neighbours. Yet behind the gentility and the respectability, his parents are involved in extra-marital affairs. The mother goes to meetings, perhaps the Housewives League or the Mothers Union.[39] The subject of the song refers to a particular type of person that survived the social challenges of the early 1960s. The 'Well Respected Man' is not a swinging beatnik, but a ruthless social climber and aspirant cad fearful that his transgressive fantasies could threaten his place within his class milieu. Similarly, the working-class culture described by Hoggart is dramatised in 'Where Have All the Good Times Gone' recorded in October 1965. In contrast to 'A Well Respected Man', 'Where Have All the Good Times Gone' moves down the class structure. The song observes the continuities and breaks in the mentality and memory of a sixties teenager and his parents. The mother and father represent the Hoggartian working-class of thrift, respectability and a collective consciousness that defined aspects of social identity in the pre-war period. As the title suggests, the old world of the English working-class was disappearing and was replaced by a nostalgia that celebrated a notion of 'better times'.[40]

Throughout the 1960s, 'moral panic' and social scandal were beginning to shape the public perception of metropolitan culture in general and youth culture in particular.[41] Mort has examined the '[a]nxieties about the radicalised forms of transgression epitomised by the Profumo, Keeler, Edgecombe triangle' and how they 'pointed to disturbing connections between the Caribbean cultures of Notting Hill and the West End's social elites'.[42] The Kinks immersed themselves in this culture, particularly Dave Davies who became an inveterate party-goer who moved easily within the class structure of the capital. Conversely, Ray distanced himself from his contemporaries in opting to observe rather than participate in counter-cultural activities. He makes an explicit statement of his position in 'I'm Not Like Everybody Else', written in January 1966. The song became a Kinks anthem of individuality and difference. Yet the song can also be read as an attack on the type of deference that had personified sections of the working-class to which Davies's parents belonged. He might have been keen to celebrate the working-class culture of Hoggart, but he remained critical of its ability to stifle ambition and crush creativity.

The Kinks witnessed the impact of slum clearance and post-war housing policy on their own families. Davies was keen to document the experiences of the urban poor who remained outside of the 'affluent' society. In his own way he was one of a number of social investigators who were rediscovering the poor.[43] He documented their lives and the struggle they faced on a daily basis. His most developed composition on this theme was 'Dead End Street' recorded in October 1966. He had no doubt been exposed to the practices of slum landlord Peter Rachman and the wretched conditions faced by his poor tenants. Lurid revelations on 'Rachmanism' were covered by newspapers in the wake of the Profumo scandal in 1963.[44] In 'Dead End Street' we have a much darker view than some of the imagery in the social realist cinema of the 1950s and the Technicolor London that we see in films like Antonioni's *Blow Up* (1966). The song is a useful companion piece to *Cathy Come Home* (1966), written by Jeremy Sandford, directed by Ken Loach and broadcast by the BBC two days before the release of the single.[45] 'Dead End Street' provides the starkest example of Davies's empathy with the urban poor. The song creates scenes of leaking pipes, collapsing walls and freezing rooms, with inhabitants unemployed, in debt, and surviving on a diet of bread, honey and tea. Slum clearances did not eradicate the problem of poor housing and the safety of domestic dwellings, as proved by the Ronan Point tower block disaster. The structure had been erected in 1966. On 16 May 1968, a gas explosion led to the collapse of a section of the building leading to four deaths and seventeen injuries.[46]

Kitts notes that 'Dead End Street' was recorded on 21 October, the day of the Aberfan disaster' in which a 'waste coal' heap collapsed and killed 116 children and 28 adults.[47] The coverage of the disaster in the press and on television was a further reminder of the unchanging character of many industrial working-class communities. The South Wales coalfield was symbolic of a pre-war working class that had clung to the communal traditions and cultures of the Victorian/Edwardian period.[48] Davies stated that the song reflected the plight of coal miners more generally in the context of recent economic pressures on particular employment sectors.[49] Harold Wilson's 'modernisation' of the British economy created social disruption and rising unemployment, leading to the creation of sophisticated critiques of British Labourism from the socialist left. In a later interview, Davies reflected on the failure of English socialism: 'I was brought up left, very socialist, extremely socialist, but they've let me down'.[50]

In *X-Ray*, Davies's 'unauthorised autobiography', he is explicit in demolishing the romantic view of the age of affluence: 'In the bistros of Belgravia and Chelsea the bright young things were partying...The working class was still in its place in the coal mines of Yorkshire, Wales and the North. The mill towns were still employing cloth-capped workers who lived in terraced back-to-backs'.[51] Davies's sense of class and ambiguous attitude to the rhetoric of progress was shared with Willmott's East End boys who showed an acute awareness of class in making sense of the world around them: 'They know that, despite the 'affluence', local people are relatively poor financially and relatively low in status'.[52] Similarly in Glasgow, 'Dead End Street' became the song of choice for one working-class gang: 'When the record came off the turn-table for perhaps the twentieth time, Big Fry, now deep in drink, rose up and tauntingly called out: 'we're the slummies!'.[53]

Davies covers similar ground to 'Dead End Street' in 'Big Black Smoke' also written in 1966. The narrative of the song depicts a London of urban danger focusing on the experiences of a young girl who finds herself on the wrong side of swinging London. Mary Morse in her ethnography of disaffected youth in the period provides context. She noted the centrality of the coffee bar as a crossing point for youths who were caught between the restrictions of the domestic sphere and the attractions of the metropolis: 'There was a group of five girls, two sets of friends, who met in the coffee bar before going to dances...A second type consisted of girls ... in twos or threes...very unstable and unhappy at home'.[54] In a number of English cities in the sixties police and social workers were aware of the role coffee bars played in exposing vulnerable youth to criminality, drugs and sexual transgression.[55] Dunn's observations that formed the basis of her novel *Up the Junction* (1963) are also illuminating. One section notes the different characters that crossed paths in a Soho clip joint: 'Johnny, the youngest tout with blue mac and blue circles under his eyes, comes in with six men...sexed up to the ears. "I'm in the motor car industry – business is very bad, the proles won't buy cars'.[56] Davies creates an image of the pining mother and the runaway girl sleeping in coffee bars and spending money on cigarettes and amphetamines. The same or similar character also appears in 'Little Miss Queen of Darkness'. The subject of this song has left the coffee bar and is now presumably working in a Soho strip joint. Davies's fallen women can be read alongside those in Dunn's novels. Joy in *Poor Cow* (1967) shares similarities to the teenager in the dangerous city in 'Big Black Smoke' and 'Little Miss Queen of Darkness'.[57]

Unlike their contemporaries, the Kinks also developed a nuanced reading of gender.[58] The Rolling Stones for example had a much more simplistic and misogynistic view of women.[59] In 'Two Sisters', written in 1966, Davies examines the impact of domesticity, affluence and social mobility within the family. Davies based 'Two Sisters' partly on the contrast between him and his brother, but also the leading female figures in his life – his wife, Rasa, his mother and sisters'.[60] Rasa was from Bradford providing a connection to this archetypal northern city which no doubt gave him an acute insight to the 'drudgery' of working-class women's lives. In 'Two Sisters', Sybilla and Priscilla represent two kinds/forms of female experience. Priscilla is married with children and seemingly chained to the cooker, the washing machine and her weekly magazines. She could be living in one of the new housing developments that were appearing in London and its periphery. In contrast,

Sybilla is enjoying the opportunities that were slowly opening-up for some women. She has 'smart friends' and a luxury flat. This type of woman was increasingly appearing in newspapers, magazines, television shows and characterised by Julie Christie in the film version of the Keith Waterhouse novel *Billy Liar* (1963) and more sensationally her character in John Schlesinger's *Darling* (1965).[61]

The life of Priscilla complements the work of Willmott and Young who documented such processes in their study of the East End in 1957.[62] They noted that 'when daughters ... absorbed themselves in the display and adventure of adolescence, excitement lay in the life of workplace and club, street and gang, cinema and holiday camp ... But when she marries ... she returns to the woman's world'.[63] Writing in *New Society* in 1964, Barker claimed that teenage married couples 'vanish from the youth clubs and even from the discotheques'.[64] Yet in Davies's world this is not necessarily a bad thing. He sees stability and respectability in the family and Priscilla realises that even though confined to domestic drudgery, children and husband meant that she is probably much happier than the wayward Sybilla. As Davies expresses in 'Two Sisters', the experience of women in the sixties remained mostly determined by social class. In a general sense, the Kinks oeuvre is critical of the way in which the Labour Party's contribution to the 'post-war political consensus' was not building on the traditional foundations of working-class life but actively undermining them.

In three more songs from 1966, 'Afternoon Tea', 'Dandy' and 'Village Green', Davies re-engages with working-class cultures, characters and the sense of a 'lost England'. In 'Afternoon Tea', Davies celebrates the centrality of tea drinking to English culture and the survival of the English café amongst the explosion of continental coffee bars. The day of a typical working-class family like the Davieses would be punctuated by regular 'brews'. Moments of crisis, celebration and reflection would be lubricated with pots of tea. In film and television shows from the period the tea pot would be a permanent fixture on the small kitchen table. The working-class family and community also provide Davies with a number of characters that enrich his compositions. The subject of 'Dandy' is an ageing womaniser who could well be based on Davies's father who had a reputation for 'chatting up the ladies'. The figure was a particular type in working-class culture often referred to as a 'Jack-the-lad' or 'patter merchant'.[65] In 'Dandy' the character chats up girls and conducts illicit affairs by climbing through windows while the husband is away. Workmates would often chide each other that while they were on the night shift the wife could well be having sex with the milkman. The elder woman who made herself freely available for sex was also a particular type. The extra-marital affair involving a workmate or friend of the husband is also observed in Sillitoe's *Saturday Night and Sunday Morning*.[66] Davies's womaniser also shares characteristics with Michael Caine's character in Lewis Gilbert's film *Alfie* (1966). Again, as with all the characters depicted in the songs of the Kinks, there is sympathy for their position and culture. The 'Dandy' maybe past his best in terms of looks and ability to attract the kind of woman that he once could, but he remains free and 'all right'.

In November 1966, Davies committed to tape a song that would form the foundation of what some critics have argued is the most ambitious and realised album of the Kinks' career. 'Village Green' imagines an English idyll outside of the bustle of the urban conurbation. The village has a green, a church, an oak tree and 'simple people'. The song highlights a familiar tension in Davies's work of embracing elements of the future but retaining a longing for a more secure past. This song provides the clearest example of his 'patriotic conservatism'. 'Village Green' goes beyond an embrace of a particular working-class culture and sees Davies reflecting a more conservative middle-class England. Davies's English idyll shares many of the features of Orwell's with its 'green fields and red pillar-boxes'.[67] Yet it also sees Davies attempting to connect with an older working-class that had originally been driven from the land through enclosure and industrialisation. Irrespective of its pretensions the village green is still nonetheless a working-class one.

Social mobility, working-class culture and the resilience of the rural idyll

In 1967, the songs of the Kinks were becoming more ambitious and developing themes that had been explored in some of the earlier compositions. In 'Situation Vacant' and 'Mr Pleasant', 'affluence' and social mobility frame the narrative. The young couple (Suzy and Johnny) in 'Situation Vacant' seem happy in their rented accommodation, but Johnny is pressured into becoming more ambitious by the social climbing ambitions of Suzy's mother. Davies here draws on a 'familiar type', perhaps best depicted by Thora Hird playing the Mrs Rothwell character in John Schlesinger's film of Stan Barstow's novel A *Kind of Loving* (1962).[68] She is convinced that her daughter has married beneath her position and particularly appalled by her son-in-law's working-class embrace of heavy drinking. In Davies's song, the mother-in-law gets her way and Johnny resigns from the job he had been in from school. Ultimately the couple reach a point of financial crisis leading to martial separation and Suzy moves back in with her mother. Similarly, the middle-class suburban idyll in 'Mr Pleasant' is not what it seems. The subject of this song enjoys a 'good job', prosperity and all the accoutrements that accompany it such as a luxury car and the latest consumer durables. Yet he is unaware that his wife is 'flirting around' with another man. The limitations, blandness and hypocrisy of the middle-classes are exposed by Davies, again signifying his working-class critique of aspiration and 'affluence'.[69]

In 'Autumn Almanac', we find a further encapsulation of Davies's attachment to and celebration of a Hoggartian working-class culture. 'Autumn Almanac' covers an array of themes, but ultimately describes the working-class attachment to locality and place. Young and Willmott's work on the East End showed that such attachments remained a core component of working-class life: 'Quite often people have themselves lived there for a long time – one out of every ten women and one out of every twenty men in the general sample still live in the street where they were born'.[70] On the surface, Davies constructs the notion of community in conventional ways, in what Bourke has referred to as 'a backward-looking romanticism' or a 'forward looking socialism'.[71] Yet Davies goes beyond the confines of such definitions by also giving voice to the marginal and eccentric. One part of 'Autumn Almanac' is based on Ray's gardener who was a popular character in and around Muswell Hill who seemed at odds with the world of affluence and technological advance that was emerging around him. Davies then moves from the individual experience to the collective. He recreates the scene of a typical working-class Friday night with people huddling together and finding solace in tea and toasted buns. As Barker discovered in his interviews with young married couples in Camberwell, South London in 1964, elements of working-class leisure remained fixed: 'The Colliers live rather how they did before they married: ladies' darts on Tuesdays; men's darts on Thursdays; a drink, a dance or a party on Saturday night'.[72] The individual voice then returns with a statement of his favourite things such as football, roast dinners and holidays in Blackpool. Football remained a core component of English working-class identity after the war. Both Ray and Dave were avid supporters of Arsenal. Davies's evocation of the working-class Sunday mirrors Hoggart's recollection of 'the smell of clothes drying by the fireside ... the *News of the World*-mingled-with-roast-beef'.[73] In 'Autumn Almanac' this thread of working-class experience is getting smaller but for Davies and many others it remained a feature of sixties England.

Davies was also aware that although in decline the English seaside resort held a particular kind of magic for working-class youth. Blackpool had been central to Lennon's childhood. The Davies family would regularly holiday in Ramsgate and Southend. The image of Blackpool in 'Autumn Almanac' is a celebration of the mass leisure and consumption patterns of the working-class. The song is evocative of Lancashire 'Wakes Weeks' and the image of Blackpool in the Gracie Fields film *Sing as We Go* (1934). Again, there is a Hoggartian sense of loss here, but also recognition of the survival of a particular working-class culture. Davies paints a far more sympathetic portrait than that of Lindsay Anderson in *O Dreamland* his 1953 cinematic portrait of the Margate amusement park.[74] Davies shares Orwell's view that the working-class culture can be read as oppositional. To Orwell, '[t]he genuinely popular culture of England is something that goes on beneath the surface, unofficially and more or less frowned upon by the authorities'.[75] Like Davies, Orwell also saw something radical in the culture of the brash seaside resort epitomised by the imagery of the Donald McGill postcards depicting hen-pecked husbands, battle-axe mother-in laws, and authoritarian landladies.[76]

The final verse of 'Autumn Almanac' returns to the individual statement of pride in class, culture and locality. The narrator will never leave his street. The notion of such security of community remained important in the collective memory of the working-class. In subsequent years, it would take more overtly political forms in the battle in particular communities such as coal mining ones to take direct action to protect jobs and 'ways of living'. As with upwardly mobile grammar schools boys and 'organic intellectuals' such as Davies, the 'working-class community' remained rooted as both a 'real' and 'mythical community' in their collective consciousness constantly calling them to 'come on home'.

During this period, Socialists and Communists were also taking notice of the social realism that formed the basis of Kinks songs. On 27 May 1967, the Kinks performed at the Young Communist League's Trend '67 Festival at the Derbyshire Miners' Holiday Camp in Skegness.[77] According to Waite this was an 'attempt to project a left-wing agenda on to youth culture'. [78] The Communist Party was particularly critical of the counter-culture: 'the do-nothing concept of drugs, drop-out and meditation. All these ideologies have one thing in common – they were not from the experience of workers in struggle but from the frustrations of the middle class'.[79] Yet the relationship between popular music and socialist activism was complex. According to Street, popular music 'is not a socialism of vanguard parties or common ownership or five-year plans; it is a socialism built of sensations and images, inspired by pleasure and personal desires'.[80] Bourke's notion of the resilience of class is important here. She claims that the 'language of class' 'remained a powerful self-defining metaphor which referred less to the individual in the present and more to the perceptions of historical construction'.[81] Davies's understanding and articulation of class was operating on this level yet it was also able to present both a historical and a contemporary sense of class to the young listener of Kinks' records.

In October 1968, the Kinks played a number of cabaret dates in North East England including appearances at the Top Hat Club in Spennymoor and the Club Fiesta in Stockton-on-Tees.[82] The Top Hat club was in the heart of a working-class England inhabited by coal miners, matriarchs and weekend hedonists. The North East was then undergoing numerous mine closures and rising unemployment. The political culture of the Durham coalfield and the city of Newcastle was personified by the politics of the Labour Party and the overweening presence of T. Dan Smith.[83] Audiences were no doubt aware of the Kinks class credentials through the social realism of their songs. The northern cabaret club was a space where three generations of the northern working-class could be found. This was a microcosm of the continuities and changes that framed working-class culture in the 1960s.

Davies's developing obsession with Englishness and the developing fissures in society would reach a new level of sophistication with a cycle of songs that would form the core of *The Kinks Are the Village Green Preservation Society*

(1968). The Kinks had already exhibited aspects of Englishness through their stage costumes and the fashions they adopted. They now introduced a variety of styles and sounds into their recordings that drew on their collective memory of a working-class childhood. The use of pub piano, trombone, and banjo was one aspect of this process. The album also introduced the listener to a number of characters that had both contemporary and historical resonance. 'Monica' is a glimpse into the world of the prostitute through which Davies presents a similarly sympathetic view of Hoggart in the *Uses of Literacy*.[84]

The prostitute figure was a marginal figure in the youth culture of London and other metropolitan centres. A sociological study published in 1961 pointed to the geographical and cultural trajectory of the young prostitute: 'After an early life in which, one after another, the social institutions fail her, a girl drifts to London...it is noticeable that they start working in milk bars and cafes, which are the last stages before prostitution'.[85] The fate of the young drawn into prostitution was also sensationalised by Don Chaffey's film *The Flesh Is Weak* (1957). Contemporary concerns regarding mixed-race relationships were also situated in the behaviour of prostitutes cavorting with West Indians. Rolph noted that 'a number of girls live with coloured men in Soho and elsewhere'.[86] The notion of the corruption of white youth had also been spotlighted in Roy Ward Baker's film of Ted Willis's screenplay *Flame in the Streets* (1961).[87] Karina Jones, an ex-prostitute told Jeremy Sandford about the 'circuit': 'I went down all the exotic places, the Flamingo...the Student Prince and The Limbo and The Apple and La Douce'.[88] Like Davies, Sandford worked tirelessly to step beyond the façade of affluence and to tell the stories of the contemporary underworld. The 1959 Street Offences Act had removed many prostitutes from the street but did not completely eradicate this aspect of selling sex.

Nostalgia is another theme connecting the songs on *The Kinks Are the Village Green Preservation Society*. Lupro characterises the album as 'Davies's response to his experience with the modernist landscapes and...developments such as New Towns'.[89] However, it can also be placed alongside the work of Orwell as depicting a particularly English strand of 'patriotic socialism'. Orwell argued that 'patriotism has nothing to do with Conservatism, since it is a devotion to something that is always changing'.[90] In 'Last of the Steam-Powered Trains', Davies presents himself as one of the 'the last of the good old renegades' lamenting the fact that his 'friends are all middle-class'. The song was written in the context of a dramatic reduction in the British railway network and the replacement of steam trains by diesel engines. The Beeching Report of 1963 had by 1967 led to closure of 5000 miles of track.[91] With the reduction of the rail network green spaces and seaside would become even less accessible to those excluded from the 'affluence' that led to car ownership. In 'Picture Book', Davies examines the way in which photographs reaffirmed locality and class. Samuel also reflected on this in his discussion of photographs as historical sources.[92] He argues that 'what seems to be involved in the case of old photographs is not so much getting back to the past... but rather of creating a lost Eden'.[93] The imagery of 'Picture Book' evokes a working-class family looking at old pictures of parents, children and holidays. For the next two Kinks albums, Davies would move beyond an idealistic English idyll and would attempt to write his own version of English history from the Victorian period through to the 1960s.

Trade unions, affluence, sexual transgression and the fragmentation of the English working-class

In *Arthur or the Decline and Fall of the British Empire* (1969), the narrative and content complements Willmott and Young's work on suburbia and cinematic characterisations of the patriotic English family in films such as David Lean's *This Happy Breed* (1944). Rogan has suggested that the album 'could almost be interpreted as a glorification of working-class fatalism'.[94] The collection of songs is of great use to the historian in marking a point in which artists were coming to terms with what they felt were significant changes transforming English life. The narrative is based on Arthur, a family relation who was 'born in a plain simple working-class position'. Arthur was ambitious and has a level of personal contentment, but his life has been determined by social class. The opening song 'Victoria' alludes to aspects of society in nineteenth-century Britain and Queen Victoria's place in the popular imagination of the period. It was written in a decade when there had been a rediscovery and celebration of Victoria in terms of fashion, literature and cinematic representations.[95] 'Victoria' symbolises the unity of the nation and the hypocrisies that underpin such patriotism.

The strongest songs on *Arthur* are concerned with developing suburban identities and how they represented a break with the past. In the 1950s, such identities were also documented by Willmott and Young in the accompanying study to their East End research.[96] They observed that '[o]n their way to work electricians and bank clerks wear the same sort of clothes... drive the same sort of cars... the interiors of their houses are indistinguishable too'.[97] It is this world that Davies explores in 'Shangri-la'. Dave Davies later claimed that 'Shangri La' was not really an attack on the suburbs, but a song expressing 'an underlying sympathy'.[98] Baxter-Moore concurs claiming that the Kinks wanted to make suburbia 'both more acceptable as a place to live and as part of a mythologized version of England'.[99] Yet, there *is* a critique of suburbia in the song and a sense that although everyday life was improving for a section of the upwardly mobile working-class something else was being lost. The song depicts the family being trapped by suburban conformity, mortgages and the rigidity of workplace elites. The houses in the street have a name, but they look the same and the neighbours are grasping, gossiping and ultimately individualistic and self-seeking.

In many ways, Davies's character in 'Shangri-la' is close to 'Selsdon man'. 'Selsdon man' represented a new type of Tory activist that was aiming to make Britain more economically liberal and socially authoritarian. The inhabitants of 'Shangri-la's' would form the bedrock of support for the Conservative Party into the 1980s.[100] In Willmott and Young's assessment of suburbia, a 'man who buys his own house has a tiny but independent estate of which he is the undisputed manager'.[101] Davies provides an insight into the bond between home and ownership in 'Shangri La'. In an interview with *Rolling Stone*, Ray stressed that he was 'not laughing at the people in the song. They're brainwashed into that'.[102] The song 'Brainwashed' rails against 'the aristocrats and bureaucrats' for creating a generally regressive and culture. This highlights a tension in Davies's writing. He seems to provide a critique and celebration of an England that is both progressive and conservative. 'Yes Sir, No Sir', confirms the resilience of deference and class and is an unsentimental depiction of a militarism that remained aware of the dispensability of the working-class. A critique of the British officer class was another theme in contemporary popular culture personified by Tony Richardson's film of *The Charge of the Light Brigade* (1968).

'Drivin' is a topical song tapping into the tradition of the Sunday car trip. Barker's Camberwell study also illustrates the way in which the young working-class male after marriage would form part of this culture. One interviewee, Philip Langham, 'used to be a Rocker…now justifies his car as a way to take the expected baby out'.[103] Affluence was impacting on the lives of the working-class leading to higher standards of living and making particular domestic tasks a lot easier, yet poverty and inequality remained. As Bourke has argued, a 'shared identity as 'working class', even if rooted in a single geographical space, could not surmount the difficulties inherent in competitive societies'.[104] Willmott and Young maintained that 'social class is the key to understanding many of the differences in the suburb'.[105] Davies concurs with this view noting that in the New Towns 'there are all these people who've been taken out of the East End of London and put into places where they don't really exist as they did before. They're trying to keep things the same…but they have to break down eventually'.[106]

In reviewing *Arthur* on its release, Crouse claimed that Ray 'loves Englishmen with all their idiosyncrasies and he hates them for constantly reaffirming the class system…Arthur's one, minimal shortcoming is that it offers no plan for improving the present situation'.[107] Yet this is the strength of the album. For historians it provides a particular characterisation of English and Englishness that does not rely on political rhetoric or dependence on a particular variant of Conservatism or Socialism, but engages with the everyday experiences of the working-class. The Kinks share with Hoggart's working-class a perception of 'them' and 'us': "Them" is the world of the bosses, whether those bosses are private individuals…or…public officials'. [108] To Davies, the working-class was now under attack from a variety of economic, social and cultural forces.

By 1970 Davies was not only attempting to make sense of the recent changes in English society but also positing critiques of a political culture that he viewed as oppressing the individual. 'Get Back In Line' shares its subject matter with the seminal American film *On the Waterfront* (1954). Davies might also have seen two English films that depicted the 'trade union problem': *I'm Alright Jack* (1959) and *The Angry Silence* (1960).[109] According to Williams 'Get Back In Line' was 'the first anti-union pop song'.[110] The song refers to the group's wrangles with American unions during their first tour of the United States, but it also reflects the kind of working-class from which the Davies emerged and the contemporary industrial relations culture of 1970. A year earlier the Labour Government had wrestled with the trade union movement in attempting to reform industrial relations through its In Place of Strife proposals.[111] Davies's father had suffered from unemployment and had not been employed in occupations noted for trade unionism. Davies himself had earlier experience of the print unions as a teenager that no doubt shaped his views. In *X-Ray* he refers to the contact he had with the 'down-tools school of trade unionism. Bastard totally perverted the meaning of the word 'union'...he...took the piss out of me for working in my tea break'.[112] Davies' characterisation of trade unionism seems to fit Street's claim that 'pop's natural sympathies...are with the scab'.[113] Yet Dave Davies later stressed that the song demanded a more complex reading and that in fact it was a 'tribute to the difficulties of the working classes'.[114] This is a more nuanced explanation and spoke to those union members who were caught between 'big labour' and 'big capital'. Baxter-Moore presents a more literal reading arguing that 'Davies accepts no political solution to the plight of the working-class other than a kind of radical populism'.[115] Yet Davies was indicative of a sizeable section of the working-class who Hoggart claimed had 'a limited realism...non-political...in their outlook'.[116]

In 'Get Back In Line', Davies portrays the archetypal 'Little Man', a particular media construction epitomising 'popular opinion' and English 'common sense'. The Little Man was a cartoon figure who appeared in the *Daily Express* between 1920 and 1947. The 'Little Man' can be set alongside John Bull and the 'English Tommy' in continuing a tradition of the depiction of national character. According to Mandler, 'Orwell also took over the basic "Little Man" stereotype, gentle and good-natured, rooted in the back garden, the fireside and the nice cup of tea'.[117] The 'Little Man' in the Davies persona is constrained by structural forces that remained in place after the optimism of victory of the Second World War and the promise of a 'New Jerusalem'. Davies toyed with the imagery of particular types to express aspects of Englishness. The 'Little Man' became increasingly prominent in the songs of the Kinks and found his voice in a number of later compositions. The contradiction in Davies's work is the pull between a commitment to the working-class, but also to an individualist sense of Englishness that can be found in the 'Little Man' persona.

In 'Lola', Davies explored the theme of sexual ambiguity and transgression. The Kinks were an overtly sexual group in terms of their name, costumes and performances. Dave Davies was openly bisexual.[118] When 'Lola' was released in June 1970 sexual politics was emerging as a distinct movement for social change. The Sexual Offences Act of 1967 had decriminalised homosexuality and the Gay Liberation Front was formed.[119] Yet homosexuality remained bounded by social class. As Houlbrook argues in his expansive exploration of 'Queer London' the 'Dilly Boy and urinal regularly appeared in the news, the discreetly respectable "homosexual" and exclusive bachelor apartment did not'.[120] The worlds of popular music, film and bohemia opened up cross-class relationships within the gay subculture of London. Writers such as William Burroughs and Colin MacInnes and fashion designers such as John Stephen were notable in this respect.[121] The 'meat rack' at Piccadilly Circus provided 'rough trade' for a variety of punters. Some would even get beyond the street and the slum dwelling and find themselves in parties thrown by the emerging cultural elite. A number of clubs were also patronised by homosexuals such as the Flamingo. Ray remembered that 'promoters thought we looked effeminate; others were convinced we were pansies'.[122] Jeff Nuttall, reflecting on youth culture in 1968 recalled that '"Kinky" was a word very much in the air. Everywhere there were zippers, leathers, boots, PVC, see-through plastics, male make-up, a thousand overtones of sexual deviation'.[123] Sex shops and strip clubs proliferated with figures such as Paul Raymond becoming major players in property speculation, business and forging links between disparate characters whose paths might not normally have crossed.[124] Mort has argued that the changing nature of striptease in Soho played a role in the 'marginalisation' of a distinctly English conception of 'feminine glamour'.[125] Yet the imagery of the Kinks represented an attempt to deter the move towards a 'continental' conception of sexual display. Davies drew on distinctly English stylistic accoutrements such as fox hunting jackets and whips. Through pose and performance, they gave these styles a particularly 'English kink'.[126] The music of the Kinks and the characters observed and created by Davies provide a corrective to the over-optimistic portrayal of sex and sexuality in the 1960s.

The Kinks' most coherent piece of social commentary is *Muswell Hillbillies* (1971). This represented a closing of the 1960s and an almost remorseful critique of slum clearance and urbanisation. Like much of Davies's work the album provides a compelling companion piece to Young and Willmott's studies of the East End working-class and the suburban culture that undermined its foundations. Young and Willmott presented a sense of a rapidly disappearing working-class world: 'That busy sociable life is now a memory. Shopping in the mornings amidst the chromium and tiles of the Parade is a lonely business compared with the familiar faces and sights of the old street market'.[127] This uprooting of the working-class was also criticised by Shelagh Delaney in her BBC Monitor profile of Salford in 1960. Davies also had personal feelings of this through the experiences of his grandmother: 'My gran used to live in Islington in this really nice old house, and they moved her to a block of flats'.[128] Davies saw through the mirage of the counter-culture later noting that it was 'a bit of a con, all that thing about the New World…I didn't share the optimism of the sixties…'.[129]

Davies claimed that the songs on *Muswell Hillbillies* were 'about people who actually existed in the lives of my parents'.[130] More forcefully, Davies develops a sophisticated critique of the post-war consensus with particular reference to urban planning and working-class housing. Kitts argues that 'the album – music, lyrics, sound, artwork – was intended to imply the economic, psychological, and overall cultural quagmire of the English working class since the advent of the Welfare State'.[131] In '20th Century Man', Davies links machinery, technology and militarism to the fall of the English Jerusalem. He rails against modern writers, painters and government bureaucracy. There is a definite Tory strand to this song with Davies lamenting the loss of privacy and liberty in which he emphasises a form of 'patriotic conservatism'.

A portrait of the individual experience of slum clearance is expressed in 'Here Come the People in Grey'. The subject of the song is informed by 'the people in grey' that his/her house will soon be demolished. A similar scene is depicted in the film version of *Till Death Us Do Part* (1969). Davies had provided the theme tune to this comedy/drama that depicted the fortunes of an East End family during the Second World War and its aftermath. A similar scene is captured in North East England in the film of *The Likely Lads* (1976). In her passionate critique of aspects of post-war housing policy Hanley has recently written from the perspective of the displaced working-class: 'With every passing year several thousand more cramped, unhealthy households were given the chance to decamp from their condemned inner-city quarters to the new suburbs; to Becontree in Essex, where 120,000 were to reside without a single pub'.[132] Through this process of displacement, the class distinctions and prejudices in English society arguably became starker. Respondents to the Willmott and Young survey articulated such sentiments: 'They treat us like dirt. They're a different class of people. They've got money…If people from the estate go to the dance hall…they all look down on them'.[133] The authors concluded that 'inside people's minds…the boundaries of class are still closely drawn'.[134] In an interview in 1988 Ray linked housing policy in the 1960s to juvenile delinquency and alienation: 'They built cheap housing and packed people in like rats. The kids there have no job and no future'.[135]

Once again the casualties of progress and those that are left desperately clinging to an earlier culture are given space throughout *Muswell Hillbillies*. 'Complicated Life' charts the physical deterioration that comes with unemployment. In 'Alcohol', Davies provides a portrait of the alcoholic and his rapid fall from grace. 'Holloway Jail' tells the story of a young girl who falls in with criminals and her life degenerates to the point at which she is imprisoned. 'Uncle Son' is centred on another character who was a 'simple working man' who had been promised a better life by Liberals, Conservatives and Socialists and told what to do by trade unionists, generals and preachers. Here is Davies's 'Little Man' being pitied as a just one cog in the great wheel of society who has little control over his own destiny. Yet characters like 'Uncle Son' find solace in traditional aspects of working-class culture. In 'Holiday' Davies returns to attractions of the seaside and the comfort that family communal tea drinking brings in 'Have A Cuppa Tea'. Ultimately, in 'Muswell Hillbilly', the displaced working-class refuses to change their way of living, retain their cockney pride and resist becoming conformists. In the Kinks' England, the working-class continue to enjoy what Hoggart referred to as their 'mild hedonism'.[136] All three aspects of Davies' politics: 'Patriotic Conservative', 'Orwellian Socialist' and 'Working Class Populist' battle for position in the lives of the 'Muswell Hillbillies'. Yet ultimately it is 'class' that is the source of identity, anxiety and experience.

Ray Davies, the Kinks and English social history

Between 1965 and 1971, Ray Davies and the Kinks presented a body of work that chartered and critiqued political, social and cultural aspects of the post-war English society. The Kinks would continue to write, record and perform through to the 1990s, and although they became less commercially successful, they retained a focus on documenting social change and trying to make sense of the recent past. 'Demolition' (1973) attacks property speculation, 'Shepherds of the Nation' (1974) is a mocking critique of Mary Whitehouse and the Festival of Light. 'Nine To Five' and 'Rush Hour Blues' (both 1974) chart the continued drudgery of working-life. Pragmatism and resignation in the face of adversity is again celebrated in 'Have Another Drink' and 'Holiday Romance' (both 1974). A critique of punk and the counter-culture is provided by 'Prince of the Punks' (1976) and 'Misfits' (1977). The new hard-right version of Toryism is satirised in 'Young Conservatives' (1983) and directly attacked by Dave Davies in 'Dear Margaret' (1988). More recently, Ray Davies returned to his 'Little Man' persona in 'Yours Truly, Confused N10' (2002) a populist rant at contemporary English society.

The critique of the post-war English politics in the music of the Kinks goes some way to explaining the complex politics of Ray Davies. In *X-Ray* he concludes that 'the sixties were a con, the establishment still ruled the country'.[137] Davies here echoes the view of Orwell whose 'England is a family with the wrong members in control'.[138] Street claims that in response to the Musicians' Union call for help with Labour's campaign in the 1974 general election Davies replied that he would be voting Conservative.[139] Yet in later interviews he claimed that he has never voted, but 'when he heard of Labour leaders' John Smith's death on the car radio, he was so moved that he sought comfort in a nearby church'.[140] In his pessimistic reading of popular music

Harker claimed that '[t]hose who 'make it' will continue to be, by and large, the mindless, spineless creatures that pop stars have traditionally been'.[141] Yet the Kinks continued to provide insights into the contemporary condition of England. They refused to play Sun City and Dave wrote a song castigating the politics of Thatcherism. In his autobiography he argued that 'Thatcher had made her killing…leaving in her wake a wave of misery unprecedented this side of the war'.[142]

This chapter has outlined the way in which the music of the Kinks represents an essential source for making sense of the sixties and the experience of the working-class in this much mythologised decade. There is a broad literature on the films and books of the period and how they were reflecting and articulating social change. The music of the Kinks can be used in the same way. However, I would make greater claims for the utility of the Kinks. The songs of Ray Davies often go beyond the rhetoric/mythology of the sixties, and as a particular type of social historian, he exhibited an acute sense of the nuances of the English social structure and the everyday experiences of the working-class. The sweep of the songs ensures that there is a sense of the national, the local and the personal. As an 'organic intellectual', Davies used popular music to make sense of the past and the present in such a way that it connected with the record-buying public in general and working-class youth in particular.

Part III
Glam/Punk England

In both America and Britain hundreds of highly masculine young men are following the more bizarre idols by making-up their faces. (*Daily Mirror*, 4 September 1972)

Sure, Brian wears spangles, feathers and rouge. But the trappings that can make a girl look like a million dollors make Brian and the lads seem frightening. If they were pretty boys The Sweet wouldn't be so sinister. But they are a tough-looking crew and their make-up makes them look worse. (*Daily Mirror*, 20 February 1973)

I don't think that most people know the true facts about the hysterical scenes which occur at pop concerts ... I was disturbed ... the fans were in a state of hysteria. (Letter to *Jackie*, 2 June 1973)

I am really sick of the canned plastic which is today churned out under the misleading title of music. Who can be stupid enough to think that such esteemed hit makers as Slade and Gary Glitter are real musicians ... they are degrading the once high standards of music. (Letter to *Jackie*, 6 October 1973)

I dreamt last night...I was in a ruined city, the suburbs. Earth had been attacked by giant red-glowing spiders, from Mars (Bowie?) and the planet was devastated. (Johnny Black diary entry, 4 July 1974)

7

Aliens in England: Slade, David Bowie, Ziggy Stardust and Glam Rock

The literature on popular music has tended to ignore the development and impact of glam rock on working-class youth culture.[1] The film director Todd Haynes claims that it fell 'through the cracks of pop cultural memory'.[2] Part of the neglect of glam rock is linked to the perceived inauthentic nature of the music and the patterns of consumption associated with the genre.[3] Where researchers have tackled glam rock, it has often been through biographical studies of David Bowie and Marc Bolan, and narrative histories of groups such as Roxy Music and T-Rex.[4] Yet glam rock more generally contained many of the attributes of the punk rock culture that followed, was arguably more politically and socially transgressive and generated a much broader popular appeal.[5]

Glam rock appeared in a period of economic instability in which working-class radicalism played a pivotal role.[6] According to Sandbrook, 'politics and culture in the 1970s were saturated in class-consciousness'.[7] Glam rock provides a distinctive lens through which a particular vision of England comes into a focus highlighting the continuities and ruptures in working-class culture in the years 1970–74. The scene was based on more than just the innovations of particular performers, impresarios and record company executives. Glam rock provided a mental and physical space that can be read as a cultural force through which sections of working-class youth sought to challenge existing gender and sexual identities.[8] Moreover, glam rock did not represent a flight from class but was a restatement of its collective values and hedonistic cultures.

This chapter explores working-class youth and their response to glam rock highlighting the personal, collective and regional experiences that framed the 'popular' embrace of this much maligned musical genre and fashion style.[9] It traces the presentation and consumption of glam rock through an exploration of the overtly working-class identity promoted by Slade and examines the social and political impact of David Bowie and his Ziggy Stardust persona in the years 1972–3. The particular image of England that glam rock provides is one where working-class youth continued to simultaneously reject and embrace elements of a culture that was forged in the factories, mines and industrial towns but on the periphery now sparkled with glitter, stardust and the appearance of aliens on the high street.

Hoskyns sees the appearance of T-Rex on *Top of the Pops* on 11 March 1971, performing 'Hot Love' as the birth of glam rock.[10] Yet others have marked the beginning with the performance of David Bowie and the Hype at London's Roundhouse in February 1970 in which the group wore outlandish clothes.[11] A suitable end point of glam rock can be marked by the cinematic release of the preposterous Gary Glitter film *Remember Me This Way* in June 1974.[12] By this time the major glam rock artists, most notably David Bowie, Marc Bolan and Slade were changing their image, musical direction and, in the case of the latter, beginning to have less commercial success.

In his popular history of the 1970s, Haslam claims that the performers who created glam rock 'consciously distanced themselves from the 1960s'.[13] This was an attempt to move beyond the seriousness that some performers had articulated in their engagement with the politics of the counter-culture. Similarly, Street who devotes only two pages of his book to glam rock claims that 'Glitter replaced the rhetoric, sequins replaced beads and decadence replaced politics'.[14] Likewise, Auslander argues that glam rock was a reaction 'against the obligation to be socially conscious'.[15] To Novick and Middles, glam rock more generally 'laughed in the face of all that pompous pseudo-intellectualism'.[16] Taylor and Wall went even further and claimed rather conspiratorially that it was 'the vehicle of a capitalist ideology'.[17] Yet other writers claim that a more complex politics was embedded in glam rock. Thompson argues that it was 'a social revolution, a cultural uprising, an erotic explosion and a moral reassessment'.[18] Auslander stresses that glam rock created 'safe spaces' for the expression of gender and sexual experimentation.[19] For Hebdige, it was crucial in shifting the focus of popular music 'away from class and...onto sexuality and gender'.[20] Yet this is only a partial reading of glam rock and one that neglects a detailed examination of the experiences of working-class youth who through exposure to and involvement in the scene played an informal but significant role in campaigns for sexual equality and challenging existing conceptions of masculinity and femininity. Leng has noted that many of the 'glam artists were working-class'. This no doubt gave them some legitimacy in presenting glam rock to the masses in the English provinces.[21] A review of a T-Rex show at Belle Vue, Manchester in June 1972 provides a portrait: 'They're a young audience...a good number of them male...a bit of facial tinsel here and there, the odd colourful slash of satin or velvet, the occasional corkscrew cut...a boy and his girl, heavily sequinned about the eyes'.[22]

Brake saw the spatial changes in leisure venues as a contributory factor to the popularity and consumption of the glam culture with 'old dance halls…replaced by the new provincial city leisure centres and discothèques' leading to an 'embourgeoisment of leisure'.[23] This process was part of the continued exploitation of a definable youth market that was both embraced and critiqued by teenage consumers. A letter to *Jackie,*[24] the popular magazine aimed at young girls, was indicative: 'I can occasionally afford a single at 50p a time, but at £2.50, albums are completely out of my price range. Then there's discos. I get 50p pocket money a week, but some of those places charge that much to get in…It's about time somebody put an end to this exploitation'.[25]

As with popular music genres discussed in previous chapters the sparkle of glitter and glam acted as a metropolitan magnet attracting working-class youths in search of adventure, romance and hedonism to some of England's bigger cities. The experience of a T-Rex fan from rural Wales is illustrative: 'the lure of the big city was very strong…When I moved to Leeds I got in touch with a Bolanite'.[26] The development of such networks of fans consolidated shared identities and often laid the basis of a collective challenge to existing perceptions of gender and sexuality. For the more isolated consumers of glam rock the scene offered escape from the drudgery of everyday life. Philip Cato grew up in Rugeley in the West Midlands and first encountered glam rock in 1970 when he heard the T-Rex single 'Ride A White Swan'. While still in his local comprehensive school he joined the T-Rex fan Club.[27] A year later his postman father had been involved in a lengthy strike that placed enormous pressure on the family, but Cato found some solace in the music.[28]

Concerns about environmental destruction and the urban and industrial decay that was beginning to blight the appearance of English cities all fed into the imagery, message, performance and consumption of glam rock.[29] In August 1972, *Jackie* carried out one of its periodic 'on-the-spot' interviews with regional readers asking them 'how do you visualise life on other planets'? Pat Straughan from County Durham imagined that 'life on another planet would be great…no wars, no arguments and no unhappiness'.[30] The yearning for both mental and physical escape expressed by some working-class youths was fed by two very different types of performers in Slade and David Bowie. Slade offered an affirmation of class and the promotion of a hedonism that could provide insulation against the alienation and boredom that youths experienced in the workplace, the home and the localities in which they resided. In contrast, Bowie offered a temporary flight from class, gender and sexual norms through the construction of transgressive characters, other worlds and alien imagery.

Idols of the working-class: Slade, Skinheads and glam rock

Slade have been marginalised in studies of English popular music. Yet the fact that they breached the rhythm and blues boom, skinhead and glam rock ensured that they made a significant contribution to working-class youth culture. The group hailed from Wolverhampton in the West Midlands and exploited their working-class roots and identity. They gained a large working-class following across the country and were a significant presence in the music charts, magazines and newspapers.[31] Slade consisted of Noddy Holder (vocals), Dave Hill (guitar), Jim Lea (bass), and Don Powell (drums) and had formed as the N'Betweens in 1966. All were working-class, with Hill, according to one biographer, being particularly 'over-conscious of his working class background'.[32] He had failed the 11-plus along with Lea and Powell. Holder, whose father was a window cleaner passed the examination but within a year was in a comprehensive school.

Slade were steeped in the industrial working-class culture of the West Midlands with its football, pubs, clubs and associated leisure activities.[33] By the early 1960s, Wolverhampton had already hosted concerts by Bill Haley, Buddy Holly, Chuck Berry and Jerry Lee Lewis and rock 'n' roll dance sessions in venues such as the Gaumont and the Civic Hall. The fact that Slade remained connected to such a culture struck a chord with their largely working-class audiences but ensured that critical acclaim would be given more grudgingly by both contemporary writers and subsequent historians. Holder had made his debut in front a live audience in 1953 at Walsall Labour Club where he gave a rendition of Frankie Laine's 'I Believe'.[34] He later recalled that the working men's clubs were an essential 'part of the community'.[35] Such spaces were a point of continuity connecting working-class youth to a pre-war culture that had been constructed in the foundries, mines and engineering plants of the West Midlands. When the photographer John Bulmer visited the Black Country in 1961, he noted the continued existence of such culture where there was 'nowhere warm to stay and the pubs served only pork scratchings for food'.[36]

Class remained a constant point of reference in Slade's career. Tremlett prefaced his 1975 history of the group with the claim that 'pop music is as thoroughly working class in its origins in this country as dog racing, soccer, fish and chips and Mitchells and Butlers Mild'.[37] He also utilised rhetoric that would be adopted by the nascent punk scene a year later in claiming that music before the glam scene was 'over-blown and self-indulgent'.[38] Their manager, Chas Chandler, also acknowledged the local identity that was implicit in Slade's image and performance: 'When I met them they were just a bunch of young Skinheads from Wolverhampton'.[39] In fact the group had never been Skinheads and the look, image and attitude was one that had been suggested by their manager to exploit the trend that had recently gained wide coverage in the media.

English Skinheads have been neglected by historians and the work that does exist presents a rather one-dimensional portrait of their musical affiliations and social behaviour.[40] The Skinhead style with its particular uniform and embrace of West Indian Ska music emerged in 1967–9 and remained a visible presence on English streets through to the emergence of glam rock in 1971–2. It was distinctly working-class and became associated with vandalism, street violence, football hooliganism, racism and far-right politics.[41] According to Bushell, 'class was a major factor in skinhead thinking'.[42] One member of London's Collinwood gang interviewed in 1970 claimed that Skinhead 'was a working-class movement', while another argued that it was the 'class gap' that was 'responsible for the world we live in'.[43] Skinhead culture was exploited by the pulp novelist Richard Allen in *Skinhead* (1970) and the associated 'suedehead' style was depicted in Barney Platts-Mills film *Bronco Bullfrog* (1969).[44] In a recent memoir, Pauline Black, the singer of the multiracial group the Selecter, recalled that it was 'a bunch of white skinhead girls who turned the only black kid in school on to ska music'.[45] Here was a nuanced example of the way in which the class and racial identities were being problematised through the consumption of popular music and youth culture.[46] The Collinwood gang was also 'racially mixed...including West Indians...Jewish, Irish and English'.[47] Yet this did not prevent them from carrying out vicious attacks on the Asians in what they termed 'paki-bashing'.[48]

Popular magazines such as *Jackie* also provide an insight into working-class Skinheads that challenge the more hysterical depictions in the contemporary tabloid press. In one letter from a reader in Leigh, the Skinhead is presented as someone who is generally law abiding and who views political protest marches as the preserve of the educated middle classes: 'It isn't skinheads that are causing disturbances at schools and colleges or damaging embassies and fighting with policemen at demos'.[49] The contributor was no doubt more attuned to the traditional forms of working-class political culture in her town such as the Lancashire Miners' Gala, the electoral campaigns of the Labour Party and the picket lines that had been organised at Parsonage and Bickershaw collieries, which contributed to a victory for the miners in the national strike that had run from 2 January through the 28 February 1972.[50] Another Skinhead and Slade fan felt moved to present a poetic representation.

Bovver boots with yellow laces
Half-mast jeans held-up with braces
Sta-prest worn to match his shirt
Doc Martins shine, they no dirt
Prince of Wales check make-up his suits
With coloured socks, he wears his boots
Crombies were his winter gear
Harrington's now that summer's here
He wears lots more than I've just said
But these are the facts about a SKINHEAD[51]

Barbara Martin told readers that in Rochester, Kent Skinhead girls were now copying the boys by committing acts of violence and vandalism: 'at my local disco, the girls are always fighting, almost killing each other'.[52] Miranda Winterburn from Somerset provided a feminist twist to the attitudes and behaviour of Skinhead girls: 'In this age of Women's Lib, I'd have thought that girls acting tough is an understood thing. Boys hit each other, why can't we?'[53] A Skinhead from County Durham penned a 'Skinhead Anthem'.

We are skinheads big and strong
And this is our little song
Dr Martins, Bovver boots
Levi gear for our suits
Short trousers held up by braces
Short hair so you can see our faces
Checky Ben Shermans too
This is what we offer you.
Levi, Wrangler and StaPress
We hate hairies "what a mess",
Scooter boys, greasers and all the rest.
We say skinheads are the best.
A skin a king.
This is what we shall sing
We shall shout and call
'Cos we skins love football
B-O-V-V-E-R[54]

Slade's music and attitude presented to Skinheads an indigenous class-based identity that complemented the West Indian ska music that soundtracked much of their daily lives. Here was a group that was accessible and rooted in the cultures and communities from which the skinhead subculture had emerged. Holder later recalled that 'skinheads ... used to stamp their feet in time to our songs. It was perfect ... because they wore such big boots'.[55] Cato remembered that gangs of Skinheads who descended on Molyneux to cheer on Wolverhampton Wanderers were all Slade fans. At his local youth club Slade's 'Get Down and Get With It', 'was a call to arms'.[56] Slade's flirtation with the Skinhead style was short-lived stretching from 1969 to 1970, but it cemented the group to a working-class fan base that quickly multiplied and was carried through into their embrace of glam rock. Their single 'Cuz I Luv You' topped the charts in November 1971 and was followed by five further number ones. The energy of their concerts was captured on the *Slade Alive* album that was a huge success in 1972.[57]

Slade constantly emphasised their 'class credentials' and identification with the industrial midlands and northern England. Hill informed *Phonograph Record* that 'being as we've worked with the working class people – they're the ones who're with us now'. In an interview with the *Record Mirror,* he referred to his background, being the lowest in his class at school and feeling that when he once dated a middle-class girl he felt that he was 'getting way out of my class'.[58] Holder also stressed that Slade 'we're a workin' class band, workin' class kids'.[59] A concert review from February 1972 noted a contrast between Slade's audience and that of the Beatles and the Rolling Stones in the 1960s: 'Not so much the screaming-type hysteria as party-type uproar. Blokes and birds get together to have a good time'.[60] The concert took place during a national miners' strike in which daily news bulletins presented images of picket line activity and the impact of working-class solidarity.

The *New Musical Express* also viewed the appeal of Slade in 'class terms': 'To ... the working class audiences they attract ... Slade is one of your mates made good'.[61] Altham described them as 'The Workers' Playtime Band' performing music at 'factory floor level, a place where it's ... at its most ... most truthful'.[62] Nick Kent claimed Slade were a counterpoint to the 'Bowies, Bolans and Roxies whose individual ventures are little more than ... offcuts from the dominant middle-class tradition'.[63] The association between working-class youth and Slade was made most explicitly by Chris Charlesworth in a piece in *Melody Maker* in September 1972, where he hailed them as 'idols of the working class'. He presented a portrait of Jack and Jill who were avid fans of the group.

> Jack is 16 years old. Having left school he's having difficulty finding a job ... He likes to wear check shirts and his braces hold up jeans ... They're a bit too short, and this reveals the boots he often uses to stamp his feet hard and occasionally kick people ... Jill is 15 years old. She's left school too and has had a couple of jobs as shop assistants ... She's cut her hair fairly short, and ... has a lot of friends who look very much like her.[64]

Similarly, a report of a Slade concert in 1973 provides another description of a typical fan and the atmosphere created by their performance.

> He's a working class hero with a lecherous grin. Not that tall, he'd be considerably shorter without the four-inch platform shoes ... He speaks with a broad Midlands accent. He is arrogant and loud mouthed ... Hours of work must go into the construction of the top hats worn at the gigs. Usually covered in silver discs – or silver paper ... Scarves are daubed with slogans written with felt pens – knickers and bras are carefully embroidered before being thrown stagewards.[65]

This example of the way in which some young people were connecting with the group shows that they did not have to shop in expensive boutiques or follow the advice of magazines in developing a glam rock style. Unlike T-Rex whose appeal was primarily aimed at teenage girls, Slade's fan base had a masculine working-class dimension that nonetheless engaged with the fashions and style that the group exploited. According to Holder, it was Slade who were the pioneers of wearing platform shoes before the other glam performers.[66] Hill took this to another level with a whole wardrobe of outlandish jackets, head-gear and boots. An insight into his preparation for the stage is provided by *Melody Maker* in September 1972: 'Hill is spraying his hair with lacquer and sprinkling spark dust on to it. He also spreads paste on his forehead and gums more sparkle on to that'.[67]

Slade aimed to retain a link with a pre-war working-class that seemed to be undergoing a process of change that came with the demolition of terraced streets and the communities and cultures that they had engendered.[68] They did not depict such a process lyrically, but through the articulation of a working-class hedonism that could still be felt in the pubs, clubs and football terraces of the English Midlands and the industrial North. As the group were beginning to enjoy national success throughout 1972, Holder told *Sounds* that the 'image came out of the Black Country and we've stayed loyal to that image' and that 'Wolverhampton provided Slade with 'their own kind of security against change'.[69]

Slade played two shows at the London Palladium on 7 January 1973, as part of the Conservative Government's Fanfare for Europe celebrations marking Britain's entry into the European Common Market.[70] They were supported by Geordie from Newcastle emphasising a working-class, regional presence. A review in *Sounds* described the scene: 'Dressed in silver toppers, knitted hats, football scarfs and waving banners...a football crowd without, thankfully, the knuckle'.[71] The Kinks also performed as part of the celebrations a week later at the Theatre Royal Drury Lane where they played a selection of songs from their *Village Green Preservation Society* album against a backdrop of historic and contemporary English imagery. The two concerts provided a snap-shot of a working-class England – where it had come from and perhaps where it was going.

Thompson argues that Slade were as much responsible for challenging gender and sexual identities as David Bowie.[72] In terms of their popular reach this is undoubtedly the case. Slade made the front page of the London *Evening Standard* and their tours into 1974/5 generated large audiences.[73] They reached across genders and were featured regularly in *Jackie, Mirabelle* and similar publications aimed at teenage girls. Throughout 1972, Slade were more prominently featured in *Jackie* than Bowie and the other stars of glam rock. The expression of class that underpinned their image, attitude and performance provided a bridge between the pre-war world of Hoggart's solidaristic communities and the contemporary class experiences of inner-city youth that had been rehoused in the tower blocks and estates of 1970s England.[74] Yet it was Bowie that proved to be the most effective in leaving a lasting impression on teenagers who felt that aspects of their working-class localities could be oppressive and restrictive in terms of enforcing particular gender and sexual identities.

David Bowie and sexual politics

A number of writers have examined the relationship between popular music and sexual politics.[75] Personal testimony has also been provided by a number of performers who forged careers in the music industry in the 1980s.[76] Gill has noted that the emergence of glam rock 'coincided with the burgeoning gay scene, and the two worlds blurred into each other'.[77] This process is most marked in the career, songs, image and performance of David Bowie and in particular through his Ziggy Stardust persona. Bowie introduced images drawn from a metropolitan gay subculture to a largely heterosexual working-class audience providing a rallying cry to those who were seeking to break with the sexual and gender norms of their particular social milieu.

Bowie's career was forged in the rhythm and blues scene of 1960s. His father was a charity worker and his mother a cinema usherette. He failed the 11-plus and set out to make a career in the entertainment business.[78] As David Jones he had catered to the Mod subculture performing with the Mannish Boys at Chicksands USAF base and at key venues such as the Scene Club.[79] In 1965, he changed his name to Bowie. He then travelled through the counter-cultural scene before performing as David Bowie and the Hype on 22 February 1970, at the Roundhouse in London where he exhibited his penchant for cross-dressing and androgyny.[80] In March of the same year, a profile of Bowie appeared in the gay magazine *Jeremy*, a move that his manager felt would lead to the possible exploitation of that particular subculture.[81] By this time, Bowie had released a hit single 'Space Oddity' (1969) and three albums *David Bowie* (1967), *Space Oddity* (1969) and *The Man Who Sold the World* (1970), which all failed to make the Top Twenty. Yet it was *Hunky Dory* (1971) that gave him a significant national profile and proved to be catalyst for the commercial success of *The Rise and Fall of Ziggy Stardust and the Spiders from Mars*, which was released a year later. In a fascinating collection of fan letters edited by Vermorel the strangeness and attractiveness of Bowie is made apparent. Bernard is one example: 'From an early age I was interested in science fiction and space things like paranormal beings. And Bowie was a personification of that kind of thing... he didn't look like a boy and he didn't look like a girl'.[82] Julie thought that he 'was science fiction personified... not of this world... an alien of some kind'.[83]

Frequenting London's gay clubs such as the Sombrero, Bowie started to write songs for the Ziggy Stardust album in January 1971.[84] This was complemented by his exposure to the subversive world of Andy Warhol, whose production of *Pork* was performed in London at the Roundhouse in August.[85] It was Bowie's ability to exploit elements of particular subcultures and present them in a more popular form that secured his connection to working-class youth culture. On 25 September, Bowie applied make-up at a performance at the Friar's Club, Aylesbury, and on 4 October, he played a benefit show for the Gay Liberation Front (GLF) in London.[86] The GLF had roots in campaigns for decriminalisation of homosexuality and in the broader culture of the British New Left.[87] According to Beckett, by '1971 the British GLF had too many members to hold its meetings in borrowed LSE classrooms'.[88] The GLF developed a presence in leftist organisations and increased its role in direct action and mass demonstrations alongside trade unionists and community activists.[89] Yet within the organisational politics of gay liberation, class remained a source of tension. Burton's memoirs illustrate the resilience of class stressing that particular forms of gay politics were 'irredeemably middle class'.[90]

Bowie was never an active figure in the politics of the GLF and the effectiveness of his message was mostly visual but nonetheless effective. According to Taylor and Wall, he had been 'strategically marketed as a new kind of media product'.[91] This may well be the case, but the consumption of Bowie's recordings, image and sensibility did have a particular impact on sections of working-class youth that provided both a statement 'of' and a temporary flight 'from' class. At the height of Bowie's pomp, class, masculinity and sexuality were discussed in youth magazines, school yards, clubs and workplaces and how and where he fitted into these particular categories of self-definition. A profile in *Melody Maker* in 1972 described Bowie as 'a gorgeously effeminate boy…as camp as a row of tents, with his limp hand and trolling vocabulary'.[92] The article informed readers that at a performance in London 'about half the gay population of the city turned up to see him…He supposes he's what people call bisexual'.[93] In response, one youth from Derby posted a letter to the Bowie fan club claiming that 'if Bowie really is gay then a few guys will have to take a second look at the gay world'.[94]

Yet Bowie distanced himself from formal political engagement. When asked in an interview with the *New Musical Express* whether he was 'into' revolutionary politics, he replied: 'I could never take all that seriously'.[95] Yet the gay press saw only positives in Bowie's impact on youth culture and popular music. A *Gay News* review of his performance at the Rainbow Theatre, London in 1972 claimed that 'whether the gay aspects of his act are just part of the show…are unimportant. His defiance of accepted social conventions…does much to break down barriers'.[96] In a later edition, Bowie was awarded the status of their 'artist of the year'.[97] This was in the context of homophobia on the streets of England. Marc Bolan told a reporter of the regular verbal assaults he faced 'with remarks like "you little poof"'.[98] Bowie also informed the press that he was 'called a queer and all sorts of things'.[99] Such experiences were shared by working-class youths drawn to his music and persona. Stuart Dalzell was a 14-year-old 'closet gay' and was 'attracted to the sexual ambiguity that Bowie radiated'.[100] Victor Wheeler also felt that Bowie's 'other worldliness and ambiguous style' gave boys like himself 'something edgy'.[101]

As Bowie was appearing in provincial clubs and theatres, teenage girls started to pose their own questions relating to inequalities in English society. In December 1971 and January 1972, *Jackie* carried out interviews asking readers what resolutions they would be making for the coming year. Karen Morley of Malvern, Worcestershire was clear in her particular intentions: 'I support women's lib…I'd like mankind to recognise the real potential of women, and start treating them as equals'.[102] Sylvia Guy from Dagenham was unhappy with the current state of the economy and women's position within the workplace: 'I would make a resolution to get rid of all unemployment in Britain. And how about more money for girls – we're never paid as much as men for the same job'.[103] Elizabeth Hart from Darlington presented her contribution with a flavour of anarchist rhetoric: 'We spend most of our lives fitting in with a system and doing what's expected of us instead of doing what we want. I think it's a great shame that most people waste their lives away following rules, so I'd like to see more freedom in 1972'.[104] Another reader felt that the presentation of pop stars in the magazine was fuelling the cause for women's liberation through its simplistic portrayal of what its female consumers wanted to read.

> Have you ever considered that *Jackie* and magazines like it, are the cause of women's lib? Every article tells you either how to get your man, or please your boyfriend. Your pages lead us to believe that blokes are the be all and end all. In fact I lost an argument on Women's Lib the other day when a boy asked me why, if I believed in it, why I read magazines that make the male species into demi-gods. I couldn't answer! So please, *Jackie*, let's have articles on horses or even embroidery – anything but men.[105]

A letter from a young girl in Birmingham pointed to the continued existence of racial tensions in English town and cities: 'I have a fantastic boyfriend ... but my friends look down on me and I can't take him home ... because he's black. You don't really appreciate the evil of discrimination, until it involves you personally'.[106] A month earlier, John Leaman from Birmingham had written to *Jackie* with his New Year wish: 'I'd get people like Enoch Powell to resolve to think more and talk less. I feel that he can do a lot of harm for race relations'.[107] Other letters to the magazine exhibited the 'do-it-yourself' ethos of glam rock that pushed against the dictates of the fashion industry. Yvonne Williams from Bolton argued that she was now 'free' and 'liberated', claiming 'I'm going to wear whatever I want to, instead of being *told* what to wear by "fashion designers" ... I am no longer going to be treated as an empty-headed fashion slave'.[108]

The national press presented its own populist characterisation of glam rock and its blurring of gender identities. The *Daily Mirror* claimed that it 'was difficult enough to tell the boys from the birds, when fellas grew their hair long. It's ... even harder now'.[109] Yet the media played an essential role in popularising the scene that it caricatured. According to Bracewell, 'Boots and the new Miss Selfridge ... were meeting the demand for ... lip gloss, re-routing space age glamour to the precinct and the High Street'.[110] In an unpublished piece by Steve Turner written in 1974, a sense of Bowie's cross gender and sexually ambiguous appeal is also evident: 'There are as many Bowie imitators in the stands at Millwall of a Saturday afternoon as there are in the canteen of the Royal College of Art on a weekday. One group would see him in terms of rebellion and glamour while the other see him as the man most responsible for making the world a safer place for closet queens'.[111] The arrival of Bowie's Ziggy Stardust character on stage and television screen extended the range and scope of his androgynous image and cemented his place in the discourse of playground banter, subcultural identity and family conversations over the breakfast table.

Ziggy Stardust and 'crisis' in England

Bowie released *The Rise and Fall of Ziggy Stardust and the Spiders from Mars* on 6 June 1972.[112] The Ziggy character was an amalgam of various individuals and fictional characters that he had encountered in recent years including the English rocker 'n' roller Vince Taylor[113], the American singer the Legendary Stardust Cowboy[114] and, according to Doggett, Johnny Angelo, a character from a pulp novel by Nick Cohn.[115] In an interview with *Rolling Stone* in 1974 Bowie articulated the basic ideas behind Ziggy.

> The time is five years to go before the end of the earth…the world will end because of a lack of natural resources…Ziggy is advised in a dream…to write the coming of a Starman…The starmen are called infinites…spacemen who will be coming down to save the earth…He takes himself up to incredible spiritual heights and is kept alive by his disciples. When the infinites arrive, they take bits of Ziggy to make themselves real…And tear him to pieces on stage.[116]

To Hebdige, 'Bowie was 'uninterested either in contemporary political and social issues or in working-class life in general'.[117] Yet Ziggy Stardust can be seen as an example of how Bowie was framing and articulating a sense of 'crisis' in English society.[118] Although the album lacked a clear narrative structure, listeners nonetheless created their own set of interpretations that captured their feelings, thoughts and anxieties.[119] Doggett notes that within Ziggy, there was a 'sense of the occult – the hidden, the esoteric, the satanic, the alien, the mythological, the divine'.[120] Ziggy was a further addition to the cultural diet of working-class youth, which included elements of the fantastic, mystical and horrific found in the films of Hammer and Amicus, Dennis Wheatley novels, Von Daniken's accounts of alien civilisations and the martial arts of Bruce Lee.[121]

Alongside references to Mars, stardust, apocalypse and suicide, Bowie also passed comment on the politics of Aneurin Bevan[122] and the escalation of violence in Northern Ireland.[123] Turner claims that Bowie was 'the first rock artist to…admit the failure of post-war dreams of progress and to offer instead an escape into fantasy'.[124] To Bracewell, Ziggy was a quintessentially English creation and 'suggested precinct mutants from Hulme or Stevenage rather than teenage rebels with an eye to America'.[125] Buckley notes that the album also dealt with minorities in a society in 'crisis': 'a black (cast as a good guy), a gay (who is repulsed by the priest and not the object of society's repulsion for once), a woman (out of control, downtrodden), and a physically handicapped person'.[126] According to Savage, 'this connected with what people were feeling'.[127] For Jake Arnott, Ziggy was a 'glimmer of hope at a time when everything else seemed so dull'.[128] Keith Woodhouse lived in a council tower block in Shoreditch, London and was transfixed by the Ziggy persona depicted on the cover and the music the album contained remembering that 'some tracks were surreal…they were mind blowing'. As a result, he started to wear the Ziggy hair style and 'dabbled with eye liner'.[129]

Bowie had watched a screening of Kubrick's *A Clockwork Orange* at the ABC Cinema in Catford, London on 13 January, and was struck by the fashion, style and attitude of the anti-heroes depicted by the director.[130] The film provides a stunning cinematic companion piece to Ziggy Stardust in exploring the micro-politics of an England seemingly beset by 'crisis'.[131] The film had been released in the context of rising concerns about juvenile delinquency and was linked to one particular seemingly copy-cat murder of 'an old tramp'.[132] The newspapers throughout the year regularly featured accounts of rampaging gangs of football hooligans and outbreaks of vandalism in English towns and cities.[133] Bowie had earlier documented such violence in 'Life on Mars' (1971).

The first Bowie concert as Ziggy was staged at Friars, Aylesbury on 29 February and was followed by a small show in the Toby Jug Pub in Tolworth, London.[134] Stephen King recalled that he 'had never seen or heard anything like it before'.[135] On 25 June, the first sell-out show was performed at the Croydon Greyhound with support by Roxy Music.[136] A review of a Bowie concert in Kent a few nights earlier proved to be a significant event for the reporter who reviewed the performance for *Melody Maker*: 'something strange was happening up there on stage…The attendants at the exits looked twice to see if they could believe their eyes…The men knew but the little girls didn't understand…It should be recorded that the first act of fellatio on a musical instrument in the British Isles took place at Dunstable Civic Hall'.[137] The review also presented a portrait of a typical Bowie fan.

> Jim had almost to pinch himself when he first heard such a grand person was actually coming…Privately his mother confided that he found it difficult to make friends at work…He was wearing his red scarf, flung nonchalantly over his shoulder, and his red platform boots. His hair was long down the back but cropped fairly short on top so that it stuck up when he brushed his fingers through it. He hated that it was dark brown. He'd promised himself that when he eventually split to London he'd have it done bright blond. He was just turned 19.[138]

On 1 July, Ziggy appeared at the Winter Gardens Pavilion, Weston-super-Mare. A few hours earlier, the first Gay Pride march weaved its way from Trafalgar Square to Hyde Park. Five days later, Bowie appeared on *Top of the Pops*. Dylan Jones was transfixed by his rendition of 'Starman' claiming that it was 'the day that made many of us go out and get our hair cut, or dyed orange, or both'.[139] Bowie's performance on the show and subsequent concerts proved to be moments of epiphany for those who had been seeking affirmation for their individual acts of social and sexual transgression. As Taylor and Wall noted, Bowie music in particular and glam rock more generally became 'known ... as 'faggot-rock' ... music for gays'.[140] Yet irrespective of the association between Bowie, glam rock and homosexuality many tough working-class boys were attracted to its appeal.

The Sweet were a working-class group who had already reached a wide audience in promoting male femininity and cross-dressing. Their guitarist Steve Priest claimed that he had been the target of homosexual advances, so he decided to play up to the image. According to Thompson, by the time of Bowie's appearance on *Top of the Pops* in July, 'Priest had been wearing his hot pants and putting like a princess for almost four months'.[141] The group's concerts were often raucous affairs, and as a result, they were banned from a number of Mecca ballrooms in 1972–3.[142] The working-class humour through which Sweet's glam rock was delivered was not taken as seriously as Bowie's transgressions, yet it was indicative of a more light-hearted engagement with the genre.[143] Sweet, Slade, Roxy Music and T-Rex all adorned themselves with outrageous clothes, but it was Bowie who gave the glam rock look a more nuanced sexual twist and partly explains why his performance of 'Starman' on BBC television became lodged in the collective memory.

After Bowie's appearance on *Top of the Pops,* his fan club received an increased volume of letters. From across the country, young converts were identifying with the seemingly confused but nonetheless potent message that they perceived to be embedded in the Ziggy character. Candy, a self-proclaimed 'Bowie freak' from Folkestone, Kent was moved to pen the following tribute.

> You have a special magic
> That the others cannot find.
> You're a star that will never fade,
> One of the rarest kind.
>
> Androgynous beauty,
> Your pale haunting face,
> Belongs to another time,
> And a different race.
> Yet some don't understand,
> Make snide remarks and jeer,
> What can you tell them
> The ones who will not hear

> You're almost a living legend,
> With your thoughts among the stars.
> David I love you very much,
> Did you really come from Mars?[144]

According to Hebdige, 'each Bowie concert performed in drab provincial cinemas and Victorian town halls attracted a host of startling Bowie lookalikes'.[145] After a show at the Festival Hall in London on 8 July, *Gay News* reported that '[e]ven the pubescent girls who'd spent their Saturday-mornings-at-Woolies wages on a seat, or crowded into the gangways screamed'.[146] There was some worry about rising levels of vandalism and violence that seemed to accompany the concerts. Bowie's manager informed the *Daily Mirror* that 'David is concerned about violence. He has often had a feeling of menace... It can be very intimidating'.[147]

Sandbrook notes the impact of Bowie but holds back on emphasising the transformative nature of his music, image and style, merely noting that 'fans who followed Bowie's lead and came out of the closet often encountered far more hostility than he did'.[148] Yet the contemporary testimonies and later recollections suggest that the experience was more nuanced than Sandbrook suggests. Victor Wheeler attended one of the shows at London's Rainbow theatre on 19–20 August: 'Tanked-topped up on cheap cans of John Courage from our local "offy"[149] – we couldn't believe our luck being down the front... We were so excited, the sweetly hemp scented, hazed atmosphere electric'.[150] At the same show Chris Welch writing for *Melody Maker* claimed that one 'of the most memorable moments... came when David appeared in natty red underwear on the highest platform, there to strike unnatural poses, while bathed in soft lighting'.[151] Jackie Cecil recalled the diversity of the crowd at concerts: 'much of the audience had seemed to be made up of sophisticated people in their twenties', but the following show 'was packed to the rafters with teenagers... They had Ziggy haircuts just like mine, satin jackets just like mine'.[152] Steve Fitzgerald lived in council house in Cranham, Essex and discovered Bowie when he was 14: 'Bowie was a bolt out of the blue to me... I wanted to be just like him. His lyrics took me to a different, exciting almost alien world'. He cut his hair into the Ziggy style, sprayed his boots silver and became one of a gang of Bowie fans on his estate.[153]

After a series of performances in the United States, Bowie and Ziggy returned to England in December. Harvey Molloy attended one of the two shows at Manchester's newly opened Hard Rock venue.

> A long queue of people waiting to get into the concert hall. Guys in black velvet top hats, silver stars on their faces; girls in dirty sheepskin coats, blue eye-shadow and maxi skirts. When he sings the finale, I feel like I'm watching Jesus. He leans over the crowd at the end of the stage, his

> outstretched hands taunting the front row audience who would give anything to touch him.[154]

Stephen Morrissey, then a 13-year-old music fan, who later found success as a significant performer and songwriter in his own right, also attended the first Manchester show.[155] After a concert at the Rainbow in January 1973, Charles Shaar Murray writing in the *New Musical Express* gave the following account.

> The Rainbow is crowded with exotic souls of all description. By far the freakiest is dressed and coiffed in classic early stardust sky-blue quilted jump suit, rust-coloured hair cut just so, one earring and simply tons of make-up...On the way back after the tubes had shut, I spied a dejected heap of silver lame in a shop doorway waiting for the morning.[156]

After more American and Japanese tours, Bowie set-off on the final Ziggy tour of Britain in May 1973.[157] A month earlier, he had released the *Alladin Sane* album, which proved to be even more successful than Ziggy, including cover art that sparked many teenage working-class copyists to dye their hair and apply make-up in the form of a lighting flash that adorned Bowie's face. In preparation for Bowie's upcoming concerts, *Gay News* put him on the front cover and penned the following editorial.

> For six weeks this King of Queens will be disturbing the peace from Aberdeen to Torquay with his own ferocious brand of violent eroticism, leaving a trail of shattered fans of all sexes in his wake...we shall be there with the best of them, strewing pampas grass and feather boas in his path.[158]

Paul from Cardiff attended the Earl's Court, London concert on 12 May: 'There were so many outlandish people, men wearing dresses, masses of silver and gold lame – totally outrageous'.[159] Pauline Fitzgerald was at the performance at the Romford Odeon on 22 May and 'couldn't get over all the people dressed up like him'.[160] After his appearance at the Brighton Dome on 25 May, Bowie was banned from any future appearances at the venue because of the damage wrought by fans.[161] The *New Musical Express* noted contrasting scenes in Glasgow and Edinburgh. In Glasgow 'seats have been demolished...couples are observed making it in the back rows...various minor scuffles broke out. Yet there is a much more sedate atmosphere in Edinburgh where the performance is preceded by a Bingo session'.[162]

On 28th May, Ziggy appeared at the Wolverhampton Civic Hall. In Hednesford in the West Midlands working-class youths would gather at Aquarius to exhibit their own engagement with glam style through outlandish hairstyles and clothing. Cato remembers a heavily graffitied wall that faced the local bus station which in four-foot letters contained the message 'BOWIE IS ZIGGY, ZIGGY IS GOD '72.[163] Jane Roberts, an avid reader of *Jackie* and *Melody Maker* and a group of her school friends from Shropshire were escorted by their parents to the Wolverhampton concert and were entranced by the flamboyant clothes and bizarre lyrics. After the show Roberts' transformation to Bowie clone was complete: 'I did go straight home and dye half my hair red with some dye from the local chemist'.[164] Michael Duke was at the show on 3 June in Coventry where the 'front rows were packed with people dressed up like Ziggy' and where he 'lost one of [his] stack heels in the crush at the front'.[165]

At the Liverpool Empire show on 10 June, Stephen Latham recalled that the 'one thing that struck you was his hair; the orange spikey style... clothes, make-up and songs screamed out at you – I'm the man – I am glam rock'.[166] Roy White also went to the Liverpool show as a 14-year-old dressed as Ziggy. He took the bus from Bootle where the excitement and anticipation of seeing Bowie temporarily dissolved the threats that he could have encountered on the streets: 'Fears of being beaten up by skinheads for dressing this way meant nothing. I'd found my niche. My father despaired but I was Ziggy Stardust'.[167] Marc Almond, then 14, also attended the concert.[168] He later claimed that he had been attacked on the way: 'I was a mess of blood, glitter and cheap, badly applied make-up, but in a state of near religious ecstasy'.[169] Stuart Dalzell also cut his hair in the Ziggy style and attended the show at Chatham Central Hall on 12 June. He sat on the front row of the balcony and remembers the seats shaking during the opening song.[170] Dave Mulley caught the bus from Swindon to attend the Salisbury concert on 14 June with his friend: 'We both dressed for the occasion. Me wearing a lilac jacket with shoulder pads and large Oxford bag trousers and my hair in the Ziggy style'.[171] Keith Woodhouse attended the show at the Southampton Guildhall on 19 June during which 'there was a lot of violence'. Ian MacDonald provided another glimpse of a typical Ziggy concert scene for the *New Musical Express*, where 'Stardust lookalikes hang defensively around as Mrs Stardust lookalikes coolly parade the aisles'.[172]

The Ziggy concerts created networks of Bowie fans. On moving to the south coast, Keith Woodhouse gained employment in a boutique in Portsmouth where 'four of the six staff there sported Bowie cuts'.[173] Paul, a 16-year-old fan from Cardiff travelled to the London show with three friends: 'I had my Ziggy haircut, dyed it red and decided to dress like Bowie'.[174] Julie recalled that 'when he killed off Ziggy Stardust at the Hammersmith Odeon on 3 July 1973 that really, really disturbed me... I was crying a lot'.[175] Another Bowie fan penned a letter to the *New Musical Express* in response to Bowie's announcement of Ziggy's retirement: 'Brushing my hair back from its Bowie style and tearing down the photos of him on my wall, I realised he's the only idol we ever had... Thanks a million, David, you made my teenage years worthwhile'.[176] *Gay News* reported that 'outside the theatre young girls and boys gathered in tears...We send our love. We want you around again soon'.[177] The consumption and articulation of Ziggy by working-class consumers represented one strand in an individual and collective contribution to challenging dominant conceptions of masculinity, femininity and sexuality.

Sex, gender, class and glam rock

By 1973 newspapers were describing Bowie as the 'King of Rock and Rouge'.[178] To Haslam, whether 'boys in make-up made a deep or lasting impression is hard to measure. Liverpool, for example, wasn't Ladbroke Grove...most places were harder and less forgiving'.[179] This view is borne out by the experiences of Stephen Latham. He was the 15-year-old son of a diesel engineer and typist and lived in a working-class area of Liverpool, where 'the Ziggy Stardust album was never off the turntable'. Yet Latham didn't change his image: 'I didn't have the courage to dress like Bowie...people thought I was strange for liking him'.[180] In Hull, the home of Spiders guitarist Mick Ronson was vandalised.[181] In their interviews with Sheffield teenagers Taylor and Wall found that the 'attraction of Bowie for the older youth lay in the form and content of his music, but, if asked, they rejected his bisexuality'.[182] Yet other experiences suggest that the reception of Bowie outside of metropolitan centres could be more nuanced. Gill claims that he knew 'heterosexuals whose attitudes about sexual difference were radically altered by the atmosphere of glam...and others began to rethink their prejudices about sexual difference'.[183] *Gay News* also viewed Bowie's popularity as a harbinger for sexual liberation and giving 'gay rock a potent spokesman'.[184]

In the historiography of gay politics there is very little on the relationship between popular music and campaigns for equality.[185] Houlbrook suggests that the 'growing number of exclusively queer commercial venues after the Second World War emblematised that broader cultural separation between queer and "normal"'.[186] Yet the rhythm and blues clubs of 1962–5 and the glam rock concerts of 1972–4 suggest a more complex process of the construction of both private and social space in reflecting and influencing sexual identity and the politics of transgression. Moreover, the phenomenon of young men wearing make-up to identify with particular performers reached far beyond the metropolitan centres of England. A letter sent to *Jackie* from Ruth Mottershead of Oldham located in the industrial north is illustrative.

> My elder brother is driving me round the bend! Once I had to hide my belongings from my younger sister Jayne. But now its my brother who uses my hair dryer and hairspray, wears my chiffon scarves, skinny rib jumpers, and pinches my nail file and emery board...whatever happened to the masculine men?[187]

In the West Midlands, Cato recalled 'walking through town with a copy of *Alladin Sane* under my arm and hearing elderly matrons tut-tutting'.[188] He also took to purchasing girls' magazines such as *Jackie* because of 'the quality of the posters of his favourite stars'.[189] Frith also remembered Bowie fans in Coventry in 1972: 'I used to see them at the bus stop: the boys with green hair ... their style shifting with the record sleeves ... I thought them the bravest of all youth cults'.[190] To Bracewell the fact 'that Bowie's Glam Rock could turn barrow boys into screaming queens was the greatest triumph'.[191] In his fictionalised account of glam rock from 1973, the pulp novelist Richard Allen recreated the thrill of transgression experienced by a working-class male when applying cosmetics to his face.

> He applied blue shadow to his eyes, got out the box with the golden stars. One by one, meticulously arranging each, he adhered the stars. He gazed into the rectangular mirror. A tremor raced through him. His hand actually shook as he used a brush to apply lipstick, curving his mouth into a desirable blow.[192]

Timothy Field from Southampton wrote to *Jackie* in March 1974 as a promoter of 'Male Lib'.

> I am writing to defend all us brave blokes wearing make-up. A rash statement you may think, but when you girls are getting ready for a date you like to make yourselves up to look special for us, then don't you think it's a complement for your bloke to make himself look better for you? It's no longer sissy to try look good for a special date.[193]

The *Daily Mirror* described the scene at a T-Rex concert in September 1972: 'The audience includes a mixture of hysterical girls and camp-looking boys – many of them wearing sequins on their faces'.[194] The novelist Jake Arnott remembered his teenage years in Aylesbury, where he would 'play Bowie' with his friend in the back garden.[195] Jones also recalls that in Deal, Kent the Ziggy hairstyle was copied by both boys and girls.[196] Pauline Fitzgerald lived in Essex and thought Bowie's image was 'amazing' and changed her style accordingly.

> I began to wear satin jackets, high waisted flared trousers, very high platform shoes and boots that were sparkly or glittery ... purple lipstick, glitter eye make-up and black or dark blue nail varnish with an Aladdin Sane flash on each nail ... hair cut at the front to try and create the sticking up hair of Ziggy Stardust ... father hated Bowie ... as he thought he was a disgusting poof.[197]

A letter to *Jackie* about 'a perplexed mum' was also indicative of the sense of despair with the apparent gender experimentation that underpinned glam: 'My mum (like most mums) can't understand why some pop singers wear make-up and glittery clothes. She says those things should only be worn by women... I've a picture of Marc Bolan on the wall holding a purse on a string. I won't tell you what she said about that'.[198] Marion Ryan from Wimbledon felt that the reason girls were 'acting tough' was 'because most of the clothes these days are unisex. Boys and girls wear trousers, platform shoes... if these so-called tough nuts dressed in old-fashioned gear, they wouldn't be so aggressive... there wouldn't be any bovver in the discos'.[199]

Along with subverting contemporary conceptions of gender, glam rock and the Ziggy concerts were also spaces for the display of sexual abandonment. Bowie later recalled that there were of plenty of 'enthusiastic fans down and at it in the back rows'.[200] Vermorel's fan letters contain an infamous but no doubt exaggerated portrait by 'Julie' of the Hammersmith concert in 1973: 'A lot of men were throwing off their underwear... it was so extraordinary because nobody had any inhibitions'.[201] The concerts took place in the context of concerns around pornography and cinematic and literary representations of young girls embracing casual sex and 'groupie culture'.[202] This was a period of a rapidly multiplying number of sex shops in Soho driven by entrepreneurial pornographers and the corrupt officers of the Metropolitan Police.[203] There were also more general anxieties around rising levels of venereal disease particularly amongst young people.[204]

To Taylor and Wall 'the appeal of a class-based Glamrock' was a form of 'exotic but passive excitement'.[205] To Leng, glam rock performers mostly shunned 'leftist politics', and 'it was assumed that glams were largely apolitical'.[206] Yet Slade, Sweet and the Spiders from Mars provided a working-class counterpoint to Bowie's metropolitan sophistication and sexual ambivalence. In the wider experiences of youth culture, class also remained a potent source of identity and a way of understanding the structural inequalities that remained in English society. McRobbie in her critical reading of *Jackie* claimed that it obscured social divisions amongst youth.[207] Yet particular contributions show that divergent identities and experiences remained. A letter from April 1972 penned by L. Smith of Sheffield provides an illustration.

> Like so many other girls of my age I left school to work in a factory... I think the present system of higher wages with more interesting jobs should be reversed! It seems more logical to me that people who have to put up with the most menial and boring jobs should be paid more than the professional employee.[208]

In a response to a question posed by *Jackie* on 'what would you do for women's lib?', Isobel Jackson called for a 'national strike of women workers'.[209] In contrast, Teresa Peyton of Birmingham in her response to the question posed by *Jackie* on 'what will things be like in 25 years' time', feared that 'the Communists will have taken over, and democratic society as we know it in this country, and the Royal family will all be just a memory'.[210] Jean Burke from Kent felt that the letters page of *Jackie* had become too political 'with all the moans about pollution, crime, poverty' and wanted to 'leave all the problems to the politicians, the church, or newspapers'.[211]

Bowie's contribution to glam rock also provided teenagers with an insight into a mythical world of stardom, celebrity and luxury that allowed them to temporarily escape the drudgery of their everyday lives. This was most notable in his detailed but fictionalised diary 'My World', which appeared in *Mirabelle* magazine. The entries were in fact written by Cherry Vanilla, Bowie's publicist. They contained opinions and thoughts on a changing world. One entry from July 1973 is indicative: 'we may not look quite the same as the people of other lands...but we are members of the same human race...we all have a share in the brotherhood of man'.[212] Readers were taken into the cosmopolitan and globe-trotting aspects of Bowie's life. Here was the twentieth-century version of a nineteenth-century polymath partaking in a grand tour of Italy, France, Russia and the United States. Bowie provides readers with details of his make-up and fashion choices: 'Some girls look ever so attractive with just a touch of mascara and a little lip gloss while others look really cute with rosy rouge cheeks and sultry black eyelids...I used to like to see my audience both girls and boys, painted and powdered up brightly for the event'.[213] In a later entry, he tells readers how to get the Bowie look: 'You must be careful to choose your hairdresser with great care and attention'. Emphasising his feminine side, he claimed that both he and his wife Angie used the same make-up: 'Angie and I use the same colours, like light powder on our faces with light blue eye shadow around the eyes, or golden powder on our cheeks with dark green shadow on our eyelids'.[214] There was also an emphasis on do-it-yourself in advice given to readers: 'Why don't you have a look at your friends' make-up and if you see something that catches your fancy ask if you can have a go with it, rather than buying lots of new stuff'.[215]

In February 1974, Bowie noted the impact that the oil crisis was having on the recording studio where 'everybody's been freezing'.[216] In a further entry he sought to downplay his public persona as a rebel: 'Believe it or not, I do get letters regularly from middle-aged mums and dads who seem to understand and fully appreciate the theatrics that go to make up the complete David Bowie'.[217] The fact that Bowie did not pen these pieces is not as important as the fact that readers thought he was the author. Bowie introduced his teenage readers to a world of glamour and excess, but also encouraged them to explore their own identities and challenge the boundaries of their own domestic and social identities.

Images of England through glam, glitter and sparkle

The class dimension of glam rock was rooted in the industrial communities of the midlands and northern England, but it also signified an embrace of camp, exaggerated femininity and aspects of a gay metropolitan subculture that was transmitted to sections of working-class youth by performers such as Slade, Sweet, T-Rex and in particular David Bowie as Ziggy Stardust. These aliens in England reached beyond the metropolitan centres, and Bowie clones could be seen in a multiplicity of provincial cities, towns and villages. The hedonism of Slade and the more sophisticated presentation of sexuality and gender constructed by Bowie allowed working-class youths to mentally and physically temporarily transcend the boundaries of their homes, communities and workplaces that were beset by industrial conflict and political violence. This was an England where even popular teenage girls' magazines like *Jackie* were beginning to reflect political tensions. A letter from J. Lyons of Basingstoke is illustrative: 'Society means the establishment and the establishment means a status quo, and it's this that most teenagers want to change and most adults want to keep'.[218]

Sandbrook provides a good illustration of the way in which the architecture and social space of provincial towns and cities was being transformed: 'The very landscape was changing; terraced streets ripped down and replaced with monolithic concrete blocks, mill chimneys and colliery engine houses crashing down in clouds of dust, pubs and chapels converted into carpet showrooms or flats for ambitious gentrifiers'.[219] Bowie would capture such scenes of 'concrete all around' in 'All the Young Dudes', a song that became a hit for Mott the Hoople in July 1972.[220] A sociological study by Robins and Cohen of a working-class estate in North London between 1972–4 also presented a similar insight: 'One evening on the wall by Monmouth estate, Tommy arrives looking like David Bowie, complete with his make-up and streaked hair, chorus of hoots, wolf whistles, and jeers from the wall gang... "Where's your handbag dearie? Going out with your fella, then? You little fairy"'.[221] Bracewell rightly claims that to 'identify with Bowie, in 1973, was to make a decision that turned bedroom dreams into personal politics'.[222]

The last appearance of Ziggy Stardust took place at the Marquee Club, London on 18–20 August 1973, under the title of the 1980 Floor Show. This performance formed a bridge between the Ziggy character and Bowie's future project, which would be loosely based on a musical version of Orwell's *Nineteen Eighty Four* (1949). In December 1973, the industrial crisis in England deepened with coal shortages, power cuts and an imminent national miner's strike and a state of emergency that would last for two months.[223] Bowie's subsequent *Diamond Dogs* album released in April 1974 was even more apocalyptic than *Ziggy Stardust* and saw Bowie again responding to an economic, political and cultural climate in England that was being experienced by working-class youth as simultaneously restrictive and liberating.[224]

The less celebrated but nonetheless equally transgressive aspects of glam rock could be found in provincial towns across England and the rest of Britain. In a rather condescending piece for the *New Musical Express*, Nick

Kent provides a description of a performance by Sweet at a Glaswegian disco.

> The building itself…is full of not-so-lithesome teenage bodies, mostly female ranging from 12 to 17 years of age. The males at the disco are a sorry sight indeed…Here are all these young kids…starting to come to terms with their bodies under garish lighting…The music is over, the kids rush the stage and the mass orgasm is over.[225]

Similarly, at a Gary Glitter concert in Birmingham 'nubile ladies and toughie boys, all along to catch a sight of this stumbling, glitzy golden wonder boy…A young lady…was heard to utter to her friend: "you can almost see it can't you. His thing I mean"'.[226] Yet it could be argued that Sweet and Glitter represented the broad appeal of glam rock and its connection to the everyday experiences of working-class youth. Reynolds has recently claimed that 'glitterbeat' was 'the rebirth of rock and roll's savage spirit in a new decade and a different country, the harsh urban landscape of 1970s Britain'.[227]

By 1974 glam rock was a national phenomenon that bled into film, television and literature. It even left its mark on the world of professional wrestling, where Adrian Street, the son of a South Wales coal miner and his assistant 'Miss Linda', would wear glitter, sparkle, lipstick and blow kisses to opponents during bouts. Here was 'ultra-camp' glam reaching pensioners and children at a string of run-down provincial public halls on Saturday afternoons.[228] Yet perhaps the most fitting symbol of the high-point and immediate death of glam rock was the release of the Gary Glitter film *Remember Me This Way* (1974). Here depicted on screen was glam rock at its most baseless, tasteless, preposterous and populist. We see Glitter as the martial arts expert, pampered rock star and generally inept live performer, yet nonetheless able to generate excitement amongst an audience of largely teenage girls and their mothers.

In January 1975, Slade released a semi-autobiographical film presenting a dark image of England and its popular music business.[229] There are various scenes of terraced streets, smoky pubs and decaying industries of cities like Sheffield and Nottingham. Beyond the glam, glitter and sparkle was a country that remained riven by inequalities and class divisions. A year later, Bowie claimed that popular music would 'return to the sensitivities of the working class'.[230] The rhetoric, imagery and mythology of punk rock would form the next stage in a process that had begun in the 1950s, whereby a musical genre created through a combination of impresarios and 'organic intellectuals' sought to once again both reflect and transform the lives of working-class youths in England.

8

Darkness over England: Punk Rock and the Sex Pistols Anarchy Tour 1976

There is an expansive literature on the Sex Pistols and punk rock.[1] Historians tend to place the group at the centre of a particular period of 'crisis' in British society (1976/77) or alternatively seek to underplay punk's significance.[2] This chapter weaves between the two positions by focusing on responses to the Sex Pistols Anarchy Tour of December 1976. It presents a particular image of England in which a sense of 'crisis' was articulated through a range of political/social organisations and media outlets.[3] The Sex Pistols were symbolic of particular shifts within popular music and youth culture. Class identity, experience and rhetoric were core features of punk rock and its attempt to challenge existing political and social orthodoxies through sound, attitude and style.

Sociologists and musicologists have long debated the meaning and significance of punk rock and although social historians have been slow in responding there is now a limited but growing historiography. Much of the literature on punk has noted a collective experience of alienation, resentment and hopelessness, which created the conditions that gave rise to new forms of youth identities, musical genres and groups such as the Sex Pistols.[4] Yet the 'framing' of the Sex Pistols and punk rock has prioritised certain features of the period – the music, the fashion, the politics – but has neglected to provide a critical engagement with the variety of responses to the Sex Pistols Anarchy Tour.[5] The whole notion of punk as a historical event, subculture, and musical genre can be read through the four weeks of the ill-fated tour. For many commentators the group formed part of a particular sense of a darkness descending over England. Jon Savage, the contemporary chronicler and future historian of punk, was attracted to the energy and excitement of the phenomenon but it also filled him with a sense of foreboding. Writing in the first issue of a punk fanzine in 1976, he saw it 'as the first stirrings, on a mass level, of a particularly English kind of fascism...here it won't be like in Germany...It'll be English: ratty, mean, pinched, hand in glove with Thatcher as mother sadist...god it does frighten me...the dance of the repressed released to become powerful beyond their dreams'.[6]

The development of a 'moral panic' around the Anarchy Tour had similarities with responses to earlier youth cultures such as Teddy Boys, Mods and Rockers.[7] The Sex Pistols were characterised by a variety of publications, organisations and individuals as representing a dangerous variant of youth culture. Punk was seen by some as being a symptom of economic and political crisis and by others as representing the outcome of the erosion of a particular type of working-class culture. Out of a total of 27 planned appearances on the tour the group performed at only five locations. Yet the episode can be read as more than just a conventional 'moral panic' in which particular social elites generated and promoted particular readings of an event based on adversarial media coverage. In the case of the Anarchy Tour some of the responses were shaped by deeper social and political convictions that went beyond the reading of the Sex Pistols provided by television and the popular press.

According to Cohen, three elements are needed to ensure the success of a 'moral panic', all which are applicable to the Sex Pistols and the Anarchy Tour. Firstly, a suitable enemy/folk devil that is easily denounced and has little power. Secondly, the panic needs a suitable victim. Thirdly, there needs to be a consensus that the enemy is a deeper symptom of wider problems within society. The media is central to the construction of 'folk devils' in setting the agenda, transmitting the images and making the initial claim that society is under threat.[8] Yet Cohen's notion of 'moral panic' has limitations.[9] Thornton inverts Cohen's model and argues that youth subcultures and the music industry play an essential role in creating and sustaining such panics.[10] A claim can be made that the Sex Pistols manager Malcolm McLaren was crucial in this aspect of image creation. Yet both McLaren and the Sex Pistols were very much on the margins of the music industry. Media coverage of the Sex Pistols was certainly exaggerated, but it also reflected 'real' anxieties.

The reading of December 1976 that follows also engages with Moran's recent work on the ways in which notions of 'crisis' in English society took particular cultural forms. However, it departs from his view that the 'mid-1970s crisis was experienced most keenly by opinion forming elites'.[11] The responses to the tour highlight a more widely shared sense of social malaise. The fraught language of conservative commentators and politicians was crucial in creating and sustaining the 'moral panic', but it was also indicative of a broader concern with a range of social and cultural developments that had emerged in a period of economic and political uncertainty. Reaction to the Sex Pistols united many shades of political and religious opinion from Conservative politicians through to feminist currents in the National Union of Students (NUS) and the 'traditional socialism' of the labour movement.

The Anarchy Tour: the economic, political and social contexts

On 25 November 1976, the week before the Sex Pistols were due to embark on their Anarchy Tour, American/Canadian rock music icons the Band and a whole batch of 1960s performers, including Bob Dylan, played a farewell concert in San Francisco. In response to events like the Band's 'last waltz', Sex Pistols vocalist, John Lydon, adumbrated what would become a cornerstone of the rhetoric of punk: 'All that peace and love rubbish – that was just the hypocrisy of that other generation – the one we hate'. He claimed that the Sex Pistols were about 'real things...the numb feeling of living on a council estate'.[12] A number of journalists concurred with Lydon's view that class identity was taking new forms. Steve Turner writing in the *Guardian*, claimed that punks were 'mostly working class and mostly unemployed'.[13] James Johnson in the London *Evening Standard* felt that punk was 'a bizarre movement...a social rather than a musical phenomenon'.[14] Many young people were unaware or disinterested in punk music, but this should not devalue the impact it had on working-class youths both in metropolitan centres and the English provinces. While the Sex Pistols were criss-crossing Britain by a coach with its destination defined as 'nowhere', the best selling artists on the music charts were epitomised by novelty acts and established artists; Showaddywaddy, Johnny Mathis, Leo Sayer and Mud.[15] Yet within six months of the Anarchy Tour, the Sex Pistols had a single at No. 2, soon followed by a No. 1 album and had spawned an international youth subculture and a musical genre that had a lasting legacy. As with glam rock, the Sex Pistols provided an image of England that some working-class youths felt reflected their experiences in the home, school and workplace.

In 1976 there was a growing consensus amongst opinion formers that Britain was in decline. Rising unemployment, inflation, calls for political devolution and trade union militancy were symbolic of continuing tensions. There had also been an upsurge of Irish Republican terror attacks on the British mainland (notably the Birmingham pub bombings in November 1974). The Conservative and Labour parties also faced pressure from within their own ranks. The February 1974 General Election had seen Heath's Conservative government removed from power on the back of a national miners' strike. Labour under Wilson also failed to adequately deal with Britain's economic problems and was being pressured by the socialist left to implement more radical measures. The loan secured from the International Monetary Fund (IMF) in November 1976 unleashed further pressures on the government. Political extremism was also more visible with running battles between the fascist National Front and sections of the revolutionary left in a number of cities and towns.[16] Within this political and economic climate of uncertainty, one more ingredient was thrown into the mix, which to politicians, the media and sections of the general public, represented a further assault on the English society – the Sex Pistols. In December 1976, the popular press painted an apocalyptic image of social breakdown; the economy was once again being threatened with a national miners' strike, the Labour Party was being taken over by Trotskyist extremists, television and cinema were becoming the domains of pornographers and teenagers were out of control. Sections of youth were labelled as football hooligans, glue sniffers, muggers and sexual deviants.

Moran claims that the general population remained immune to such 'apocalyptic narratives' and continued to engage with the 'banality of daily life'.[17] Yet the perception that elements of youth culture were undergoing a metamorphosis into something more threatening was shared by more than just the usual suspects from the conservative and religious right. Youth violence was internalised not only through press coverage and news bulletins but also through the experience of urban vandalism, gang violence and football hooliganism. Even a concert by the staid 1950s rock 'n' roller Bill Haley at the Victoria Theatre, London was disrupted by fighting between hundreds of Teddy Boys and security staff.[18] The response to the Anarchy Tour formed part of an engagement with what was perceived by many as a new set of social problems that signalled the end of a particular understanding of England and Englishness. Mothers, students, trade unionists, feminists and community leaders joined with conservatives, religious activists and journalists in attempting to prevent the Sex Pistols from performing. Yet the Sex Pistols themselves were the personification of particular aspects of Englishness that could be found in working-class radicalism, humour and populism. They shared Orwell's view that England remained 'a land of snobbery and privilege, ruled largely by the old and the silly'.[19]

The print media was at the forefront of fuelling and framing the response to the Sex Pistols. On 2 December 1976, the *Daily Mirror* used the words 'Rock Cult Filth' to describe the antics of the group and labelled them as boorish, ill-mannered, foul-mouthed, dirty, obnoxious and arrogant'.[20] The *Daily Mail* described them as 'a bizarre band preaching the new rock religion of violence and anarchy...directed against the rich and powerful'.[21] Over the next two weeks the press reinforced this apocalyptic view of the Sex Pistols. The catalyst had been the group's pre-tour appearance on television in the early evening of 1 December 1976, interviewed on the *Today* show by Bill Grundy.[22] Grundy goaded members of the group into 'saying something controversial' and they responded with a few obscenities.[23] A number of viewers jammed the switchboard at Thames Television and one viewer reportedly destroyed his set because he was so incensed.[24] The *Daily Telegraph* reported that 'happy family viewing was somewhat disrupted last night when parents found their children being exposed to foul language'. One parent, a Mr Leslie Blunt, was interviewed: 'Our children were waiting for *Crossroads*[25] to come on when suddenly they heard every swear word in the book'. He said that after the programme two of his children aged 7 and 9 'were running round using words they did not understand'.[26] Grundy was duly suspended and Tom Steel, executive producer, and Mike Housego, programme producer, were severely reprimanded.[27] The impact of the Grundy incident also heightened the rhetoric of the literate punks who were already creating their own fanzines and fuelling the creation of a 'moral panic'. The first issue of *Bondage* from 1976 claimed that 'they feel that security is threatened just by what the Pistols represent. I hope that after this whole thing dies down the Pistols carry on being more and more obnoxious... You're either a threat to the establishment or you're part of it – there's no in-between'.[28]

The 'moral panic' had now developed what Cohen terms as its 'own internal trajectory'. The subsequent Anarchy Tour provides an example of his notion of the 'microphysics of outrage'.[29] Journalists warned against the dangers that the group posed to the youth of Britain. Shaun Usher in the *Daily Mail* claimed that 'if pop is the modern opium of the masses and of course it is – then Punk rock is pure heroin'.[30] A week later in *The Times*, Ronald Butt, commenting on the Grundy incident, felt that 'the speciality of the performers who were wheeled on for interview is not musical talent but outrage, anarchy and behaviour calculated to disgust and shock'.[31] Local authorities, universities, and concert hall owners now started to cancel planned appearances by the group. The BBC refused to play their debut single 'Anarchy in the UK', placing the Sex Pistols future recording career in jeopardy. The song encapsulated Lydon's particular image of the nation with terrorist bombs exploding in England and Northern Ireland and a sense of impending doom and social breakdown. The multiplicity of responses to the Anarchy Tour suggested that the Sex Pistols were symbolic of developing fissures in class identities, popular music, youth culture and radical politics.

Trade unions and universities

The initial response to the Sex Pistols' Grundy interview came from members of the Transport and General Workers' Union (TGWU). The union had been steadily moving to the left throughout the early 1970s, leading to an increase in the power of shop stewards and strike action. In June 1976, the Trades Union Congress had already voted to return to a policy of free collective bargaining, abandoning the income policy that it had previously agreed to with the Labour Government. Within the TGWU, women had been expressing their desire for equality in disputes in a number of Ford motor plants in the late 1960s and campaigning for the passing of the Equal Pay Act in 1970. Sixteen female members of the TGWU at the EMI Records dispatch plant in Hayes, Middlesex refused to handle any material produced by the Sex Pistols. The company had a long history of employing women and had initially refused to recognise unions using various strategies to retain workers' loyalties.[32] By 1976, trade unions had full recognition at the plant. The women were spread across two shifts and after witnessing the Grundy interview they refused to handle 'Anarchy in the UK'.[33] Union officials convened a meeting with EMI to discuss the matter. As female packers were registering their indignation, support was provided by electricians who were members of the Electrical, Electronic, Telecommunication and Plumbing Union (EETPU). On Friday 3 December, the EETPU and the clerical workers union APEX made representations to the company claiming that it was degrading that staff should be involved in the production of such records. After a meeting between the various unions and management a day later the women decided to resume normal duties. The TGWU felt that any further action would merely provide the Sex Pistols with more publicity.[34] Despite the return to work, some were unhappy with the outcome. Two women in particular negotiated an exemption from handling any Sex Pistols product.[35] The episode reveals that working-class women trade unionists in the mid-1970s were using industrial militancy not only to gain wage equality but were also willing to withhold their labour in order to protect a particular notion of femininity and working-class respectability.[36]

The first stop on the Anarchy Tour was due to take place in the main hall of the University of East Anglia (UEA) on Friday 3 December. Along with the Sex Pistols, other groups sharing the bill were the Clash, the Damned and the Heartbreakers. In response to the Grundy show the Norwich local press bombarded the UEA with questions as to whether the concert would go ahead. The local president of the National Union of Students (NUS), Aidan Lines, said that he wanted the concert to be cancelled, but he was prevented from doing so because of the financial implications. The union had paid the group £750 and a number of tickets had been sold in advance. Nonetheless, they had written into the contract a NUS stipulation that the group would use no fascist insignia on stage and no fascist lyrics in their songs.[37] This had raised concerns because one of the group's entourage, Siouxsie Sioux, had worn a Nazi armband during the Grundy interview. Moreover, it was in a context where rock performers were toying with far-right imagery and occasionally supporting anti-immigration statements; most notably David Bowie's alleged Nazi salute at Victoria Station in May and Eric Clapton's vocal support for Enoch Powell during a concert at the Birmingham Odeon in August.[38] The Sex Pistols were averse to fascist politics. The lyrics of their songs did not contain any racist rhetoric and there is no evidence that they made any racist comments during performances. Nonetheless, it was clear that the UEA NUS were suspicious of the Sex Pistols in that they did not seem to fit the archetype of progressive peaceful middle-class groups that personified the student music scene in 1976.

The political pressure and the hysteria of the press soon became too much for the university and the concert was cancelled. Although the union had been uneasy about the event, the cancellation came from an executive decision by the Vice-Chancellor of the university Frank Thistlethwaite. He felt that the concert could have led to violence. This created a rift between the university authorities and the NUS. The NUS publicity officer Sally Partington informed the *Eastern Evening News* that 'we wish to make it known that we are disgusted with the manner in which the Vice Chancellor's decision was taken'.[39] She felt that the union had been railroaded into agreeing to the cancellation. The executive decision had been taken at the end of a hastily convened meeting. The two NUS representatives had tried in vain to put their position across, but the university council had been swayed by the 'moral panic' that was now in place. The conservative members of the university council were no doubt keen to avoid being labelled with the tag of allowing the Sex Pistols to play. This exposed the fragility of the consensus that existed between the university and the student body and how the culture of liberalism on the campus owed more to rhetoric than reality. University administrators were comfortable with a woolly notion of freedom of expression, but the Sex Pistols were clearly an affront to the middle-class sensibilities of academics and a number of students.

The decision created conflict on the campus and students were disgruntled by the fact that their views had been disregarded. To union activists this action threatened the autonomy of the student body. In response, around 50 NUS members occupied the university's administration block, although a more intense drama was averted when through negotiations the occupation was halted.[40] The protest was not geared towards defending the Sex Pistols but was a demonstration of the union's unhappiness with the executive decision taken by the Vice-Chancellor. The outcome meant an effective ban on the use of campus buildings for NUS events. The university stressed that this was not the case and the decision to ban the concert was taken on the grounds of safety. Nonetheless, it seems obvious that the Vice-Chancellor had been convinced of the undesirability of a Sex Pistols performance. He was clearly influenced by and now reinforced the 'moral panic' that was surrounding the group. The media amplification and genuine concerns regarding the nature of the Sex Pistols had led to cultural censorship.

The attempt by the Sex Pistols to perform at the University of Lancaster also ended in failure. On 3 December the *Lancaster Guardian* had given wide coverage to the case of a 15-year-old girl who had allegedly been raped 20 times by Hell's Angels at a charity concert held at Leigh Rugby League Club's training ground.[41] The proposed concert by the Sex Pistols only added to this climate of fear of rampaging youths. However, in this case, it was the NUS who acted as the moral guardians of decency and taste. Maggie Gallagher, the President of the Union, argued that the punk movement was sexist.[42] Barry Lucas, the Social Manager, had objected to the names of the groups on the bill. After a series of meetings it was agreed that they would adopt NUS policy and not to stage concerts where sexism was promoted.[43] The reaction of trade unionists, UEA and Lancaster students illustrates the use of particular political discourses and procedures to censure the Sex Pistols. The perceived radicalism of the group could not be located within existing characterisations of progressive politics so the response from the left was largely negative.

Local government and Labour socialism

As women workers in the EMI pressing plant were taking industrial action, local councils were making arrangements to ban the Sex Pistols from their towns and cities. On 4 December, the group travelled to Derby for their planned appearance at the local authority owned King's Hall. After a meeting of the Derby Borough Council Leisure Committee, it was decided that the Sex Pistols and their supporting acts would have to pass a vetting procedure. They would be asked to perform in front of members of the council in the afternoon. Councillor Les Shepley, Chairman of the Leisure Committee, and the Entertainments Officer, Norman Rushton, claimed that they had been bombarded with phone calls and letters from parents, education officials and religious leaders. Retired clergyman, Canon E. T. Hughes called for the banning of the concert. He felt that the behaviour, image and lyrics of the group would fuel the concerns regarding the increase of violence and obscenity in British society.[44] Hughes was voicing a view that had been mobilised by Christian activists, spearheaded by individuals such as Mary Whitehouse who were calling for increased censorship of television programmes, films and other forms of popular culture. This movement had taken on a public role as the National Festival of Light, an organisation of mostly Christian activists that increased its public profile and activity as a powerful pressure group in the 1970s.[45]

Dave Corke and Mick Barnett, the Birmingham-based promoters of the concert, called for the show to go ahead as they had already sold over 500 tickets. In a statement to the press they endeavoured to ease concerns regarding the likelihood of violence: 'We say to any parent who as any doubts about their children to come along... there is nothing obscene about the show... Pornography had nothing to with it'.[46] The reference to pornography was linked to the growing concern about teenage promiscuity and an increase in sexual imagery in the cinema. Recent films had sparked outrage with scenes of rape, group sex, violence and blasphemy. Most notably: *A Clockwork Orange* (1971), *Straw Dogs* (1971), *The Devils* (1971), *The Exorcist* (1973), *Enter the Dragon* (1973), *Death Wish* (1974) and *Frightmare* (1975). Stanley Kubrick's *A Clockwork Orange* became especially controversial by seemingly holding a mirror to juvenile delinquency in England.[47] Here was a vision of England where rampaging youths in boiler suits and bowler hats caused mayhem and destruction. The nascent punk scene would provide similar images for the tabloid press and the nightmares of politicians and religious leaders.

The view of the council was pushed towards an outright ban when a number of parents started to organise in order to prevent the show. The

Derby Evening Telegraph used its front page to warn that people were prepared to use force. A small group were averse to even allowing the band to perform privately in front of the leisure committee. A caller to the paper's news desk warned that parents would use stink bombs, smoke bombs, air raid sirens and violence if necessary. They would also mount a large picket. According to the *Derby Evening Telegraph*, 'the irate parents did not want Derby to be labelled a filthy town'.[48] The paper passed on these messages to the police and the council. The editor no doubt felt that this would influence the decision on the concert. However, there was a voice of pragmatism amongst the welter of 'moral outrage'. Councillor Mick Walker, leader of the council's minority Labour group viewed the whole thing as a farce that was trivialising the work of the local authority. Walker felt that their role as elected representatives did not include being 'guardians of public morals'. He said that he would not be attending the audition and hoped that all his Labour colleagues would take a similar decision.[49] John Lydon's mother provided a similar critique of the way in which councillors were prioritising the wrong issues.

> The councillors annoy me because they sit back and don't do their job that they're supposed to do. They keep banning kids who want to see them [Sex Pistols] but they won't rehouse people, they leave people homeless on the streets... they just sit back and say this band can't play... because of the violence. I think it's more violent people sleeping on the streets and giving them no homes.[50]

Mrs Lydon's comments articulated the working-class alienation experienced by many inhabitants of high-rise housing blocks on council estates, who, like the Lydons, had been left behind by Harold Wilson's particular brand of 'socialism'. Her son would often dedicate the song 'Liar' to the former Prime Minister at a number of Sex Pistols performances. Here again was an example of the link between class and popular music. For working-class youths such as Lydon, music was one way in which class could be encapsulated in a short song accompanied by a backbeat that tapped into the consciousness of record buyers and those attending live performances by the Sex Pistols.

On the day of the concert the councillors waited two hours for the group to perform. Contrary to the pleas of Walker, five Labour councillors attended, along with five Conservatives. The road crew had already set-up the instruments and the scene was set. The Sex Pistols issued a statement that they would only be judged by those who wanted to attend the official concert and not by people 'unfamiliar with their music'. Bernie Rhodes, manager of the Clash, said 'that we don't agree to the terms we have to perform under. It's ludicrous that people who are 102 years old should pass judgement'.[51] The event was now turned into a circus with the venue besieged by over 40 journalists who were awaiting a verdict. Councillor Shepley eventually read out a prepared statement in front of the group's equipment claiming that the committee 'had bent over backwards to accommodate them' but had decided that their non-attendance at the audition meant that they would not be allowed to perform.[52]

The Derby debacle had also caused conflict amongst the groups that were accompanying the Sex Pistols on the tour. McLaren had decided that all the performers should refuse to appear in front of the councillors. One of the supporting acts, the Damned, broke ranks and agreed to play. Glen Matlock, bass player with the Sex Pistols, returned to the subject of the Derby debacle in his autobiography and claimed that the decision was based on 'narrow-minded, pig ignorant, provincial censorship'.[53] The reaction of the Derby councillors indicates the way in which local authorities outside of the capital were unwilling to accept metropolitan influences in their districts that they viewed as damaging to the 'morality' of the local population.

The next concert at Newcastle was also cancelled. The press coverage here emphasised the sex and not the violence. The headline of the *Evening Chronicle* proclaimed 'Sex Group Banned'. This gave the impression that they were some kind of live pornographic stage show. Similar to the situation in Derby, a political decision was taken and Councillor Arthur Stables informed the press that the proposed concert at the City Hall would be banned. Stables felt that this was a wise decision as the council would not be able to 'control what might be said from the stage and if we stopped the concert in the middle it might cause audience trouble'. He added that the Sex Pistols were 'certainly not the type of people we want in this city'.[54] The local labour movement at this time was being investigated for wide-scale corruption involving leading party and trade union figures including T. Dan Smith, Andy Cunningham, and the architect John Poulson.[55] The Labour Party response in Derby and Newcastle fitted an emerging pattern of criticism that was couched in terms of a 'working-class world we have lost' discourse. Unfortunately for Labour elites a particular section of working-class youth were now immune to calls for party loyalty. Young miners, factory workers, shipbuilders and steelmakers continued to drink in working mens' clubs and pubs, but aspects of youth culture and popular music held up the possibility of an alternative England. The rhetoric of the Sex Pistols and the basis of their appeal were indicative of such a process.

Sex Pistols as symptom and motif of post-war decline

After three cancelled shows, the group performed at Leeds Polytechnic. On 3 December, Ian Steele of the NUS announced that the show on 6 December would go ahead despite the Grundy incident. The Polytechnic and the local council took a much more enlightened view of the Sex Pistols. Chris Tipple, deputy Director of Education for the city, along with Patrick Nuttgens, the Director of Leeds Polytechnic, stressed that they did not want to stop the group appearing as long as there was no violence. A more outraged reaction was forthcoming from a number of Leeds councillors. Bill Hudson, the Conservative chairman of the Education Committee said the city would be far better off without them. Another Conservative, Patrick Coxtey, was dismayed that 'people in higher education found it necessary to listen to such rubbish'. The Reverend Michael Taylor, a Liberal councillor, detected a sinister force in this new youth movement. He felt that the Sex Pistols 'were a product of a society that had lost its moral values'.[56] Keith Waterhouse, in his analysis of punk in the *Daily Mirror*, put the phenomenon down to the failure of post-war urban planning: 'The Punk Rock phenomenon...could not exist at all if the so-called 'blank generation' – the unemployed, under-educated, aimless tribe of vandals to be found on every disastrous concrete housing project – had not been there to feed off'.[57]

In Leeds, the local press fed the sense of outrage by reporting scenes of violence that had plagued the group. A story appeared that they had caused damage to a four-star hotel in the city. The *Evening Post* in its report of the concert emphasised the obnoxiousness of Lydon's performance.

> [The Sex Pistols] set the tone for this abysmal performance of depravity rock by dedicating the first number to Councillor Bill Hudson of Leeds, Bill Grundy, and the Queen. They immediately broke orders from their manager not to swear by using a string of obscenities...Rotten took a swig of ale and spat it out all over the fans at the front.[58]

The Bournemouth show was the first in a private venue. It was due to take place on 7 December in a local discothèque owned by the Rank Organisation. The relationship between Rank and its young customers was already at a crisis point. The company had recently banned those under 25 from its ballrooms throughout Britain because of rising vandalism and violence.[59] The day after the Grundy incident, a spokesman for the venue announced that the appearance would more than likely be cancelled. On 3 December this was made official. The company stated that the tour would be banned from all their venues. Rank Information Controller, Chris Moore, pointed to the prospect of violence as the reason for the decision: 'The group themselves appear to incite crowds...at the end of the day it does not appear to be the kind of entertainment we want to be associated with'.[60] The decision now presented the Sex Pistols management with logistical problems. Many of the arranged dates were due to take place in premises owned by the Rank Organisation. A search for alternative venues was undertaken, but the itinerary was now compromised. The group were also informed that their recording contract was in jeopardy. Sir John Reed, Chairman of EMI told the *Times* that he was considering their position. Speaking at the annual meeting of the company in London he described the group's behaviour as 'disgraceful'.[61]

In Manchester there was apprehension in staging the group, but the city also provided an opportunity for the Sex Pistols to perform.[62] The *Manchester*

Evening News gave wide coverage to the Grundy incident (Grundy himself was from Marple in neighbouring Stockport) and had carried advertisements for the proposed show planned for 9 December at the Electric Circus. In recent editions the paper had been reporting the rise of football violence, glue sniffing and general youth delinquency. The Sex Pistols had already played two shows at the city's Free Trade Hall on 4 June and 20 July. The Palace Theatre and the Free Trade Hall unsurprisingly declined the invitation of further concerts in light of the adverse publicity. The manger of the latter, Ron O' Neil claimed that during the group's previous appearance 'they started arguments with the audience and the language was a bit strong'. Paul Galsworthy of the Palace told the paper that he had 'heard that they were very rough and the lowest type of group'.[63] The request to perform was duly rejected.

The Electric Circus was a privately owned former cinema in Collyhurst, north Manchester. The location perfectly suited the 'rough music' and performance of the Sex Pistols. By the mid-1970s, Collyhurst was becoming a 'problem area' with dilapidated housing stock, petty crime, unemployment and youth delinquency. The promoters had used the rejection from other venues to publicise the show; 'Banned from the Palace, Banned from the Free Trade Hall'. The group had already been asked to leave the city's prestigious Midland Hotel the day before the show. The manager, Harry Berry, changed his mind on the booking once he realised who they were.[64] They were then refused accommodation at the Belgrade Hotel in Stockport, eventually securing rooms at the Arosa in Fallowfield. They were also ejected from these premises when the manager, Mohammed Anwar, claimed that they 'started using the filthiest language, ran riot and upset other guests'.[65] The show went ahead with the press reporting that the 500 people in attendance faced an immediate slew of obscenities. In preparation for any kind of violence, the press claimed that 'local detectives had been dispatched in 'pop gear' to mix with crowd while senior uniformed officers kept vigil from the back of the hall'.[66]

Punk music had created divisions amongst Manchester's youth, which was articulated along lines of social class. Howard Paul, a public school boy from Cheshire, was featured in the *Manchester Evening News* castigating the Sex Pistols.[67] In response, he had formed a band with ex-grammar and public schools boys with the name Contempt; a reference to what he felt for this new form of music. Paul claimed that the Sex Pistols were taking advantage of a section of gullible youth: 'They are just playing on the frustrations of young kids who have no jobs and no prospects.' [68] John Scott said that he was sickened by the whole spectacle of punk rock. He felt the Sex Pistols were deliberately stirring up trouble and violence for publicity purposes. In contrast, Stephen Morrissey, a 17-year-old working-class music fan from Stretford, later to lead another influential group, the Smiths, penned a letter to the *Manchester Evening News* claiming that the Sex Pistols were 'speaking for the youth today'.[69] Their manager, Malcolm McLaren, told reporters that the Sex Pistols 'dress loudly and they are loud mouthed like all young kids in a similar predicament'.[70]

The *Liverpool Daily Post* also gave considerable space to the Sex Pistols. The front page of 3 December again quoted McLaren describing the group as 'working class spivs, dole-queue kids'.[71] The Sex Pistols were due to play the Liverpool Stadium on 11 December. There was an immediate response from the city's religious representatives. The Reverend Donald Gray expressed worries concerning the political message that the group seemed to be promoting. He felt that far from liberating the youth of the nation 'anarchy doesn't give freedoms, it takes them away'.[72] Councillor Doreen Jones made a direct appeal to her local constituents: 'Let's show the rest of the country Liverpool is too good for this sort of rubbish'.[73] The venue's managers buckled under pressure and decided to cancel the event.[74] An attempt to perform a replacement concert at the famous Cavern Club also ended in failure.

The Celtic fringe and the crusade against Sex Pistols

The most confrontational event during the Anarchy Tour occurred when the Sex Pistols crossed the English border into Wales. The show at a Caerphilly cinema promoted by Andy Walton witnessed a mobilisation that drew on a radical tradition of Welsh protest. The group was initially due to perform at the Top Rank Club in Cardiff on 14 December. The show was cancelled as a result of the decision taken by the Rank Organisation to ban the Sex Pistols from all its premises. An alternative was quickly found. The Castle Cinema in Caerphilly was a private establishment owned by Pauline Uttley. From the outset she took a libertarian view of the Sex Pistols phenomenon and said that she was unwilling to act as a censor: 'I am not going to force people to see the show. If they want to, that is up to them'.[75]

The struggle to prevent the show was reported in the national and local press. The Rhymney Valley District Council took a negative view of the Sex Pistols. They initially wanted to take legal action against Uttley. Madeleine Ryland, Vice-Chair of the council, said that the behaviour of the group had forced them to consider stopping them through court action, but after legal advice they were informed that this would probably fail. Because of the short notice, it would be difficult to stop the show going ahead. Ryland said, 'the council had been horrified of reports of previous concerts and we do not feel the people in this valley should be subjected to this kind of treatment'.[76] The next move was a public mobilisation. The subsequent picket of the show was organised by Caerphilly County Councillors Ray Davies and Colin Hobbs. Davies had been a coal miner, steel worker and socialist activist. He represented a new generation of trade unionists who were showing less deference to their officials and calling for increased use of the strike weapon and direct action to protect hard won gains and to secure higher wages.[77] After liaising with local councillors, publicans agreed that they would not open for business on the day of show, as drunkenness would probably accentuate the culture of violence that appeared to follow the band to each performance. A section of the local population was reacting as it had done previously to alien incursions into its community. Indeed it is possible to draw analogies between Welsh working-class attempts to repel the Sex Pistols and the resistance they mustered to the presence of troops and police during industrial disputes in the first quarter of the twentieth century.[78]

As the protest against the group gathered pace the Sex Pistols launched a counter-attack. Lydon argued that the 'anti-concert lobby should be concerned with far more important things like housing problems and unemployment'.[79] He also attacked the limitations of the Labour councillors: [T]hey don't offer the young generation of Caerphilly nothing... While they've been in office they've done sweet FA for anybody except themselves'.[80] On the morning of the concert, Hobbs sent a telegram to Uttley urging a last minute cancellation. She refused to countenance such a request and added that tickets were still available.[81] By mid-afternoon the town became eerily quiet as cafés and pubs were closed. According to McLaren, the group had difficulty in reaching the cinema. The bus driver was told by his company to leave the entourage at the edge of town and let the members walk to the venue.[82] Local protesters, estimated at between 150 and 300, gathered outside of the venue for a show in which less than 100 people had turned up, out of a possible capacity of over four-hundred. One observer, Kevin Dicks, later recalled 'a large police presence of miners' strike proportions'.[83] The protest was given added colour by a 'fire and brimstone' speech by a religious leader that was boomed-out of a public address system. This was complemented by a choir singing hymns and Christmas carols as the Sex Pistols played on. Worshippers from the local Elm Church handed out leaflets linking punk to prophecy.

> Does the Sex Pistols' 'Anarchy in the UK' tour offer the real answer to the needs of youth? What is the meaning of this latest controversial trend in the pop world? Oddly enough, this group's own reported use of the word "antichrist" indicates the answer.
>
> This term describes the essence of the spirit of rebellion against all that God stands for. Even though apparently just a passing fad, therefore, such trends are clearly in part fulfilment of Jesus' prophecy that before his return to earth, wickedness would multiply beyond all previous limits.[84]

John Birkin, the author of the leaflet, later claimed that his aim was 'to make a clear stand against this further decline in moral standards'.[85] Despite the protest the concert went ahead with the promoter claiming that 'Caerphilly will be exactly the same tomorrow morning; nobody will be fallen dead in the street'.[86] The *Western Mail*'s front page declared that 'Hymns Score

Biggest Hit at Punk Show'.[87] Out of ten fans interviewed by the *Rhymney Valley Express* only one said that they enjoyed the concert. Nonetheless, the group had delivered three encores and '30 fans had danced in the aisles'.[88] A week later Wayne Nowaczyk provided a review of the show for the same newspaper: 'After irate councillors, pub and café closures, and fire and brimstone chastisement from the local clergy...I did not see anyone who was obviously shocked at or depraved by the goings on'.[89] Members of the local council did not share the pragmatism of Nowaczyk's review. Councillor Davies told the *Western Mail* that 'the fact so few people turned up for the concert is a victory for the people...we hope we have given a lead to the rest of Wales to take positive action against filth in their town'.[90] But political responses to the event were not unanimous. John Ranelagh, the prospective Conservative candidate for Caerphilly attacked Labour councillors for seeking to gain publicity from the concert. He pointed out that the Sex Pistols had played three times in South Wales in the last six months with no local protests. (The group had appeared in Cardiff, Newport, and Swansea on 21–23 September.) The Labour councillors denied the charge of trying to make political capital out of the Sex Pistols but insisted that 'they stood shoulder-to-shoulder with people from all beliefs and political affiliations in opposition to the concert'.[91] Davies later claimed that he was reacting to pressure from young mothers who were concerned about the safety of their children.[92]

The Sex Pistols faced a similar reaction when they attempted to perform in Scotland. They were due to play Glasgow and Dundee on 15–16 December. A week earlier Lydon was interviewed by the *Daily Record* where he again used class rhetoric to make a political point: 'They try to ruin you from the start. They take away your soul. They destroy you...You have got to fight back or die. You have no future, nothing. You are made unequal...Every kid who goes to a comprehensive school...They are taken as mugs'.[93] In Glasgow, the city's fathers decided that the group would not perform at the Apollo concert hall. The District Council utilised a condition in the venue's license to close the premises on the night that the concert was meant to take place. The ban was implemented through a fear of social disorder. Robert Gray, the chairman of the council's licensing committee told the press that 'we have enough problems in Glasgow without importing yobbos'.[94] In Dundee the lead to ban the Sex Pistols was taken by the Lord Provost Charles Farquhar. He made it clear that he would do everything in his power to prevent the group from performing at the Caird Hall: 'Far be it from me to interfere with the normal day-to-day management of affairs in the city. But so far as I am concerned this group will certainly not be welcomed by me in the city'.[95] He played an active role in pressing certain members of the licensing committee to prevent the concert. Nonetheless, some were concerned at the Lord Provost's intervention. Harold Rubidge, Director of Civil Amenities was not wholly in favour of a ban on the basis that 'they had only used a couple of swear words'. Farquhar argued that he had received many letters from the public concerning the event and opposed the group on the basis that they 'might incite violence and bigotry'.[96] Initially the licensing committee voted 8–7 in favour of deferring a decision. Rubidge then held a meeting with John Henderson, Labour leader of the District Council and Alex Forrester convenor of the Cultural Services Committee and reversed this decision. The Lord Provost also pressed the council to ask the Student Union, nightclub proprietors and other bodies to co-operate and ensure that the group could not play.[97] The Sex Pistols therefore would not appear in Scotland.

Sex, vulgarity and the corruption of youth

The apocalyptic press coverage of the Anarchy Tour stressed that no town or city was immune to the Sex Pistols and that they were rapidly infecting whole swathes of the nation's youth. Reporters painted a picture of a darkness descending over England that was being fuelled by punk rock, juvenile delinquency, trade union militancy and Irish terrorism. Class was central to the construction of such narratives and the experiences and actions that led to their creation. The Sex Pistols and the working-class youths they attracted to their performances had experienced the limitations of the post-war consensus and the continued existence of inequalities in English society.[98]

The proposed show at Bristol Colston Hall on 13 December was also cancelled. Protests from parents and religious organisations had combined to put pressure on local councillors. Ray Muir, the entertainments manager, stressed that 'the decision has been taken in consideration of the best interest of young teenagers whom it is thought would have made up the biggest number of the audience, and in deference of the concern expressed by young people who would have attended'.[99] In Sheffield, local politicians framed the Sex Pistols as being purveyors of obscenity. Councillor Francis Butler, the former leader of the Liberal Party in the city, told the press that 'punk rock is one of the most obscene performances that can be put on a stage'. In response, Sam Mason, the manager of the City Hall, announced the cancellation of the show. Councillor Sidney Dyson justified the move by saying that 'we are not having obscenity, vulgarity, and deprivation in our Hall'.[100] Appearances in Southend and Guildford on the 18 and 19 December were also cancelled. The story was a similar one in Birmingham, where the Sex Pistols planned to appear at the town hall. After interviewing Lydon for the *Birmingham Evening Mail*, the music columnist advised 'fans who care about rock should stay away from the Pistols and their like'.[101] Ted Hanson, chair of Birmingham Leisure Services, said that he had 'decided to cancel the concert because of the absolute degradation these people put across to the public. The people of this city are not going to be subjected to pure, unadulterated filth'.[102]

If the Anarchy Tour had failed in the industrial North and the Midlands, it seemingly had little hope of success on the south coast. Yet the Sex Pistols managed to play two concerts at the Woods Centre, Plymouth on the 21 and 22 December. They were less successful in Torquay. The town already had its own version of Mary Whitehouse in the shape of Sheila Hardaway, a former councillor and leader of the 'Clean-Up Torbay' campaign. The day after the Grundy interview she urged the local 400 Ballroom to ban the planned concert. In an interview with Torbay's *Herald Express,* she warned that 'to allow these people to perform here is putting the children of this town at risk…it is up to the public to form themselves in a group to stop all this, we must protect the children'.[103] The concert was duly cancelled but an appearance at Penelope's discothèque in Paignton was mooted.

The mayor of Torbay, W. Beesley, with the support of the town's Recreation Committee, publicly urged the club not to allow the performance to go ahead. One clergyman had contacted Councillor John Farrell claiming to represent three thousand people who wanted the group banned. Another council member, Joan Cooper said that the Sex Pistols were 'sickening'. She strongly deplored 'the kind of image publicised by this group: one of slovenly appearance, filth, and habit'. The council wanted to ban the concert, but the town clerk, David Hudson, informed Beesley that because it was being held on private premises it had no authority to act. The Sex Pistols then found an ally in C. V. Tanna, the manager of Penelope's. In response to a letter from the mayor, he took a more contrary position: 'I don't think the mayor is musically competent enough to advise me…how would you like a High Court judge to remove your appendix'.[104] Tanna urged the people of Torbay to attend the concert and accused the mayor of trying to gain political publicity from the Sex Pistols. He offered to arrange a vote in the town on the matter and that he would stand by the decision. He planned to open a register in the foyer of Penelope's where voters could express their preference. Tanna found support from Ian MacTaggart, a local student leader. MacTaggart was president and social secretary of South Devon Technical College Student's Union and viewed the attack on the Sex Pistols as 'another way of discriminating against the youth of Torbay'.[105] However, on 13 December, Tanna announced that the show would not go ahead: 'I am creating a lot of controversy…I am a businessman and I do not want to create controversy. I want everybody to be happy'.[106] Perhaps the most pragmatic response to the Anarchy Tour came from the good citizens of Cleethorpes. Ian Galloway of the town's Winter Gardens insisted that 'we have booked this group simply to give a musical performance of heavy rock'. Alan Green, the local mayor said that 'there would not be much to worry about' concerning the appearance on 20 December. The concert in Cleethorpes was completed with the *Grimsby Evening Telegraph* reporting that 'the swearing, beer throwing, and spitting came from the 350 strong audience not the band'.[107]

Out of a total of 27 planned shows for the Anarchy Tour, the Sex Pistols performed at 5 locations: Leeds, Manchester, Caerphilly, Cleethorpes, and Plymouth. Between 3 and 26 December, the tour bus had made its way around the country being turned away from cities and towns as if it was carrying a new form of plague that posed great danger to British youth. The last concert was planned for the then newly opened Roxy in London on 26 December, but this was also cancelled. To the punks and the plethora of fanzines that had appeared as part of this new youth culture phenomenon, the Sex Pistols represented a vanguard in challenging, attacking and subverting aspects of English society. The Christmas edition of *Sniffin' Glue* noted that 'they've done what no other bands have dared to do. They've broken the rules, not just the establishment rules but all the rock 'n' roll laws. They hate and despise everything'.[108]

The outrage and 'moral panic' surrounding the Sex Pistols did not subside with the end of the Anarchy Tour. In the jubilee year that followed, the media and politicians would continue to pour scorn on the group. Yet contrary to popular myth, the Sex Pistols were not the subject of major debate in Parliament. In one of the few speeches that mentioned punk, Bruce George, MP for Walsall South, presented a measured view. He raised the issue of punk in the Commons during a debate on safety at pop concerts in June 1977.

> Unemployed young people or those with limited job prospects provide a fertile ground for the proponents of punk rock… Despite the total opposition of the Press, a punk rock record by the Sex Pistols has shot to the top of the hit parade ['God Save the Queen' in June 1977]. Young people are listening to this new phenomenon and it is one about which we should be concerned.[109]

Kenneth Marks, the Under Secretary of State for the Environment, speaking in response expressed awareness of the anger and alienation that the Sex Pistols represented, but noted that 'one of the problems with punk rock… is that the whole idea is to be against the Establishment and the adult population'.[110] Negative publicity would continue to impact on the Sex Pistols ability to perform concerts and the group would finally implode after appearing at the Winterland Ballroom, San Francisco in January 1978.[111]

Images of England through the Sex Pistols and punk rock

The Sex Pistols Anarchy Tour highlights the limitations of sociological writing on punk and the historiography of the 1970s in which two positions remain dominant. Writers on the period generally accept the 'mythology of punk' and the centrality of 'crisis' or alternatively seek to downplay the view that the decade was a 'unified entity with a distinctive character'.[112] This chapter has negotiated a path through the two positions by examining a variety of local responses to the Sex Pistols. In December 1976, youth was defined by the media, influential commentators and politicians as a symptom and cause of a shifting morality that threatened the social fabric of the country. The Sex Pistols were the concrete personification of this 'condition of England' and their attitude, recordings and performances provided a critique of contemporary politics and culture. There is a historical consensus that views the country at a crossroads between a form of Labour socialism that had ran out of steam in the 1970s and had failed to deliver improvements to a significant section of its own constituency, and a more right-wing Conservatism that would dismantle much of what such socialism had constructed. The chapter has demonstrated that the sign-posts of 'crisis' and decline were cultural as well economic and political.

The Sex Pistols Anarchy Tour can be characterised as both 'moral panic' and a particular cultural/political event that formed one response to a sense of escalating change. The concept of 'moral panic' is a useful tool in understanding media reactions to popular music, but in its most limited form, it only takes us so far. A more comprehensive utilisation of the 'moral panic' framework for assessing popular reactions to particular types of cultural phenomena needs to engage with the micro-politics of a variety of groups, individuals and localities. The Sex Pistols faced a critical response from business interests, politicians, religious leaders, the media, and a section of the general public that seemed intent on eradicating these 'folk devils' from English society. The discourse utilised was indicative of earlier 'moral panics'. The keywords of 'filth', 'obscenity', 'immorality', 'pornography', 'violence', 'sex', 'dirty', 'cult' and 'anarchy' were associated with the group. The attacks on the Sex Pistols were often couched in the emotive message of 'protecting the children', a constant theme in 'moral panics' across the century. Yet the local response to the Sex Pistols demonstrates that the media was just one player, albeit a fairly dominant one, in articulating a sense of crisis and anxiety in the England of December 1976. Reactions to the group were not completely determined by populist journalists and conservative commentators. Women trade unionists, mothers, students and feminists voiced legitimate concerns about the Sex Pistols and punk. Similarly, councillors in Derby and community activists in south Wales were averse to a metropolitan influence that was seen as a threat to the culture of their localities. Their actions set the scene for further conflicts between north/south and town/country in the 1980s.

The responses to the Sex Pistols Anarchy took a variety of forms and were not just the preserve of social elites. The Conservative leader of the Greater London Council Bernard Brook-Partridge's view that the Sex Pistols were the 'antithesis of humankind' might have been hyperbolic, but it was a characterisation that drew on a wider feeling that England was entering a period of moral and political flux. Unlike many of their musical contemporaries, the Sex Pistols articulated a political identity, but one that was based on a largely inarticulate sense of class, place and generation.[113] Nonetheless, the group was able to present a critique of existing youth culture, popular music and contemporary English society through the force of their personalities, interviews and performances. Ultimately, the political impact of the Sex Pistols was undermined by a combination of media driven 'moral panic' and the mobilisation of social, community, political and religious groups. The 'moral panic' was also crucial to the development of the 'subcultural identity' of punk and the positioning of the Sex Pistols as totemic figures within the movement.

The Sex Pistols and the associated punk rock movement that emerged in the winter of 1976 was a further example of the complex relationship between class, youth and rock 'n' roll. Punk might have partly emerged from the art schools and fashion boutiques of London, but it also depended on a local articulation of its sound, style and rhetoric to develop and maintain its popularity.[114] Working-class youths decoded punk as a genre of music and fashion style to make sense of the difficulties and frustrations that they faced in school, home and workplace. Here was an image of England that remained divided by class but an England where popular music retained its power as a form of social protest and a discourse of escape. The ideological message of the Sex Pistols might have been confused and fragmentary, but it symbolised emerging fractures in English society that would be further tested in the wake of Margaret Thatcher's election victory in 1979.

Encore: On the Road to Wigan Pier to see Georgie Fame and Billy Boston, Sunday 2 March 2003

The car[1] left Didsbury and headed down School Lane passing the site of the ABC television studios where Bob Dylan had performed on 14 May 1964.[2] The traffic slowed on approach to Rusholme where many people were already heading for an early lunch at the many restaurants of Manchester's 'curry mile'. This was the place where the first edition of *Top of the Pops* was broadcast from a converted church on New Year Day 1964. The show was beamed into living rooms introducing working-class youths to the visual spectacle of the Rolling Stones, the Beatles and Dusty Springfield. Along Princess Road and through Moss Side, where the shebeens and street sounds had given the city a particularly multicultural dimension to its youth culture. Here was the former site of the Reno Club that had been opened in 1962. Primarily frequented by Manchester's West Indians and their children, it had also introduced the city's working-class youth to the sounds of rhythm and blues, ska and reggae music[3] – into the city centre and now passing the Edwardian Radisson Hotel. This had formerly been the Free Trade Hall where Dylan was branded a 'Judas' in 1966, and ten years later, a performance by the Sex Pistols would lead to the creation of a multiplicity of groups that would later find their own place in the mythology of English popular music.[4]

Leaving behind the city centre, the car picks up speed along the 'East Lancs' road, and within 15 minutes, the remains of the county's working-class and industrial heritage sweep into view. The head-gear of Astley Green Colliery had stopped winding in 1970, but it remains as a reminder of a past built on coal, class and a radical politics that had contributed to the growth of the trade union movement and the electoral success of the Labour Party in the twentieth century. A little further down the road, a once thriving but long closed cotton mill stands as a monument to the region's contribution to the Industrial Revolution. A sign at the side of the road welcomes visitors to Leigh with images of a coal mine, a cotton mill and rugby players.

Arriving in the town the number of boarded-up pubs is noticeable yet the place still seems to have a spirit and character that has survived the ravages of Thatcherism and the closure of its coal mines and cotton mills that had forged such a collective political and social identity. Just out of town now on 'the road to Wigan Pier' and passing the site of Parsonage Colliery.[5] The mine never really survived the dramatic year-long miners' strike of 1984–5, and it closed in 1992 along with Bickershaw and Golbourne that were part of the same complex.[6] On the last day of production before closure, miners and their families, many of them in tears, marched behind banners depicting a century of industrial, political and social struggle.[7] These mines had provided thousands of jobs to the working-class of Leigh and Wigan across the decades of the twentieth century. A retail park now stands in place of the colliery with the only reminder of its existence being the retention of the 'Parsonage' name and a colliery 'winding wheel'. The shopping complex consists of the usual array of fast-food outlets and chain stores with little evidence of an underground world that once existed below its foundations. Yet a stone's throw from the retail park Georgie Fame's house on Cotton Street still stands. The inhabitants of Number 5 are no longer employed in coal mining and cotton and are perhaps unaware of the importance of the address in providing a home to an important figure in the history of English popular music and a crucial link between northern working-class culture and the shifting social identities of 'swinging London'.

More terraced streets lead on to examples of the modern type of post-war council housing, and within a short time, Leigh becomes Wigan. The town is synonymous with coal mines, working-class culture, a mythical pier and a teenage hedonism that was located in its clubs and dance halls.[8] Again there are more closed pubs but enough pie shops to suggest that the town's working-class retains a link to the dietary culture of coal miners that no longer dig coal because of retirement, disablement and the rapid process of de-industrialisation that impacted on parts of North West England from the 1960s through to the 1980s.[9] Now passing the Ritz, the site of Buddy Holly's electrifying show in 1958, which is now closed, boarded-up and showing little sign of the bright lights, thumping music and Teddy Boy culture of its heyday. A quick swing by the site of the legendary Wigan Casino, the club that dominated the Northern Soul Scene between 1973 and 1981 and was once voted the 'Best Disco in the World' by the American Billboard Magazine.[10] The club had played a key role in the development and popularity of a music scene that had attracted working-class youth from Northern England, the Midlands, Wales and Scotland.[11]

The journey on the 'road to Wigan pier' is almost complete. The car stops at the venue that forms part of the 'Wigan Pier Experience', which had been opened by the Queen in 1986. The complex consists of a collection of buildings hosting the 'Way We Were Museum', 'Trencherfield Mill' and the 'Museum of Memories'.[12] Here was heritage and nostalgia at its best and worst. Depictions of working-class life and its associated hardships and hopes, along with a gift shop where visitors could purchase 'Wigan coal dust'. The rich industrial and cultural history of Wigan and Leigh is traced through machinery, photographs, ephemera and individual and collective memories of a working-class world that had now largely disappeared and perhaps never existed in the form presented here. Yet on Sunday 2 March 2003, aspects of this culture and how it was connected to the rhythm and blues of the United States and the ska music of the West Indies from the 1950s–70s were brought to life by Georgie Fame and Billy Boston.

Fame had been invited to perform a musical tribute to the great Boston, who to 'Wiganers' was a working-class sporting icon and legend of Rugby League, the sport perhaps more than any other that was firmly grounded in the culture of coal, cotton and industrial struggle. Boston had been born in Tiger Bay, Cardiff, the son of an African father and Irish mother and after playing Rugby in Wales had signed for Wigan on 13 March 1953, becoming a giant of the game.[13] The small audience, that nonetheless fill the venue, is here to celebrate the careers of both Boston and Fame and in doing so they are reconnecting with a working-class world and collective memory in which popular music was a constant feature.

The MC delivers a welcome, and being a man of few words, Boston declines to make a speech and just mutters a perfunctory 'thanks very much for turning up'. Five minutes earlier he had been in conversation at the bar and urinal with assorted figures from Wigan's past and others who had travelled some distance in order to witness a performance by Fame. Great tries and mazy runs were recalled with relish, and Boston is happy to talk to all those who request his company. Wigan and Leigh dialect can be heard thick and strong, along with laughter, banter and the odd 'blue joke'. People make a last dash for the bar and return to their seats with their pints of bitter, lager and Guinness, as Fame climbs onto the stage. Given Fame's early employment in weaving, it is fitting that the concert was taking place in the Trencherfield Mill section of the complex that had originally opened in 1908 and still contained a steam engine and other equipment that had once contributed to Lancashire's role in the global cotton industry. Accompanied by his sons on drums and guitar, Fame settles behind the Hammond organ that had already left an indelible mark on the Mods of the Flamingo Club in 1963 and was now ready to deliver both a musical history lesson and an autobiographical romp through the working-class culture of Leigh and Wigan, the excesses of 'swinging London' and his meetings and conversations with the greats of American rhythm and blues music.

Fame opens the show with a short speech about the poor quality of the hotel he stayed in the night before in Haydock and how it might be better utilised as a centre for asylum seekers. The music begins with a traditional hymn, no doubt taking him back to Cotton Street and his early years playing in the church and then straight into a number by the American jazz pianist

Mose Allison. Between songs he constructs a narrative in his still recognisable broad Lancashire accent of playing the pubs of Wigan and Leigh, competing in talent contests at Butlin's holiday camps and his incursion into the world of 'swinging London'. He recalls his experiences with Eddie Cochran, Gene Vincent, Sonny Boy Williamson, John Lee Hooker, John Lennon and Jimi Hendrix. He then sings his own personal tribute to Boston in which he marvels at Billy's ability with the rugby ball and the way in which he moved so quickly and freely up and down the field of play. During the interval, Fame encourages the audience to enjoy 'a cup of tea or a couple of pints'. The songs played in the second half of the show range from standards to blues, to rock 'n' roll, to soul classics. A cover of Edwin Starr's 'S.O.S. – Stop Her on Sight' is particularly engaging and reflective.[14] Starr was a native of Nashville and Cleveland and had been a huge figure on the Northern Soul Scene performing in a number of clubs across North West England. Since 1973, he had lived in England eventually settling in Bramcote near Nottingham, where he would die of a heart attack four weeks after Fame's appearance at Wigan Pier.

The concert ends and everyone shuffles out of Trencherfield Mill a bit worse for wear after the beer and the both uplifting and reflective music. Comments are made about Fame still being 'one of us', and stories of drinking sessions, concerts, parties and workplace shenanigans are retold with much laughter. For a couple of hours on a winter's Sunday afternoon in Wigan, England a working-class past, present and perhaps future came together to listen to a soundtrack that had accompanied poverty, affluence, broken hearts, births, deaths, marriages, divorce and dreams of escape and better times. Here was an image of England that contained continuities and ruptures but ultimately depicted the resilience of a particular working-class identity that had been lived through popular music.

Conclusion

The excavation of popular music that has been presented in this book has attempted to centre rock 'n' roll and its associated cultures in the everyday lives of a significant section of working-class youth. Historians have generally neglected the role of popular music in reflecting and shaping the economic and social changes that posed a challenge to working-class lifestyles and identities in the post-war period. The preceding chapters have presented a more nuanced reading of popular music and youth culture than has been so far offered by Marwick, Sandbrook and Fowler. As such it stands as a call for popular music and youth culture to be taken far more seriously by social, political and economic historians. The images and impressions of England that can be accessed through popular music and youth culture shed light on an array of social identities that were being confirmed, challenged and transformed by working-class youths in their creation, performance and consumption of rock 'n' roll.

Through a focus on particular localities and music scenes, the claims and critiques of the CCCS have been empirically tested by drawing on an extensive range of primary and secondary sources. What emerges is a clearer view of the relationship between popular music and social class. To many of the performers and consumers of popular music in post-war England, class remained a source of identity, anxiety and rebellion. From the Lancashire coalfield to the rhythm and blues clubs of London, class remained a source of collective identity for many young men and women. Far from symbolising a flight from class, affluence, youth culture and popular music represented a restatement of its centrality to English society. Thompson in his classic *Making of the English Working Class* (1963) argued that class-consciousness was grounded in the way that particular social experiences were expressed in cultural terms. From the 1950s, working-class youth performed and consumed popular music as a source of escape from the mine, mill and factory, but also as an affirmation of a particular connection to community and locality. Rock 'n' roll, rhythm and blues and West Indian ska music provided a range of spaces and soundscapes where class could be traversed, challenged and absorbed into particular aspects of youth culture.

Influential performers such as Pete Townshend, Ray Davies, David Bowie and John Lydon should be seen as 'organic intellectuals' who expressed and re-shaped a particular 'structure of feeling' that was attuned to the changes taking place in English society in the post-war period. Through their songs, styles and performances they accessed the everyday experiences of working-class youth and made a significant contribution to then current debates on the 'condition of England'. The images of England that they created, documented and expressed formed a critique of the inequalities and social problems that remained a feature of English social life into the late twentieth century. Popular music and youth culture can and should inform future research on English identity in the post-war period. The coffee bars, dance halls and theatres of London and the English provinces were spaces where social conventions were being challenged and a new society was being constructed. Lancashire coal miners and cotton workers absorbing African American rhythm and blues, Mod girls wearing suits and cropping their hair, northern tough lads applying mascara and lip gloss and punk rockers sneering at social elites all made a particular contribution to new forms of politics and personal expression. Popular music might not have changed the course of English history, but it reflected its tensions, explored its nuances, and soundtracked the everyday experiences of its working-class.

Notes

Introduction

1. The literature on American 'rock 'n' roll' and 'rhythm and blues' is vast. Two books stand out in presenting detailed explorations of the origins and development of these musical genres and their impact on wider US society. For rock 'n' roll, see G. C. Altschuler, *All Shook Up: How Rock 'n' Roll Changed America* (Oxford, 2003) and for 'rhythm and blues', B. Ward, *Just My Soul Responding: Rhythm and Blues, Black Consciousness and Race Relations* (London, 1998).
2. The emphasis on England and the English experience of popular music does not necessarily suggest that the relationship between class and youth culture was always different in Wales, Scotland and Northern Ireland, but in some respects it clearly did differ. For examples in the literature, see S. Hill, *Blerwytirhwg? The Place of Welsh Pop Music* (Aldershot, 2007); M. Kielty, *Big Noise: The History of Scottish Rock 'n' Roll* (Edinburgh, 2006); D. Cooper, *The Musical Traditions of Northern Ireland and Its Diaspora: Community and Conflict* (Aldershot, 2010).
3. There are really only two academic books written by historians devoted to this aspect of British society. See B. Osgerby, *Youth Culture in Britain Since 1945* (Oxford, 1998) and D. Fowler, *Youth Culture in Modern Britain, c1920–1970* (Basingstoke, 2008).
4. W. Straw, 'Consumption', in Frith, Straw and Street (eds), *The Cambridge Companion to Pop and Rock*, p. 55. For a critical survey of the limited histories of popular music, see S. Frith, 'Writing the History of Popular Music', in H. Dauncy and P. Le Guern (eds), *Stereo: Comparative Perspectives on the Sociological Study of Popular Music in France and Britain* (Aldershot, 2011), pp. 11–22.
5. Popular music histories on television range from the nostalgia of the Yesterday channel through to the more serious, comprehensive and analytical documentaries produced for BBC4.
6. Mort's excellent book on permissiveness is a detailed exploration of the sexual politics of London but has very little on popular music. See F. Mort, *Capital Affairs: London and the Making of the Permissive Society* (New Haven, 2010).
7. Kynaston's work is notable for drawing on the autobiographies/biographies of some of the leading musicians of the 1950s/60s. See D. Kynaston, *Family Britain 1951–57* (London, 2009).
8. A. Marwick, *The Sixties: Cultural Revolution in Britain, France, Italy and the United States, c.1958–c.1974* (Oxford, 1998); D. Sandbrook, *White Heat: A History of Britain in the Swinging Sixties* (London, 2006) and Fowler, *Youth Culture in Modern Britain*.
9. The seminal collection of papers from CCCS can be found in S. Hall and T. Jefferson (eds), *Resistance through Rituals: Youth Subcultures in Post-war Britain* (London, 1976).
10. R. Hoggart, *The Uses of Literacy: Aspects of Working-Class Life with Special Reference to Publications and Entertainments* (Harmondsworth, 1957).
11. For a recent re-appraisal, see J. Moran, 'Milk Bars, Starbucks and the Uses of Literacy', *Cultural Studies*, 20, 6 (2006), 552–73.

12. R. Williams, *Culture and Society, 1780–1950* (London, 1984), p. 310.
13. R. Williams, *Marxism and Literature* (Oxford, 1977), p. 132.
14. For a discussion of 'structure of feeling' and its applicability to the literature of the late twentieth century, see John Kirk, 'Class, Community and 'Structure of Feeling', in Working-class Writing from the 1980s', *Literature and History*, 3, 8, 2 (1999), 44–63.
15. Although Williams was not associated with the Birmingham school, his work shared their methodology of applying a critical Marxist analysis to the relationship between class and culture. A broader advocacy of 'structure of feeling' can be found in Williams, *The Long Revolution* (Harmondsworth, 1961), pp. 64–88. A critical appraisal of the concept can be found in P. Filmer, 'Structures of Feeling and Socio-cultural Formations: The Significance of Literature and Experience to Raymond William's Sociology of Culture', *British Journal of Sociology*, 54, 2 (2003), 199–219. For a biography of Williams, see F. Inglis, *Raymond Williams* (London, 1995).
16. See Williams, *Culture and Society*.
17. For another seminal CCCS exposition of class, capitalism and subculture, see P. Cohen, *Subcultural Conflict and Working Class Community* (Birmingham, 1972).
18. D. Hebdige, *Subculture: The Meaning of Style* (London, 1979).
19. Both Fowler and Sandbrook have attempted to comprehensively dismantle the claims of the CCCS but have merely replaced one partial interpretation with another and are equally guilty of hyperbole and rhetoric in imposing what they perceive to be a 'common sense' view of popular music and its place in post-war English history. See Sandbrook, *White Heat* and Fowler, *Youth Culture in Modern Britain*.
20. See for example A. McRobbie, *Feminism and Youth Culture: From Jackie to Just Seventeen* (Cambridge, 1991).
21. For a good summary, see P. Hodkinson, 'Youth Cultures: A Critical Outline of Key Debates', in P. Hodkinson and W. Deicke (eds), *Youth Cultures: Scenes, Subcultures and Tribes* (London, 2009), pp. 1–21. Also, K. Gelder, *Subcultures: Cultural Histories and Social Practice* (London, 2007), chapter 5.
22. For a critique of the CCCS, see C. Bugge, 'Selling Youth in the Age of Affluence: Marketing to Youth in Britain Since 1959', in L. Black and H. Pemberton (eds), *An Affluent Society? Britain's Post-War Golden-Age Revisited* (Aldershot, 2004), pp. 185–202. Also the collection of essays in K. Gelder and S. Thornton (eds), *The Subcultures Reader* (London, 2005). For a critical defence of the CCCS, see the essays on youth culture, popular music and the post-war consensus in *Contemporary British History*, 26, 3 (2012).
23. Frith, 'Writing the History of Popular Music', p. 12.
24. Interestingly a number of leading popular music scholars outside of the academy also have very privileged educational backgrounds, but have made a career out of extolling the virtues of various popular music performers and genres. Barney Hoskyns (Oxford), Johnny Rogan (Oxford), John Harris (Oxford), Simon Reynolds (Oxford) and Dave Haslam (King Edwards' School Birmingham) are most notable in this respect.
25. See P. Henessey, *Having It So Good: Britain in the Fifties* (London, 2006). This book has 740 pages with only three devoted to a discussion of 'rock 'n' roll'. Sandbrook's work has devoted more space to popular culture, but is sceptical of the claims made for popular music by other writers. He shows his own prejudices by putting more emphasis on particular youth cultures while ridiculing others.

See D. Sandbrook, *Seasons in the Sun: The Battle for Britain, 1974–1979* (London, 2012). A much better examination of popular culture in the 1970s can be found in A. W. Turner, *Crisis? What Crisis? Britain in the 1970s* (London, 2008).

26. For a recent call for popular music and youth culture to be taken more seriously by historians, see introduction to the special issue of *Contemporary British History: Youth Culture, Popular Music and 'Consensus' in Post-War Britain* 26, 3 (2012), 265–71.
27. D. Sandbrook, *Never Had It So Good: A History of Britain from Suez to the Beatles* (London, 2005), p. xix.
28. For example, see the testimonies in K. Farley, *They Rocked, We Rolled: A Personal and Oral Account of Rock 'n' Roll in and around Wolverhampton and the West Midlands 1956–1969* (Wolverhampton, 2010). Similarly, in the late 1950s Aberdare remained a vibrant community with coal mines, labour movement institutions and a developing youth culture based on a local record shop, music venues and accessibility to the city of Cardiff where working-class youth could see both American and British performers.
29. For English resorts in the twentieth century, see J. Walton, *The British Seaside: Holidays and Resorts in the Twentieth Century* (Manchester, 2000).
30. In the 1960s, writers such as Nell Dunn and television directors such as Ken Loach were aware of the importance of popular music in working-class life and used it accordingly in their attempts at documenting the experiences of English youth. As John Hill stresses in his critical analysis of the Loach directed BBC play of Dunn's *Up the Junction*, which was broadcast in November 1965: 'the play avoids representing 'mass culture' as simply a culture imposed from above but seeks to show how the characters succeed in making pop songs their own… and are able to use pop music as a cultural resource in the struggles of everyday life'. J. Hill, *Ken Loach: The Politics of Film and Television* (London, 2011), p. 45.
31. S. Hall, 'Notes on Deconstructing 'the Popular', in R. Samuel (ed.), *People's History and Socialist Theory* (London, 1981), p. 230.
32. R. Hewison, *Culture and Consensus. England, Art and Politics Since 1940* (London, 1995), p. xiv.
33. For a recent exception, see J. P. Wilson, 'Beats Apart: A Comparative History of Youth Culture and Popular Music in Liverpool and Newcastle upon Tyne, 1956–1965' (Unpublished PhD thesis, University of Northumbria, 2009).
34. For examples of this particular genre, see A. Flowers and V. Histon, *It's My Life! 1960s Newcastle: Memories from People Who Were There* (Newcastle, 2009), D. Hale and T. Thornton, *Club 60 & The Esquire: Sheffield Sounds in the 60s* (Sheffield, 2002) and Farley, *They Rocked, We Rolled.*
35. J. Davis, *Youth and the Condition of Britain: Images of Adolescent Conflict* (London, 1990).
36. Fowler, *Youth Culture in Modern Britain* (Basingstoke, 2008).
37. Osgerby, *Youth Culture in Britain Since 1945*. For a summary of his main points, see B. Osgerby, 'Well, It's Saturday Night and I Just Got Paid': Youth, Consumerism and Hegemony in Post-War-Britain', *Contemporary Record,* 6, 2 (1992), 287–303. Fowler, *Youth Culture in Modern Britain.*
38. R. Weight, *Patriots: National Identity in Britain 1940–2000* (Basingstoke, 2002).
39. J. Street, 'Shock Waves: The Authoritarian Response to Popular Music', in D. Strinati and S. Wagg (eds), *Come on Down? Popular Media Culture in Post-War Britain* (London, 1992), p. 303.
40. J. Street, *Rebel Rock: The Politics of Popular Music* (Oxford, 1986), p. 174.
41. J. Street, 'Rock, Pop and Politics', in Frith, Straw and Street (eds), *The Cambridge Companion to Pop and Rock*, p. 246.

42. D. Harker, 'Still Crazy After All These Years: What Was Popular Music in the 1960s?', in B. M. Gilbert and J. Seed (eds), *Cultural Revolution? The Challenge of the Arts in the 1960s* (Oxford, 1992), p. 249. See also D. Harker, *One for the Money. Politics and Popular Song* (London, 1980).
43. For a similar attempt to examine the contribution of song to political ideals and conflicts but neglects both rock 'n' roll and rhythm and blues, see I. Watson, *Song and Democratic Culture in Britain: An Approach to Popular Culture in Social Movements* (London, 1983).
44. Harker, 'Still Crazy After All These Years', in Gilbert and Seed (eds), *Cultural Revolution?* p. 251.
45. For a critical reading of the relationship between rock and notions of counter-culture, see K. Keightley, 'Reconsidering Rock', in Frith, Straw and Street (eds), *The Cambridge Companion to Pop and Rock*, p. 125.
46. Both Frith and Marcus are giants in the field of popular music studies yet both seem to be more concerned with sociological theory (Frith) or the more literary and symbolic aspects of popular music (Marcus). For a detailed overview of the theoretical approaches to rock music in particular, see L. Grossberg, 'Another Boring Day in Paradise: Rock and Roll and the Empowerment of Everyday Life', *Popular Music*, 4 (1984), 225–58.
47. S. Frith, *Sound Effects: Youth, Leisure, and the Politics of Rock 'n' Roll* (London, 1983).
48. Ibid., pp. 271–2.
49. G. Marcus, *Mystery Train: Images of America in Rock 'n' Roll Music* (London, 1975, 1997), p. 4.
50. According to John Harris the seminal texts include N. Cohn, *Awopbopaloobop Alopbamboom: Pop from the Beginning* (London, 1969); I. MacDonald's, *Revolution in the Head* (London, 1994); and J. Savage, *England's Dreaming: Sex Pistols and Punk Rock* (London, 1991). See J. Harris, 'Don't Look Back', *The Guardian*, 27 June 2009.
51. C. Gillett, *The Sound of the City: The Rise of Rock and Roll* (Gateshead, 1970).
52. See, for example, J. Savage, *Teenage: The Creation of Youth, 1875–1945* (London, 2007) and his ground breaking study of punk, *England's Dreaming*.
53. For a collection of his writings, see J. Savage, *Time Travel: Pop, Media and Sexuality 1976–96* (London, 1996).
54. G. Melly, *Revolt into Style. The Pop Arts in the 50s and 60s* (London, 1970, 1989), p. 247.
55. For film, see J. Richards, *Films and British National Identity: From Dickens to Dad's Army* (Manchester, 1997), pp. 25–6.
56. For discussion of this method, see A. Aldgate and J. Richards, *Best of British: Cinema and Society from 1930 to the Present* (London, 1999), pp. 8–9.
57. For film, see Richards, *Films and British National Identity* and Aldgate and Richards, *Best of British*.
58. D. Russell, *Popular Music in England, 1840–1914* (Manchester, 1987).
59. R. Colls, *Identity of England* (Oxford, 2004).
60. See M. Cloonan, 'State of the Nation: Englishness, Pop and Politics in the mid-1990s', *Popular Music and Society*, 21, 2 (1997), 47–70; A. Bennett and J. Stratton (eds), *Britpop and the English Music Tradition* (Aldershot, 2010); Weight, *Patriots* (Basingstoke, 2002).
61. P. Mandler, *The English National Character: The History of an Idea from Edmund Burke to Tony Blair* (New Haven, 2006), p. 221.
62. M. Bracewell, *England Is Mine: Pop Life in Albion from Wilde to Goldie* (London, 1998), p. 82.

63. P. Gilroy, *The Black Atlantic: Modernity and Double Consciousness* (London, 1993), p. 76.
64. For a survey of the literature on race and popular music, see B. Shank, 'From Rice to Ice: The Face of Race in Rock and Pop', in Frith, Straw and Street (eds), *The Cambridge Companion to Pop and Rock*, pp. 256–71.
65. J. Carey, *What Good Are the Arts* (London, 2005), pp. 178–9.
66. For two major interventions on this relationship, see Harker, *One for the Money* and J. Street, *Music and Politics* (London, 2011).
67. For an attempt to locate 'political' songs in their social context and as reflecting particular types of protest, see D. Lynskey, *33 Revolutions Per Minute: A History of Protest Songs* (London, 2010).
68. L. Black, *The Political Culture of the Left in Affluent Britain, 1951–64* (Basingstoke, 2003), p. 77.
69. J. Benson, *The Rise of Consumer Society in Britain* (London, 1994), p. 226.
70. E. E. Cashmore, *No Future. Youth and Society* (London, 1984), p. 31.
71. B. Osgerby, 'From the Roaring Twenties to the Swinging Sixties: Continuity and Change in British Youth Culture 1929–59', in B. Brivati and H. Jones (ed.), *What Difference Did the War Make?* (London, 1995), p. 84.
72. T. Blackwell and J. Seabrook, *A World Still To Win: The Reconstruction of the Post-War Working Class* (London, 1985), p. 87.
73. N. Nehring, *Flowers in the Dustbin. Culture, Anarchy, and Postwar England* (Ann Arbor, 1993), p. 168.
74. P. Wicke, *Rock Music: Culture, Aesthetics and Sociology* (Cambridge, 1995), p. ix.
75. Ibid., p. 91.
76. The United States seems to be ahead of England in this respect with the production of detailed histories of popular music and how it engaged with wider economic, social and cultural developments. For example, see Altschuler, *All Shook Up*.
77. For a discussion of this process in the mid-1950s, see D. Bradley, *Understanding Rock 'n' Roll: Popular Music in Britain 1955–1964* (Buckingham, 1992), especially pp. 91–3.
78. For a good collection of pieces on the origins and development of black music in Britain, see P. Oliver (ed.), *Black Music in Britain: Essays on the Afro-Contribution to Popular Music* (Buckingham, 1990).
79. The standard text remains A. McRobbie, *Feminism and Youth Culture: From Jackie to Just Seventeen* (London, 1991).
80. L. Heron, *Truth, Dare or Promise: Girls Growing Up in the Fifties* (London, 1985), p. 7.
81. For a pithy synopsis see the essay by Jon Savage, 'Tainted Love. The Influence of Male Homosexuality and Sexual Divergence on Pop Music and Culture Since the War', in A. Tomlinson (ed.), *Consumption, Identity and Style* (London, 1990), pp. 153–71. For a broader analysis of the homosexual culture of London, see R. Hornsey, *The Spiv and the Architect: Unruly Life in Postwar London* (Minneapolis, 2010).
82. K. Davey, *English Imaginaries* (London, 1999), p. 2.
83. The selection of particular artists for a history such as this is bound to be controversial and open to critique. As with all art, critical appraisal of popular music is highly subjective. The performers were selected on the basis of both their commercial and critical success and the way in which they made a crucial contribution to changing the direction of popular music in particular or working-class youth culture more generally.
84. Colls, *Identity of England*, p. 365.

85. For a clear exposition of Thompson's view, one needs to go no further than the preface to his classic *The Making of the English Working Class* (Harmondsworth, 1963).
86. A. Gramsci, *Selections from the Prison Notebooks,* Q. Hoare and G. N. Smith (eds) (London, 1986), p. 3.
87. For a dated but useful survey of Gramsci's ideas, see Carl Boggs, *Gramsci's Marxism* (London, 1980).
88. For a discussion of the problem of sources for the study of popular music, see S. Thornton, 'Strategies for Reconstructing the Popular Past', *Popular Music*, 9, 1 (1990), 87–95 and T. Gourvish, 'The British Popular Music Industry, 1950–75: Archival Challenges and Solutions', *Business Archives*, 99 (2009), 25–39.
89. R. Samuel, *Theatres of Memory Vol. 1: Past and Present in Contemporary Culture* (London, 1994), p. 443.
90. J. M. Picker, *Victorian Soundscapes* (Oxford, 2003). The United States was the key contributor to the style, image and promotion of youth culture in the 1950s. For an analysis of this process, see L. G. Cooper and B. L. Cooper, 'The Pendulum of Cultural Imperialism: Popular Music Interchanges between the United States and Britain, 1943–1967', in S. P. Ramet and G. P. Crnkovic (eds), *Kazaam! Splat! Ploof! The American Impact on European Popular Culture Since 1945* (London, 2003), pp. 69–82.
91. For a collection of essays with a transnational focus on this theme, see T. Mitchell, *Popular Music and Local Identity: Rock, Pop and Rap in Europe and Oceania* (Leicester, 1996).
92. A. Bennett, *Popular Music and Youth Culture: Music, Identity and Place* (Basingstoke, 2000), p. 2.
93. M. Stokes, 'Introduction', in Martin Stokes (ed), *Ethnicity, Identity and Music. The Musical Construction of Place* (Oxford, 1994), p. 5.
94. I. Chambers, *Urban Rhythms: Pop Music and Popular Culture* (Basingstoke, 1985) p. 41.
95. J. Connell and C. Gibson, *Sound Tracks: Popular Music, Identity and Place* (London, 2003), p. 1.
96. Ibid., p. 73.
97. M. Houlbrook, *Queer London: Perils and Pleasures in the Sexual Metropolis, 1918–1957* (Chicago, 2005).
98. For an interesting recent study of the relationship between England and Ireland through popular music, see S. Campbell, *Irish Blood English Heart: Second Generation Irish Musicians in England* (Cork, 2011).
99. Music chart statistics have been taken from D. McAleer, *Hit Singles Top 20 Charts from 1954 to the Present Day* (London, 2003).
100. Chambers, *Urban Rhythms,* p. 18.

Soundcheck: Buddy Holly and the 'Lemon Drop Kid', Wigan, England, Tuesday 18 March 1958

1. This reconstruction of the day is based on an interview the author conducted with Ronnie 'The Lemon Drop Kid', Carr, 4 September 2012.
2. *Daily Mail*, 5 September 1956.
3. See concert bill in *Wigan Observer and District Advertiser*, 28 February 1958.
4. Six years later Allan Horsfall, a clerk for the National Coal Board established the North West Committee for Homosexual Law Reform from his miners' home in the neighbouring town of Atherton. The initiative was covered on the front page

of the *Leigh Reporter*. A number of Labour MPs had warned Horsfall that 'the miners would not stand for it', but to Horsfall's surprise there was 'no trouble' from the working-class inhabitants of the town. See obituaries in *The Independent*, 11 September and *The Guardian*, 20 October 2012.

5. *Bradford Telegraph and Argus*, 10 March 1958.

1 Coal, Cotton and Rock 'n' Roll in North West England

1. There is no biography/autobiography of Clive Powell/Georgie Fame, which is surprising given the central role that he played in various key-moments in the development of rock 'n' roll, rhythm and blues and associated youth subcultures in post-war England.
2. Both of these classic texts have been the subject of much critique. For example see, J. Moran, 'Milk Bars, Starbucks and the Uses of Literacy', *Cultural Studies*, 20, 6 (2006), 552–73 and Sandbrook's scathing assessment of MacInnes's novel in *Never Had It So Good: A History of Britain from Suez to the Beatles* (London, 2005), pp. 323–6. See also Flower, *Youth Culture in Modern Britain, c.1920–c.1970: From Ivory Tower to Global Movement – A New History* (Basingstoke, 2008), chapter 6.
3. C. MacInnes, *Absolute Beginners* (1959, 1986), p. 74.
4. R. Hoggart, *The Uses of Literacy: Aspects of Working-class Life with Special Reference to Publications and Entertainments* (Harmondsworth, 1957, 1969), chapter 8.
5. Historians have tended to neglect the industrial towns of North West England in the post-war period and have primarily concentrated on the culture and politics of the larger cities. For recent examples, see A. Kidd, *Manchester: A History* (Lancaster, 2006) and J. Belchem (ed.), *Liverpool 800: Culture, Character and History* (Chicago, 2012).
6. See J. Saville, 'Henry Twist (1870–1934)', in J. and J. M. Bellamy, *Dictionary of Labour Biography Vol. II* (Basingstoke, 1974), pp. 370–1. The last miners' sponsored Labour MP for Leigh was Lawrence Cunliffe, who held the seat between 1979–2001.
7. J. Singleton, 'The Decline of the British Cotton Industry since 1940', in M. B. Rose (ed.) *The Lancashire Cotton Industry. A History Since 1700* (Preston, 1996), p. 307.
8. A. Fowler, *Lancashire Cotton Operatives and Work, 1900–1950. A Social History of Lancashire Cotton Operatives in the Twentieth Century* (Aldershot, 2003), p. 10.
9. Singleton, 'The Decline of the British Cotton Industry since 1940', p. 298.
10. G. Moorhouse, *Britain in the Sixties: The Other England* (Harmondsworth, 1964), p. 121.
11. For an examination of trade union politics in the area, see D. Howell, *The Politics of the NUM: A Lancashire View* (Manchester, 1989), especially chapters 1–3.
12. Closures increased in the 1950s and 60s further diluting the number of miners in Leigh and Wigan: Victoria (1958), Garswood Hall (1958), Maypole (1959), Welch Whittle (1963), Landgate (1960), Mains (1960), Giants Hall (1961), Standish Hall (1961), Ince Moss (1962), Wigan Junction (1962), Dairy (1962), Gibfield (1963), Robin Hill (1963), Cleworth (1963). For detail on individual collieries, see Stephen Catterall, 'The Lancashire Coalfield, 1945–1972: The Politics of Industrial Change' (Unpublished DPhil thesis, University of York, 2001).
13. For Williams such a 'structure of feeling' was distinct from an affirmation of class that could be gauged through particular organisations and ideologies.

See R. Williams, *Marxism and Literature* (Oxford, 1977), chapter 9. For a critical appraisal of the concept, see P. Filmer, 'Structures of feeling and Socio-cultural Formations: The Significance of Literature and Experience to Raymond Williams's Sociology of Culture', *British Journal of Sociology*, 54, 2 (2003), 199–219.

14. Clive Powell birth certificate, Family Records Centre, London.
15. Parsonage Colliery was situated close to Leigh town centre. It had been in operation from 1920 and by the 1950s employed over 1200 workers.
16. The first episode of *Coronation Street* had been broadcast on 9 December 1960, and put on screen some of the features of Hoggart's inter-war working-class values and types. For an insightful analysis, see J. Moran, 'Imagining the Street in Post-war Britain', *Urban History*, 39, 1 (2012), 166–86.
17. *Rave*, No. 13 February 1965. *Rave* was a popular magazine aimed at the 'teenage market' and contained photographs and profiles of the leading popular music stars of the 1960s.
18. For an insight into the inter-war working-class of Wigan, see G. Orwell, *The Road to Wigan Pier* (London, 1937).
19. For a detailed description of working-class culture in this period, see R. McKibbin, *Classes and Cultures: England 1918–1951* (Oxford, 1998), especially chapters IV, V, IX and X.
20. *Rave*, No. 13 February 1965.
21. *Leigh Chronicle*, 29 August 1963.
22. The family piano proved crucial in the musical education of a number of seminal figures in English popular music including Ray and Dave Davies of the Kinks (see chapter 6).
23. *Rave*, No. 13 February 1965.
24. For the role of the church in American rhythm and blues music, see some of the biographical sketches in P. Guralnick, *Sweet Soul Music: Rhythm and Blues and the Southern Dream of Freedom* (London, 1986).
25. For a rich social history of the popular music in this period, see P. Frame, *The Restless Generation: How Rock Music Changed the Face of 1950s Britain* (London, 2007).
26. For a description of popular radio and its impact in this period, see P. Hennessey, *Having It So Good: Britain in the Fifties* (London, 2006), chapter 2.
27. N. Cohn, *Awopbopaloobop Alopbamboom: Pop from the Beginning* (London, 1969), p. 58. Cohn's work is partial and problematic, but it nonetheless captures the zeitgeist of the developing connection between particular aspects of youth culture and popular music. English popular music in the 1950s is beginning to be re-appraised. For example see, G. A. M. Mitchell, 'A Very British Introduction to Rock 'n' Roll: Tommy Steele and the Advent of Rock 'n' Roll Music in Britain, 1956–60', *Contemporary British History*, 25, 2 (2011), 205–25.
28. The year is also notable as forming a turning point in the lives of leading figures in post-war popular music. Many rock autobiographies make some reference to the arrival of Elvis on jukeboxes, in magazines and the racks of record shops. For example, see K. Richards, *Life* (London, 2010).
29. For the charts in both the United Kingdom and the United States, see D. McAleer, *Hit Singles Top 20 Charts from 1954 to the Present Day* (London, 2003).
30. This is particularly the case when the multiplicity of local and regional publications on the 1950s are examined. The oral testimonies that underpin many of these books point to the way in which rock 'n' roll both energised and offered an alternative sense of reality to teenage consumers. For example, see A. Flowers

and V. Histon (eds), *It's My Life! 1960s Newcastle: Memories from People Who Were There* (Newcastle, 2009).

31. For a very good analysis of the transmission of popular music through juke boxes, see A. Horn, *Juke Box Britain: Americanisation and Youth Culture, 1945–60* (Manchester, 2009).
32. For a literary characterisation of the rides and atmosphere of Nottingham's Goose Fair, see A. Sillitoe, *Saturday Night and Sunday Morning* (London, 1958), chapter 11.
33. Similar experiences were apparent across England. In Northampton, Ray Gosling felt that rock 'n' roll 'was like the start of a revolution'. See R. Gosling, *Sum Total* (London, 1962), p. 71.
34. A. Clayson, *Call Up the Groups: The Golden Age of British Beat, 1962–67* (London, 1985), p. 103.
35. For an overview of rock 'n' roll in England, see Frame, *The Restless Generation* and D. Bradley, *Understanding Rock n' Roll: Popular Music in Britain 1955–64* (Milton Keynes, 1992).
36. D. Russell, *Looking North: Northern England and the National Imagination* (Manchester, 2004), p. 208.
37. For examples, see Russell, *Looking North*, chapter 7.
38. For an overview of cinemas and audiences for film in this period, see S. Hanson, *From Silent Screen to Multi-Screen: A History of Cinema Exhibition in Britain Since 1896* (Manchester, 2007), chapter 4 and P. Stead, *Film and the Working Class: The Feature Film in British and American Society* (London, 1989), chapter 8.
39. London County Council, *London Children and the Cinema* (1951–7), Mark Abrams Papers, Box 53, Churchill College, Cambridge.
40. For example, see S. Chibnall, 'Whistle and Zoot: The Changing Meaning of a Suit of Clothes', *History Workshop Journal*, 20 (1985), 56–81.
41. *Wigan Examiner*, 11 May 1954. The revue also featured a young Shirley Bassey who went on to achieve significant success in both Britain and the United States.
42. For examples, see Stephen Catterall and K. Gildart, 'Outsiders: The Experience of Polish and Italian Coal Miners in Britain', in S. Berger, A. Croll, and N. LaPorte (eds), *Towards a Comparative History of Coalfield Societies* (Aldershot, 2005), pp. 164–76.
43. For profile of Ellington, see D. McAleer, *Hit Parade Heroes* (London, 1993), p. 18.
44. 'Ray Ellington (1916–1985)', *Oxford Dictionary of National Biography* (Oxford, 2004–12).
45. Fowler seriously underestimates the importance of the multiplicity of transmission routes for the consumption of American popular culture in signifying sharp shifts in the youth culture of the 1950s. See Fowler, *Youth Culture in Modern Britain*, especially the preface and chapter 9.
46. *Leigh Chronicle*, 13 August 1954.
47. For a succinct survey of the impact of the film and its connection to youth culture, see Sandbrook, *Never Had It So Good*, chapter 13.
48. *Leigh Chronicle*, 14 and 21 September 1956.
49. Manchester was the scene of a number of disturbances with vandalism in the cinema and scuffles on the street. For a critical discussion of the press reports of the violence that accompanied the screening of the film, see J. Davis, *Youth and the Condition of Britain: Images of Adolescent Conflict* (London, 1990), chapter 7.
50. *The Independent*, 17 April 2005.
51. For an account of the developing 'moral panic' around 'Teddy Boy' violence, see G. Pearson, *Hooligan: A History of Respectable Fears* (Basingstoke, 1983), chapter 2.

The literature on Teds is still extremely limited. For partial accounts, see Davis, *Youth and the Condition of Britain*, chapter 7; C. Steel-Perkins and R. Smith, *The Teds* (Stockport, 1979); T. Jefferson, 'Cultural Responses of the Teds', in S. Hall and T. Jefferson (eds), *Resistance Through Rituals: Youth Subcultures in Post-War Britain* (London, 1975, 2004), pp. 81–6; T.R. Fyvel, *The Insecure Offenders: Rebellious Youth in the Welfare State* (Harmondsworth, 1961); T. Parker, *The Ploughboy* (London, 1965); P. Rock and S. Cohen, 'The Teddy Boy', in V. Bogdanor and R. Skidelsky (eds), *The Age of Affluence, 1951–64* (Basingstoke, 1970), pp. 288–320 and Horn, *Juke Box Britain*, chapter 5.

52. Ronnie Carr, interview with author, 4 September 2006.
53. *Leigh Chronicle*, 24 September 1954. Report of prosecution of Leigh youths for breaking into a number of premises. Liverpool Quarter Sessions described the accused as Teddy Boys. Some were jailed, and others sent to approved schools.
54. *Leigh Chronicle*, 12 March and 2 April 1954.
55. For an example of an insight into these sexual underworlds, see R. Hornsey, *The Spiv and the Architect: Unruly Life in Postwar London* (Minneapolis, 2010), chapters 1–2.
56. L. A. Hall, *Sex, Gender and Social Change in Britain Since 1880* (Basingstoke, 2000), pp. 160–2.
57. For link between Teds and crime, see Fyvel, *The Insecure Offenders*, chapter 4.
58. For an account of the development of Teddy Boy culture, see Rock and Cohen, 'The Teddy Boy'.
59. *London Evening Standard*, 23 January 1956.
60. *London Evening Standard*, 24 January 1956.
61. Sandbrook, *Never Had It So Good*, p. 103.
62. *Sunday Times*, 14 December 1958.
63. *London Evening Standard*, 25 January 1956.
64. *Sunday Times*, 14 December 1958.
65. Ibid.
66. *Leigh Chronicle*, 2 July 1954.
67. *Leigh Chronicle*, 29 June 1956.
68. For juvenile delinquency on film, see the perceptive piece in *Sight and Sound* (Winter, 1959–60) and J. Hill, *Sex, Class and Realism: British Cinema 1956–1963* (London, 1986), chapter 4.
69. C2654 Female, 60, Mass Observation Project, University of Sussex Archives.
70. *Leigh Chronicle*, 17 May 1957.
71. A. Davies, *Leisure, Gender and Poverty. Working-Class Culture in Salford and Manchester, 1900–1939* (Manchester, 1992), p. 90.
72. For summary of the development of these shows, see entries in J. Evans, *The Penguin TV Companion* (Harmondsworth, 2003).
73. *Sunday Times*, 14 December 1958.
74. *Wigan Observer and District Advertiser*, 18 April 1958.
75. For a recent revisionist view of this process, see S. Todd and H. Young, 'Babyboomers to Beanstalkers: Making the Modern Teenager in Post-War Britain', *Cultural and Social History*, 9, 3 (2012), 451–67.
76. *Wigan Observer and District Advertiser*, 11 April 1958.
77. For a rather simplistic critique of MacInnes' novel, see Fowler, *Youth Culture in Modern Britain*, pp. 5–7.
78. C. P. Lee, *Shake, Rattle and Rain: Popular Music Making in Manchester 1955–1995* (Devon, 2002), p. 26.
79. D. Haslam, *Manchester England: The Story of a Pop Cult City* (London, 1999), p. 84.

80. For a history, see V. Toulmin, *Pleasurelands: All the Fun of the Fair* (Hastings, 2003).
81. Moorhouse, *Britain in the Sixties*, p. 118.
82. M. Abrams, 'Why Labour Has Lost Elections Part 4. Young Voter', *Socialist Commentary*, (July 1960), pp. 5–12.
83. M. Abrams, 'The Younger Generation', *Encounter* (May 1956), p. 40.
84. C. McDevitt, *Skiffle. The Definitive Inside Story* (London, 1997), p. 143.
85. For coffee bars in North East England, see early chapters of B. Welch, *Rock 'n' Roll I Gave You the Best Years of My Life: A Life in the Shadows* (London, 1989), p. 65.
86. Ronnie Carr, interview with author, 4 September 2006.
87. B. A. Young, 'Coffee-Bar Theory and Practice', *Punch*, Vol. CCXXXI, No. 6067, 5 (December 1956), 670–2.
88. A. Atkinson and R. Searle, 'The New Mayhem – Night in a London Coffee-House', *Punch*, Vol. CCXXXIV, No. 6128, 29 (January 1958), 178–9.
89. *Daily Express*, 13 May 1959.
90. Hoggart, *The Uses of Literacy*, pp. 248–9.
91. See Hill, *Sex, Class and Realism* and John Kirk, *The British Working Class in the Twentieth Century: Film, Literature and Television* (Cardiff, 2009). The key novels of the period included John Braine's *Room at the Top* (1957), A. Sillitoe's *Saturday Night and Sunday Morning* (1958) and C. MacInnes's *Absolute Beginners* (1959).
92. For a critical discussion of youth and the 'social problem film', see Hill, *Sex, Class and Realism,* chapters 4 and 5.
93. Skiffle instruments were very basic and affordable consisting of an acoustic guitar, washboard and a home-made tea-chest bass.
94. McDevitt, *Skiffle*, p. xiv. Formby himself promoted a particularly caricatured Wigan identity in the inter-war period, yet his style of humour was maintained into the post-war period and was embraced by working-class youth in Leigh and Wigan. For career details, see D. Bret, *George Formby: A Troubled Genius* (London, 1999).
95. For the crucial role played by Donegan in English popular music, see P. Humphries, *Lonnie Donegan and the Birth of British Rock and Roll* (London, 2012).
96. M. Dewe, *The Skiffle Craze* (London, 1998), p. 63.
97. The Lilford Weaving Mill, Pennington had been built in 1914, and during the Great War, it was used to house German prisoners. In the 1950s, it was operated by the English Sewing Cotton Company and produced industrial cloths.
98. Fowler, *Lancashire Cotton Operatives and Work,* p. 201.
99. At the beginning of a British tour, it was revealed in the press that Lewis was married to his 13-year-old cousin. There was widespread coverage in the tabloid press and the tour was cancelled after three concerts. For an account of Lewis's time in Britain and the press furore, see N. Tosches, *Hell Fire: The Jerry Lee Lewis Story* (Harmondsworth, 1982, 2007), pp. 151–61.
100. See S. Catterall, 'Edwin Hall (1895–1961)', in K. Gildart and D. Howell (eds), *Dictionary of Labour Biography Vol. III* (Basingstoke, 2010), pp. 146–52.
101. For Lancashire miners in the post-war period, see Howell, *The Politics of the NUM.*
102. Ronnie Carr, interview with author, 4 September 2006.
103. Georgie Fame, 'Its Tough at the Top', *Radio Luxembourg Annual 1965.*
104. Mike O'Neil, interview with author, 14 September 2006.

105. *The Observer*, 21 December 1958.
106. Ronnie Carr, interview with author, 4 September 2006.
107. Ronnie Carr, diary entries for August and September 1957.
108. Interview with Georgie Fame, *Leigh Journal*, 14 January 1965.
109. Interview with Ronnie Carr, *Leigh Journal*, 13 October 2000.
110. *Leigh Chronicle*, 14 June 1957.
111. M. Abrams, *Teenage Consumer Spending in 1959*. For surveys and reports, see relevant boxes in Mark Abrams Papers, Churchill College, Cambridge.
112. *Leigh Chronicle*, 20 June 1959.
113. For details of the fortunes of cinema going in the 1950s, see Hanson, *From Silent Screen to Multi-Screen*, chapter 4.
114. *Daily Express*, 4 March 1959.
115. Ronnie Carr, diary entries, 1959.
116. R. Gate, *Rugby League. An Illustrated History* (London, 1989), p. 104.
117. Mike O'Neil, interview with author, 14 September 2006.
118. For a social history of the camps, see S. T. Dawson, *Holiday Camps in Twentieth Century Britain: Packaging Pleasure* (Manchester, 2011).
119. Such behaviour on a holiday camp in 1959 is brilliantly evoked in R. Connolly's novel, *That'll Be the Day* (Glasgow, 1973). The film version directed by Claude Whatham released in the same year is also very good on periodisation and the link between popular music and youth culture.
120. Rory Blackwell was a key figure in the development of rock 'n' roll in England. He had been playing rock 'n' roll in London and at various holiday camps since 1956 in what was regarded as the first British rock 'n' roll group. For a short profile, see McAleer, *Hit Parade Heroes*, p. 24.
121. Ronnie Carr, interview with author, 4 September 2006.
122. The success of Carr, Turner and Powell was noted by the local press. *Leigh Chronicle*, 17 July 1959. A year later at a further summer residency, Starkey changed his name to Starr and in 1962 replaced Pete Best as drummer in the Beatles.
123. 'Wakes weeks' dated back to the nineteenth century but were consolidated in the Edwardian period when holiday entitlement was granted to Lancashire cotton workers and coal miners.
124. The song had been written by the radical troubadour Woody Guthrie and had been a hit for Lonnie Donegan in April 1958. For a detailed biography of Guthrie and his work and politics, see J. Klein, *Woody Guthrie: A Life* (London, 1989).
125. The names and choruses of the song changes over the years and is often linked to match results. Georgie Fame performed a version of this at Wigan Jazz Club on 2 March 2003 as a tribute to Wigan rugby legend Billy Boston. See encore section of this book for further discussion.
126. Ronnie Carr, interview with author, 7 February 2007.
127. Ronnie Carr, diary entry, 18 July 1959.
128. *Leigh Chronicle*, 17 July 1959.
129. The Beat Boys released a Joe Meek produced single 'That's My Plan' on Decca in 1963.
130. *Leigh Chronicle*, 20 March 1959
131. *Leigh Chronicle*, 1 May 1959.
132. Welch, *Rock 'n' Roll*, p. 101.
133. For details of these artists and their oeuvre, see McAleer, *Hit Parade Heroes*.

134. For an analysis of the different types of venues where jukeboxes were installed to attract working-class youth, see Horn, *Juke Box Britain*, chapter 7.
135. For a partial, but nonetheless valuable, insight into the variety of premises that formed part of Manchester's 'clubland' in the 1950s and 60s, see J. Donnelly, *Jimmy the Weed. Inside the Quality Street Gang: My Life in the Manchester Underworld* (Lancashire, 2012) chapter 5.
136. Savile went on to have a long career as a disc jockey for BBC radio, presenter of the long-running *Top of the Pops* and charity campaigner. His reputation was destroyed in 2012 when it was revealed that he had sexually assaulted a significant number of young girls. His early years in Manchester and in the popular music industry are recalled in his autobiography *Jimmy Savile: Love is an Uphill Thing* (London, 1978).
137. Haslam, *Manchester, England*, p. 88.
138. The most notable example of the link between working-class youth and American rhythm and blues was the Twisted Wheel Club, which opened in 1963. The key figure here was record collector and enthusiast Roger Eagle. For biography, see B. Sykes, *Sit Down! Listen to This! The Roger Eagle Story* (Manchester, 2012) and K. Rylatt and P. Scott, *CENtral 1179: The Story of Manchester's Twisted Wheel Club* (London, 2001).
139. A. Lawson, *It Happened in Manchester: The True Story of Manchester's Music 1958–1965* (Bury, 1990), p. 11.

2 Exploring London's Soho and the Flamingo Club with Georgie Fame and the Blue Flames

1. Most notably by A. Marwick, *The Sixties: Cultural Revolution in Britain, France, Italy, and the United States, c.1958–c.1974* (Oxford, 1998). For critique of this characterisation, see D. Fowler, *Youth Culture in Modern Britain, c.1920–c.1970: From Ivory Tower to Global Movement – A New History* (Basingstoke, 2008).
2. For the sexual politics of the city in this period, see F. Mort, *Capital Affairs: London and the Making of the Permissive Society* (New Haven, 2010). For the pre-rock 'n' roll years, see M. Houlbrook, *Queer London: Perils and Pleasures in the Sexual Metropolis, 1918–1957* (Chicago, 2005).
3. For a detailed examination of the Mod subculture in London and in the provinces, see chapters 4 and 5.
4. For a popular history, see A. Ings, *Rockin' At The 2 I's Coffee Bar* (Brighton, 2010). A cinematic representation of the coffee bar scene can be found in *The Tommy Steel Story* (1957) and *Expresso Bongo* (1959). The Rank organisation also produced a short film on Soho's coffee bars for its *Look at Like* series in 1959 which included scenes from the Two I's.
5. F. Norman and J. Bernard, *Soho Night and Day* (London, 1966), p. 16.
6. The coffee bar has now become one of the foundation myths of English rock 'n' roll and in 2006 the City of Westminster unveiled a plaque on the site in recognition of its contribution to popular culture.
7. Writers, film-makers and television dramatists were keen to document the experiences and exploits of northerners in the capital city through fictional characters. For example, see the BBC serial *Diary of a Young Man*, which was broadcast in 1964. For a discussion of its form, content and impact, see J. Hill, *Ken Loach: The Politics of Film and Television* (London, 2011), pp. 13–19.
8. *Pipeline Instrumental Review*, 17 (spring 1993) p. 19.

9. B. Welch, *Rock 'n' Roll – I Gave You the Best Years of My Life: A Life in the Shadows* (London, 1989), p. 22.
10. For an autobiographical account of homosexuals and 1960s club culture, see P. Burton, *Parallel Lives* (London, 1985). For a collection of essays on sexuality and popular music, see J. Gill, *Queer Noises: Male and Female Homosexuality in Twentieth-Century Music* (London, 1995).
11. Working-class cinema-goers had recently seen the sexual and criminal underbelly of Soho depicted on screen in Don Chaffey's *The Flesh Is Weak* (1957). For characters associated with prostitution and pornography in the city in the post-war period, see M. Tomkinson, *The Pornbrokers: The Rise of the Soho Sex Barons* (London, 1982).
12. S. Jackson, *An Indiscreet Guide to Soho* (London, 1948), p. 65.
13. This aspect of working-class continuity and change in London is discussed in more detail in chapter 6.
14. *Daily Express*, 9 March 1959.
15. Clay Nicholls had also made a similar journey to O'Neil travelling from Scotland in search of fame and fortune at the 2 I's coffee bar.
16. Mike O'Neil, interview with author, 14 September 2006.
17. *Pipeline Instrumental Review* (spring 1993), pp. 19–20.
18. For jazz music and associated clubs in London, see K. Newton, *The Jazz Scene* (Harmondsworth, 1959). Kenneth Newton was a pseudonym for Eric Hobsbawm the Marxist historian and Communist activist who made a major contribution to British labour and economic history.
19. *Daily Express*, 13 March 1959.
20. *Rave*, No. 13 February 1965.
21. Georgie Fame, 'It's Tough at the Bottom', *Radio Luxembourg Annual*, 1965.
22. A. L. Oldham, *Stoned* (London, 2001), p. 50.
23. Georgie Fame: A Brief Biography, unpublished MS, local studies collection, Leigh Public Library.
24. C. MacInnes, *Absolute Beginners* (1959, 1986), p. 74. For a scathing but generally unconvincing critique of MacInnes, see Fowler, *Youth Culture in Modern Britain*, chapter 6.
25. Johnny Dankworth (1927–2010) was one of the giants of British jazz and also played a role in attempting to combat the threat of far-right organisations such as the White Defence League in 1959 through his involvement in the creation of the Stars Campaign for Inter-Racial Friendship. See obituary in *The Guardian*, 8 February 2010. The development of British jazz is also charted in his autobiography *Jazz in Revolution* (London, 1999).
26. *Daily Express*, 10 August 1959.
27. *Daily Express*, 9 February 1960.
28. For succinct profiles of all these performers, see D. McAleer, *Hit Parade Heroes: British Beat Before the Beatles* (London, 1993).
29. For career profile of Parnes, see J. Rogan, *Starmakers and Svengalis. The History of British Pop Management* (London, 1988), pp. 15–38.
30. *Daily Express*, 8 December 1960.
31. For biography, see J. Repsch, *The Legendary Joe Meek: The Telstar Man* (London, 2001).
32. Ronnie Carr, interview with author, 7 February 2007.
33. For biography, see D. and C. Stafford, *Fings Ain't Wot They Used T'Be: The Lionel Bart Story* (London, 2011).
34. 'Lionel Bart (1930–1999)', *Oxford Dictionary of National Biography* (2004–12).

35. Mort, *Capital Affairs*, p. 236.
36. S. Napier-Bell, *Black Vinyl White Powder* (London, 2002), p. 52.
37. Ibid., p.15.
38. Jackson, *An Indiscreet Guide to Soho*, p. 55.
39. *New Musical Express*, 13 March 1959.
40. *Daily Express*, 7 April 1960.
41. *Daily Express*, 8 April 1960.
42. For the business relationship between the camp and extravagant Parnes and the East End working-class Bart, see D. and C. Stafford, *Fings Ain't Wot They Used T'Be*, pp. 112–13.
43. A. L. Oldham, *Stoned* (London, 2001), p. 26
44. Georgie Fame: A Brief Biography.
45. *Leigh Journal*, 27 November 1959.
46. *Daily Express*, 29 June 1959.
47. *Daily Express*, 21 July 1960.
48. For tour dates and press coverage, see J. Collis, *Gene Vincent and Eddie Cochran. Rock 'n' Roll Revolutionaries* (London, 2004).
49. P. Norman, *John Lennon: The Life* (London, 2008), p. 175.
50. J. Mundy and D. Higham, *Don't Forget Me: The Eddie Cochran Story* (New York, 2000), p. 174.
51. The English motorcycle gangs of the 1950s/60s still await serious historical analysis. For general accounts of their development and culture, see J. Stuart, *Rockers!* (London, 1987); M. Clay, *Café Racers: Rockers, Rock 'n' Roll and the Coffee Bar Cult* (London, 1988); W. G. Ramsay, *The Ace Café Then and Now* (Harlow, 2002). For cinematic representations, see Sidney J. Furie's, *The Leather Boys* (1963) and Joseph Losey's, *The Damned* (1963). For more formal motor cycling organisations, see the papers of the Motor Cycling Association, Modern Records Centre, University of Warwick, MSS.204.
52. Collis, *Gene Vincent and Eddie Cochran*, p. 74
53. *Leigh Journal*, 6 May 1960.
54. For career profile of Nero and the Gladiators, see *Pipeline Instrumental Review* 17, (Spring 1993), pp. 19–29.
55. Formby was another Lancashire entertainer who had used exaggerated aspects of regional identity for comedic and musical purposes. See D. Bret, *George Formby. A Troubled Genius* (London, 1999).
56. For biographical details, see S. Leigh and J. Fimminger, *Wondrous Face: The Billy Fury Story* (Folkestone, 2005).
57. See Billy Fury entry, *Oxford Dictionary of National Biography* (2004–2012).
58. S. Leigh and J. Firminger, *Halfway to Paradise: Britpop, 1955–1962* (Folkestone, 1996), p. 48.
59. For an overview of the development of blues music in England, see B. Brunning, *Blues: The British Connection* (Poole, 1986). For an autobiographical account of a conversion to the blues, see the early chapters of K. Richards, *Life* (London, 2010) and B. Wyman, *Stone Alone: The Story of a Rock 'n' Roll Band* (Harmondsworth, 1990). The Rolling Stones were the most successful group in adopting American blues to their own style. For a narrative of this process, see the early chapters of P. Norman, *The Stones: The Acclaimed Biography* (London, 2002).
60. S. Bright, 'In with the In Crowd', *Mojo*, No. 33 (August 1996), 44.
61. *Rave*, No. 13 February 1965.

62. *New Musical Express*, 12 February 1965.
63. See Mort, *Capital Affairs*, pp. 227–8.
64. For an interesting spatial exploration of Soho, see F. Mort, *Cultures of Consumption: Masculinities and Social Space in Late-Twentieth Century Britain* (London, 1996), chapter 2.
65. See D. Hughes, 'The Spivs', in M. Sissons and P. French (eds), *Age of Austerity 1945–51* (Harmondsworth, 1963), pp. 85–105.
66. For Spivs and youth culture, see A. Horn, *Juke Box Britain: Americanisation and Youth Culture, 1945–60* (Manchester, 2009), chapter 5.
67. Jackson, *An Indiscreet Guide to Soho*, pp. 113–4.
68. G. Melly, 'Preface' in D. Farson, *Soho in the Fifties* (London, 1987), p. xiii.
69. Jackson, *An Indiscreet Guide to Soho*, p. 120.
70. Mike O'Neil, interview with author, 14 September 2006.
71. The press also noted the trend for suburban housewives taking legally prescribed amphetamine immortalised in the Rolling Stones song 'Mother's Little Helper' that was recorded in 1965.
72. *Daily Express*, 3 January 1960.
73. For an examination of drugs and the Mod subculture, see chapters 4 and 5.
74. For the negative reviews of *Peeping Tom*, see J. Petley, 'A Crude Sort of Entertainment for a Crude Sort of Audience: The British Critics and Horror Cinema', in S. Chibnall and J. Petley (eds), *British Horror Cinema* (London, 2002), p. 36.
75. *Daily Express*, 17 November 1960. For a cinematic representation of concerns around the spread of sexually transmitted diseases amongst vulnerable youths, see Gerry O'Hara's, *That Kind of Girl* (1963).
76. For accounts of racial attacks on migrants and minorities, see P. Fryer, *Staying Power: The History of Black People in Britain* (London, 1991).
77. Jackson, *An Indiscreet Guide to Soho*, pp. 104–5.
78. L. Constantine, *Colour Bar* (London, 1954), p. 65.
79. S. Patterson, *Dark Strangers. A Sociological Study of the Absorption of a Recent West Indian Migrant Group in Brixton, South London* (London, 1963), p. 245.
80. M. Gellhorn, 'So Awful to Be Young or, Morning to Midnight in Espresso Bars', *Encounter*, May 1956, pp. 45–6.
81. S. Selvon, *The Lonely Londoners* (London, 1956), p. 130.
82. C. MacInnes, *City of Spades* (London, 1957), p. 50.
83. See E. Pilkington, *Beyond the Mother Country: West Indians and the Notting Hill White Riots* (London, 1988).
84. M. Koningh and M. Griffiths, *Tighten Up!. The History of Reggae in the UK* (London, 2003), p. 14.
85. MacInnes, *Absolute Beginners*, p. 198.
86. P. Gilroy, *There Ain't No Black in the Union Jack* (London, 2002), p. 215.
87. For a more measured account of Teddy Boy behaviour, see R. Gosling, *Personal Copy: A Memoir of the Sixties* (Nottingham, 1980), pp. 34–5.
88. Patterson, *Dark Strangers*, p. 3
89. For youth culture and racism in film, see Vernon Sewell's, *The Wind of Change* (1961).
90. For a literary tour of the London jazz scene, see *Jazz News and Review*, August 1963.
91. Jackson, *An Indiscreet Guide to Soho*, pp. 48–9.
92. *Daily Express*, 5 January 1959.
93. *Daily Express*, 1, 2 and 20 August 1960.

94. P. Gorman, *The Look: Adventures in Rock and Pop Fashion* (London, 2006), p. 34.
95. The origin and development of the Mod subculture is discussed in chapters 4 and 5.
96. G-2481, 65-year-old-male, Images of the 1950s/60s, Mass Observation Project (2003), University of Sussex Archives.
97. *Melody Maker*, 27 July 1963.
98. Gunnell had been involved in jazz clubs in the 1950s and had attracted the interest of the Metropolitan Police who were concerned about the links between drugs, prostitution and Soho's music venues. For obituary, see *The Independent*, 28 June 2007.
99. Bright, 'In with the In Crowd', p. 46.
100. Marwick, *The Sixties*, pp. 55–80.
101. For biography, see Speedy Acquaye obituary in *The Independent*, 18 November 1993.
102. *New Musical Express*, 15 January 1965.
103. Fame, 'It's Tough at the Bottom', p. 15.
104. A. Clayson, *Call Up the Groups* (London, 1985), p. 103.
105. Booker T. Jones was a key figure in American soul music in the 1960s through his involvement with Stax records in Memphis. With his band the MGs, he provided music for Otis Redding, Sam and Dave and Eddie Floyd. He had a hit in 1962 with the instrumental 'Green Onions', which found its way into Fame's set during his residency at the Flamingo. See R. Bowman, *Soulsville USA: The Story of Stax Records* (New York, 2003).
106. Fame, 'It's Tough at the Bottom', p. 15.
107. *Disc and Music Echo*, 3 September 1966.
108. Koningh and Griffiths, *Tighten Up!*, p. 15.
109. P. Hewitt, *The Soul Stylists* (Edinburgh, 2000), p. 75.
110. S. Maitland, *Very Heaven. Looking Back at the 1960s* (London, 1988), p. 34.
111. For biography, see S. Green, *Rachman* (London, 1979) and J. Davis, 'Rents and Race in 1960s London: New Light on Rachmanism', *Twentieth Century British History*, 12, 1 (2001), 69–92.
112. Bright, 'In with the In Crowd', p. 43.
113. Rico is another figure who has been marginalised in the historiography of British popular music. He was a significant presence in the 1960s as well as being crucial to the multiracial Two Tone movement of the late 1970s. For Two Tone, see R. Eddington, *Sent From Coventry: The Chequered Past of Two Tone* (London, 2003); D. Thompson, *2 Tone, The Specials and the World in Flame* (London, 2004); H. Panter, *Ska'd for Life: A Personal Journey with the Specials* (Basingstoke, 2007); N. Staple, *Original Rude Boy: From Borstal to the Specials* (London, 2008) and for a feminist perspective P. Black, *Black by Design: A 2-Tone Memoir* (London, 2011).
114. *Disc Weekly*, 27 March 1965.
115. P. Hewitt, 'The Birth of Modernism', in *New Musical Express Originals* Vol. 2, No. 2 (no date), p. 40.
116. M. Farren, *Give the Anarchist a Cigarette* (London, 2001), p. 26.
117. For brief biography, see Johnny Edgecombe obituary *The Guardian*, 30 September 2010.
118. J. Edgecombe, *Black Scandal* (London, 2002), p. 60.
119. Ibid., p. 86. For an detailed analysis of the Profumo case and the cultures from which it emerged, see Mort, *Capital Affairs*, chapter 7.

120. J. Maycock, 'Pop Music: Fame at the Flamingo: Golden Years in Soho', *The Independent*, 16 January 1998.
121. M. Ritson and S. Russell, *The In Crowd: The Story of the Northern and Rare Soul Scene Volume 1* (London, 1999), p. 81.
122. Ronnie Carr, interview with author, 4 September 2006.
123. *Leigh Chronicle*, 29 August 1963.
124. For the spread of rhythm and blues across London clubs in 1963, see T. Bacon, *London Live: From the Yardbirds to Pink Floyd to the Sex Pistols. The Inside Story of Live Band's in the Capital's Trail-Blazing Music Clubs* (London, 1999), pp. 46–58.
125. Bright, 'In with the In Crowd', p. 42
126. For a history of Island Records, see C. Salewicz and S. Newman, *The Story of Island Records: Keep on Running* (New York, 2010).
127. *Melody Maker*, 24 August 1963.
128. *Melody Maker*, 27 July 1963.
129. *Melody Maker*, 14 November 1964.
130. *Melody Maker*, 17 July 1965.
131. See Tommy Thomas obituary, the *Guardian*, 22 September 2005.
132. For Oldham's career in this period, see his autobiography, *Stoned* (London, 2001). Meaden was a key figure in the development of the Mod subculture. For his contribution to the Soho club scene and London's youth culture, see chapters 4 and 5.
133. *Melody Maker*, 18 April 1964.
134. According to Terri Quaye, such networks would extend beyond the Flamingo into the wider environs of London's youth culture and struggles for racial equality in England, South Africa and the United States. Terri Quaye, interview with author, 12 April 2011.
135. Hewitt, *The Soul Stylists*, pp. 57–8.
136. For the importance of the link between fashion and music, see Gorman, *The Look*.
137. Koningh and Griffiths, *Tighten Up!*, p. 25.
138. Bright, 'In with the In Crowd', p. 44.
139. 'Working Party on Juvenile jazz and Dance Clubs in the West End of London', PRO HO 300/8.
140. See L. Jackson, 'The Coffee Club Menace: Policing Youth, Leisure and Sexuality in Post-war Manchester', *Cultural and Social History*, 5, 3 (2008), 289–308.
141. T. Raison (ed.), *Youth in New Society* (London, 1966), pp. 77–8.
142. 'Pep Pill Menace', *British Medical Journal*, 28 March 1964. The importance of theft is also noted by J. Davis, 'The London Drug Scene and the Making of Drug Policy 1965–73', *Twentieth Century British History*, 17, 1 (2006), p. 33.
143. Metropolitan Police Report 15 June 1964. Young Persons in the Soho Area. PRO HO 300/8.
144. Working Party on Juvenile Jazz and Dance Clubs in the West End of London. Minutes of meeting 23 July 1965. PRO HO 300/8.
145. Raison, *Youth in New Society*, p. 78.
146. See the files in 'Working Party on Juvenile jazz and Dance Clubs in the West End of London', PRO HO 300/8.
147. Working Party on Juvenile Jazz and Dance Clubs in the West End of London. Minutes of meeting 23 July 1965. PRO HO 300/8.
148. *New Musical Express*, 11 December 1964.
149. *New Musical Express*, 15 January 1965.

150. *Melody Maker*, 18 January 1965.
151. *Leigh Journal*, 14 January 1965.
152. For history of the Twisted Wheel, see K. Rylatt and P. Scott, *CENtral 1179: The Story of Manchester's Twisted Wheel Club* (London, 2001).
153. For link between Motown sound and city of Detroit, see S. E. Smith, *Dancing in the Street. Motown and the Cultural Politics of Detroit* (Cambridge, 2000).
154. *New Musical Express* 26 March 1965.
155. *Melody Maker*, 3 April 1965.
156. Ritson and Russell, *The In Crowd*, pp. 51–52.
157. *New Musical Express*, 23 April 1965.

3 Liverpool, the Beatles and the Cultural Politics of Class, Race and Place

1. Each member of the Beatles has been the subject of numerous biographies. The most substantial and insightful is P. Norman, *John Lennon: The Life* (London, 2009).
2. For a critical but partial discussion of Beatles historiography, see J. Harris, 'Paperback Writers', *The Guardian*, 29 September 2012.
3. For a critical analysis of the Beatles heritage industry, see R. J. Kruse II, 'The Beatles as Place Makers: Narrated Landscapes in Liverpool, England', *Journal of Cultural Geography*, 22, 2 (Spring/Summer, 2005), 87–114.
4. For a visual representation of the Liverpool of the Beatles, see Terence Davies's masterful and compelling cinematic eulogy *Of Time and the City* (2008). Interestingly, for Davies a working-class Catholic, who gave up on popular music in 1963, the Beatles meant nothing. For a reconstruction of working-class Liverpool, see his autobiographical film *Distant Voices, Still Lives* (1988). For a critical appraisal, see P. Farley, *Distant Voices, Still Lives* (London, 2006).
5. For a collection of academic essays on the Beatles, see I. Inglis (ed.), *The Beatles, Popular Music and Society: A Thousand Voices* (Basingstoke, 2000). For a problematic and idiosyncratic critique of the Beatles' influence on youth culture, see D. Fowler, *Youth Culture in Modern Britain, c.1920–c.1970: From Ivory Tower to Global Movement – A New History* (Basingstoke, 2008), chapter 9.
6. A. Marwick, *The Sixties: Cultural Revolution in Britain, France, Italy and the United States, c. 1958–c.1974* (Oxford, 1998), p. 19.
7. I. MacDonald, *Revolution in the Head: The Beatles' Records and the Sixties* (London, 1995), p. 12.
8. D. Sandbrook, *White Heat: A History of Britain in the Swinging Sixties* (London, 2006), p. 58.
9. D. Sandbrook, *Never Had It So Good: A History of Britain from Suez to the Beatles* (London, 2005), p. 468.
10. Sandbrook, *White Heat*, p. 748.
11. For discussion of the poll, see *Daily Telegraph*, 27 December 1961.
12. For a critical appraisal of the politics of the Beatles, see Marcus Collins, 'The Beatles Politics', *The British Journal of Politics and International Relations* (2012), 1–19.
13. Fowler, *Youth Culture in Modern Britain*, p. 174.
14. E. Wald, *How the Beatles Destroyed Rock 'n' Roll: An Alternative History of American Popular Music* (Oxford, 2009), p. 246.
15. C. Gillett, *The Sound of the City. The Rise of Rock and Roll* (London, 1970), p. 250.

16. M. Brocken, *Other Voices: Hidden Histories of Liverpool's Popular Music Scenes, 1930s–1970s* (Aldershot, 2010).
17. For example, see J. P. Wilson, 'Beats Apart: A Comparative History of Youth Culture and Popular Music in Liverpool and Newcastle upon Tyne, 1956–65', (Unpublished PhD thesis, University of Northumbria, 2009).
18. B. Harry, *Bigger Than the Beatles: Liverpool the Story of the City's Musical Odyssey* (Liverpool, 2009), p. 9.
19. See D. Russell, *Looking North: Northern England and the National Imagination* (Manchester, 2004). Also a collection of analytical essays can be found in N. Kirk (ed.), *Northern Identities: Historical Interpretations of 'The North' and 'Northerness'* (Aldershot, 2000).
20. P. Du Noyer, *Liverpool Wondrous Place: Music from the Cavern to the Coral* (London, 2004), p. 5.
21. J. Belchem, *Merseypride: Essays in Liverpool Exceptionalism* (Liverpool, 2000), p. xi.
22. This was particularly the case in the realm of popular music. Bill Harry claims that the song selection of groups in neighbouring Manchester was very different to those selected in Liverpool. Bill Harry, interview with author, 26 July 2010.
23. G. Moorhouse, *Britain in the Sixties: The Other England* (Harmondsworth, 1964), p. 140.
24. D. Russell, 'Music and Northern Identity 1890–c.1965', in Kirk (ed.), *Northern Identities*, p. 30.
25. For an early population study, see D. C. Jones (ed.), *The Social Survey of Merseyside* (Liverpool, 1934).
26. For Liverpool's place in a broader conception of 'Northerness', see Russell, *Looking North.*
27. For religious sectarianism, see F. Neal, *Sectarian Violence: The Liverpool Experience, 1819–1914: An Aspect of Anglo-Irish History* (Manchester, 1988)
28. See early chapters of R. Tomlinson, *Ricky* (London, 2003). Tomlinson would go on to have a career as a victimised trade union activist, television celebrity and film star.
29. Bill Harry, interview with author, 26 July 2010.
30. Russell, 'Music and Northern Identity 1890–c.1965', p. 23.
31. Sandbrook, *Never Had It So Good*, p. 468.
32. This was a point consistently made by Mike O'Neil, Ronnie Carr and Bill Harry in their interviews with the author.
33. T. Lane, *Liverpool. City of the Sea* (Liverpool, 1997), p. ix.
34. S. Cohen, *Rock Culture in Liverpool: Popular Music in the Making* (Oxford, 1991), p. 12.
35. Du Noyer, *Liverpool Wondrous Place*, p. 51.
36. For a detailed analysis of these recordings, see the relevant sections in MacDonald, *Revolution in the Head.*
37. Lane, *Liverpool*, p. 81.
38. B. Spitz, *The Beatles. The Biography* (New York, 2005) p. 132.
39. P. McCartney, 'Foreword', in Du Noyer, *Liverpool Wondrous Place*, p. vi.
40. P. Norman, *Shout! The Beatles in Their Generation* (London, 1981), p. 50.
41. M. Woolf, 'Is Liverpool a Frontier for Rock', *Mersey Beat* Vol. 2, No. 44, 28 March–11 April 1963 p. 11.
42. A. Clayson and Spencer Leigh, *The Walrus Was Ringo: 101 Beatles Myths Debunked* (New Malden, 2003), pp. 52–4.
43. S. Leach, *The Rocking City. The Explosive Birth of the Beatles* (Liverpool, 1999), p. 22.

44. Harry, *Bigger Than the Beatles*, p. 43.
45. Ibid., p. 13.
46. See K. McManus, *Nashville of the North: Country Music in Liverpool* (Liverpool, 2004).
47. Harry, *Bigger Than the Beatles*, p. 10.
48. Bill Harry, interview with author, 26 July 2010.
49. Presented by Daniel Farson it offers a glimpse into a world that was disappearing and being re-made through the vibrancy of youth culture. Farson himself had been a chronicler of bohemianism in Soho and inhabited the same homosexual milieu as Colin MacInnes. For autobiography, see D. Farson, *Never a Normal Man* (London, 1997).
50. For the Welsh, see R. M. Jones and D. B. Rees, *Liverpool Welsh and their Religion* (Wales, 1984). For the Irish, see J. Belchem, *Irish, Catholic and Scouse: The History of the Liverpool Irish, 1800–1939* (Liverpool, 2007).
51. For an examination of such identity, see D. Frost, 'Ambiguous Identities: Constructing and De-constructing Black and White 'Scouse' Identities in Twentieth Century Liverpool', in Kirk (ed.), *Northern Identities*, pp. 197–8.
52. Once again, researchers are left to examine traces of such a history through the numerous local publications that have attempted to reconstruct the lives and experiences of these minority groups. See M. L. Wong, *Chinese Liverpudlians: History of the Chinese Community in Liverpool* (Liverpool, 1989) and R. H. Costello, *Black Liverpool: The Early History of Britain's Oldest Black Community, 1730–1918* (Liverpool, 2001).
53. The black history of Liverpool has been noticeably marginalized by academic historians. See S. Small, 'Racialised Relations in Liverpool: A Contemporary Anomaly', *New Community*, 17, 4 (July 1991), 511–37.
54. MacDonald, *Revolution in the Head*, p. 8.
55. G. Smith, *When Jim Crow Met John Bull: Black American Soldiers in World War II Britain* (London, 1987), p. 107.
56. For origins of Liverpool's black community, see Costello, *Black Liverpool*.
57. A. H. Richmond, *Colour Prejudice in Britain: A Study of West Indian Workers in Liverpool, 1941–1951* (London, 1954), p. 90.
58. In her anthropological study of black Liverpudlians, Nassey Brown exposed the connections between the largely African population with the politics and culture of African Americans. From her observations and interviews she realised that '[n] ested at key moments in their accounts were references to the formative influence that Black America...has had on the racial and cultural identity of their city'. Her interviews also show that in the 1940s seamen were bringing jazz recordings and the music of Billie Holliday into Liverpool thus suggesting some validity to a particular variant of the 'Cunard Yank' theory. J. Nassey Brown, *Dropping Anchor, Setting Sail: Geographies of Race in Black Liverpool* (Princeton, 2003), p. 37.
59. Tomlinson, *Ricky*, p. 21.
60. *Daily Express*, 15 April 1959.
61. R. Guthrie, 'The Biggest Years in a Boy's Life', in T. Raison (ed.), *Youth in New Society* (London, 1966), pp. 101–2.
62. Bill Harry, interview with author, 26 July 2010.
63. Ibid.
64. For profile, see *Mersey Beat*, 23 July 1964. For the role of Hamburg and its importance in the development of popular music in Britain see, A. Clayson, *Hamburg: The Cradle of British Rock* (London, 1998).

65. See television documentary *Who Put the Beat in Merseybeat?* (1996).
66. J. B. Mays, *Growing Up in the City: A Study of Juvenile Delinquency in an Urban Neighbourhood* (Liverpool, 1954), p. 23.
67. Ibid., p. 43.
68. For biography, see obituary, *The Guardian*, 10 July 2000.
69. For details of the disturbances, see P. Fryer, *Staying Power: The History of Black People in Britain* (London, 1984), pp. 367–71.
70. Obituary, *The Guardian*, 10 July 2000.
71. Richmond, *Colour Prejudice in Britain*, p. 95.
72. A point reiterated at numerous junctures in Bill Harry's interview with author.
73. Norman, *Shout! The Beatles in Their Generation* (London, 1981), p. 66.
74. *Mersey Beat*, Vol. 1, No. 26, 12–26 July 1962.
75. A. P. Ferguson, *Burtonwood* (London, 1986), pp. 38, 75.
76. Ibid., p. 98.
77. Mike O'Neil, interview with author, 14 September 2006.
78. Ferguson, *Burtonwood*, p. 103.
79. A point also made by director Terence Davies on the DVD commentary track to his insightful documentary on Liverpool, *Of Time and the City* (2008).
80. J. Gardner, *Over Here: The GI's in Wartime Britain* (London, 1992), p. 108.
81. For a history of the programme, see D. Little, *The Coronation Street Story: Celebrating Thirty-Five Years of the Street* (London, 1998). For an insightful analysis of post-war representations of conceptions of the street in British culture, see J. Moran, 'Imagining the Street in Post-war Britain', *Urban History*, 39, 1 (2012), 166–86.
82. Correspondence with Jack McMichael, 10 February 2007.
83. Correspondence with Ed Floyd, former Major, United States Air Force, 8 February 2007.
84. Letter from Phil Kroper to author, 13 September 2009.
85. Letter from Jeanette Land to author, 14 September 2009.
86. Mays, *Growing Up in the City*, p. 73.
87. S. Maitland (ed.), *Very Heaven: Looking Back at the 1960s* (London, 1988), p. 23.
88. Eddie Amoo, interview with author, 2008.
89. Harry, *Bigger Than the Beatles*, p. 57; Bill Harry, interview with author, 26 September 2010.
90. *Mersey Beat*, 17 September 1964.
91. The role of the club in promoting soul music in the city was the subject of a radio broadcast *Motown on the Mersey* (BBC, 2007).
92. Geno Washington was a popular and energetic live performer who would cover rhythm and blues classics and attracted a loyal following amongst the Mod subculture examined in chapters 4 and 5.
93. Bill Harry, interview with author, 26 July 2010.
94. A. Williams, *The Man Who Gave the Beatles Away. The Amazing True Story of the Beatles Early Years* (London, 1976), pp. 14–15.
95. P. Gilroy, *There Ain't No Black in the Union Jack* (London, 2002), p. 228.
96. D. Chapman, 'The Autonomous Generation', *The Listener*, 17 January 1963.
97. Bill Harry, interview with author, 26 July 2010.
98. Belchem, *Merseypride*, p. xiii.
99. For a detailed examination of this process, see S. Davies, *Liverpool Labour: Social and Political Influences on the Development of the Labour Party in Liverpool, 1900–1939* (Keele, 1996).

100. Du Noyer, *Liverpool Wondrous Place*, p. 55.
101. The pre-1960s Liverpool pub is brilliantly evoked in Terence Davies's film *Distant Voices, Still Lives* (1988). To Farley this was 'the alehouse before jukeboxes and games machines ate into its spaces'. See Farley, *Distant Voices, Still Lives*, p. 75.
102. Bill Harry, interview with author, 26 July 2010.
103. Maitland (ed.), *Very Heaven*, p. 23.
104. M. Kerr, *The People of Ship Street* (London, 1958), p. 32.
105. Ibid., p. 115.
106. Ibid., p. 167.
107. M. Abrams, 'The Younger Generation', *Encounter*, May 1956. Mark Abrams Papers, Box 54, Churchill College, Cambridge University.
108. C. Fletcher, 'Beat Gangs on Merseyside', in T. Raison (ed.), *Youth in New Society* (London, 1966), p. 153.
109. Bill Harry, interview with author, 26 July 2010.
110. For example, see Sandbrook, *Never Had It So Good*, pp. 456–7.
111. T. Riley, 'For the Beatles: Notes on Their Achievement', *Popular Music*, 6, 3 (1987), p. 260.
112. M. Brocken, 'Some Other Guys! Some Theories about Signification: Beatles Cover Versions', *Popular Music and Society*, 20, 4, (1996), p. 8. For a cinematic representation of youth delinquency in Liverpool, see Basil Dearden's, *Violent Playground* (1958).
113. For a fascinating examination of this process in London's West End, see F. Mort, *Capital Affairs: London and the Making of the Permissive Society* (New Haven, 2010).
114. For an detailed exploration of the links between art school and popular music in post-war England, see S. Frith and H. Horne, *Art into Pop* (London, 1987).
115. Bill Harry, interview with author, 26 July 2010.
116. Bill Harry, interview with author, 26 July 2010. Stuart Sutcliffe (1940–1962) was the most bohemian of the Beatles. For biographical details, see A. Clayson and P. Sutcliffe, *Backbeat: Stuart Sutcliffe – The Lost Beatle* (London, 1994).
117. Norman, *Shout*, p. 23.
118. Norman, *John Lennon*, p. 8
119. The complex pull of class is personified in Hoggart's conception of the grammar school boy. See R. Hoggart, *The Uses of Literacy: Aspects of Working-class Life with Special Reference to Publications and Entertainments* (Harmondsworth, 1957), chapter 10.
120. For critical survey of the English education system in this period, see B. Jackson and D. Marsden, *Education and the Working Class* (Harmondsworth, 1962).
121. C. MacInnes, *Absolute Beginners* (London, 1959).
122. Spitz, *The Beatles*, p. 65.
123. The class tensions between jazz and rock 'n' roll fans in the 1950s are recreated in a key scene in Claude Whatham's film *That'll Be the Day* (1973).
124. Frith and Horne, *Art Into Pop*, p. 73.
125. Miles, 'John Lennon/Yoko Ono interview, unpublished, September 1969, www.rocksbackpages.com
126. See Hoggart, *The Uses of Literacy*, chapter 10.
127. The early chapters of Spitz, *The Beatles* (2005) are particularly good on McCartney's childhood.
128. Ibid., p. 273.
129. 'Harrison, George (1943–2001)', in *Oxford Dictionary of National Biography* (2004–9).

130. For an insightful exploration of the role of the grammar school on the Liverpool music scene, see Brocken, *Other Voices*, pp. 137–44.
131. *Saturday Evening Post*, March 1964.
132. Brocken, 'Some Other Guys', p. 5.
133. McCartney interviewed in J. Wilde, 'Tomorrow Never Knows', *Uncut*, 86, July 2004 p. 47.
134. D. Kynaston, *Family Britain 1951–57* (London, 2009), pp. 637–8.
135. *Mersey Beat*, Vol. 2, No. 24, 26 July–9 August 1962.
136. Bill Harry, interview with author, 26 July 2010.
137. Ibid.
138. *Mersey Beat*, Vol. 2, No. 24, 26 July–9 August 1962.
139. See interviews in the collective biographical documentary of the group, *The Beatles Anthology* (1995).
140. For an exploration of this process, see MacDonald, *Revolution in the Head*.
141. Harry, *Bigger Than the Beatles*, pp. 64–66. Also, Bill Harry, interview with author, 26 July 2010.
142. *Mersey Beat*, Vol. 3, No. 68, 27 February–12 March 1964.
143. *Daily Express*, 24 May 1963.
144. Epstein's own account of his place in the Beatles story has been subject to critique and revision. B. Epstein, *A Cellarful of Noise* (London, 1964). For comparison of Epstein with his contemporaries in music management, see J. Rogan, *Starmakers and Svengalis. The Story of British Pop Management* (London, 1988), pp. 105–34.
145. For an oral history of Epstein's life, see D. Geller, *The Brian Epstein Story* (London, 1999).
146. R. Coleman, *Brian Epstein: The Man Who Made the Beatles* (Harmondsworth, 1990), p. 247.
147. Ibid., p. 57.
148. M. Brocken, 'Coming Out of the Rhetoric of Merseybeat: Conversations with Joe Flannery', in Inglis (ed.), *The Beatles, Popular Music and Society*, p. 34.
149. Coleman, *Brian Epstein*, p. 381.
150. Fletcher, 'Beat Gangs on Merseyside', p. 148. However, Bill Harry disputes this particular claim and does not recall hardly any musicians who had been involved in street gangs. Bill Harry, interview with author, 26 July 2010.
151. Fletcher, 'Beat Gangs on Merseyside', pp. 151–2.
152. Ibid., p. 153.
153. Bill Harry, interview with author, 26 July 2010.
154. G. Melly, *Revolt Into Style. The Pop Arts in the 50s and 60s* (London, 1989), p. 71.
155. *Mersey Beat*, Vol. 2, No. 40, 31 January–14 February 1963.
156. *Mersey Beat*, Vol. 1, No. 24, 14–28 June 1962.
157. This aspect of the publication came out of discussion with Bill Harry, interview with author, 26 July 2010.
158. *Mersey Beat*, Vol. 2, No. 28, 9–23 August 1962.
159. *Daily Mail*, 6 March 1963.
160. *Daily Mail*, 7 January 1963.
161. Moorhouse, *Britain in the Sixties*, p. 133.
162. Melly, *Revolt Into Style*, p. 82.
163. *Mersey Beat*, Vol. 2, No. 27, 26 July–9 August 1962.
164. *Mersey Beat*, Vol. 2, No. 29, 23 August–6 September 1962.
165. Ibid.
166. *Mersey Beat*, Vol. 2, No. 44, 28 March–11 April 1963.

167. Ronnie Carr, interview with author, 4 September 2012.
168. *Mersey Beat*, Vol. 2, No. 43, 14–28 March 1963.
169. The first 'Face of Beauty' in *Mersey Beat* was Bernie Boyle who had been a girlfriend of both Paul McCartney and George Harrison.
170. Letter from Elaine Waring and the Gang, Queen's Park, Wrexham to the Lord Mayor, 13 February 1964, Liverpool Record Office (LRO) 352BEA/1/4/iii.
171. *Mersey Beat*, Vol. 2, No. 41, 14–28 February 1963.
172. Maitland (ed.), *Very Heaven*, p. 20.
173. For account of the 292 Cavern shows, see S. Leigh, *Let's Go Down the Cavern* (London, 1984), p. 93.
174. S. Hall and P. Whannel, *The Popular Arts* (London, 1964), p. 312.
175. See contribution in the television documentary *Beat City* (1963).
176. Moorhouse, *Britain in the Sixties*, p. 132.
177. R. Guthrie, 'The Biggest Years in a Boy's Life', in Raison (ed.), *Youth in New Society*, p. 102.
178. Further insights can be garnered from S. Leigh, *The Best of Fellas: The Story of Bob Wooler – Liverpool's First DJ. The Man Who Introduced the Beatles* (London, 2002).
179. *Mersey Beat*, Vol. 3, No. 56, 12–26 September 1963.
180. Bill Harry, interview with author, 26 July 2010.
181. See entry on Braddock in *Oxford Dictionary of National Biography* (2004–10).
182. For the working-class political milieu of the Labour Party in Liverpool, see J. and B. Braddock, *The Braddocks* (London, 1963).
183. Amoo had a picture of the Chants with Bessie Braddock on display in his home when the author carried out his interview.
184. For the response of the left to youth culture, see L. Black, *The Political Culture of the Left in Affluent Britain: Old Labour, New Britain* (Basingstoke, 2002) chapter 4. Braddock invited Wilson to the Cavern Club in 1966. See S. Leigh on the fiftieth birthday of the Cavern Club, *The Independent*, 28 June 2007.
185. *Daily Express*, 31 May 1963.
186. Labour Party Press Release, 30 May 1964, Mark Abrams Papers, Box 54, Churchill College, Cambridge University.
187. K. B. Oettinger, 'Youth and Youth Services in England', *Children*, 14, 2 (March–April, 1967). Mark Abrams Papers, Box 54, Churchill College, Cambridge University.
188. See M. Waite, 'Sex 'n' Drugs 'n' Rock 'n' Roll (and Communism) in the 1960s', in G. Andrews, N. Fishman and K. Morgan (eds), *Opening the Books: Essays on the Social and Cultural History of the British Communist Party* (London, 1995), pp. 210–24.
189. *Music and Life. Newsletter of the Communist Music Group*, 22, (1964).
190. E. Heffer, *Never A Yes Man. The Life and Politics of an Adopted Liverpudlian* (London, 1991), p. 107.
191. Ibid.
192. In 1950 Labour held Liverpool Exchange (Braddock), Liverpool Kirkdale (Keenan), Liverpool Scotland (Logan), and Liverpool Edge Hill (Irvine). In 1964, Labour added Liverpool Toxteth (Crawshaw), Liverpool Walton (Heffer), Liverpool West Derby (Odgen).
193. Heffer, *Never a Yes Man*, pp. 106–7.
194. Lord Mayor's correspondence Liverpool Record Office, 352/BEA.
195. Letter from Eric Heffer to Lord Mayor, 2 February 1964, LRO 352 BEA/1/2 (ii).

196. Letter from Ernest Hayes to the Lord Mayor, 14 February 1964, LRO 352 BEA/1/2.
197. Letter from A.R. McFall to the Lord Mayor, 13 November 1963, LRO 352 BEA/2/3 iii.
198. Letter from the Lord Mayor of Liverpool to Burgermeister of Hamburg, 15 November 1963, LRO 352 BEA2/3/vi.
199. Letter from the Lord Mayor to C.J. Epstein, 23 March 1964, LRO 352BEA/3/1.
200. I. MacDonald, *The People's Music* (London, 2003), p. 194.
201. *Saturday Evening Post*, March 1964.
202. For complete details of Beatles recordings in this period, see MacDonald, *Revolution in the Head.*
203. Ibid., p. 9.
204. Ibid., p. 22.

4 My Generation: Pete Townshend, the Who and English Mods

1. For a pithy discussion of Mod that draws on a limited range of sources, see D. Fowler, *Youth Culture in Modern Britain, c.1920–c.1970: From Ivory Tower to Global Movement – A New History* (Basingstoke, 2008), chapter 7. See also C. J. Feldman, *We Are the Mods: A Transnational History of a Youth Subculture* (New York, 2009). The best introduction to Mod remains R. Barnes, *Mods!* (London, 1979). See also S. Cohen, *Folk Devils and Moral Panics: The Creation of the Mods and Rockers* (London, 2010), pp. 150–61. Aspects of Mod culture also found its way into a number of key films of the 1960s such as Michelangelo Antonioni's *Blow Up* (1967) and Peter Collinson's *Up the Junction* (1967).
2. Townshend presented his own social history of Mod with the release of the album *Quadrophenia* (1973) and the subsequent film directed by Frank Roddam in 1979.
3. For the cultural politics of West Indian and African American popular music in England, see P. Gilroy, *There Ain't No Black in the Union Jack* (London, 2002), chapter 5. For the relationship between Mod and race, see D. Hebdige, *Subculture: The Meaning of Style* (London, 1979, 2003), pp. 52–4.
4. For biographical details, see P. Townshend, *Who I Am* (London, 2012); G. Gialiano, *Behind Blue Eyes: A Life of Pete Townshend* (London, 1996) and M. Wilkerson, *Who Are You: The Life of Pete Townshend: A Biography* (London, 2009). There is also some useful information in the early chapters of D. Marsh, *Before I Get Old: The Story of the Who* (London, 1985).
5. P. Doggett, *There's a Riot Going on: Revolutionaries, Rock Stars and the Rise and Fall of the 60s Counter Culture* (London, 2007).
6. Townshend, *Who I Am*, p. 4.
7. *New Musical Express*, 12 March 1983.
8. Along with John Lennon, Ray Davies and John Lydon, Townshend was one of the four most significant 'organic intellectuals' in the post-war popular music industry who through their work explored and critiqued aspects of English society. To Townshend the tough working-class rock 'n' roller was symbolised by Roger Daltrey, the sheet metal-worker and tough Teddy Boy who became lead singer of the Who. For biography, see S. Hildred and T. Ewbank, *Roger Daltrey: The Biography* (London, 2012).

9. In the 1930s Townshend's father had briefly been a member of the British Union of Fascists. See Townshend, *Who I Am*, p. 8.
10. Ibid., p. 35.
11. Townshend had also been in the church choir. In his autobiography he states that: 'As I fell asleep at night I sang my prayers into the mouth of my hot-water bottle'. Townshend, *Who I Am*, p. 33.
12. For the roots of the Who and the various permutations that led to their formation, see the early chapters of Marsh, *Before I Get Old*.
13. At art school an American friend introduced Townshend to the more obscure sounds of American jazz and blues. See Townshend, *Who I Am*, p. 56. For the culture of art schools and their connection to the popular music scene of the 1960s, see S. Frith and H. Horne, *Art into Pop* (London, 1987), chapter 3.
14. K. Davey, *English Imaginaries: Six Studies in Anglo-British Modernity* (London, 1999), p. 81. Townshend does not shed light on whether he was a member of these organisations in his autobiography.
15. R. Denselow, *When the Music's Over: The Story of Political Pop* (London, 1989), p. 93.
16. For inter-war working-class consumption, see D. Fowler, 'Teenage Consumers? Young Wage-earners and Leisure in Manchester, 1919–1939', in A. Davies and S. Fielding (eds), *Workers' Worlds: Cultures and Communities in Manchester and Salford, 1880–1939* (Manchester, 1992), pp. 133–55.
17. For a critical analysis of the *Quadrophenia,* see J. Wood, 'The Kids Are Alright', *The Guardian*, 30 May 2009. Another source has claimed that it was a show a year later at in Brighton on 17 April 1965 that was the impetus for *Quadrophenia*. See J. McMichael and J. Lyons, *The Who Concert File* (London, 1997, 2004), p. 29. Yet Townshend has more recently reiterated that 1964 was the year. See Townshend, *Who I Am*, p. 245.
18. Songs on the album, such as 'Cut My Hair', The Punk and the Godfather', 'I'm One', 'The Dirty Jobs', 'Helpless Dancer' and 'I've Had Enough', provide examples of the limitations of social, organisational and subcultural identities and how a working-class teenager simultaneously feels a sense of both 'belonging' and 'distance' from them.
19. Denselow, *When the Music's Over*, p. 95.
20. Townshend claims that the title came from *Generations,* a collection of plays by the socialist playwright David Mercer. Townshend, *Who I Am*, p. 83.
21. For the place of Mods in this process, see Gilroy, *There Ain't No Black in the Union Jack*, p. 215.
22. For a very good oral history, see P. Hewitt, *The Soul Stylists: Six Decades of Modernism – From Mods to Casuals* (Edinburgh, 2000), chapter 1.
23. R. Elms, *The Way We Wore: A Life in Threads* (London, 2005), p. 26.
24. Hewitt has been the most ambitious in tracing the origins of Mod to the jazz scene in 1940s Soho. See Hewitt, *The Soul Stylists*. For a general history of jazz and its impact on England in this period, see F. Newton, *The Jazz Scene* (London, 1959).
25. P. Du Noyer, '*In the City. A Celebration of London Music* (London, 2009), p. 116.
26. T. Rawlings, *Mod: A Very British Phenomenon* (London, 2000), p. 11.
27. Hewitt, *The Soul Stylists*, p. 16. For the developing schisms in the English jazz scene, see G. McKay, *Circular Breathing: The Cultural Politics of Jazz in Britain* (Durham, 2005). McKay explores the division in jazz through its 'revivalists', 'traditionalists' and 'modernists' that led to trouble at the 1959 and 1960 Beaulieu Jazz Festivals.

28. P. Gorman, *The Look: Adventures in Rock and Pop Fashion* (London, 2006), p. 34.
29. Barnes, *Mods!*, p. 8. A point also made by Reed in his biography of John Stephen. See J. Reed, *The King of Carnaby Street: The Life of John Stephen* (London, 2010).
30. G. Melly, *Revolt into Style: The Pop Arts in the 50s and 60s* (Harmondsworth, 1970, 1989), p. 168.
31. P. Burton, *Parallel Lives* (London, 1985), pp. 30–1.
32. Hebdige, *Subculture*, p. 52.
33. Fowler, *Youth Culture in Modern Britain*, p. 128.
34. Colin MacInnes, *Absolute Beginners* (London, 1959), pp. 70–1.
35. S. Hall, 'Absolute Beginnings: Reflections on the Secondary Modern Generation', *Universities and Left Review* (Autumn, 1959), p. 23.
36. *Daily Express*, 22 January 1960.
37. M. Morse, *The Unattached* (Harmondsworth, 1960), p. 101.
38. P. Laurie, *The Teenage Revolution* (Harmondsworth, 1965), p. 26.
39. This document is the foundation text of the Mod movement and has been analysed by a number of authors. 'The Young Take the Wheel': Young Men Who Live For Clothes and Pleasure', *Town*, 3, 9 (September 1962). For a critical assessment, see Fowler, *Youth Culture in Modern Britain*, pp. 128–32.
40. For glam rock, see chapter 7. Fowler wrongly claims that it represents the 'earliest piece of evidence on the mods'. As has been noted in this chapter, a range of writers were already referring to Mod in 1959. Fowler, *Youth Culture in Modern Britain*, p. 129.
41. Townshend remembered 'Bolan with full make-up working as a 'rent boy' to buy clothes, in and round the Scene Club'. See A. L. Oldham, *Stoned* (London, 2001), p. 220.
42. M. Paytress, *Bolan: The Rise and Fall of a Twentieth Century Superstar* (London, 1992), p. 23.
43. Barnes, *Mods!*, p. 10.
44. There is no biography of Meaden, but some detail can be found in an interview he gave to the *New Musical Express*, 17 November 1979. This was subsequently reprinted in P. Hewitt (ed.), *The Sharper Word: A Mod Anthology* (London, 2002), pp. 162–80.
45. Andrew Loog Oldham was one of a new generation of music managers in the 1960s who laid the foundations for the success of the Rolling Stones. Oldham, *Stoned*, pp. 76–7. For Austin's and its role in youth styles of the 1960s, see Reed, *The King of Carnaby Street*, pp. 12–13.
46. Meaden quoted in Hewitt (ed.), *The Sharper Word*, pp. 167–8.
47. By 1964, Mod consisted of Italian, American, French and English fashions, modern jazz, American rhythm and blues, British beat music and a street slang through which Mods identified with each other and excluded others who did not fit their exacting tastes.
48. For full details of early appearances, see McMichael and Lyons, *The Who Concert File*, pp. 9–10.
49. The High Numbers was a reference to the way in which Mods defined themselves. 'High Numbers' being the discerning Mods who were setting the pace in terms of fashion trends and musical affiliations and more lowly 'numbers' and 'tickets' merely followers. Townshend referenced Mod discourse in a number of songs but most notably in 'Sea and Sand' from *Quadrophenia* (1973).
50. T. Fletcher, *Dear Boy: The Life of Keith Moon* (London, 1998), p. 87.
51. For recollections, see M. Sargeant, 'Looking back with Irish Jack', *Scootering*, 163 (September 1999). 'Irish Jack' Lyons was one of a number of Mods who

Townshend drew on in creating the Jimmy character for the *Quadrophenia* album in 1972–3.

52. M. Scala, *Diary of a Teddy Boy: A Memoir of the Long Sixties* (London, 2000), p. 80.
53. McMichael and Lyons, *The Who Concert File*, p. 14.
54. For contemporary account of the link between the High Numbers and Mods, see *Fabulous*, 10 October 1964.
55. For typical concert set lists in this period, see McMichael and Lyons, *The Who Concert File*, pp. 13–23.
56. J. Swenson, *The Who* (London, 1981), p. 22.
57. For biography, see A. Motion, *The Lamberts: George, Constant and Kit* (London, 1986), part 3.
58. For biography, see obituary, *The Guardian*, 28 November 2012.
59. For details of all the places the Who played in this period, see McMichael and Lyons, *The Who Concert File*, pp. 15–45.
60. For Stewart's unsentimental and pragmatic view of his role in political protest and the Mod movement, see R. Stewart, *Rod: The Autobiography* (London, 2012), chapter 2. For the Kinks, see chapter 6 of this book.
61. For Stewart's early life in working-class North London, see Stewart, *Rod,* chapters 1 and 2.
62. T. Ewbank and S. Hildred, *Rod Stewart: The New Biography* (London, 2003), p. 16–17.
63. J. Melly, *Last Orders, Please: Rod Stewart, the Faces and the Britain We Forgot* (2003), p. 11.
64. Fowler suggests that the role of *Ready Steady Go!* in Mod has been exaggerated and that black music was not prominent. Fowler, *Youth Culture in Modern Britain,* p.135. Yet he fails to note the Motown Special that aired in April 1965 featuring artists such as the Supremes, Stevie Wonder, Martha Reeves and the Vandellas, and the Miracles.
65. For details, see S. Levy, *Ready, Steady, Go! Swinging London and the Invention of Cool* (London, 2002), pp. 127–33.
66. See Gorman, *The Look*, pp. 60–3.
67. See obituary, *The Telegraph*, 15 May 2009.
68. For Stevens and his play-list at the Scene Club, see M. Ritson and S. Russell, *The In Crowd: The Story of the Northern and Rare Soul Scene Volume 1* (London, 1999), pp. 55–7.
69. For details, see B. Sykes, *Sit Down! Listen To This! The Roger Eagle Story* (Manchester, 2012), chapters 3 and 4.
70. D. Hale with T. Thornton, *Club 60 and the Esquire: Sheffield Sounds in the 60s* (Sheffield, 2002), chapters 2 and 8.
71. A. Flowers and V. Histon (eds), *It's My Life! 1960s Newcastle* (Newcastle, 2009), pp. 64–6.
72. K. Farley, *They Rocked, We Rolled! A Personal and Oral Account of Rock 'n' Roll in and around Wolverhampton and the West Midlands 1956–1969* (Wolverhampton, 2010), pp. 145–7.
73. Paytress, *Bolan,* p. 25.
74. This view was articulated by Hebdige in his exploration of youth subcultures and their relationship to economic change and social class. See Hebdige, *Subculture,* p. 133.
75. Perry was a socialist and had campaigned with his father, Sam, in the general election of 1929. He went on to win the Wimbledon championship in 1934, 35

and 36. See F. Perry, *An Autobiography* (London, 1984). For Sam Perry's political and parliamentary career as Labour MP for Kettering, see K. Gildart, 'Samuel Frederick Perry (1877–1954)', in K. Gildart and D. Howell (eds), *Dictionary of Labour Biography Vol. XII* (Basingstoke, 2005), pp. 226–33.

76. Fowler has claimed that Stephen was not 'the prime mover' in Mod culture as he only belatedly discovered the movement'. Fowler, *Youth Culture in Modern Britain*, p. 133. Yet the fact that he was crucial to its popularisation means that his role was more important than Fowler suggests. For a sophisticated analysis of Stephen's contribution to Mod in particular and youth culture more generally, see Reed, *The King of Carnaby Street.*
77. For a detailed examination of the link between fashion, youth culture and popular music, see Gorman, *The Look.*
78. John Stephen obituary, *The Guardian*, 9 February 2004.
79. Burton, *Parallel Lives*, p. 31.
80. See R. Lester, *Boutique London. A History: King's Road to Carnaby Street* (Bath, 2010).
81. Reed, *The King of Carnaby Street*, p. 57.
82. Ibid., p. 28.
83. A. Marwick, *The Sixties: Cultural Revolution in Britain, France, Italy and the United States c.1958–c.1974* (Oxford, 1998), p. 77.
84. Flowers and Histon, *It's My Life!*, p. 96.
85. *The Mod's Monthly*, No. 1, March 1964.
86. P. Willmott, *Adolescent Boys of East London* (Harmondsworth, 1966), p. 22
87. For the origins of particular Mod terms, see Laurie, *The Teenage Revolution*, p. 27.
88. *The Mod's Monthly*, No. 2, April 1964.
89. *The Mod's Monthly*, No. 8, October 1964.
90. For cinematic representations of the transnationality of Mod couture, see William Wyler, *Roman Holiday* (1959), Jean-Luc Goddard, *Breathless* (1960) and Robert Wise, *West Side Story* (1961).
91. D. Hebdige, 'The Meaning of Mod', in Stuart Hall and Tony Jefferson (eds), *Resistance Through Rituals: Youth Subcultures in Post-War Britain* (London, 1975), p. 89.
92. Hewitt, *The Soul Stylists*, p. 58.
93. Townshend, *Who I Am*, p. 65.
94. D. Hughes, *Friday on My Mind: A Rock 'n' Roll Lifestyle* (London, 2010), p. 119.
95. *The Mod's Monthly*, No. 6, August 1964.
96. *The Mod's Monthly*, No. 8, October 1964.
97. *The Mod's Monthly*, No. 4, June 1964.
98. *The Mod's Monthly*, No. 2, April 1964.
99. *The Mod's Monthly*, No. 6, August 1964.
100. *The Mod's Monthly*, No. 3, May 1964.
101. C. Hamblett and J. Deverson, *Generation X* (London, 1964), p. 18.
102. J. Spencer, J. Tuxford and N. Dennis, *Stress and Release in an Urban Estate: A Study in Action Research* (London, 1964), p. 170.
103. T. Wolfe, 'The Noonday Underground' in *The Pump House Gang* (London, 1969, 1989), p. 101.
104. Interview with Lloyd Johnson, 12 April 2011.
105. Reed, *The King of Carnaby Street*, p. 63.
106. Willmott, *Adolescent Boys of East London*, p. 22.

107. Interview with Lloyd Johnson, 12 April 2011.
108. Interview with Linden Kirby, 12 April 2011.
109. *Rave*, No. 17, August 1964.
110. Hall, 'Absolute Beginnings', p. 23.
111. Laurie, *The Teenage Revolution*, p. 88.
112. For the Kinks, see chapter 6 of this book. For the Small Faces, see P. Hewitt and J. Hellier, *Steve Marriott: All Too Beautiful* (London, 2004) and I. McLagan, *All the Rage: A Riotous Romp Through Rock & Roll History* (New York, 2000), chapters 5–12.
113. Townshend, *Who I Am*, p. 77.
114. T. Bacon, *London Live* (London, 1999), p. 46.
115. Ibid., p. 58.
116. *Melody Maker*, 2 March 1963.
117. *Jazz News and Review*, 2 January 1963.
118. The Crawdaddy in Richmond provided a springboard for the enduring success of the Rolling Stones. See P. Norman, *The Stones* (Basingstoke, 2002) chapter 2. For the geography of London's rhythm and blues clubs, see Bacon, *London Live*, p. 59.
119. As noted in the last chapter, Georgie Fame's set-list at the Flamingo was an amalgam of jazz, blues, soul and ska music.
120. This more discerning characteristic of Mods and the choice of music were reiterated through interviews with Linden Kirby and Lloyd Johnson. Both were Mods in the early 1960s and attended a number of Mod clubs in London.
121. *The Mod's Monthly*, No. 8, October 1964.
122. A. Marks, 'Young Gifted and Black: Afro-American and Afro-Caribbean Music in Britain 1963–88', in P. Oliver (ed.), *Black Music in Britain: Essays on the Afro-Asian Contribution to Popular Music* (Milton Keynes, 1990), p. 104.
123. For an examination of ska and West Indian music more generally, see D. Hebdige, *Cut 'n' Mix: Culture, Identity and Caribbean Music* (London, 1987).
124. Marks, 'Young Gifted and Black', p. 106.
125. Ibid., p. 104.
126. Fowler, *Youth Culture in Modern Britain*, p. 127. Surprisingly, the author takes a strident tone but does not uncover any primary sources to sustain his contrary opinions.
127. J. Green, *Days In the Life: Voices from the English Underground, 1961–1971* (London, 1998) p. 36.
128. Ibid., p. 39.
129. Rawlings, *Mod*, p. 39.
130. See obituaries the *Guardian*, 18 June 2007 and *Independent*, 28 June 2007.
131. *Rave*, No. 4, May 1964.
132. Interview with Terri Quaye, 12 April 2011.
133. *New Musical Express*, 3 August 1973.
134. Interview with Terri Quaye, 12 April 2011.
135. Interview with Linden Kirby, 12 April 2011.
136. The Scene Club was run by Ronan O'Rahilly. He was another interesting entrepreneur who noted the business potential of youth culture. O'Rahilly went on to establish the pirate radio station Radio Caroline.
137. B. Miles, *London Calling: A Countercultural History of London Since 1945* (London, 2010), p. 168.
138. *Rave*, No. 4, May 1964.

139. Interview with Linden Kirby, 12 April 2011.
140. Burton, *Parallel Lives*, pp. 30–1.
141. Oldham, *Stoned*, p, 77.
142. *Rave*, No. 4, May 1964.
143. Hughes, *Friday on My Mind*, pp. 225–6.
144. *Rave*, No. 4, May 1964.
145. Willmott, *Adolescent Boys of East London*, p. 44.
146. For career details of the Yardbirds, see A. Clayson, *The Yardbirds: The Band That Launched Eric Clapton, Jeff Beck, Jimmy Page* (London, 2002).
147. *The Mod's Monthly*, No. 2, April 1964.
148. *The Mod's Monthly*, No. 1, March 1964.
149. Interview with Linden Kirby, 12 April 2011.
150. Laurie, *The Teenage Revolution*, pp. 56–57.
151. *Daily Mirror*, 4 May 1964.
152. Metropolitan Police, West End Central, Young Persons in the Soho Area, 15 June 1964, TNA HO 300/8.
153. London County Council meeting with Home Secretary and Minister of Health on Jazz and Dance Clubs in the West End, 15 September 1964, TNA HO 300/8.
154. Ibid.
155. Metropolitan Police, West End Central, Young Persons in the Soho Area, 15 June 1964, TNA HO 300/8.
156. Ibid.
157. Harry Shapiro, *Waiting for the Man: The Story of Drugs and Popular Music* (London, 1988), p. 119.
158. *Daily Mirror*, 20 September 1955.
159. *Daily Express*, 4 April 1960.
160. *Daily Mirror*, 28 February 1964.
161. Willmott, *Adolescent Boys of East London*, pp. 175–76.
162. P. Connell, 'What to Do About Pep Pills', *New Society*, 20 February 1964. Reprinted in T. Raison (ed.), *Youth in New Society* (London, 1966), pp. 74–80.
163. Connell, 'What to Do About Pep Pills', p. 78.
164. Hamblett and Deverson, *Generation X*, p. 73.
165. Scala, *Diary of a Teddy Boy*, p. 73.
166. Barnes, *Mods!*, p. 126.
167. *New Musical Express*, 3 August 1974.
168. J. Pidgeon, 'Memories of the Flamingo Club', www.rocksbackpages.com.
169. Shapiro, *Waiting for the Man*, p. 127.
170. Interview with Linden Kirby, 12 April 2011.
171. Hughes, *Friday on My Mind*, p. 178.
172. London County Council notes of a meeting with the Home Secretary, 15 September 1964, TNA HO 300/8.
173. London County Council notes by Children's Department on Jazz and Dance Clubs in the West End 5 August 1964, TNA HO 300/8.
174. Ibid.
175. Interview with Linden Kirby, 12 April 2011.
176. Ibid.
177. For an analysis of the clashes between Mods and Rockers, see Cohen, *Folk Devils and Moral Panics*; R. S. Grayson, 'Mods, Rockers and Juvenile Delinquency in 1964: The Government Response', *Contemporary British History*, 12, 1 (1998), 19–47; Fowler, *Youth Culture in Modern Britain*, pp. 136–43.

178. *Daily Mirror*, 31 March 1964.
179. Townshend, *Who I Am*, p. 71.
180. Marwick, *The Sixties*, p. 77.
181. *Trouser Press*, May 1978.
182. Townshend, *Who I Am*, p. 340.
183. Ibid., p. 80.
184. Cohen, *Folk Devils and Moral Panics*, p. 159. Mods and the seaside disturbances are discussed in chapter 5.
185. Townshend would return to this theme on the expansive *Quadrophenia* album released in 1973.
186. For details of each recording, see early sections of C. Charlesworth and E. Hanel, *The Who: The Complete Guide to Their Music* (London, 2004).
187. For a critical analysis of the album, see J. Dougan, *The Who Sell Out* (London, 2006).
188. For an interesting analysis of pirate radio and the British state, see A. Johns, *Death of a Pirate: British Radio and the Making of the Information Age* (New York, 2011) and R. Chapman, *Selling the Sixties: The Pirates and Pop Music Radio* (London, 1992).
189. For background to the writing of the album, see N. Cawthorne, *The Who and the Making of Tommy* (London, 2005).
190. Film-makers were also realising that popular music was having a particular impact on youth culture. For example, see Peter Watkins, *Privilege* (1967) and Tony Palmer's documentary *All My Loving* (1968).
191. Englishness is even more apparent in the cinematic version of Townshend's 'rock opera' in Ken Russell's, *Tommy* (1975).
192. Townshend, *Who I Am*, p. 184.
193. For details of the Lifehouse project, see Townshend, *Who I Am*, chapter 14 and R. Unterberger, *Won't Get Fooled Again: The Who from Lifehouse to Quadrophenia* (London, 2011).
194. Marsh, *Before I Get Old*, p. 423.
195. Davey, *English Imaginaries*, p. 100, 102.
196. *Uncut*, June 2009.
197. The photographs were taken by Ethan Russell. For background and his work on popular music, see E. Russell, *Dear Mr Fantasy. Diary of A Decade: Our Time and Rock 'n' Roll* (London, 1985).
198. See Unterberger, *Won't Get Fooled Again*, p. 241.
199. The song was recorded in the summer of 1972 during a year of a national miners' strike that had seen the effective use of mass picketing and a younger more militant strand of trade unionism challenging the diktats of their moderate leaders.
200. For example, see D. Fowler, *Youth Culture in Modern Britain, c.1920–c.1970: From Ivory Tower to Global Movement – A New History* (Basingstoke, 2008) and D. Sandbrook, *White Heat: A History of Britain in the Swinging Sixties* (London, 2006), pp. 194–201.

5 Mods over England: Local Experiences and Social Control

1. The literature on Mod has primarily focused on the scene in London, 1959–64. For example, see R. Barnes, *Mods!* (London, 1979) and Fowler, *Youth Culture in Modern Britain*, chapter 7

2. Fowler, *Youth Culture in Modern Britain*, p. 128.
3. E. Nelson, *The British Counter-Culture 1966–73: A Study of the Underground Press* (Basingstoke, 1989), p. 21.
4. P. Hewitt and J. Hellier, *Steve Marriott: All Too Beautiful* (London, 2004), p. 89.
5. For example the glamour and excitement of these groups appeared on a number of occasions in northern English industrial towns populated by coal miners and factory workers such as Chesterfield, Stoke-on-Trent, Wigan, Doncaster and Bolton.
6. The classic analysis of the media construction of Mod remains S. Cohen, *Folk Devils and Moral Panics: The Creation of the Mods and Rockers* (London, 2010). For a critique, see Fowler, *Youth Culture in Modern Britain*, pp. 136–43. For a detailed examination of the parliamentary response to the Mod violence at coastal resorts, see R. S. Grayson, 'Mods, Rockers and Juvenile Delinquency in 1964: The Government Response', *Contemporary British History*, 12, 1 (Spring 1988), 19–47.
7. Cohen, *Folk Devils and Moral Panics*, p. 157.
8. *The Mod's Monthly*, No. 1, March 1964.
9. *The Mod's Monthly*, No. 6, August 1964.
10. Ibid.
11. *The Mod's Monthly*, No. 2, April 1964.
12. Ibid.
13. *The Mod's Monthly*, No. 3, May 1964.
14. Ibid.
15. *The Mod's Monthly*, No. 4, June 1964.
16. *The Mod's Monthly*, No. 5, July 1964.
17. *Rave*, No. 6, July 1964.
18. *The Mod's Monthly*, No. 6, August 1964.
19. Ibid.
20. *The Mod's Monthly*, No. 5, July 1964.
21. *The Mod's Monthly*, No. 6, August 1964.
22. *The Mod's Monthly*, No. 4, June 1964.
23. *The Mod's Monthly*, No. 3, 1964.
24. *Rave*, No. 4, May 1964.
25. Ibid.
26. Ibid.
27. Ibid.
28. Ibid.
29. Ibid.
30. *Rave*, No. 17, June 1965.
31. *Daily Mirror*, 13 January 1964.
32. *Fabulous*, 27 June 1964.
33. In March 1960, in what must be one of the first manifestations of the punk style in England, Kevin Mahoney, an 11-year-old from Boldon Colliery, was apparently sent home from school for having a Mohican haircut. See *Daily Express*, 25 March 1960.
34. Interview with Lloyd Johnson, 12 April 2011.
35. P. Willmott, *Adolescent Boys of East London* (1966), p. 23.
36. Ibid.
37. Ibid., p. 140.
38. M. Blandy, *Razor Edge: The Story of a Youth Club* (London, 1967), p. 145.
39. G. Melly, *Revolt Into Style: The Pop Arts in the 50s and 60s* (London, 1989), p. 170.

40. M. Sargeant, 'Looking Back with Irish Jack', *Scootering*, 163 (September 1999).
41. D. Hughes, *Friday on My Mind: A Rock 'n' Roll Lifestyle* (London, 2010), p. 210.
42. Ibid., p. 187.
43. *Rave*, No. 6, July 1964.
44. C. Hamblett and J. Deverson, *Generation X* (London, 1964), p. 43.
45. *Rave*, No. 6, July 1964.
46. D. Hale with T. Thornton, *Club 60 and the Esquire: Sheffield Sounds in the 60s* (Sheffield, 2002), p. 47.
47. D. Nowell, *Too Darn Soulful: The Story of Northern Soul* (London, 1999), p. 16.
48. Interview with Lloyd Johnson, 12 April 2011.
49. *Rave*, No. 4, May 1964.
50. Ibid.
51. M. Ritson and S. Russell, *The In Crowd: The Story of the Northern and Rare Soul Scene Vol. 1* (London, 1999), p. 78.
52. For reminiscences see S. Myatt, *The Mod Years* (London, 2005).
53. See K. Rylatt and P. Scott, *CENtral 1179: The Story of Manchester's Twisted Wheel Club* (London, 2001).
54. For profile see *Rave*, No. 4, May 1964.
55. See Rylatt and Scott, *CENtral 1179*, p. 62.
56. Ibid., p. 179.
57. A. Flowers and V. Histon, *It's My Life! 1960s Newcastle: Memories from People Who Were There* (Newcastle, 2009), p. 64.
58. Ibid., p. 75.
59. For a recent example, see Fowler, *Youth Culture in Britain*, pp. 136–43. The classic characterisation of the events was provided by Cohen and his articulation of the concept of 'moral panic'. See Cohen, *Folk Devils and Moral Panics*, especially chapters 2–5.
60. The literature on English Rockers is even more limited than that on Mod. In general Rockers were linked to the motorcycle gangs and 'Ton-Up boys' of the late 1950s. Unlike Mods many of them were uninterested in new forms of popular music and fashion styles. They wore leather jackets, heavy boots, denim jeans, white silk scarves and soundtracked their social life with the 1950s rock 'n' roll of Elvis Presley, Chuck Berry, Jerry Lee Lewis and Gene Vincent. See J. Stuart, *Rockers* (London, 1987) and their cinematic representation in Sidney J. Furie's *The Leather Boys* (1964).
61. N. Dunn, *Up the Junction* (London, 1963), p. 82. For oral histories of rockers, see W. Ramsey, *The Ace Café: Then and Now* (London, 2002).
62. Interview with Lloyd Johnson, 12 April 2011.
63. Interview with Linden Kirby, 12 April 2011.
64. For a critical reading of the media response, see Cohen, *Folk Devils and Moral Panics*.
65. *Melody Maker*, 25 April 1964.
66. For details of numbers involved, arrests, etc., see Grayson, 'Mods, Rockers and Juvenile Delinquency, p. 26.
67. *The Mod's Monthly*, No. 4, June 1964.
68. *Daily Mirror*, 18 September 1963.
69. *Daily Mirror*, 31 March 1964.
70. Hamblett and Deverson, *Generation X*, p. 73.
71. Memorandum from Chief Superintendent of Essex County Constabulary on Clacton disturbances, 1 April 1964, TNA, BN 29/1765.

72. Ibid.
73. Ibid.
74. Ibid.
75. Ibid.
76. Ibid.
77. Ibid.
78. Ibid.
79. *Daily Mirror*, 19 May 1964.
80. *Daily Mirror*, 21 May 1964.
81. Ibid.
82. *Daily Mirror*, 22 May 1964.
83. For example, see Cohen, *Folk Devils and Moral Panics* and Grayson, 'Mods, Rockers and Juvenile Delinquency in 1964'.
84. *Daily Mirror*, 18 May 1964.
85. *Daily Mirror*, 23 May 1964.
86. Ibid.
87. *Daily Mirror*, 25 July 1964.
88. For media coverage see extensive report in *Daily Mirror*, 3 August 1964.
89. *Daily Mirror*, 26 August 1964.
90. *Daily Mirror*, 28 April 1964.
91. J. Mandelkau, *Buttons: the Making of a President* (London, 1971), p. 46.
92. J. Green, *Days In the Life: Voices from the English Underground, 1961–1971* (London, 1988, 1998), p. 84.
93. Interview with Linden Kirby, 12 April 2011.
94. *Daily Mirror*, 23 May 1964.
95. *Daily Mirror*, 27 May 1964.
96. *Daily Mirror*, 18 August 1964.
97. *New Musical Express*, 3 November 1973.
98. P. Barker, 'The Margate Offenders: A Survey', *New Society*, 30 July 1964. Reprinted in T. Raison (ed.), *Youth in New Society* (1966), pp. 115–27.
99. Ibid., p. 119.
100. Ibid., p. 122.
101. Hamblett and Deverson, *Generation X*, p. 9.
102. *Daily Mirror*, 24 May 1964.
103. Blandy, *Razor Edge*, p. 177.
104. Willmott, *Adolescent Boys of East London*, p. 152.
105. *Daily Mirror*, 25 May 1964.
106. Melly, *Revolt into Style*, p. 171.
107. *Daily Mirror*, 3 September 1964.
108. Mods in Brighton still made the front pages but were praised for their lack of violence. See *Daily Mirror*, 19 April 1965.
109. Hughes, *Friday on My Mind*, p. 186.
110. For violence between Mods and Rockers and Welsh's role, see Mandelkau, *Buttons*, pp. 24–8.
111. J. Reed, *The King of Carnaby Street: The Life of John Stephen* (London, 2010), p. 94.
112. Ibid., p. 151.
113. For example, see Grayson, 'Mods, Rockers and Juvenile Delinquency in 1964' and Fowler, *Youth Culture in Modern Britain*, pp. 136–43.
114. National Association of Youth Clubs, "Weekenders", TNA MEPO 2/100477

115. Ibid.
116. Ibid.
117. Ibid.
118. Ibid.
119. Portobello Project, 1964, TNA MEPO 2/100477
120. Testimony of Peter Jennings, voluntary helper in youth club, Portobello Project, 1964, TNA MEPO 2/100477.
121. Ibid.
122. Ibid.
123. Ibid.
124. Ibid.
125. Ibid.
126. Ibid.
127. *Daily Mirror*, 5 January 1966.
128. Hamblett and Deverson, *Generation X*, p. 25
129. *New Musical Express*, 3 August 1974.
130. London County Council meeting with Home Secretary and Minister of Health on Jazz and Dance Clubs in the West End, 15 September 1964, TNA HO 300/8.
131. Ibid.
132. Portobello Project, 1964, TNA MEPO 2/100477.
133. Metropolitan Police Memorandum, Notting Hill Social Council Project, 4 March 1965, TNA MEPO 2/100477.
134. Portobello Project, 1964, TNA MEPO 2/100477.
135. London County Council meeting with Home Secretary and Minister of Health on Jazz and Dance Clubs in the West End, 15 September 1964, TNA HO 300/8.
136. Ibid.
137. *Daily Mirror*, 14 June 1965.
138. See early chapters of Mandelkau, *Buttons*.
139. See *Daily Mirror*, 9 November 1965 and 4 February 1966.
140. Mandelkau, *Buttons*, p. 48.
141. Hale, *Club 60 and the Esquire*, p. 47.
142. See C. P. Lee, *Shake, Rattle and Rain: Popular Music Making in Manchester, 1955–1995* (Ottery, 2002), especially chapter 4.
143. Manchester City Police, File on Sovereign Club 1964, Box File on Manchester Clubs, Police Museum, Manchester.
144. City of Manchester Chief Constable's Report 1965, Box File on Manchester Clubs, Police Museum, Manchester.
145. Manchester City Police File on Twisted Wheel Incidents Concerning Drugs 1964, Box File on Manchester Clubs, Police Museum, Manchester.
146. Manchester City Police Report 23 June 1964, Box File on Manchester Clubs, Police Museum, Manchester.
147. For a fascinating novel depicting teenage girls and the all-night club scene in 1960s Manchester, see V. Tenny, *Just Ask the Lonely* (London, 1970).
148. Manchester City Police Report of Occurrence 10 May 1964, Box File on Manchester Clubs, Police Museum, Manchester.
149. See L. Jackson, 'The Coffee Club Menace: Policing Youth, Leisure and Sexuality in Post-war Manchester', *Cultural and Social History*, 5, 3 (2008), 289–308.
150. City of Manchester Chief Constable's Report 1965, Box File on Manchester Clubs, Police Museum, Manchester.
151. P. H. Connell, 'What to Do About Pep Pills', *New Society*, 20 February 1964. Reprinted in T. Raison (ed.), *Youth in New Society* (1966), p. 78.

152. Alec Macguire, 'Emancipated and Reactionaries', *New Society*, 28 May 1964. Reprinted in T. Raison (ed.), *Youth in New Society* (1966) p. 110.
153. Ibid., p. 113.
154. Mods also appeared on cinema and television screens presenting aspects of the style to a wide audience. For example, in the BBC play *The End of Arthur's Marriage*, which was broadcast in November 1965, Mods are seen riding Lambretta scooters and enjoying themselves at a party. See J. Hill, *Ken Loach: The Politics of Film and Television* (London, 2011), pp. 19–23.
155. Barker, 'The Margate Offenders', p. 122.
156. Interview with Lloyd Johnson, 12 April 2011.
157. Hughes, *Friday on My Mind*, pp. 196–7.
158. Interview with Linden Kirby, 12 April 2011.
159. Hamblett and Deverson, *Generation X*, pp. 39–40.
160. Rylatt and Scott, *CENtral 1179*, p. 130.
161. Blandy, *Razor Edge*, p. 146.
162. *Daily Express*, 9 April 1960.
163. Hamblett and Deverson, *Generation X*, p. 27.
164. Blandy, *Razor Edge*, p. 146.
165. R. Barnes, *Mods!* (London, 1979), p. 16.
166. Interview with Linden Kirby, 12 April 2011.
167. *The Mod's Monthly*, No. 5, July 1964.
168. London County Council meeting with Home Secretary and Minister of Health on Jazz and Dance Clubs in the West End, 15 September 1964, TNA HO 300/8.
169. Barnes, *Mods!*, p. 11.
170. P. Laurie, *The Teenage Revolution* (Harmondsworth, 1965), p. 155.
171. London County Council meeting with Home Secretary and Minister of Health on Jazz and Dance Clubs in the West End, 15 September 1964, TNA HO 300/8.
172. Hamblett and Deverson, *Generation X*, p. 23.
173. Hughes, *Friday on My Mind*, p. 156.
174. Ibid., p. 179.
175. *Mojo*, 217, December 2011.
176. P. Burton, *Parallel Lives* (London, 1985), p. 36.
177. Ibid., p. 27.
178. G. Mckay, *Circular Breathing: The Cultural Politics of Jazz in Britain* (Durham, 2005), p. 303.
179. Hamblett and Deverson, *Generation X*, p. 22.
180. London County Council meeting with Home Secretary and Minister of Health on Jazz and Dance Clubs in the West End, 15 September 1964, TNA HO 300/8.
181. Hamblett and Deverson, *Generation X*, p. 35.
182. Interview with Jimmy James, 3 April 2008.
183. Interview with Terri Quaye, 12 April 2011.

6 Class, Nation and Social Change in the Kinks' England

1. The Kinks were a four-piece group formed around Muswell Hill, London. From 1961 to 1964 the group performed under a number of names including the Boll-Weevils, the Ravens, and then becoming the Kinks in 1964. The driving force of the band was provided by Ray Davies (1944–), who played guitar, took lead vocals and became the principal songwriter. His younger brother Dave (1947–) played lead guitar, penned a number of songs and was supported by Pete Quaife (1943–2010)

on bass and Mick Avory (1944–) on drums. They released their first single 'Long Tall Sally' in the same year followed by 'You Really Got Me', which reached the top of the charts. The Kinks consolidated their commercial success releasing numerous singles and by 1971 had produced nine studio albums. For a recent biography of the group, see N. Hasted, *The Story of The Kinks: You Really Got Me* (London, 2011). However, the best books on the background and formation of the group remain Ray and Dave's autobiographies. See R. Davies, *X-Ray: The Unauthorised Autobiography* (London, 1996) and D. Davies, *Kink: An Autobiography* (London, 1996).

2. M. Shanks, *The Stagnant Society* (London, 1961); A. Sampson, *The Anatomy of Britain* (London, 1962); A. Koestler, *Suicide of a Nation* (London, 1963). These books were representative of a literary trend that sought to make sense of the current state of England, its recent past and prospects for the future.
3. For the CCCS, see S. Hall and T. Jefferson (eds), *Resistance Through Rituals: Youth Subcultures in Post-war Britain* (London, 1993).
4. There is a broad literature on the notion of 'political consensus' and its impact on the period between 1945 and 1979. See P. Addison, *The Road to 1945: British Politics and the Second World War* (London, 1975). For a summary of the critiques of the idea of a 'post-war consensus', see D. Fraser, 'The Postwar Consensus: A Debate Not Long Enough', *History*, 84, 274 (1999), 301–24.
5. For a sophisticated analysis of Davies's work, see T. M. Kitts, *Ray Davies: Not Like Everybody Else* (London, 2008).
6. *New Musical Express*, 6 October 1979.
7. For a survey of the main social and political developments in this period, see A. Marwick, *British Society Since 1945* (Harmondsworth, 1982).
8. For punk, class and England, see chapter 8 of this book.
9. R. Hoggart, *The Uses of Literacy: Aspects of Working-Class Life with Special Reference to Publications and Entertainments* (Harmondsworth, 1957). For a classic CCCS text on the working-class community and youth culture, see P. Cohen, 'Subcultural Conflict and Working Class Community', *Working Papers in Cultural Studies*, 2 (Birmingham, 1972).
10. Hoggart, *Uses of Literacy*, p. 324.
11. Ibid., p. 222.
12. The best sources for the family backgrounds of the Kinks are the autobiographies of Ray Davies and Dave Davies and the various profiles of the Kinks that have been published since the 1980s. See Davies, *X-Ray*; Davies, *Kink*, and J. Savage, *The Kinks: The Official Biography* (London, 1984).
13. These film directors made a significant contribution to the depiction of working-class life in popular film. For examples see the following films, Karel Reisz's *Saturday Night and Sunday Morning* (1960), Tony Richardson's *A Taste of Honey* (1961), John Schlesinger's *A Kind of Loving* (1962) and Lindsay Anderson's *This Sporting Life* (1963). For a critical discussion of the films, see J. Hill, *Sex, Class and Realism: British Cinema 1956–1963* (London, 1997).
14. R. Samuel, *Island Stories. Unravelling Britain: Theatres of Memory Vol. II,* A. Light, S. Alexander and G. Stedman Jones (eds) (London, 1998), p. 160.
15. Davies, *Kink*, p. 134.
16. G. Orwell, *The Lion and the Unicorn: Socialism and the English Genius* (Harmondsworth, 1990).
17. Ibid., p. 36.
18. See M. J. Krause, 'The Greatest Rock Star of the 19th Century: Ray Davies, Romanticism, and the Art of being English', *Popular Music and Society*, 29, 1 (2006), 201–12.

19. M. Cloonan, 'State of the Nation: Englishness, Pop, and Politics in the Mid-1990s', *Popular Music and Society*, 21, 2 (1997), 47–70.
20. N. Baxter-Moore, 'This Is Where I Belong: Identity, Social Class, and the Nostalgic Englishness of Ray Davies and the Kinks', *Popular Music and Society*, 29, 2 (2006), 145–65.
21. G. Orwell, *The Road to Wigan Pier* (London, 1937).
22. For discussion of Orwell's politics, see S. Ingle, *George Orwell: A Political Life* (Manchester, 1993), chapters 5 and 6.
23. Hoggart, *Uses of Literacy*, p. 343.
24. Davies, *X-Ray*, pp. 311–12.
25. Ibid., p. 342.
26. Hoggart, *Uses of Literacy*, p. 33.
27. J. Rogan, *The Kinks: The Sound and the Fury* (London, 184), p. 4.
28. N. Dunn, *Up the Junction* (London, 1968), pp. 51–2.
29. P. Willmott, *Adolescent Boys of East London* (Harmondsworth, 1966), p. 19.
30. Hoggart, *Uses of Literacy*, p. 158.
31. For an autobiographical insight into 'northern clubland' in the 1960s, see the memoirs of Manchester comedian Les Dawson. L. Dawson, *A Clown Too Many* (Glasgow, 1985).
32. Davies, *X-Ray*, 340.
33. L. Hanley, *Estates: An Intimate History* (London, 2007), p. 76.
34. Willmott, *Adolescent Boys of East London*, pp. 173–6.
35. Davies, *X-Ray*, p. 85.
36. Hoggart, *Uses of Literacy*, p. 201.
37. For chronology of the Kinks' career including recording sessions and live performances, see D. Hinman, *The Kinks All Day and All of the Night: Day-by-Day Concerts, Recordings and Broadcasts, 1961–1996* (San Francisco, 2004).
38. Savage, *The Kinks*, p. 61.
39. For the conservatism of middle-class women, see J. Hinton, 'Militant Housewives: The British Housewives' League and the Attlee Government', *History Workshop Journal*, 38, 1 (1994), 129–156.
40. The sense of a 'better past' underpinned Davies's characterisation of the working-class throughout his writing. Two later examples can be found in 'Better Things' (1981) and 'Come Dancing' (1982).
41. For the history of moral panics in England, see G. Pearson, *Hooligan: A History of Respectable Fears* (Basingstoke, 1983).
42. F. Mort, *Capital Affairs: London and the Making of the Permissive Society* (New Haven, 2010), p. 340.
43. See also G. Moorhouse, *Britain in the Sixties: The Other England* (Harmondsworth, 1964) and K. Coates and R. Silburn, *Poverty: The Forgotten Englishmen* (Harmondsworth, 1970).
44. For biography of Rachman, see entry in *Oxford Dictionary of National Biography* (Oxford, 2004–10).
45. The films of Ken Loach also convincingly depict the continuities in pre-war and post-war working-class consciousness and the 'structure of feeling' that remained a feature of everyday life and the culture that emerged from the home, the workplace and the street. For a critical reading of Loach's films see J. Hill, *Ken Loach: The Politics of Film and Television* (London, 2011).
46. For an examination of the planning culture that led to Ronan Point, see D. Sandbrook, *White Heat*, (London, 2006), chapter 29.
47. Kitts, *Ray Davies*, p. 75.

48. For the Aberfan disaster and its aftermath see I. McLean, 'On Moles and the Habits of Birds: The Unpolitics of Aberfan', *Twentieth Century British History*, 8, 3 (1997), 285–309.
49. Hinman, *The Kinks,* p. 91
50. *Time Out*, 21–28 September 2005.
51. Davies, *X-Ray,* p. 79.
52. Willmott, *Adolescent Boys of East London,* p. 168.
53. J. Patrick, *A Glasgow Gang Observed* (London, 1973), pp. 110–11.
54. M. Morse, *The Unattached* (Harmondsworth, 1965), p. 116.
55. For Manchester, see L. Jackson, 'The Coffee Club Menace: Policing Youth, Leisure and Sexuality in Post-war Manchester', *Cultural and Social History*, 5, 3 (2008), 289–308.
56. Dunn, *Up the Junction*, p. 63.
57. N. Dunn, *Poor Cow* (London, 1967).
58. For an insightful analysis of class, gender and popular culture in the 1960s, see S. Rowbotham, *Promise of a Dream: Remembering the Sixties* (Harmondsworth, 2000).
59. For a recent re-appraisal of the Rolling Stones' depiction of women, see A. August, 'Gender and 1960s Youth Culture: The Rolling Stones and the New Woman', *Contemporary British History*, 23, 1 (2009), 79–100.
60. Davies, *X-Ray,* p. 336–7.
61. For a perceptive assessment of the characterisation of film in this period, see Geraghty, 'Women and Sixties British Cinema: The Development of the "Darling" Girl', in Robert Murphy (ed.), *The British Cinema Book* (London, 1997), pp. 154–63.
62. For a recent re-appraisal of their work, see M. Savage, *Identities and Social Change in Britain Since 1940: The Politics of Method* (Oxford, 2010).
63. M. Young and P. Willmott, *Family and Kinship in East London* (Harmondsworth, 1986), p. 61.
64. Paul Barker, 'Young Marriage', in T. Raison (ed.), *Youth in New Society* (London, 1966), p. 179.
65. For discussion of these figures, see R. McKibbin, *Classes and Cultures: England, 1918–1951* (Oxford, 1998), pp. 127–37.
66. A. Sillitoe, *Saturday Night and Sunday Morning* (London, 1958).
67. Orwell, *The Lion and the Unicorn,* p. 37.
68. S. Barstow, *A Kind of Loving* (London, 1960).
69. A critique of middle-class conformity was also provided by the BBC play *The End of Arthur's Marriage,* which had been broadcast in November 1965. For discussion, see Hill, *Ken Loach,* pp. 19–23.
70. Young and Willmott, *Family and Kinship in East London,* p. 108.
71. J. Bourke, *Working-Class Cultures in Britain, 1890–1960: Gender, Class and Ethnicity* (London, 1996), p. 137.
72. Barker, 'Young Marriage', pp. 182–3.
73. Hoggart, *Uses of Literacy*, p. 39.
74. For discussion, see E. Hedling, *Lindsay Anderson: Maverick Film-maker* (London, 1998), pp. 43–5.
75. Orwell, *The Lion and the Unicorn,* p. 40.
76. See G. Orwell, 'The Art of Donald McGill', in G. Orwell, *Decline of the English Murder* (Harmondsworth, 2011).
77. Hinman, *The Kinks,* p. 101.

78. M. Waite, 'Sex 'n' Drugs 'n' Rock 'n' Roll (and Communism) in the 1960s', in G. Andrews, N. Fishman and K. Morgan (eds), *Opening the Books: Essays on the Social and Cultural History of the British Communist Party* (London, 1995), pp. 218–19.
79. Young Communist League District Congress, December 1967, People's History Museum CP/YCL/09/04.
80. J. Street, *Rebel Rock: The Politics of Popular Music* (Oxford, 1986), p. 221.
81. Bourke, *Working-Class Cultures in Britain,* p. 213.
82. Hinman, *The Kinks,* 120–21.
83. T. Dan Smith was the autocratic and enigmatic Labour figure in Newcastle politics who was eventually imprisoned for corruption. For background and details of the case, see R. Fitzwalter and D. Taylor, *Web of Corruption: The Story of John Poulson and T. Dan Smith* (London, 1981).
84. Hoggart, *Uses of Literacy,* pp. 96–8.
85. C. H. Rolph, *Women of the Streets: A Sociological Study of the Common Prostitute for the British Social Biology Council* (London, 1961), pp. 112–13.
86. Ibid., p. 131.
87. For cinematic images of post-war youth, see Hill, *Sex, Class and Realism,* chapters 3 and 4.
88. J. Sandford, *Prostitutes* (London, 1977), p. 112.
89. M. M. Lupro, 'Preserving the Old Ways, Protecting the New: Post-War British Urban Planning in *The Kinks Are the Village Green Preservation Society*', *Popular Music and Society,* 29, 2 (2006), p. 190.
90. Orwell, *The Lion and the Unicorn,* p. 115.
91. P. S. Bagwell, *The Railwaymen: The History of the National Union of Railwaymen Vol. 2: The Beeching Era and After* (London, 1982), p. 24.
92. R. Samuel, *Theatres of Memory Vol. 1: Past and Present in Contemporary Culture,* (London, 1994), p. 271.
93. Ibid., p. 356.
94. Rogan, *The Kinks,* p. 105.
95. For and overview of these developments, see Sandbrook, *White Heat,* chapter 21.
96. P. Willmott and M. Young, *Family and Class in a London Suburb* (London, 1967), p. 23.
97. Ibid.
98. Davies, *Kink,* p. 119.
99. Baxter-Moore, 'This Is Where I Belong', p. 157.
100. For the creation of 'Selsdon man' and its impact, see J. Campbell, *Edward Heath. A Biography* (London, 1993), pp. 265–7.
101. Willmott and Young, *Family and Class in a London Suburb,* p. 31
102. *Rolling Stone,* 10 November 1969.
103. Barker, 'Young Marriage', p. 183.
104. Bourke, *Working-Class Cultures in Britain,* p. 165.
105. Willmott and Young, *Family and Class in a London Suburb,* p. 98.
106. *Circus Magazine,* February 1972.
107. *Show Guide Magazine,* 1969.
108. Hoggart, *Uses of Literacy,* p. 72.
109. For discussion, see P. Stead, *Film and the Working Class: The Feature Film in British and American Society* (London, 1989), chapter 8 and A. Aldgate and J. Richards, *Best of British: Cinema and Society From 1930 to the Present* (London, 1999), chapter 10.

110. R. Denselow, *When the Music's Over: The Story of Political Pop* (London, 1989), p. 95.
111. See R. Tyler, 'Victims of Our History? Barbara Castle and *In Place of Strife*', *Contemporary British History*, 20, 3 (2006), 461–76.
112. Davies, *X-Ray,* p. 54.
113. Street, *Rebel Rock*, p. 214.
114. Davies, *Kink,* p. 134.
115. Baxter-Moore, 'This Is Where I Belong', p. 161.
116. Hoggart, *Uses of Literacy*, pp. 102–3.
117. P. Mandler, *The English National Character: The History of an Idea from Edmund Burke to Tony Blair* (New Haven, 2006), p. 189.
118. For references to Dave Davies and bisexuality, see S. Napier-Bell, *Black Vinyl White Powder* (London, 2002), p. 72.
119. For background, see J. Weeks, *Coming Out: Homosexual Politics in Britain from the Nineteenth Century to the Present* (London, 1983), chapters 14–16.
120. M. Houlbrook, *Queer London: Perils and Pleasures in the Sexual Metropolis, 1918–1957* (Chicago, 2005), p. 223.
121. For description of this milieu, see J. Reed, *The King of Carnaby Street. The Life of John Stephen* (London, 2010), p. 85.
122. Davies, *X-Ray,* pp. 138–9.
123. J. Nuttall, *Bomb Culture* (London, 1970), p. 34.
124. For Raymond, see P. Willetts, *Members Only: The Life and Times of Paul Raymond* (London, 2010).
125. F. Mort, 'Striptease: The Erotic Female Body and Live Sexual Entertainment in Mid-Twentieth-Century London', *Social History*, 23, 1 (2007), 53.
126. For a detailed exploration of English pornography in this period, see G. Freeman, *The Undergrowth of Literature* (London, 1969).
127. Young and Willmott, *Family and Kinship in East London*, p. 132.
128. *Circus Magazine*, February 1972.
129. *International Musician*, December 1981.
130. Davies, *X-Ray,* p. 386.
131. Kitts, *Ray Davies,* p. 160.
132. Hanley, *Estates,* p. 59.
133. Young and Willmott, *Family and Kinship in East London,* p. 151.
134. Willmott and Young, *Family and Class in a London Suburb,* p. 107.
135. *Rock Bill*, May 1988.
136. Hoggart, *Uses of Literacy*, p. 135.
137. Davies, *X-Ray,* p. 311.
138. Orwell, *The Lion and the Unicorn,* p. 81.
139. Street, *Rebel Rock,* 153.
140. John Smith became leader of the Labour Party in 1992. Interview with Davies, *Independent*, 27 August 1994.
141. D. Harker, *One for the Money. Politics and Popular Song* (London, 1980), p. 111.
142. Davies, *Kink,* p. 248.

7 Aliens in England: Slade, David Bowie, Ziggy Stardust and Glam Rock

1. For the earliest academic piece on glam rock, see I. Taylor and D. Wall, 'Beyond the Skinheads: Comments on the Emergence and Significance of the Glam Rock

Cult', in G. Mungham and G. Pearson (eds), *Working Class Youth Culture* (London, 1976), pp. 105–23. For more recent explorations of glam rock, see P. Auslander, *Performing Glam Rock: Gender and Theatricality in Popular Music* (Ann Arbor, 2006); S. Leng, *The Twisted Tale of Glam Rock* (Santa Barbara, 2010) and D. Pih (ed.), *Glam: The Performance of Style* (Liverpool, 2013).

2. T. Haynes, 'Foreword', in B. Hoskyns, *Glam! Bowie, Bolan and the Glitter Rock Revolution* (London, 1998), p. xi. Haynes provided a fictionalised account of glam rock culture in his film *Velvet Goldmine* (1998).
3. The most detailed accounts of glam rock can be found in a range of popular publications that are strong on chronology and facts but weak on analysis and social context. The best book in this genre remains Hoskyns, *Glam*. There is also useful detail of performers and recordings in D. Thompson, *Children of the Revolution: The Glam Rock Story, 1970–75* (London, 2010).
4. For example, see P. Doggett, *The Man Who Sold the World: David Bowie and the 1970s* (London, 2011); M. Bracewell, *Re-make/Re-model: Art, Pop, Fashion and the Making of Roxy Music, 1953–1972* (London, 2007) and M. Paytress, *Bolan: The Rise and Fall of a 20th Century Superstar* (London, 1992).
5. For a visual representation of the meshing of glam and punk styles, see *Roxette*, the short film made by art students at Manchester Polytechnic in 1977, which documents youths attending a Roxy Music concert at the city's Opera House. (North West Film Archive, Manchester Metropolitan University). For glam's connection to youth culture's past, present and future, see S. Reynolds, 'The Rift of Retro: 1962? Or Twenty Years On?', in D. Pih (ed.), *Glam*, pp. 63–73.
6. For narrative histories of the period, see A. W. Turner, *Crisis? What Crisis? Britain in the 1970s* (London, 2008); A. Beckett, *When the Lights Went out: Britain in the Seventies* (London, 2009) and D. Sandbrook, *State of Emergency: The Way We Were, Britain, 1970–74* (London, 2010).
7. Sandbrook, *State of Emergency*, p. 32. For glam rock's place in the politics of the period, see A. W. Turner, 'Rocking while Rome Burns: The Politics of Glam', in D. Pih (ed.), *Glam*, pp. 75–9.
8. A useful text on popular music, masculinity and performance is S. Hawkins, *The British Pop Dandy: Masculinity, Popular Culture and Culture* (Aldershot, 2009), although it contains little on the social context of glam rock.
9. For the origins of the glam style, see Judith Watt, 'For Your Pleasure: The Quest for Glamour in British Fashion 1969–1972', in D. Pih (ed.), *Glam*, pp. 39–52.
10. Hoskyns, *Glam*, p. 19.
11. See D. Buckley, *Strange Fascination: David Bowie, The Definitive Story* (1999, 2005), p. 76.
12. *Remember Me This Way* (1974) directed by Ron Inkpen and Bob Foster. Unfortunately for Glitter, he was remembered in a very different way as a notorious paedophile convicted of possessing child pornography in 1999 and a few years later prosecuted in Vietnam for having sex with minors.
13. D. Haslam, *Not Abba: The Real Story of the 1970s* (London, 2005), p. 112.
14. J. Street, *Rebel Rock: The Politics of Popular Music* (Oxford, 1986), p. 172.
15. Auslander, *Performing Glam Rock*, p. 51.
16. J. Novick and M. Middles, *Wham Bam Thank You Glam: A Celebration of the 70s* (London, 1998), p. 20.
17. Taylor and Wall, 'Beyond the Skinheads', p. 121.
18. Thompson, *Children of the Revolution*, p. 22.
19. Auslander, *Performing Glam Rock*, pp. 229–30.
20. D. Hebdige, *Subculture: The Meaning of Style* (London, 1979), p. 62.

21. Leng, *The Twisted Tale of Glam Rock*, p. 13.
22. *New Musical Express*, 24 June 1972.
23. M. Brake, *Comparative Youth Culture: The Sociology of Youth Subcultures in America, Britain and Canada* (London, 1985), p. 76.
24. For a critical analysis of *Jackie* magazine, see A. McRobbie, *Feminism and Youth Culture: From Jackie to Just Seventeen* (Cambridge, 1991), chapters 5 and 6.
25. *Jackie*, No. 497, 14 July 1973.
26. F. Vermorel, *Starlust. The Secret Fantasies of Fans* (London, 1985, 2011), p. 149.
27. P. Cato, *Crash Course for the Ravers: A Glam Odyssey* (Lockerbie, 1997), p. 15.
28. Ibid., p. 19. The national post workers strike ended on 8 March 1971 and had lasted for seven weeks.
29. For broader aspects of popular culture including television and literature in this period, see Turner, *Crisis? What Crisis?*, chapter 3. For a cinematic representation of an England beset by famine, environmental destruction and roving gangs of rampaging bikers, see Cornel Wilde's *No Blade of Grass* (1970).
30. *Jackie*, No. 451, 26 August 1972.
31. A serious critical study of Slade remains to be written. For career details, see G. Tremlett, *The Slade Story* (London, 1975) and N. Holder, *Who's Crazee Now? My Autobiography* (London, 1999).
32. Tremlett, *The Slade Story*, p. 42.
33. For the beat boom in the West Midlands and Slade's place in its development, see K. Farley, *They Rocked, We Rolled!: A Personal and Oral Account of Rock 'n' Roll in and around Wolverhampton and the West Midlands 1956–1969* (Wolverhampton, 2010). For Birmingham, see E. Fewtrell and S. Thompson, *King of the Clubs: The Eddie Fewtrell Story* (Studley, 2007).
34. Holder, *Who's Crazee Now*, p. 3
35. Ibid., p. 8.
36. J. Bulmer, *The North* (Liverpool, 2012), p. 32.
37. Tremlett, *The Slade Story*, p. 8.
38. Ibid., p. 77.
39. M. Wale, *Vox Pop: Profiles of the Pop Process* (London, 1972), p. 235. Chandler himself had been a 'turner' in the shipyards of North East England before forging a successful career as a member of the Animals and later managing Jimi Hendrix. For obituary, see *The Independent*, 18 July 1996.
40. The most interesting contemporary insight into Skinhead culture remains the 1970 study of a West End gang that was published as a Penguin Special in 1972, but it contains nothing on their musical affiliations. See *The Paint House: Words from an East End Gang* (Harmondsworth, 1972).
41. For details, see M. Brake, 'The Skinheads: An English Working Class Subculture', *Youth and Society*, 6, 2 (1974) 179–200; Hebdige, *Subculture*, pp. 54–9; N. Knight, *Skinhead* (London, 1982); G. Marshall, *Spirit of 69: A Skinhead Bible* (Lockerbie, 1994); P. Fowler, 'Skins Rule', in C. Gillett and S. Frith (eds), *The Beat Goes On: The Rock File Reader* (London, 1996), pp. 153–67; P. N. Stearns, 'Pop Music and Politics: Skinheads and "Nazi Rock" in England and Germany', *Journal of Social History*, 38, 1 (2004), 157–78; G. Watson, *Skins* (London, 2007); G. Bushell, *Hoolies: True Stories of Britain's Biggest Street Battles* (London, 2010), chapter 3.
42. Bushell, *Hoolies*, p. 30. A point also made by Skinhead from the Collinwood gang from East London. See *The Paint House*.
43. *The Paint House*, pp. 35, 127.

44. For a critical analysis of Richard Allen's oeuvre, see B. Osgerby, 'Bovver Books of the 1970s: Subcultures, Crisis and Youth-Sploitation Novels', *Contemporary British History*, 26, 3 (2012), 299–331.
45. P. Black, *Black by Design: A 2-Tone Memoir* (London, 2011), p. 86.
46. A fascinating depiction of Skinheads can also be seen in the BBC's exploration of the subculture in an episode of its *Man Alive* series titled 'What's the truth about Hell's Angels and Skinheads', which was broadcast in 1969.
47. *The Paint House*, p. 16.
48. Ibid., pp. 28, 69–74 and chapters 7 and 8.
49. *Jackie*, No. 447, 29 July 1972.
50. For the 1972 miners' strike in the Lancashire coalfield, see D. Howell, *The Politics of the NUM: A Lancashire View* (Manchester, 1989), chapter 3.
51. *Jackie*, No. 451, 26 August 1972.
52. *Jackie*, No. 513, 3 November 1973.
53. *Jackie*, No. 529, 23 February 1974.
54. *Jackie*, No. 545, 15 June 1974.
55. Holder, *Who's Crazee Now*, pp. 98–9.
56. Cato, *Crash Course for the Ravers*, pp. 18–19.
57. For Slade discography, see D. Thompson, *20th Century Rock and Roll: Glam Rock* (London, 2000), chapter 3.
58. *Record Mirror*, 9 September 1972.
59. *Phonograph Record*, November 1972.
60. *Record Mirror*, 12 February 1972.
61. *New Musical Express*, 19 February 1972.
62. *New Musical Express*, 16 September 1972.
63. *New Musical Express*, 7 July 1973.
64. *Melody Maker*, 16 September 1972.
65. *New Musical Express*, 13 January 1973.
66. Holder, *Who's Crazee Now*, p. 31.
67. *Melody Maker*, 16 September 1972.
68. Such imagery is also evident in the Slade feature film, *Flame* (1974).
69. *Sounds*, 30 December 1972.
70. For narrative of the Fanfare for Europe celebrations, see Sandbrook, *State of Emergency*, pp. 170–72.
71. *Sounds*, 13 January 1973.
72. Thompson, *Children of the Revolution*, p. 106.
73. See *Evening Standard*, 17 April 1973.
74. Another group that successfully attracted rowdy working-class audiences in this period were the Faces, consisting of Rod Stewart, Ronnie Lane, Ronnie Wood, Kenny Jones and Ian McLagan. Their concerts were often shambolic, drunken affairs, mixing rock with rhythm and blues. For an insightful recollection of their appeal, see Jim Melly, *Last Orders, Please: Rod Stewart, the Faces and the Britain We Forgot* (London, 2003).
75. For a fascinating recent exploration of this relationship in the American context, see A. Echols, *Hot Stuff: Disco and the Remaking of American Culture* (New York, 2010).
76. For example, see M. Almond, *Tainted Life: The Autobiography* (London, 1999); H. Johnson, *A Bone in My Flute* (London, 1994) and B. George and S. Bright, *Take It Like A Man: The Autobiography of Boy George* (London, 1994).
77. J. Gill, *Queer Noises: Male and Female Homosexuality in Twentieth Century Music* (London, 1995), p. 112.

78. For early biographical details, see P. Trynka, *Starman: David Bowie the Definitive Biography* (London, 2010).
79. For a comprehensive survey of Bowie scholarship, see the introductory essay in E. Thompson and D. Gutman, *The Bowie Companion* (London, 1993).
80. K. Cann, *Any Day Now: David Bowie. The London Years, 1947–1974* (London, 2010), p. 166. For details of the clothes worn by Bowie and the recollections of an audience member, see T. Viscounti, *Bowie, Bolan and the Brooklyn Boy: The Autobiography* (London, 2007), pp. 146–7.
81. Cann, *Any Day Now,* p. 185.
82. Vermorel, *Starlust,* p. 63.
83. Ibid., p. 99.
84. For the origins and recording of the album, see *Uncut,* April 2012.
85. For the relationship between Warhol and glam rock, see Hoskyns, *Glam,* p. 27
86. Cann, *Any Day Now,* pp. 228–9.
87. J. Weeks, *Coming Out: Homosexual Politics in Britain from the Nineteenth Century to the Present* (London, 1977, 1983), p. 190.
88. A. Beckett, *When the Lights Went Out: Britain in the Seventies* (London, 2009), p. 210.
89. For a detailed analysis, see L. Robinson, *Gay Men and the Left in Post-war Britain: How the Personal Got Political* (Manchester, 2011), chapters 3 and 4.
90. P. Burton, *Parallel Lives* (London, 1985), p. 107.
91. Taylor and Wall, 'Beyond the Skinheads', p. 111.
92. *Melody Maker,* 22 January 1972.
93. Ibid.
94. 'Period Fan Letters and Fan Club Memorabilia', http://5years.com/oypt2.htm
95. *New Musical Express,* 11 August 1973.
96. *Gay News,* No. 6, 1972.
97. *Gay News,* No. 13, 1972.
98. *Daily Mirror,* 4 September 1972.
99. *Daily Mirror,* 24 April 1971.
100. Correspondence between author and Stuart Dalzell, 5 January 2012.
101. Correspondence between author and Victor Wheeler, 5 January 2012.
102. *Jackie,* No. 417, 1 January 1972.
103. Ibid.
104. Ibid.
105. *Jackie,* No. 439, 3 June 1972.
106. *Jackie,* No. 467, 16 January 1972.
107. *Jackie,* No. 469, 30 December 1972.
108. *Jackie,* No. 455, 23 September 1972.
109. *Daily Mirror,* 4 September 1972.
110. M. Bracewell, *England Is Mine: Pop Life in Albion from Wilde to Goldie* (London, 1998), p. 198.
111. S. Turner, 'David Bowie: How to Become a Cult Figure in Only Two Years', unpublished piece for *Nova,* 1974, available at http://www.rocksbackpages.com.
112. The Spiders were Mick Ronson (guitar), Trevor Bolder (bass) and Woody Woodmansey (drums).
113. Vince Taylor (Brian Holden) was a minor figure in English pop in the late 1950s. He suffered a series of breakdowns and during a concert in Paris declared himself a Christ-like figure. Bowie claims to have met him on a London Street, clutching a map purportedly showing alien landing locations on earth.

114. The Legendary Stardust Cowboy (Norman Odam) was a 1960s American rockabilly singer with an interest in space travel.
115. Johnny Angelo is the fictional working-class, androgynous, anti-hero, rock star and cult leader of N. Cohn's novel, *I Am Still the Greatest Says Johnny Angelo* (Harpenden, 1967, 2003). Cohn's work is in need of serious critical appraisal given his contribution to the youth culture and popular music of 1960s/70s England. For a collection of his writings, see *Ball the Wall: Nik Cohn in the Age of Rock* (London, 1989). For the contribution of the Johnny Angelo character to Bowie's Ziggy persona, see Doggett, *The Man Who Sold the World,* pp. 144–5.
116. C. Copetas, 'Beat Godfather Meets Glitter Mainman', *Rolling Stone,* 28 February 1974 reprinted in Thomson and David Gutman, *The Bowie Companion,* pp. 105–17.
117. Hebdige, *Subculture,* p. 61.
118. For a critical reading of popular culture and 'crisis' in the 1970s, see J. Moran, 'Stand Up and Be Counted: Hughie Green, the 1970s and Popular Memory', *History Workshop Journal,* 70 (2010), 173–98.
119. For a critical reading of the album and the themes it addresses, see the song-by-song analysis in Doggett, *The Man Who Sold the World.*
120. Ibid., p. 83.
121. Hammer horror films were regularly broadcast on television and even tried to exploit elements of youth culture by moving away from 'gothic' settings most notably in the much maligned but brilliant *Dracula A.D. 1972* (1972). Amicus also concentrated on contemporary settings for their brand of English horror in films such as *Tales from the Crypt* (1972) and *From Beyond the Grave* (1973). Popular occult novels by Wheatley were *The Devil Rides Out* (1934) and *To The Devil A Daughter* (1953), both filmed by Hammer in 1967 and 1975. For a critical analysis of Hammer, see D. Pirie, *A New Heritage of Horror: The English Gothic Cinema* (London, 2009), chapters 2–4. For Amicus, see P. Hutchings, 'The Amicus House of Horror', in S. Chibnall and J. Petley (eds), *British Horror Cinema* (London, 2002), pp. 131–44. From 1971, the BBC also commissioned a series of *Ghost Stories for Christmas.* For a critical analysis of the supernatural on British television, see H. Wheatley, *Gothic Television* (Manchester, 2006), chapter 2. E. V. Daniken's *Chariots of the Gods* (1968) was hugely successful and was the subject of more discerning pub and workplace conversations. Bruce Lee became an international star and youth culture hero with the release of *Enter The Dragon* (1973).
122. Bevan was a South Wales coal miner, socialist, Labour MP and architect of the National Health Service.
123. For a narrative of events in Northern Ireland and their impact on the British mainland, see Sandbrook, *State of Emergency,* chapters 6 and 12.
124. Turner, *Crisis? What Crisis?* pp. 24–5.
125. Bracewell, *England Is Mine,* p. 193.
126. Buckley, *Strange Fascination,* p. 130.
127. J. Savage, *England's Dreaming: Sex Pistols and Punk Rock* (London, 1991), pp. 76–7.
128. J. Arnott, 'Blown Away', *Observer Music Monthly,* April 2006.
129. Keith Woodhouse correspondence with author, 5 January 2012.
130. The soundtrack of the film would be played as the lights went down, and Bowie entered the stage during the subsequent Ziggy concerts.
131. Cann, *Any Day Now,* p. 239.
132. For details of the case, see *Daily Mirror,* 4 July 1973.

133. For example, see the extensive report on 'The Wild Ones', in the *Daily Mirror*, 25 November 1971.
134. The Ziggy concerts occurred between January 1972 and July 1973 (three stand-alone performances for American television at the Marquee Club, London in October 1973 are also considered part of the Ziggy period) consisting of three tours of the United Kingdom, two of the United States and one of Japan. For full chronology, see M. Rock and D. Bowie, *Moonage Daydream: The Life and Times of Ziggy Stardust* (Bath, 2005), pp. 313–14.
135. Stephen King, 'Ziggy Stardust at the Toby Jug', http://www.5years.com/stephenking.htm.
136. The best visual record of the Ziggy tours 1972–3, which includes an essay by Bowie remains Rock and Bowie, *Moonage Daydream*.
137. *Melody Maker*, 1 July 1972. In point of fact, according to the editor of the online Ziggy Stardust Companion the 'act of fellatio' was first performed on 17 June at Oxford Town Hall. See editor's note http://www.5years.com/wftm.htm.
138. *Melody Maker*, 1 July 1972.
139. D. Jones, *When Ziggy Played Guitar: David and Four Minutes That Shook the World* (London, 2012), p. 2. For critical perspective on the collective memory of Bowie's *Top of the Pops* appearance, see J. Moran, 'David Bowie Misremembered: When Ziggy Played with Our Minds', *The Guardian*, 6 July 2012.
140. Taylor and Wall, 'Beyond the Skinheads', p. 123.
141. D. Thompson, *Blockbuster! The True Story of the Sweet* (London, 2010), p. 90.
142. Ibid., pp. 83–5.
143. Andy Scott of Sweet hailed from the traditional working-class coal mining town of Wrexham, North Wales.
144. 'Period Fan Letters and Fan Club Memorabilia', http://www.5years.com/fanletters.htm.
145. Hebdige, *Subculture*, p. 60.
146. *Gay News*, July 1972.
147. *Daily Mirror*, 18 July 1972.
148. Sandbrook, *State of Emergency*, p. 402.
149. Off Licenses (offys) provided teenagers with an opportunity to purchase beer, wine and spirits through persuading an older youth to buy drinks on their behalf.
150. Correspondence between author and Victor Wheeler, 3 January 2012.
151. *Melody Maker*, 26 August 1972.
152. Letter from Jackie Cecil, *Uncut*, December 2008.
153. Correspondence between author and Stephen Fitzgerald, 6 January 2012.
154. Harvey Molloy, 'Ziggy '72: A Catalogue of Lost Objects', http://www.5years.com/molloy.htm.
155. Cann, *Any Day Now*, p. 283. For a detailed description of the Manchester of Morrissey's youth, see J. Rogan, *Morrissey and Marr: The Severed Alliance* (London, 1992), chapters 1–3.
156. *New Musical Express*, 6 January 1973.
157. For a complete chronology of the Ziggy concerts, see Rock and Bowie, *Moonage Daydream*, pp. 313–14.
158. *Gay News*, No. 22, 1973.
159. Paul, 'My Memories of Ziggy Stardust', http://www.5years.com/paulm.htm.
160. Correspondence between author and Pauline Fitzgerald, 5 January 2012.
161. Cann, *Any Day Now*, p. 298.
162. *New Musical Express*, 26 May 1973.

163. Cato, *Crash Course for the Ravers,* p. 61.
164. Correspondence between author and Jane Roberts, 28 December 2011.
165. Letter from Michael Duke, *Uncut,* December 2008.
166. Stephen Latham, 'Liverpool Empire Theatre 10 June 1973', http://www.5years.com/slatham.htm.
167. Roy White, 'Liverpool Empire 10 June 1973', http://www.5years.com/roywhite.htm.
168. See Almond, *Tainted Life,* p. 29.
169. *Uncut,* 133, June 2008 p. 42.
170. Correspondence between author and Stuart Dalzell, 28 December 2011.
171. Dave Mulley, 'Ziggy Stardust Concert, Salisbury City Hall, 14 June 1973', http://www.5years.com/davemulley.htm.
172. *New Musical Express,* 14 July 1973.
173. Correspondence between author and Keith Woodhouse, 5 January 2012.
174. Paul, 'My Memories of Ziggy Stardust', http://www.5years.com/paulm.htm.
175. Vermorel, *Starlust,* p. 104.
176. *New Musical Express,* 14 July 1973. The Hammersmith concerts were filmed by D. A. Pennebaker and given a cinematic and video release in 1983.
177. *Gay News,* No. 27, 1973.
178. *Daily Mirror,* 22 January 1973.
179. Haslam, *Not Abba,* p. 132.
180. Correspondence between author and Stephen Latham, 5 January 2012.
181. Jones, *When Ziggy Played Guitar,* p. 59.
182. Taylor and Wall, 'Beyond the Skinheads', p. 118.
183. Gill, *Queer Noises,* p. 110.
184. *Gay News,* July 1972.
185. For example, see Weeks, *Coming Out.*
186. M. Houlbrook, *Queer London: Perils and Pleasures in the Sexual Metropolis, 1918–1957* (Chicago, 2005), p. 270.
187. *Jackie,* No. 548, 6 July 1974.
188. Cato, *Crash Course for the Ravers,* p. 43.
189. Ibid., p. 85.
190. *New Society,* 23 April 1981.
191. Bracewell, *England Is Mine,* p. 194.
192. R. Allen, *Glam* (London, 1973), pp. 42–3.
193. *Jackie,* No. 533, 23 March 1974.
194. *Daily Mirror,* 4 September 1972.
195. Arnott, 'Blown Away'.
196. Jones, *When Ziggy Played Guitar,* p. 53.
197. Correspondence between author and Pauline Fitzgerald, 5 January 2012.
198. *Jackie,* No. 478, 3 March 1973.
199. *Jackie,* No. 532, 16 March 1974.
200. Rock and Bowie, *Moonage Daydream,* p. 215.
201. Vermorel, *Starlust,* pp. 182–3.
202. For example, see J. Fabian and J. Byrne, *Groupie* (London, 1969) and Lindsay Shonteff's exploitation film *Permissive* (1970). For the dark side of youth experiences in Soho, see also M. Deakin and J. Willis, *Johnny Go Home* (London, 1976).
203. For the Soho sex industry in the early 1970s, see M. Tomkinson, *The Pornbrokers: The Rise of the Soho Sex Barons* (London, 1982), chapters 3 and 4. For corruption in the Metropolitan Police and its role in Soho's pornography business, see B. Cox, J. Shirley and M. Short, *The Fall of Scotland Yard* (Harmondsworth, 1977), chapter 4.

204. L. A. Hall, *Sex, Gender and Social Change in Britain Since 1880* (London, 2000), p. 184.
205. Taylor and Wall, 'Beyond the Skinheads', p. 119.
206. Leng, *The Twisted Tale of Glam Rock*, p. 4.
207. McRobbie, *Feminism and Youth Culture,* p. 83.
208. *Jackie*, No. 430, 1 April 1972.
209. *Jackie*, No. 457, 7 October 1972.
210. *Jackie*, No. 436, 13 May 1972.
211. *Jackie*, No. 453, 9 September 1972.
212. *Mirabelle*, 21 July 1973. A complete run of the diaries from January 1973–March 1975 has been compiled by Paul Kinder and can be accessed electronically at http://www.bowiewonderworld.com/diaries.diary/diary0773.htm.
213. *Mirabelle*, (diary entry) 3 November 1973.
214. *Mirabelle*, (diary entry) 10 November 1973.
215. *Mirabelle*, (diary entry) 1 December 1973.
216. *Mirabelle*, (diary entry) 23 February 1974.
217. *Mirabelle*, (diary entry) 30 March 1974.
218. *Jackie*, No. 446, 22 July 1972.
219. Sandbrook, *State of Emergency*, p. 363.
220. Mott the Hoople would also provide an elegiac and anthemic reflection on the glam rock phenomenon through their single 'Saturday Gigs', which made the charts in October 1974.
221. D. Robins and P. Cohen, *Knuckle Sandwich: Growing Up in the Working Class City* (Harmondsworth, 1978), p. 81.
222. Bracewell, *England Is Mine,* p. 192.
223. For the best narrative/analysis of this period, see Beckett, *When the Lights Went Out*, chapters 4–7.
224. For a critical reading of *Diamond Dogs,* see Doggett, *The Man Who Sold the World,* pp. 195–212. For similarly apocalyptic literary companion piece to *Diamond Dogs,* see James Herbert's phenomenally successful novel *The Rats* (London, 1974).
225. *New Musical Express*, 10 February 1973.
226. *New Musical Express*, 9 June 1973.
227. Reynolds, 'The Rift of Retro', p. 66.
228. For the career trajectory and visual image of Adrian Street, see relevant sections of S. Garfield, *The Wrestling* (London, 1996).
229. *Flame* (1975) directed by Richard Loncraine.
230. Interview with David Bowie, *Playboy*, September 1976, reprinted in D. Brackett (ed.), *The Pop, Rock and Soul Reader* (Oxford, 2005), p. 281.

8 Darkness over England: Punk Rock and the Sex Pistols Anarchy Tour 1976

1. In 1976 the group consisted of John Lydon (Rotten), Steve Jones, Paul Cook and Glen Matlock. Their manager, Malcolm McLaren, was also crucial in the development of their presentation and rhetoric. There are various autobiographies and biographies of the band as well as numerous articles and edited collections of essays on punk rock.
2. For example, see J. Savage, *England's Dreaming Sex Pistols and Punk Rock* (London, 1981) and J. Moran, 'Stand Up and Be Counted: Hughie Green, the 1970s and Popular Memory', *History Workshop Journal* 70, (2010), 173–198.

3. In many ways the response to the Sex Pistols was a classic case of 'moral panic'. The seminal work on moral panic remains S. Cohen, *Folk Devils and Moral Panics* (London, 2002). For the development of the term and its use by the media, see A. Hunt, 'Moral Panic and Moral Language in the Media', *British Journal of Sociology*, 28, 4 (1997), 629–48. For a recent use of the concept in social history, see A. Bartie, 'Moral Panics and Glasgow Gangs: Exploring "the New Wave of Glasgow Hooliganism", 1965–1970', *Contemporary British History*, 24, 3 (2010), 385–408.
4. For a critical survey of the 'meaning' of punk, see D. Simonelli, 'Anarchy, Pop and Violence: Punk Rock Subculture and the Rhetoric of Class, 1976–8', *Contemporary British History*, 16, 2 (2002), 121–44. The following texts also have useful accounts of punk: D. Laing, *One Chord Wonders: Power and Meaning in Punk Rock* (London, 1985); D. Hebdige, *Subculture: The Meaning of Style* (London, 1979); B. Osgerby, *Youth in Britain since 1945* (London, 1988); S. Home, *Cranked Up Really High: Genre Theory and Punk Rock* (Hove, 1995); R. Sabin (ed.), *Punk Rock: So What?: The Cultural Legacy of Punk* (London, 1999). For a recent exploration of the political responses to punk rock, see M. Worley, 'Shot By Both Sides: Punk, Politics and the End of 'Consensus', *Contemporary British History*, 26, 3 (September 2012), 333–54.
5. The 'foundation myth' of punk is based on a clear connection between economic decline, radical politics and a challenge to the perceived inertia of the music industry. The attempt to pitch the Sex Pistols as a manifestation of Situationist politics has also been surprisingly influential. For example, see G. Marcus, *Lipstick Traces. A Secret History of the Twentieth Century* (London, 1997).
6. *London's Outrage!* (1976) England's Dreaming Archive, Liverpool John Moores University (LJMU), ED/3/28/2 (1).
7. For the history of 'moral panics' in English society, see J. Springhall, *Youth, Popular Culture and Moral Panics: Penny Gaffs to Gangsta-Rap, 1830–1996* (London, 1998) and G. Pearson, *Hooligan: A History of Respectable Fears* (London, 1983).
8. Cohen, *Folk Devils,* pp. xi, xxiii-xxiv.
9. See A. McRobbie and S. L. Thornton, 'Rethinking 'Moral Panic' for Multi-Mediated Social Worlds', *British Journal of Sociology*, 46, 4 (1995), 559–74.
10. See S. Thornton, 'Moral Panic, The Media and British Rave Culture', in A. Ross and T. Rose' (eds), *Microphone Fiends: Youth Music and Youth Culture* (London, 1994), pp. 176–92.
11. J. Moran, 'Stand Up', p. 190.
12. *Birmingham Evening Mail*, 4 December 1976. For a sense of Lydon's view on England in the 1970s, see the early chapters of his autobiography. J. Lydon, *Rotten: No, Irish, No Blacks, No Dogs* (New York, 1994).
13. *The Guardian*, 2 December 1976.
14. *Evening Standard (London)*, 2 December 1976.
15. A point also made by Moran to show that in his view the impact of the Sex Pistols was minimal. Moran, 'Stand Up', p. 189.
16. For narratives of these events, see D. Sandbrook, *Seasons in the Sun: The Battle for Britain, 1974–1979* (London, 2012).
17. Moran, 'Stand Up', pp. 189–90.
18. *Manchester Evening News*, 4 December 1976. The Teddy Boy revival of the early 1970s brought the drape-suit and Elvis back on to the English high street. The London Rock 'n' Roll show held at Wembley Stadium on 5 August 1972 including performances by Chuck Berry and Jerry Lee Lewis was symbolic of the continued association between English working-class youth and 1950s Americana.
19. G. Orwell, *The Lion and the Unicorn. Socialism and the English Genius* (Harmondsworth, 1982), p. 52.

20. *Daily Mirror*, 2 December 1976.
21. Ibid.
22. For Grundy's account, see C. Bromberg, *The Wicked Ways of Malcolm McLaren* (New York, 1989), pp. 114–116.
23. For copies of documents from Thames Television relating to the 'Grundy incident', see *Classic Rock*, November 2010.
24. *Daily Express*, 2 December 1976.
25. *Crossroads* was a popular soap opera based on the fortunes of a motel in the English Midlands that was broadcast between 1964 and 1988.
26. *Daily Telegraph*, 2 December 1976.
27. *Daily Mirror*, 3 December 1976.
28. *Bondage*, No. 1 (1976), England's Dreaming Archive, LJMU, ED6/5/10/3.
29. Cohen, *Folk Devils*, p. xxxi.
30. *Daily Mail*, 3 December 1976.
31. *The Times*, 9 December 1976.
32. M. Glucksmann, *Women Assemble: Women Workers and the New Industries in Inter-War Britain* (London, 1990), p. 117.
33. *London Evening Standard*, 3 December 1976.
34. EMI was also concerned about the negative publicity that the episode was attracting. The company expressed its concerns about the Sex Pistols and punk rock at its Annual General Meeting in the same month: 'whether EMI does in fact release any more of their records will have to be very carefully considered…we shall do everything we can to restrain their public behaviour, although this is a matter over which we have no real control'. News from EMI Annual General Meeting, 7 December 1976, comment on content of records by Sir John Reed, England's Dreaming Archive, LJMU ED2/22/15.
35. *Hayes and Harlington Gazette*, 9 December 1976.
36. For women and the trade union movement in this period, see C. Wrigley, 'Women in the Labour Market and Unions', in J. McIlroy, N. Fishman and A. Campbell (eds), *The High Tide of British Trade Unionism. Trade Unions and Industrial Politics, 1964–79* (Monmouth, 2007), pp. 43–69.
37. *Eastern Evening News* (Norwich), 2 December 1976.
38. For Bowie's flirtation with Fascist imagery and discourse, see P. Doggett, *The Man Who Sold the World: David Bowie and the 1970s* (London, 2011), pp. 254–6.
39. *Eastern Evening News* (Norwich), 3 December 1976.
40. *Eastern Evening News* (Norwich), 4 December 1976.
41. *Lancaster Guardian*, 3 December 1976.
42. *Daily Mirror*, 3 December 1976.
43. *Lancaster Guardian*, 10 December 1976.
44. *Derby Evening Telegraph*, 3 December 1976.
45. For Whitehouse and the milieu in which she operated, see B. Thompson, *Ban This Filth!: Letters From the Mary Whitehouse Archive* (London, 2012); M. Whitehouse, *Quite Contrary: An Autobiography* (London, 1984) and L. Black, 'There Was Something About Mary: Social Movement Theory and the National and Viewers' and Listeners' Association in Sixties Britain', in N. Crowson, M. Hilton and J. McKay (eds), *NGOs in Contemporary Britain: Non-State Actors in Society and Politics Since 1945* (Basingstoke, 2009), pp. 182–200.
46. *Derby Evening Telegraph*, 3 December 1976.
47. For cinema in this period, see A. Walker, *National Heroes: British Cinema in the Seventies and Eighties* (London, 1985) and L. Hunt, *British Low Culture: From Safari Suits to Sexploitation* (London, 1998), chapters 7–10.

48. *Derby Evening Telegraphy*, 4 December 1976.
49. Ibid.
50. Mrs Lydon quoted in F. and J. Vermorel, *Sex Pistols: The Inside Story* (London, 1978), p. 41.
51. *Sounds*, 11 December 1976.
52. *Derby Evening Telegraph*, 6 December 1976.
53. G. Matlock, *I Was A Teenage Sex Pistol* (London, 1990) p. 158.
54. *Newcastle Evening Chronicle*, 3 December 1976.
55. For a detailed analysis of corruption in labour politics in Newcastle, see R. Fitzwalter and D. Taylor, *Web of Corruption: The Story of John Poulson and T. Dan Smith* (London, 1981), The politics of local government in the north had also been brilliantly satirised in Lindsay Anderson's film *O'Lucky Man* (1973).
56. *Leeds Evening Post*, 6 December 1976.
57. *Daily Mirror*, 6 December 1976.
58. *Leeds Evening Post*, 7 December 1976.
59. *Daily Mirror*, 6 December 1976.
60. *Bournemouth Evening Echo*, 2 and 3 December 1976.
61. *The Times*, 8 December 1976.
62. For the impact of the Sex Pistols performances in Manchester and how they led to the creation of a number of successful groups in the late 1970s and early 1980s, see D. Nolan, *I Swear I Was There: The Gig That Changed the World* (Church Stretton, 2006) and D. Haslam, *Manchester England: The Story of the Pop Cult City* (London, 1999), chapter 5.
63. *Manchester Evening News*, 3 December 1976.
64. *Daily Mirror*, 9 December 1976.
65. *Daily Mirror*, 11 December 1976.
66. *Manchester Evening News*, 9 and 10 December 1976.
67. In interviews the Sex Pistols were consistently scathing about the inadequacies of the English education system. In an interview conducted during the Anarchy Tour for the American magazine *Punk*, Johnny Rotten was particularly acerbic: 'I refused to let them educate me'. *Punk*, No. 8, March 1977.
68. *Manchester Evening News*, 8 December 1976.
69. *Manchester Evening News*, 10 December 1976.
70. *Daily Telegraph*, 3 December 1976.
71. *Liverpool Daily Post*, 3 December 1976.
72. *Liverpool Daily Post*, 4 December 1976.
73. *Liverpool Echo*, 7 December 1976.
74. *Liverpool Daily Post*, 7 December 1976.
75. *Western Mail*, 8 December 1976.
76. *Western Mail*, 11 December 1976.
77. Davies was interviewed for the Ken Loach documentary series *A Question of Leadership* (1981) which was made for Channel 4 but never broadcast. For a critical analysis of this series, see J. Hill, *Ken Loach: The Politics of Film and Television* (London, 2011), pp. 161–3. More recently, Davies expressed regret about his role in preventing the Sex Pistols from performing in Caerphilly. See letter from Ray Davies at www.sex-pistols.net.
78. For industrial disputes and class conflict in the South Wales coalfields, see R. P. Arnot, *South Wales Miners: A History of the South Wales Miners' Federation, 1898–1914* (London, 1967) and H. Francis and D. Smith, *The Fed: A History of the South Wales Miners in the Twentieth Century* (London, 1980).
79. *Rhymney Valley Express*, 16 December 1976.

80. *Buzz* (Issue 2), February 1977.
81. *Western Mail*, 14 December 1976.
82. *Western Mail*, 15 December 1976.
83. Kevin Dicks contribution to BBC News at http://news.bbc.co.uk/1/hi/wales/6180555.stm.
84. Copy of the leaflet can be found at www.sex-pistols.net.
85. John Birkin contribution to BBC News at http://news.bbc.co.uk/1/hi/wales/6180555.stm.
86. *Buzz* (Issue 2) February 1977.
87. *Western Mail*, 15 December 1976.
88. *Rhymney Valley Express*, 16 December 1976.
89. *Rhymney Valley Express*, 23 December 1976.
90. *Western Mail*, 15 December 1976.
91. *Rhymney Valley Express*, 22 December 1976.
92. Ray Davies interview with BBC Wales in 2006 at www.bbc.co.uk/wales/music/sites/history/pages/sex-pistols-caerphilly.shtml.
93. *Daily Record*, 8 December 1976.
94. *Daily Record*, 7 December 1976.
95. *Dundee Evening Telegraph and Post*, 3 December 1976.
96. *Dundee Evening Telegraph and Post*, 7 December 1976.
97. *Dundee Evening Telegraph and Post*, 8 December 1976.
98. The best critical narrative of class, politics and social change in this period is A. Beckett, *When the Lights Went Out: Britain in the Seventies* (London, 2009).
99. *Bristol Evening Post*, 6 December 1976.
100. *The Star* (Sheffield), 3 December 1976.
101. *Birmingham Evening Mail*, 4 December 1976.
102. *Birmingham Evening Mail*, 3 December 1976.
103. *Torbay Herald Express*, 2 December 1976.
104. *Torbay Herald Express*, 8 December 1976.
105. *Torbay Herald Express*, 11 December 1976.
106. *Torbay Herald Express*, 13 December 1976.
107. *Grimsby Evening Telegraph*, 16, and 21 December 1976.
108. *Sniffin' Glue, Xmas Special* (1976), England's Dreaming Archive, LJMU, ED3/44/13.
109. *Parliamentary Debates*, 14 June 1977, cols. 337–8.
110. Ibid., col. 345.
111. For the Sex Pistols in America and a reconstruction of the Winterland concert see Marcus, *Lipstick Traces*, pp. 27–152. The American media also constructed English punk and the Sex Pistols in class terms. For example, *Time* magazine noted that 'in Britain, punk is the voice (some would say) of working-class kids who cannot find jobs and care not a bit for the traditions of their homeland'. *Time*, 16 January 1978.
112. Moran, 'Stand Up', p. 194.
113. For film footage of the response of Brook-Partridge and other politicians to the Sex Pistols Anarchy Tour and punk rock more generally, see Julien Temple, *The Filth and the Fury* (2000).
114. For an excellent collection of interviews with punk musicians from across England, see J. Robb, *Punk Rock: An Oral History* (London, 2006).

Encore: On the Road to Wigan Pier to see Georgie Fame and Billy Boston, Sunday 2 March 2003

1. The author attended this concert and spoke to a number of audience members about their backgrounds, memories and musical tastes.
2. The site is now home to an apartment block built in response to the rising investment opportunities in what now is one of Manchester's most desirable suburbs.
3. For a musical history of the city and its prominent venues, see D. Haslam, *Manchester England: The Story of a Pop Cult City* (1999).
4. For the Dylan concert, see C. P. Lee, *Like the Night (Revisited): Bob Dylan and the Road to the Manchester Free Trade Hall* (2004). For the Sex Pistols concert, see D. Nolan, *I Swear I Was There: The Gig That Changed the World* (2006).
5. *The Road to Wigan Pier* is the title of George Orwell's account of working-class life in the town that was first published in 1937. For a feminist exploration of Wigan's and England's working-class in the 1980s, see B. Campbell, *Wigan Pier Revisited: Poverty and Politics in the 80s* (1984).
6. For a detailed examination of the miner's strike in Leigh's pits, see D. Howell, *The Politics of the NUM: A Lancashire View* (1989), chapters 6–8.
7. The fields close to Bickershaw Colliery attracted thousands of music fans in the summer of 1972. The Bickershaw Festival included performances by the Kinks, the Grateful Dead and Captain Beefheart.
8. Wigan's pier was merely a small wooden jetty on the side of the Leeds-Liverpool Canal that was used to load locally produced coal into boats that then would transport it for use in industry. The mechanism was dismantled in 1929. The notion of a Wigan Pier was popularised in the songs and shtick of George Formby one of the town's most famous celebrities.
9. The population of Leigh and Wigan have a particular attachment to pies and they remain a feature of the working-class diet in both towns. According to popular legend, Wiganers became known as 'pie-eaters' after returning to work before other Lancashire miners in the 1926 lockout and thus forced to 'eat humble pie'.
10. For a history of the Wigan Casino, see D. Shaw, *Casino* (2000) and R. Winstanley and D. Nowell, *Soul Survivors: The Wigan Casino Story* (2003).
11. The Northern Soul Scene is still in need of serious historical analysis. However, there have been some good sociological accounts, journalistic examinations and memoirs from those who played a key role in this particularly esoteric youth subculture. For examples, see A. Wilson, *Northern Soul: Music, Drugs and Subcultural Identity* (2007) and D. Nowell, *Too Darn Soulful: The Story of Northern Soul* (1999).
12. For an insightful and critical analysis of the Wigan Pier Experience, see S. Catterall, 'Otherness Plus the Three Cs Minus Orwell: 'The Wigan Pier Experience', *Labour History Review*, 70, 1 (2005), 103–12.
13. See R. Gale, *Billy Boston: Rugby League Footballer* (London, 2009).
14. 'S.O.S–Stop her on Sight' had been a Top-20 hit in England in 1966. Fame recalled that he had hired Starr to play at a party he organised in the 1960s in which John Lennon, in the wake of the 'Beatles being more popular than Jesus' furore, turned-up dressed as a Vicar.

Bibliography

1. Archive sources

Churchill College, Cambridge University

Mark Abrams Papers

Leigh Library

Ronnie Carr Papers
Georgie Fame Material

Liverpool John Moores University

England's Dreaming: The Jon Savage Archive

Liverpool Record Office, Central Library, Liverpool

Lord Mayor's correspondence, 352/BEA.
Letter from A. R. McFall to the Lord Mayor, 13 November 1963, 352 BEA/2/3 iii.
Letter from the Lord Mayor of Liverpool to Burgermeister of Hamburg, 15 November 1963, 352 BEA2/3/vi.
Letter from Eric Heffer to Lord Mayor, 2 February 1964, 352 BEA/1/2 (ii).
Letter from Ernest Hayes to the Lord Mayor, 14 February 1964, 352 BEA/1/2.
Letter from Elaine Waring and the Gang, Queen's Park, Wrexham to the Lord Mayor, 13 February 1964, Liverpool Record Office 352BEA/1/4/iii.
Letter from the Lord Mayor to C. J. Epstein, 23 March 1964, 352BEA/3/1.

Manchester Metropolitan University

North West Film Archive

Greater Manchester Police Museum

Manchester City Police, Box File on Manchester Clubs.
City of Manchester Chief Constable's Report 1965, Box File on Manchester Clubs, Police Museum, Manchester.
Manchester City Police File on Twisted Wheel: Incidents Concerning Drugs 1964.
Manchester City Police Report of Occurrence, 10 May 1964.
Manchester City Police Report, 23 June 1964.

Modern Records Centre, University of Warwick

Motorcycle Association Papers

People's History Museum, Manchester

Young Communist League District Congress, December 1967, CP/YCL/09/04.

The National Archives, London

Working Party on Juvenile Jazz and Dance Clubs in the West End of London, HO 300/8.

Memorandum from Chief Superintendent of Essex County Constabulary on Clacton Disturbances, 1 April 1964, BN 29/1765.
Metropolitan Police Report 15 June 1964. Young Persons in the Soho Area, HO 300/8.
Metropolitan Police, West End Central, 15 June 1964, HO 300/8.
London County Council notes by Children's Department on Jazz and Dance Clubs in the West End, 5 August 1964, HO 300/8.
London County Council meeting with Home Secretary and Minister of Health on Jazz and Dance Clubs in the West End, 15 September 1964, HO 300/8.
National Association of Youth Clubs, "Weekenders", MEPO 2/100477.
Portobello Project, 1964, MEPO 2/100477.
Metropolitan Police Memorandum, Notting Hill Social Council Project, 4 March 1965, MEPO 2/100477.

University of Sussex

Mass Observation Project
Johnny Black Diaries

2. Interviews and correspondence

Ronnie Carr (the Lemon Drop Kid), 4 September 2006.
Mike O'Neil, 14 September 2006.
Jack McMichael, 10 February 2007.
Ed Floyd, 8 February 2007.
Eddie Amoo, 2008.
Jimmy James, 3 April 2008.
Count Prince Miller, 3 April 2008.
Phil Kroper, 13 September 2009.
Jeanette Land, 14 September 2009.
Bill Harry, 26 July 2010.
Terri Quaye, 12 April 2011.
Lloyd Johnson, 12 April 2011.
Linden Kirby, 12 April 2011.
Stuart Dalzell, 28 December 2011, and 5 January 2012.
Victor Wheeler, 5 January 2012.
Stephen Latham, 5 January 2012.
Pauline Fitzgerald, 5 January 2012.
Stephen Fitzgerald, 6 January 2012.

3. Newspapers, periodicals and fanzines

Birmingham Evening Mail
Bondage
Bournemouth Evening Echo
Bradford Telegraph and Argus
Bristol Evening Post
British Medical Journal
Buzz
Circus Magazine
Classic Rock
Daily Express

Daily Mail
Daily Mirror
Daily Record
Daily Telegraph
Derby Evening Telegraph
Disc and Music Echo
Disc Weekly
Dundee Evening Telegraph and Post
Eastern Evening News (Norwich)
Encounter
Fabulous
Gay News
Grimsby Evening Telegraph
Hayes and Harlington Gazette
International Musician
Jackie
Jazz News and Review
Lancaster Guardian
Leeds Evening Post
Leigh Chronicle
Leigh Journal
Leigh Reporter
Liverpool Daily Post
London Evening Standard
London's Outrage!
Manchester Evening News
Melody Maker
Mersey Beat
Mirabelle
Mojo
New Community
New Musical Express
New Musical Express Originals
New Society
Newcastle Evening Chronicle
Nova
Observer Music Monthly
Oxford Dictionary of National Biography
Parliamentary Debates
Phonograph Record
Pipeline Instrumental Review
Popular Music
Popular Music and Society
Punch
Punk
Radio Luxembourg Annual
Rave
Record Mirror
Rhymney Valley Express
Ripped and Torn
Rock Bill

Rolling Stone
Saturday Evening Post
Scootering
Show Guide Magazine
Sight and Sound
Sniffin' Glue
Socialist Commentary
Sounds
Sunday Times
The Guardian
The Independent
The Listener
The Mod's Monthly
The Observer
The Star (Sheffield)
The Times
Time
Torbay Herald Express
Town
Uncut
Universities and Left Review
Western Mail
Wigan Examiner
Wigan Observer and District Advertiser

4. Articles

Abrams, M., 'The Younger Generation', *Encounter* (May 1956), p. 40.

———, 'Why Labour Has Lost Elections Part 4. Young Voter', *Socialist Commentary* (July 1960), pp. 5–12.

August, A., 'Gender and 1960s Youth Culture: The Rolling Stones and the New Woman', *Contemporary British History*, 23, 1 (2009), pp. 79–100.

Bartie, A., 'Moral Panics and Glasgow Gangs: Exploring "the New Wave of Glasgow 'Hooliganism"', 1965–1970', *Contemporary British History*, 24, 3 (2010), pp. 385–408.

Baxter-Moore, N., 'This Is Where I Belong: Identity, Social Class, and the Nostalgic Englishness of Ray Davies and the Kinks', *Popular Music and Society*, 29, 2 (2006), pp. 145–65.

Brake, M., 'The Skinheads: An English Working Class Subculture', *Youth and Society*, 6, 2 (1974), pp. 179–200.

Bright, S. 'In with the In Crowd', *Majo,* 33 (1996).

Brocken, M., 'Some Other Guys! Some Theories about Signification: Beatles Cover Versions', *Popular Music and Society*, 20, 4 (1996), pp. 5–40.

Catterall, S., 'Otherness Plus the Three Cs Minus Orwell: 'The Wigan Pier Experience', *Labour History Review*, 70, 1 (2005), pp. 103–12.

Chibnall, S., 'Whistle and Zoot: The Changing Meaning of a Suit of Clothes', *History Workshop Journal*, 20 (1985), pp. 56–81.

Cloonan, M., 'State of the Nation: Englishness, Pop and Politics in the Mid-1990s', *Popular Music and Society*, 21, 2 (1997), pp. 47–70.

Collins, M., 'The Beatles Politics', *The British Journal of Politics and International Relations* (2012), pp. 1–19.

Davis, J., 'Rents and Race in 1960s London: New Light on Rachmanism', *Twentieth Century British History*, 12, 1 (2001), pp. 69–92.

———, 'The London Drug Scene and the Making of Drug Policy 1965–73', *Twentieth Century British History*, 17, 1 (2006), pp. 26–49.

Filmer, P., 'Structures of Feeling and Socio-cultural Formations: The Significance of Literature and Experience to Raymond William's Sociology of Culture', *British Journal of Sociology*, 54, 2 (2003), pp. 199–219.

Fraser, D., 'The Postwar Consensus: A Debate Not Long Enough', *History*, 84, 274 (1999), pp. 301–24.

Gourvish, T., 'The British Popular Music Industry, 1950–75: Archival Challenges and Solutions', *Business Archives*, 99 (2009), pp. 25–39.

Grayson, R. S., 'Mods, Rockers and Juvenile Delinquency in 1964: The Government Response', *Contemporary British History*, 12, 1 (1998), pp. 19–47.

Grossberg, L., 'Another Boring Day in Paradise: Rock and Roll and the Empowerment of Everyday Life', *Popular Music*, 4 (1984), pp. 225–58.

Hewitt, P. 'The Birth of Modernism', in *New Musical Express Originals*, 2, 2 (no date).

Hinton, J., 'Militant Housewives: The British Housewives' League and the Attlee Government', *History Workshop Journal*, 38, 1 (1994), pp. 129–156.

Hunt, A., 'Moral Panic and Moral Language in the Media', *British Journal of Sociology*, 28, 4 (1997), pp. 629–48.

Jackson, L. A., 'The Coffee Club Menace: Policing Youth, Leisure and Sexuality in Post-war Manchester', *Cultural and Social History*, 5, 3 (2008), pp. 289–308.

Kirk, J., 'Class Community and 'Structure of Feeling', in Working Class Writing from the 1980'; *Literature and History*, 3, 8, 2(1999) pp.44–63.

Kraus, M. J., 'The Greatest Rock Star of the 19th Century: Ray Davies, Romanticism, and the Art of Being English', *Popular Music and Society*, 29, 1 (2006), pp. 201–12.

Kruse II, R. J., 'The Beatles as Place Makers: Narrated Landscapes in Liverpool, England', *Journal of Cultural Geography*, 22, 2 (Spring/Summer, 2005), pp. 87–114.

Lupro, M. M., 'Preserving the Old Ways, Protecting the New: Post-War British Urban Planning in the *Kinks Are the Village Green Preservation Society*', *Popular Music and Society*, 29, 2 (2006), pp. 189–200.

McLean, I., 'On Moles and the Habits of Birds: The Unpolitics of Aberfan', *Twentieth Century British History*, 8, 3 (1997), pp. 285–309.

McRobbie, A. and Thornton, S. L., 'Rethinking 'Moral Panic' for Multi-Mediated Social Worlds', *British Journal of Sociology*, 46, 4 (1995), pp. 559–74.

Mitchell, G. A. M., 'A Very British Introduction to Rock 'n' Roll: Tommy Steele and the Advent of Rock 'n' Roll Music in Britain, 1956–60', *Contemporary British History*, 25, 2 (2011), pp. 205–25.

Moran, J., 'Milk Bars, Starbucks and the Uses of Literacy', *Cultural Studies*, 20, 6 (2006), pp. 552–73.

———, 'Stand Up and Be Counted: Hughie Green, the 1970s and Popular Memory', *History Workshop Journal*, 70 (2010), pp. 173–98.

———, 'Imagining the Street in post-war Britain', *Urban History*, 39, 1 (2012), pp. 166–86.

Mort, F., 'Striptease: The Erotic Female Body and Live Sexual Entertainment in Mid-Twentieth-Century London', *Social History*, 23, 1 (2007), pp. 27–53.

Osgerby, B., 'Well, It's Saturday Night and I Just Got Paid': Youth, Consumerism and Hegemony in Post-War-Britain', *Contemporary Record*, 6, 2 (1992), pp. 287–303.

———, 'Bovver Books of the 1970s: Subcultures, Crisis and Youth-Sploitation Novels', *Contemporary British History*, 26, 3 (2012), pp. 299–331.

Riley, T., 'For the Beatles: Notes on Their Achievement', *Popular Music*, 6, 3 (1987), pp. 257–72.
Sargeant, M., 'Looking Back with Irish Jack', *Scootering*, 163 (September 1999).
Simonelli, D., 'Anarchy, Pop and Violence: Punk Rock Subculture and the Rhetoric of class, 1976–8', *Contemporary British History*, 16, 2 (2002), pp. 121–44.
Small, S., 'Racialised Relations in Liverpool: A Contemporary Anomaly', *New Community*, 17, 4 (July 1991), pp. 511–37.
Stearns, P. N., 'Pop Music and Politics: Skinheads and "Nazi Rock" in England and Germany', *Journal of Social* History, 38, 1 (2004), pp. 157–78.
Thornton, S., 'Strategies for Reconstructing the Popular Past', *Popular Music*, 9, 1 (1990), pp. 87–95.
Todd, S. and Young, H., 'Babyboomers to Beanstalkers: Making the Modern Teenager in Post-War Britain', *Cultural and Social History*, 9, 3 (2012), pp. 451–67.
Tyler, R., 'Victims of Our History? Barbara Castle and *In Place of Strife*', *Contemporary British History*, 20, 3 (2006), pp. 461–76.
Wilde, J., 'Tomorrow Never Knows; *Uncut*, 86 (2004)'.
Worley, M., 'Shot by Both Sides: Punk, Politics and the End of 'Consensus', *Contemporary British History*, 26, 3 (September 2012), pp. 333–54.
Young, B. A., 'Coffee-Bar Theory and Practice', *Punch*, Vol. CCXXXI No. 6067, 5 (December 1956), pp. 670–2.

5. Chapters in books

Adorno, T. W., 'On Popular Music', in S. Frith and A. Goodwin (eds), *On Record: Rock, Pop and the Written Word* (London, 1990), pp. 301–14.
Barker, P., 'The Margate Offenders: A Survey', in T. Raison (ed.), *Youth in New Society* (London, 1966), pp. 115–27.
———, 'Young Marriage', in T. Raison (ed.), *Youth in New Society* (London, 1966), pp. 178–84.
Black, L., 'There Was Something About Mary: Social Movement Theory and the National and Viewers' and Listeners' Association in Sixties Britain', in N. Crowson, M. Hilton and J. McKay (eds), *NGOs in Contemporary Britain: Non-State Actors in Society and Politics Since 1945* (Basingstoke, 2009), pp. 182–200.
Brocken, M., 'Coming Out of the Rhetoric of Merseybeat: Conversations with Joe Flannery', in I. Inglis (ed.), *The Beatles, Popular Music and Society* (Basingstoke, 2000), pp. 23–34.
Bugge, C., 'Selling Youth in the Age of Affluence: Marketing to Youth in Britain Since 1959', in L. Black and H. Pemberton (eds), *An Affluent Society? Britain's Post-War Golden-Age Revisited* (Aldershot, 2004), pp. 185–202.
Catterall, S., 'Edwin Hall (1895–1961)', in K. Gildart and D. Howell (eds), *Dictionary of Labour Biography Vol. XIII* (Basingstoke, 2010), pp. 146–52.
Catterall, S., and Gildart, K., 'Outsiders: The Experience of Polish and Italian Coal Miners in Britain', in S. Berger, A. Croll and N. LaPorte, (eds), *Towards a Comparative History of Coalfield Societies* (Aldershot, 2005), pp. 164–76.
Connell, P. H., 'What To Do About Pep Pills', in T. Raison, (ed.), *Youth in New Society* (London, 1966), pp. 74–80.
Cooper, L. G., and Cooper, B. L., 'The Pendulum of Cultural Imperialism: Popular Music Interchanges between the United States and Britain, 1943–1967', in S. P. Ramet and G. P. Crnkovic (eds), *Kazaam! Splat! Ploof! The American Impact on European Popular Culture Since 1945* (London, 2003), pp. 69–82.

Fletcher, C., 'Beat Gangs on Merseyside', in T. Raison (ed.), *Youth in New Society* (London, 1966), pp. 148–59.

Fowler, D. 'Teenage Consumers? Young Wage-earners and Leisure in Manchester, 1919–1939', in A. Davies and S. Fielding (eds), *Workers' Worlds: Cultures and Communities in Manchester and Salford, 1880–1939* (Manchester, 1992), pp. 133–55.

Fowler, P., 'Skins Rule', in C. Gillett and S. Frith (eds), *The Beat Goes On: The Rock File Reader* (London, 1996), pp. 153–67.

Frith, S., 'Writing the History of Popular Music', in H. Dauncy and P. Le Guern (eds), *Stereo: Comparative Perspectives on the Sociological Study of Popular Music in France and Britain* (Aldershot, 2011), pp. 11–21.

Frost, D., 'Ambiguous Identities; Constructing and De-constructing Black and White 'Scouse' Identities in Twentieth Century Liverpool', in N. Kirk (ed.), *Northern Identities: Historical Interpretations of 'The North' and 'Northerness'* (Aldershot, 2000).

Geraghty, C., 'Women and Sixties British Cinema: The Development of the "Darling" Girl', in R. Murphy (ed.), *The British Cinema Book* (London, 1997), pp. 154–63.

Gildart, K., 'Samuel Frederick Perry (1877–1954)', in K. Gildart and D. Howell (eds), *Dictionary of Labour Biography Vol. XII* (Basingstoke, 2005), pp. 226–33.

Guthrie, R., 'The Biggest Years in a Boy's Life', in T. Raison (ed.), *Youth in New Society* (London, 1966), pp. 101–8.

Hall, S., 'Notes on Deconstructing "the popular"', in R. Samuel (ed.), *People's History and Socialist Theory* (London, 1981), pp. 227–41.

Harker, D., 'Still Crazy After All These Years: What Was Popular Music in the 1960s?', in B. M. Gilbert and J. Seed (eds), *Cultural Revolution? The Challenge of the Arts in the 1960s* (Oxford, 1992).

Haynes, T., 'Foreword', in B. Hoskyns, *Glam! Bowie, Bolan and the Glitter Rock Revolution* (London, 1998), p. xi.

Hebdige, D., 'The Meaning of Mod', in S. Hall and T. Jefferson (eds), *Resistance Through Rituals: Youth Subcultures in Post-War Britain* (London, 1975), pp. 97–98.

Hodkinson, P., 'Youth Cultures: A Critical Outline of Key Debates', in P. Hodkinson and W. Deicke (eds), *Youth Cultures: Scenes, Subcultures and Tribes* (London, 2009), pp. 1–21.

Hughes, D., 'The Spivs', in M. Sissons and P. French (eds), *Age of Austerity 1945–51* (Harmondsworth, 1963), pp. 85–105.

Hutchings, P., 'The Amicus House of Horror', in S. Chibnall and J. Petley (eds), *British Horror Cinema* (London, 2002), pp. 131–44.

Jefferson, T., 'Cultural Responses of the Teds', in S. Hall and T. Jefferson (eds), *Resistance Through Rituals: Youth Subcultures in Post-War Britain* (London, 1975, 2004), pp. 81–6.

Keightley, K., 'Reconsidering Rock', in S. Frith, W. Straw and J. Street (eds), *The Cambridge Companion to Pop and Rock* (Cambridge, 2001), pp. 109–42.

Macguire, A., 'Emancipated and Reactionaries', in T. Raison (ed.), *Youth in New Society* (London, 1966), pp. 109–14.

Marks, A., 'Young Gifted and Black: Afro-American and Afro-Caribbean Music in Britain 1963–88', in P. Oliver (ed.), *Black Music in Britain: Essays on the Afro-Asian Contribution to Popular Music* (Milton Keynes, 1990), pp. 102–17.

Melly, G., 'Preface' in D. Farson (ed.), *Soho in the Fifties* (London, 1987).

Middleton, R., 'Pop, Rock and Interpretation', in S. Frith, W. Straw and J. Street, (eds), *The Cambridge Companion to Pop and Rock* (Cambridge, 2001), pp. 211–25.

Orwell, G., 'The Art of Donald McGill', in G. Orwell, *Decline of the English Murder* (Harmondsworth, 2011).

Osgerby, B., 'From the Roaring Twenties to the Swinging Sixties: Continuity and Change in British Youth Culture 1929–59', in B. Brivati and H. Jones (ed.), *What Difference Did the War Make?* (London, 1995), pp. 80–98.

Petley, J., 'A Crude Sort of Entertainment for a Crude Sort of Audience: The British Critics and Horror Cinema', in S. Chibnall and J. Petley (eds), *British Horror Cinema* (London, 2002), pp. 23–41.

Reynolds, S., 'The Rift of Retro: 1962? Or Twenty Years On?', in D. Pih (ed.), *Glam: The Performance of Style* (Liverpool, 2013), pp. 63–74.

Rock, P., and Cohen, S., 'The Teddy Boy', in V. Bogdanor and R. Skidelsky (eds), *The Age of Affluence, 1951–64* (Basingstoke, 1970), pp. 288–320.

Russell, D., 'Music and Northern Identity 1890–c.1965', in N. Kirk (ed.), *Northern Identities: Historical Interpretations of 'The North' and 'Northerness'* (Aldershot, 2000).

Savage, J., 'Tainted Love: The Influence of Male Homosexuality and Sexual Divergence on Pop Music and Culture Since the War', in A. Tomlinson (ed.), *Consumption, Identity and Style* (London, 1990), pp. 153–71.

Saville, J., 'Henry Twist (1870–1934)', in J. Saville and J. M. Bellamy (eds), *Dictionary of Labour Biography Vol. II* (Basingstoke, 1974), pp. 370–1.

Shank, B., 'From Rice to Ice: The Face of Race in Rock and Pop', in S. Frith, W. Straw and J. Street (eds), *The Cambridge Companion to Pop and Rock* (Cambridge, 2001), pp. 256–71.

Singleton, J., 'The Decline of the British Cotton Industry since 1940', in M. B. Rose (ed.), *The Lancashire Cotton Industry: A History Since 1700* (Preston, 1996).

Stokes, M., 'Introduction', in M. Stokes (ed.), *Ethnicity, Identity and Music: The Musical Construction of Place* (Oxford, 1994).

Straw, W., 'Consumption', in S. Frith, W. Straw and J. Street (eds), *The Cambridge Companion to Pop and Rock* (Cambridge, 2001), pp. 53–90.

Street, J., 'Youth Culture and the Emergence of Popular Music', in T. Gourvish and A. O' Day (eds), *Britain Since 1945* (Basingstoke, 1981), pp. 305–23.

———, 'Shock Waves. The Authoritarian Response to Popular Music', in D. Strinati and S. Wagg (eds), *Come on Down? Popular Media Culture in Post-War Britain* (London, 1992), pp. 302–24.

———, 'Rock, Pop and Politics', in S. Frith, W. Straw and J. Street (eds), *The Cambridge Companion to Pop and Rock* (Cambridge, 2001), pp. 243–55.

Taylor, I., and Wall, D., 'Beyond the Skinheads: Comments on the Emergence and Significance of the Glam Rock Cult', in G. Mungham and G. Pearson (eds), *Working Class Youth Culture* (London, 1976), pp. 105–23.

Thornton, S., 'Moral Panic, The Media and British Rave Culture', in A. Ross and T. Rose (eds), *Microphone Fiends: Youth Music and Youth Culture* (London, 1994), pp. 176–92.

Turner, A. W., 'Rocking While Rome Burns: The Politics of Glam', in D. Pih (ed.), *Glam: The Performance of Style* (Liverpool, 2013), pp. 75–82.

Waite, M., 'Sex 'n' Drugs 'n' Rock 'n' Roll (and Communism) in the 1960s', in G. Andrews, N. Fishman and K. Morgan (eds), *Opening the Books: Essays on the Social and Cultural History of the British Communist Party* (London, 1995), pp. 210–24.

Watt, J., 'For Your Pleasure: The Quest for Glamour in British Fashion 1969–1972', in D. Pih (ed.), *Glam: The Performance of Style* (Liverpool, 2013), pp. 39–52.

Wrigley, C., 'Women in the Labour Market and Unions', in J. McIlroy, N. Fishman and A. Campbell (eds), *The High Tide of British Trade Unionism. Trade Unions and Industrial Politics, 1964–79* (Monmouth, 2007), pp. 43–69.

6. Books

Addison, P., *The Road to 1945. British Politics and the Second World War* (London, 1975).

Aldgate, A., and Richards, J., *Best of British: Cinema and Society from 1930 to the Present* (London, 1999).

Allen, R., *Glam* (London, 1973).

Almond, M., *Tainted Life: The Autobiography* (London, 1999).

Altschuler, G. C., *All Shook Up: How Rock 'n' Roll Changed America* (Oxford, 2003).

Arnot, R. P., *South Wales Miners: A History of the South Wales Miners' Federation, 1898–1914* (London, 1967).

Auslander, P., *Performing Glam Rock: Gender and Theatricality in Popular Music* (Ann Arbor, 2006).

Bacon, T., *London Live: From the Yardbirds to Pink Floyd to the Sex Pistols. The Inside Story of Live Band's in the Capital's Trail-Blazing Music Clubs* (London, 1999).

Bagwell, P. S., *The Railwaymen: The History of the National Union of Railwaymen Vol. 2: The Beeching Era and After* (London, 1982).

Barnes, R., *Mods!* (London, 1979).

Barstow, S., *A Kind of Loving* (London, 1960).

Beckett, A., *When the Lights Went Out: Britain in the Seventies* (London, 2009).

Belchem, J., *Irish, Catholic and Scouse: The History of the Liverpool Irish, 1800–1939* (Liverpool, 2007).

———, *Merseypride: Essays in Liverpool Exceptionalism* (Liverpool, 2000).

———, (ed.), *Liverpool 800: Culture, Character and History* (Chicago, 2012).

Bennett, A., *Popular Music and Youth Culture: Music, Identity and Place* (Basingstoke, 2000).

Bennett, A., and Stratton, J., (eds), *Britpop and the English Music Tradition* (Aldershot, 2010).

Benson, J., *The Rise of Consumer Society in Britain* (London, 1994).

Berger-Hamerschlag, M., *Journey into a Fog* (London, 1955).

Black, L., *The Political Culture of the Left in Affluent Britain, 1951–64* (Basingstoke, 2003).

Black, P., *Black by Design: A 2-Tone Memoir* (London, 2011).

Blackwell, T., and Seabrook, J., *A World Still to Win: The Reconstruction of the Post-War Working Class* (London, 1985).

Blandy, M., *Razor Edge: The Story of a Youth Club* (London, 1967).

Boggs, Carl., *Gramsci's Marxism* (London, 1980).

Bourke, J., *Working-Class Cultures in Britain 1890–1960: Gender, Class and Ethnicity* (London, 1994).

Bowman, R., *Soulsville USA: The Story of Stax Records* (New York, 2003).

Bracewell, M., *Re-make/Re-model: Art, Pop, Fashion and the Making of Roxy Music, 1953–1972* (London, 2007).

———, *England Is Mine. Pop Life in Albion from Wilde to Goldie* (London, 1998).

Brackett, D. (ed.), *The Pop, Rock and Soul Reader* (Oxford, 2005).

Braddock, J., and B., *The Braddocks* (London, 1963).

Bradley, D., *Understanding Rock 'n' Roll: Popular Music in Britain 1955–1964* (Buckingham, 1992).

Braine, J., *Room at the Top* (London, 1957).

Brake, M., *Comparative Youth Culture: The Sociology of Youth Subcultures in America, Britain and Canada* (London, 1985).

Bret, D., *George Formby: A Troubled Genius* (London, 1999).
Brew, J. M., *Youth and Youth Groups* (London, 1957, 1968).
Brocken, M., *Other Voices: Hidden Histories of Liverpool's Popular Music Scenes, 1930s–1970s* (Aldershot, 2010).
Bromberg, C., *The Wicked Ways of Malcolm McLaren* (New York, 1989).
Brown, J. N., *Dropping Anchor, Setting Sail. Geographies of Race in Black Liverpool* (Princeton, 2003).
Brunning, B., *Blues: The British Connection* (Poole, 1986).
Buckley, D., *Strange Fascination: David Bowie, The Definitive Story* (1999, 2005).
Bulmer, J., *The North* (Liverpool, 2012).
Burton, P., *Parallel Lives* (London, 1985).
Bushell, G., *Hoolies: True Stories of Britain's Biggest Street Battles* (London, 2010).
Campbell, B., *Wigan Pier Revisited: Poverty and Politics in the 80s* (1984).
Campbell, J., *Edward Heath. A Biography,* (London, 1993).
Campbell, S., *Irish Blood English Heart: Second Generation Irish Musicians in England* (Cork, 2011).
Cann, K., *Any Day Now: David Bowie. The London Years, 1947–1974* (London, 2010).
Carey, J., *What Good Are the Arts* (London, 2005).
Cashmore, E. E., *No Future: Youth and Society* (London, 1984).
Cato, P., *Crash Course for the Ravers: A Glam Odyssey* (Lockerbie, 1997).
Cawthorne, N., *The Who and the Making of Tommy* (London, 2005).
Chambers, I., *Urban Rhythms: Pop Music and Popular Culture* (Basingstoke, 1985).
———, *Popular Culture. The Metropolitan Experience* (London, 1986).
Chaplin, S., *The Day of the Sardine* (London, 1961).
Chapman, R. *Selling the Sixties: The Pirates and Pop Music Radio* (London, 1992).
Charlesworth, C., and Hanel, E., *The Who: The Complete Guide to Their Music* (London, 2004).
Clay, M., *Café Racers: Rockers, Rock 'n' Roll and the Coffee Bar Cult* (London, 1988).
Clayson, A., *The Yardbirds: The Band that Launched Eric Clapton, Jeff Beck, Jimmy Page* (London, 2002).
———, *Hamburg: The Cradle of British Rock* (London, 1998).
———, *Call Up the Groups: The Golden Age of British Beat, 1962–67* (London, 1985).
———, *Back in the High Life: A Biography of Steve Winwood* (London, 1988).
Clayson, A., and Leigh, S., *The Walrus Was Ringo: 101 Beatles Myths Debunked* (New Malden, 2003).
Clayson, A., and Sutcliffe, P., *Backbeat: Stuart Sutcliffe – The Lost Beatle* (London, 1994).
Coates, K., and Silburn, R., *Poverty: The Forgotten Englishmen* (Harmondsworth, 1970).
Cohen, P., *Subcultural Conflict and Working Class Community* (Birmingham, 1972).
Cohen, S., *Rock Culture in Liverpool: Popular Music in the Making* (Oxford, 1991).
———, *Folk Devils and Moral Panics: The Creation of the Mods and Rockers* (London, 2010).
Cohn, N., *I Am Still the Greatest Says Johnny Angelo* (Harpenden, 1967, 2003).
———, *Ball the Wall: Nik Cohn in the Age of Rock* (London, 1989).
———, *Awopbopaloobop Alopbamboom: Pop from the Beginning* (London, 1969).
Coleman, R., *Brian Epstein: The Man Who Made the Beatles* (Harmondsworth, 1990).
Collis, J., *Gene Vincent and Eddie Cochran: Rock 'n' Roll Revolutionaries* (London, 2004).
Colls, R., *Identity of England* (Oxford, 2004).
Connell, J., and Gibson, C., *Sound Tracks: Popular Music, Identity and Place* (London, 2003).

Connolly, R., *That'll Be the Day* (Glasgow, 1973).
Constantine, L., *Colour Bar* (London, 1954).
Cooper, D., *The Musical Traditions of Northern Ireland and Its Diaspora: Community and Conflict* (Aldershot, 2010).
Cornelius, J., *Liverpool 8* (London, 2001).
Costello, R. H., *Black Liverpool: The Early History of Britain's Oldest Black Community, 1730–1918* (Liverpool, 2001).
Cox, B., Shirley, J., and Short, M., *The Fall of Scotland Yard* (Harmondsworth, 1977).
Dankworth, J., *Jazz in Revolution* (London, 1999).
Davey, K., *English Imaginaries: Six Studies in Anglo-British Modernity* (London, 1999).
Davies, A., *Leisure, Gender and Poverty: Working-Class Culture in Salford and Manchester, 1900–1939* (Manchester, 1992).
Davies, A. and Fielding, S., (eds), *Workers Worlds: Cultures and Communities in Manchester and Salford, 1880–1939* (Manchester, 1992).
Davies, D., *Kink: An Autobiography* (London, 1996).
Davies, R., *X-Ray: The Unauthorised Autobiography* (London, 1996).
Davies, S., *Liverpool Labour: Social and Political Influences on the Development of the Labour Party in Liverpool, 1900–1939* (Keele, 1996).
Davis, J., *Youth and the Condition of Britain: Images of Adolescent Conflict* (London, 1990).
Dawson, L., *A Clown Too Many* (Glasgow, 1985).
Dawson, S. T., *Holiday Camps in Twentieth Century Britain: Packaging Pleasure* (Manchester, 2011).
Deakin, M. and Willis, J., *Johnny Go Home* (London, 1976).
Denselow, R., *When the Music's Over: The Story of Political Pop* (London, 1989).
Dewe, M., *The Skiffle Craze* (London, 1998).
Doggett, P., *The Man Who Sold the World: David Bowie and the 1970s* (London, 2011).
———, *There's A Riot Going On: Revolutionaries, Rock Stars and the Rise and Fall of the 60s Counter Culture* (London, 2007).
Donnelly, J., *Jimmy the Weed. Inside the Quality Street Gang: My Life in the Manchester Underworld* (Lancashire, 2012).
Dougan, J., *The Who Sell Out* (London, 2006).
Du Noyer, P., *In the City: A Celebration of London Music* (London, 2009).
———, *Liverpool Wondrous Place: Music from the Cavern to the Coral* (London, 2004).
Dunn, N., *Poor Cow* (London, 1967).
———, *Up the Junction* (London, 1963).
Echols, A., *Hot Stuff: Disco and the Remaking of American Culture* (New York, 2010).
Eddington, R., *Sent From Coventry: The Chequered Past of Two Tone* (London, 2003).
Edgecombe, J., *Black Scandal* (London, 2002).
Elms, R., *The Way We Wore: A Life in Threads* (London, 2005).
Epstein, B., *A Cellarful of Noise* (London, 1964).
Evans, J., *The Penguin TV Companion* (Harmondsworth, 2003).
Ewbank, T., and Hildred, S., *Rod Stewart: The New Biography* (London, 2003).
Fabian, J., and Byrne, J., *Groupie* (London, 1969).
Farley, K., *They Rocked, We Rolled: A Personal and Oral Account of Rock 'n' Roll in and around Wolverhampton and the West Midlands 1956–1969* (Wolverhampton, 2010).
Farley, P., *Distant Voices, Still Lives* (London, 2006).
Farren, M., *Give the Anarchist a Cigarette* (London, 2001).
Farson, D., *Never A Normal Man* (London, 1997).
Feldman, C. F., *We Are the Mods: A Transnational History of a Youth Subculture* (New York, 2009).

Ferguson, A. P., *Burtonwood* (London, 1986).
Fewtrell, E., and Thompson, S., *King of the Clubs: The Eddie Fewtrell Story* (Studley, 2007).
Fitzwalter, R., and Taylor, D., *Web of Corruption: The Story of John Poulson and T. Dan Smith* (London, 1981).
Fletcher, T., *Dear Boy: The Life of Keith Moon* (London, 1998).
Flowers, A., and Histon, V., (eds), *It's My Life! 1960s Newcastle: Memories from People Who Were There* (Newcastle, 2009).
Fowler, A., *Lancashire Cotton Operatives and Work, 1900–1950: A Social History of Lancashire Cotton Operatives in the Twentieth Century* (Aldershot, 2003).
Fowler, D., *Youth Culture in Modern Britain, c.1920–c.1970: From Ivory Tower to Global Movement – A New History* (Basingstoke, 2008).
Frame, P., *The Restless Generation: How Rock Music Changed the Face of 1950s Britain* (London, 2007).
Francis, H., and Smith, D., *The Fed: A History of the South Wales Miners in the Twentieth Century* (London, 1980).
Freeman, G., *The Undergrowth of Literature* (London, 1969).
———, *The Leather Boys* (London, 1961).
Frith, S., *Sound Effects: Youth, Leisure, and the Politics of Rock 'n' Roll* (London, 1983).
Frith, S., and Horne, H., *Art into Pop* (London, 1987).
Fryer, P., *Staying Power: The History of Black People in Britain* (London, 1991).
Fyvel, T. R., *The Insecure Offenders. Rebellious Youth in the Welfare State* (Harmondsworth, 1961).
Gale, R., *Billy Boston: Rugby League Footballer* (London, 2009).
Gardner, J., *Over Here: The GI's in Wartime Britain* (London, 1992).
Garfield, S., *The Wrestling* (London, 1996).
Gate, R., *Rugby League: An Illustrated History* (London, 1989).
Gelder, K., *Subcultures: Cultural Histories and Social Practice* (London, 2007).
Gelder, K., and Thornton, S., (eds), *The Subcultures Reader* (London, 2005).
Geller, D., (edited by Anthony Wall), *The Brian Epstein Story* (London, 1999).
George, B (with Spencer Bright), *Take It Like a Man: The Autobiography of Boy George* (London, 1994).
Gialiano, G., *Behind Blue Eyes: A Life of Pete Townshend* (London, 1996).
Gill, J., *Queer Noises: Male and Female Homosexuality in Twentieth-Century Music* (London, 1995).
Gillett, C., *The Sound of the City: The Rise of Rock and Roll* (Gateshead, 1970).
Gilroy, P., *The Black Atlantic: Modernity and Double Consciousness* (London, 1993).
———, *There Ain't No Black in the Union Jack* (London, 2002).
Glucksmann, M., *Women Assemble: Women Workers and the New Industries in Inter-War Britain* (London, 1990).
Gorman, P., *The Look: Adventures in Rock and Pop Fashion* (London, 2006).
Gosling, R., *Sum Total* (London, 1962).
———, *Personal Copy: A Memoir of the Sixties* (Nottingham, 1980).
Gramsci, A., (edited by Quintin Hoare and Geoffrey Nowell Smith), *Selections from the Prison Notebooks* (London, 1986).
Green, J., *Days In The Life: Voices from the English Underground, 1961–1971* (London, 1998).
Green, S., *Rachman* (London, 1979).
Guralnick, P., *Sweet Soul Music: Rhythm and Blues and the Southern Dream of Freedom* (London, 1986).

Hale, D., and Thornton, T., *Club 60 & The Esquire: Sheffield Sounds in the 60s* (Sheffield, 2002).
Hall, L. A., *Sex, Gender and Social Change in Britain Since 1880* (Basingstoke, 2000).
Hall, S., and Jefferson, T., (eds), *Resistance Through Rituals: Youth Subcultures in Post-war Britain* (London, 1976).
Hall, S. and Whannel, P., *The Popular Arts* (London, 1964).
Hamblett, C., and Deverson, J., *Generation X* (London, 1964).
Hanley, L., *Estates: An Intimate History* (London, 2007).
Hanson, S., *From Silent Screen to Multi-Screen: A History of Cinema Exhibition in Britain Since 1896* (Manchester, 2007).
Harker, D., *One for The Money: Politics and Popular Song* (London, 1980).
Harry, B., *Bigger Than the Beatles: Liverpool the Story of the City's Musical Odyssey* (Liverpool, 2009).
Haslam, D., *Manchester England: The Story of a Pop Cult City* (London, 1999).
———, *Not Abba: The Real Story of the 1970s* (London, 2005).
Hasted, N., *The Story of the Kinks: You Really Got Me* (London, 2011).
Hawkins, S., *The British Pop Dandy: Masculinity, Popular Culture and Culture* (Aldershot, 2009).
Hebdige, D., *Subculture: The Meaning of Style* (London, 1979).
———, *Cut 'n' Mix: Culture, Identity and Caribbean Music* (London, 1987).
Hedling, E., *Lindsay Anderson: Maverick Film-maker* (London, 1998).
Heffer, E., *Never a Yes Man: The Life and Politics of an Adopted Liverpudlian* (London, 1991).
Henessey, P., *Having It So Good: Britain in the Fifties* (London, 2006).
Herbert, J., *The Rats* (London, 1974).
Heron, L., *Truth, Dare or Promise: Girls Growing Up in the Fifties* (London, 1985).
Hewison, R., *Culture and Consensus: England, Art and Politics Since 1940* (London, 1995).
Hewitt, P., and Hellier, J., *Steve Marriott: All Too Beautiful* (London, 2004).
———, (ed.), *The Sharper Word: A Mod Anthology* (London, 2002).
———, *The Soul Stylists: Six Decades of Modernism – From Mods to Casuals* (Edinburgh, 2000).
Hildred, S., and Ewbank, T., *Roger Daltrey: The Biography* (London, 2012).
Hill, J., *Sex, Class and Realism. British Cinema 1956–1963* (London, 1986, 1997).
———, *Ken Loach: The Politics of Film and Television* (London, 2011).
Hill, S., *Blerwytirhwg? The Place of Welsh Pop Music* (Aldershot, 2007).
Hinman, D., *The Kinks All Day and All of the Night: Day-by-Day Concerts, Recordings and Broadcasts, 1961–1996* (San Francisco, 2004).
Hoggart, R., *The Uses of Literacy: Aspects of Working-Class Life with Special Reference to Publications and Entertainments* (Harmondsworth, 1957).
Holder, N., *Who's Crazee Now? My Autobiography* (London, 1999).
Home, S., *Cranked Up Really High: Genre Theory and Punk Rock* (Hove, 1995).
Horn, A., *Juke Box Britain: Americanisation and Youth Culture, 1945–60* (Manchester, 2009).
Hornsey, R., *The Spiv and the Architect: Unruly Life in Postwar London* (Minneapolis, 2010).
Hoskyns, B., *Glam! Bowie, Bolan and the Glitter Rock Revolution* (London, 1998).
Houlbrook, M., *Queer London: Perils and Pleasures in the Sexual Metropolis, 1918–1957* (Chicago, 2005).
Howell, D., *The Politics of the NUM: A Lancashire View* (Manchester, 1989).

Hughes, D., *Friday on My Mind: A Rock 'n' Roll Lifestyle* (London, 2010).
Humphries, P., *Lonnie Donegan and the Birth of British Rock and Roll* (London, 2012).
Hunt, L., *British Low Culture: From Safari Suits to Sexploitation* (London, 1998).
Ingle, S., *George Orwell: A Political Life* (Manchester, 1993).
Inglis, F., *Raymond Williams* (London, 1995).
Inglis, I., (ed.), *The Beatles, Popular Music and Society: A Thousand Voices* (Basingstoke, 2000).
Ings, A., *Rockin' At The 2 I's Coffee Bar* (Brighton, 2010).
Jackson, B., and Marsden, D., *Education and the Working Class* (Harmondsworth, 1962).
Jackson, S., *An Indiscreet Guide to Soho* (London, 1948).
Johns, A., *Death of a Pirate: British Radio and the Making of the Information Age* (New York, 2011).
Johnson, H., *A Bone in My Flute* (London, 1994).
Jones, D., *When Ziggy Played Guitar: David and Four Minutes That Shook the World* (London, 2012).
Jones, H., *Crime in a Changing Society* (Harmondsworth, 1965).
Jones, R. M., and Rees, D. B., *Liverpool Welsh and Their Religion* (Wales, 1984).
Jones, D. C., (ed.), *The Social Survey of Merseyside* (Liverpool, 1934).
Kerr, M., *The People of Ship Street* (London, 1958).
Kidd, A., *Manchester: A History* (Lancaster, 2006).
Kielty, M., *Big Noise: The History of Scottish Rock 'n' Roll* (Edinburgh, 2006).
Kirk, J., *The British Working Class in the Twentieth Century: Film, Literature and Television* (Cardiff, 2009).
Kirk, N., (ed.), *Northern Identities: Historical Interpretations of 'The North' and 'Northerness'* (Aldershot, 2000).
Kitts, T. M., *Ray Davies: Not Like Everybody Else* (London, 2008).
Klein, J., *Woody Guthrie: A Life* (London, 1989).
Knight, N., *Skinhead* (London, 1982).
Koestler, A., *Suicide of a Nation* (London, 1963).
Koningh, M. D., and Griffiths, M., *Tighten Up!. The History of Reggae in the UK* (London, 2003).
Kureishi, H., and Savage, J., (eds), *The Faber Book of Pop* (London, 1993).
Kynaston, D., *Family Britain 1951–57* (London, 2009).
Laing, D., *One Chord Wonders: Power and Meaning in Punk Rock* (London, 1985).
Lane, T., *Liverpool. City of the Sea* (Liverpool, 1997).
Laurie, P., *The Teenage Revolution* (Harmondsworth, 1965).
Lawson, A., *It Happened in Manchester: The True Story of Manchester's Music 1958–1965* (Bury, 1990).
Leach, S., *The Rocking City: The Explosive Birth of the Beatles* (Liverpool, 1999).
Lee, C. P., *Shake, Rattle and Rain: Popular Music Making in Manchester 1955–1995* (Devon, 2002).
———, *Like the Night (Revisited): Bob Dylan and the Road to the Manchester Free Trade Hall* (2004).
Leigh, S., *The Best of Fellas: The Story of Bob Wooler – Liverpool's First DJ. The Man Who Introduced the Beatles* (London, 2002).
———, *Let's Go Down the Cavern* (London, 1984).
Leigh, S., and Firminger, J., *Halfway to Paradise: Britpop, 1955–1962* (Folkestone, 1996).
———, *Wondrous Face: The Billy Fury Story* (Folkestone, 2005).

Leng, S., *The Twisted Tale of Glam Rock* (Santa Barbara, 2010).
Lester, R., *Boutique London. A History: King's Road to Carnaby Street* (Bath, 2010).
Levy, S., *Ready, Steady, Go! Swinging London and the Invention of Cool* (London, 2002).
Little, D., *The Coronation Street Story: Celebrating Thirty-Five Years of the Street* (London, 1998).
Lydon, J., (with Keith and Kent Zimmerman), *Rotten: No Irish, No Blacks, No Dogs* (New York, 1994).
Lynskey, D., *33 Revolutions Per Minute: A History of Protest Songs* (London, 2010).
MacDonald, I., *Revolution in the Head* (London, 1994, 1995).
———, *The People's Music* (London, 2003).
MacInnes, C., *City of Spades* (London, 1957).
———, *Absolute Beginners* (London, 1959).
Maitland, S., *Very Heaven: Looking Back at the 1960s* (London, 1988).
Mandelkau, J., *Buttons: The Making of a President* (London, 1971).
Mandler, P., *The English National Character: The History of an Idea from Edmund Burke to Tony Blair* (New Haven, 2006).
Marcus, G., *Lipstick Traces: A Secret History of the Twentieth Century* (London, 1997).
———, *Mystery Train: Images of America in Rock 'n' Roll Music* (London, 1997).
Marsh, D., *Before I Get Old: The Story of the Who* (London, 1985).
Marshall, G., *Spirit of 69: A Skinhead Bible* (Lockerbie, 1994).
Marwick, A., *British Society Since 1945* (Harmondsworth, 1982).
———, *The Sixties: Cultural Revolution in Britain, France, Italy and the United States, c.1958–c.1974* (Oxford, 1998).
Matlock, G., *I Was A Teenage Sex Pistol* (London, 1990).
Mays, J. B., *Growing Up in the City: A Study of Juvenile Delinquency in an Urban Neighbourhood* (Liverpool, 1954).
Mcaleer, D., *Hit Parade Heroes: British Beat before the Beatles* (London, 1993).
———, *Beat Boom: Pop Goes the Sixties* (London, 1994).
———, *Hit Singles Top 20 Charts from 1954 to the Present Day* (London, 2003).
McDevitt, C., *Skiffle: The Definitive Inside Story* (London, 1997).
McKay, G., *Circular Breathing: The Cultural Politics of Jazz in Britain* (Durham, 2005).
McKibbin, R., *Classes and Cultures: England 1918–1951* (Oxford, 1998).
McLagan, I., *All The Rage: A Riotous Romp Through Rock & Roll History* (New York, 2000).
McManus, K., *Nashville of the North: Country Music in Liverpool* (Liverpool, 2004).
McMichael, J., and Lyons, J., *The Who Concert File* (London, 1997, 2004).
McRobbie, A., *Feminism and Youth Culture* (Cambridge, 1991).
Medovoi, L., *Rebels: Youth and the Cold War Origins of Identity* (Durham, 2005).
Melly, G., *Revolt Into Style: The Pop Arts in the 50s and 60s* (London, 1989).
Melly, J., *Last Orders, Please: Rod Stewart, the Faces and the Britain We Forgot* (London, 2003).
Miles, B., *London Calling: A Countercultural History of London Since 1945* (London, 2010).
Mitchell, T., *Popular Music and Local Identity: Rock, Pop and Rap in Europe and Oceania* (Leicester, 1996).
Moorhouse, G., *Britain in the Sixties: The Other England* (Harmondsworth, 1964).
Morse, M., *The Unattached* (Harmondsworth, 1960).
Mort, F., *Cultures of Consumption: Masculinities and Social Space in Late-Twentieth Century Britain* (London, 1996).
———, *Capital Affairs: London and the Making of the Permissive Society* (New Haven, 2010).

Morton, J., *Gangland Soho* (London, 2008).
Motion, A., *The Lamberts: George, Constant and Kit* (London, 1986).
Mundy, J., and Higham, D., *Don't Forget Me. The Eddie Cochran Story* (New York, 2000).
Myatt, S., *The Mod Years* (London, 2005).
Napier-Bell, S., *Black Vinyl White Powder* (London, 2002).
Neal, F., *Sectarian Violence: The Liverpool Experience, 1819–1914. An Aspect of Anglo-Irish History* (Manchester, 1988).
Nehring, N., *Flowers in the Dustbin: Culture, Anarchy, and Postwar England* (Ann Arbor, 1993).
Nelson, E., *The British Counter-Culture 1966–73: A Study of the Underground Press* (Basingstoke, 1989).
Newton, K., *The Jazz Scene* (Harmondsworth, 1959).
Nolan, D., *I Swear I Was There: The Gig That Changed the World* (2006).
Norman, F., and Bernard, J., *Soho Night and Day* (London, 1966).
Norman, P., *Shout! The Beatles in Their Generation* (London, 1981).
———, *The Stones: The Acclaimed Biography* (London, 2002).
———, *John Lennon. The Life* (London, 2008).
Novick, J., and Middles, M., *Wham Bam Thank You Glam: A Celebration of the 70s* (London, 1998).
Nowell, D., *Too Darn Soulful: The Story of Northern Soul* (London, 1999).
Nuttall, J., *Bomb Culture* (London, 1970).
Oldham, A. L., *Stoned* (London, 2001).
Oliver, P., (ed.), *Black Music in Britain: Essays on the Afro-Contribution to Popular Music* (Buckingham, 1990).
Orwell, G., *The Road to Wigan Pier* (London, 1937).
———, *The Lion and the Unicorn. Socialism and the English Genius* (Harmondsworth, 1990).
———, *Decline of the English Murder* (Harmondsworth, 2011).
Osgerby, B., *Youth Culture in Britain Since 1945* (Oxford, 1998).
Panter, H., *Ska'd for Life: A Personal Journey with the Specials* (Basingstoke, 2007).
Parker, T., *The Ploughboy* (London, 1965).
Patrick, J., *A Glasgow Gang Observed* (London, 1973).
Patterson, S., *Dark Strangers. A Sociological Study of the Absorption of a Recent West Indian Migrant Group in Brixton, South London* (London, 1963).
Paytress, M., *Bolan: The Rise and Fall of a Twentieth Century Superstar* (London, 1992).
Pearson, G., *Hooligan: A History of Respectable Fears* (Basingstoke, 1983).
Perry, F. *An Autobiography* (London, 1984).
Picker, J. M. *Victorian Soundscapes* (Oxford, 2003).
Pih, D., (ed.), *Glam: The Performance of Style* (Liverpool, 2013).
Pilkington, E., *Beyond the Mother Country: West Indians and the Notting Hill White Riots* (London, 1988).
Pirie, P., *A New Heritage of Horror: The English Gothic Cinema* (London, 2009).
Pratt, R., *Rhythm and Resistance: Explorations in the Political Uses of Popular Music* (London, 1990).
Raison, T., (ed.), *Youth in New Society* (London, 1966).
Ramsay, W. G., *The Ace Café Then and Now* (Harlow, 2002).
Rawlings, T., *Mod: A Very British Phenomenon* (London, 2000).
Raymond Williams, *Culture and Society, 1780–1950* (London, 1984).
Reed, J., *The King of Carnaby Street: The Life of John Stephen* (London, 2010).
Repsch, J., *The Legendary Joe Meek: The Telstar Man* (London, 2001).

Richards, J., *Films and British National Identity: From Dickens to Dad's Army* (Manchester, 1997).

Richards, K., *Life* (London, 2010).

Richmond, A. H., *Colour Prejudice in Britain. A Study of West Indian Workers in Liverpool, 1941–1951* (London, 1954).

Ritson, M., and Russell, S., *The In Crowd: The Story of the Northern and Rare Soul Scene Volume 1* (London, 1999).

Robb, J., *Punk Rock: An Oral History* (London, 2006).

Roberts, R., *The Classc Slum: Salford Life in the First Quarter of the Century* (Harmondsworth, 1971).

Robins, D., and Cohen, P., *Knuckle Sandwich: Growing Up in the Working Class City* (Harmondsworth, 1978).

Robinson, L., *Gay Men and the Left in Post-war Britain: How the Personal Got Political* (Manchester, 2011).

Rock, M., and Bowie, D., *Moonage Daydream: The Life and Times of Ziggy Stardust* (Bath, 2005).

Rogan, J., *Morrissey and Marr: The Severed Alliance* (London, 1992).

———, *The Kinks: The Sound and the Fury* (London, 1984).

———, *Starmakers and Svengalis: The History of British Pop Management* (London, 1988).

Rolph, C. H., *Women of the Streets: A Sociological Study of the Common Prostitute for the British Social Biology Council* (London, 1961).

Rowbotham, S., *Promise of a Dream: Remembering the Sixties* (Harmondsworth, 2000).

Rushton, N., *Northern Soul Stories* (London, 2009).

Russell, D., *Popular Music in England, 1840–1914* (Manchester, 1987).

———, *Looking North: Northern England and the National Imagination* (Manchester, 2004).

Russell, E., *Dear Mr Fantasy. Diary of a Decade: Our Time and Rock 'n' Roll* (London, 1985).

Rylatt, K., and Scott, P., *CENtral 1179: The Story of Manchester's Twisted Wheel Club* (London, 2001).

Sabin, R., (ed.), *Punk Rock: So What?: The Cultural Legacy of Punk* (London, 1999).

Salewicz, C., and Newman, S., *The Story of Island Records: Keep on Running* (New York, 2010).

Sampson, A., *The Anatomy of Britain* (London, 1962).

Samuel, R., *Theatres of Memory Vol. 1: Past and Present in Contemporary Culture,* (London, 1994).

———, *Theatres of Memory Vol. 1: Past and Present in Contemporary Culture* (London, 1994).

———, *Island Stories: Unravelling Britain: Theatres of Memory Vol. II* (edited by Alison Light, Sally Alexander and Gareth Stedman Jones), (London, 1998).

Sandbrook, D., *White Heat: A History of Britain in the Swinging Sixties* (London, 2006).

———, *Never Had It So Good: A History of Britain from Suez to the Beatles* (London, 2005).

———, *State of Emergency: The Way We Were, Britain, 1970–74* (London, 2010).

———, *Seasons in the Sun: The Battle for Britain, 1974–1979* (London, 2012).

Sandford, J., *Prostitutes* (London, 1977).

Savage, J., *The Kinks: The Official Biography* (London, 1984).

———, *England's Dreaming: Sex Pistols and Punk Rock* (London, 1991).

———, *Time Travel: Pop, Media and Sexuality 1976–96* (London, 1996).

———, *Teenage: The Creation of Youth, 1875–1945* (London, 2007).

Savage, M., *Identities and Social Change in Britain Since 1940: The Politics of Method* (Oxford, 2010).
Savile, J., *Love is an Uphill Thing* (London, 1978).
Scala, M., *Diary of a Teddy Boy: A Memoir of the Long Sixties* (London, 2000).
Selvon, S., *The Lonely Londoners* (London, 1956).
Shanks, M., *The Stagnant Society* (London, 1961).
Shapiro, H., *Waiting for The Man: The Story of Drugs and Popular Music* (London, 1988).
Shaw, D., *Casino* (London, 2000).
Sillitoe, A., *Saturday Night and Sunday Morning* (London, 1958).
Smith, G., *When Jim Crow Met John Bull: Black American Soldiers in World War II Britain* (London, 1987).
Smith, S. E., *Dancing in the Street: Motown and the Cultural Politics of Detroit* (Cambridge, 2000).
Spencer, J., Tuxford, J., and Dennis, N., *Stress and Release in an Urban Estate: A Study in Action Research* (London, 1964).
Spitz, B., *The Beatles: The Biography* (New York, 2005).
Springhall, J., *Youth, Popular Culture and Moral Panics: Penny Gaffs to Gangsta-Rap, 1830–1996* (London, 1998).
Stafford, D., and C., *Fings Ain't Wot They Used T'Be: The Lionel Bart Story* (London, 2011).
Staple, N., *Original Rude Boy: From Borstal to the Specials* (London, 2008).
Stead, P., *Film and the Working Class: The Feature Film in British and American Society* (London, 1989).
Steel-Perkins, C., and Smith, R., *The Teds* (Stockport, 1979).
Stewart, R., *Rod: The Autobiography* (London, 2012).
Street, J., *Rebel Rock: The Politics of Popular Music* (Oxford, 1986).
———, *Music and Politics* (London, 2011).
Stuart, J., *Rockers!* (London, 1987).
Swenson, J., *The Who* (London, 1981).
Sykes, B., *Sit Down! Listen To This! The Roger Eagle Story* (Manchester, 2012).
Tenny, V., *Just Ask The Lonely* (London, 1970).
The Paint House: Words from an East End Gang (Harmondsworth, 1972).
Thompson, B., *Ban This Filth!: Letters From the Mary Whitehouse Archive* (London, 2012).
Thompson, D., *20th Century Rock and Roll: Glam Rock* (London, 2000).
———, *2 Tone, The Specials and the World in Flame* (London, 2004).
———, *Blockbuster! The True Story of the Sweet* (London, 2010).
———, *Children of the Revolution: The Glam Rock Story, 1970–75* (London, 2010).
Thompson, E. P., *The Making of the English Working Class* (Harmondsworth, 1963).
Thompson, E., and Gutman, D., *The Bowie Companion* (London, 1993).
Tomkinson, M., *The Pornbrokers: The Rise of the Soho Sex Barons* (London, 1982).
Tomlinson, R., *Ricky* (London, 2003).
Tosches, N., *Hell Fire: The Jerry Lee Lewis Story* (Harmondsworth, 1982, 2007).
Toulmin, V., *Pleasurelands: All The Fun of the Fair* (Hastings, 2003).
Townshend, J., *The Young Devils: Experiences of a School Teacher* (London, 1958).
Townshend, P., *Who I Am* (London, 2012).
Tremlett, G., *The Slade Story* (London, 1975).
Trynka, P., *Starman: David Bowie The Definitive Biography* (London, 2010).
Turner, A. W., *Crisis? What Crisis? Britain in the 1970s* (London, 2008).
Unterberger, R., *Won't Get Fooled Again: The Who from Lifehouse to Quadrophenia* (London, 2011).

Vermorel, F., and J., *Sex Pistols: The Inside Story* (London, 1978).
———, *Starlust. The Secret Fantasies of Fans* (London, 1985, 2011).
Viscounti, T., (with Richard Havers), *Bowie, Bolan and the Brooklyn Boy. The Autobiography* (London, 2007).
Von Daniken, E., *Chariots of the Gods* (London, 1968).
Wald, E., *How the Beatles Destroyed Rock 'n' Roll: An Alternative History of American Popular Music* (Oxford, 2009).
Wale, M., *Vox Pop: Profiles of the Pop Process* (London, 1972).
Walker, A., *National Heroes: British Cinema in the Seventies and Eighties* (London, 1985).
Walton, J., *The British Seaside: Holidays and Resorts in the Twentieth Century* (Manchester, 2000).
Ward, B., *Just My Soul Responding: Rhythm and Blues, Black Consciousness and Race Relations* (London, 1998).
Watson, G., *Skins* (London, 2007).
Watson, I., *Song and Democratic Culture in Britain: An Approach to Popular Culture in Social Movements* (London, 1983).
Weeks, J., *Coming Out: Homosexual Politics in Britain from the Nineteenth Century to the Present* (London, 1983).
Weight, R., *Patriots: National Identity in Britain 1940–2000* (Basingstoke, 2002).
Welch, B., *Rock 'n' Roll I Gave You the Best Years of My Life: A Life in the Shadows* (London, 1989).
Wheatley, H., *Gothic Television* (Manchester, 2006).
Whitehouse, M., *Quite Contrary: An Autobiography* (London, 1984).
Wicke, P., *Rock Music: Culture, Aesthetics and Sociology* (Cambridge, 1995).
Wilkerson, M., *Who Are You: The Life of Pete Townshend. A Biography* (London, 2009).
Willetts, P., *Members Only: The Life and Times of Paul Raymond* (London, 2010).
Williams, A., with Marshall, W., *The Man Who Gave the Beatles Away: The Amazing True Story of the Beatles Early Years* (London, 1976).
Williams, R., *The Long Revolution* (Harmondsworth, 1961)
Williams, R., *Marxism and Literature* (Oxford, 1977).
Willmott, P., *Adolescent Boys of East London* (Harmondsworth, 1966).
Wilson, A., *Northern Soul: Music, Drugs and Subcultural Identity* (Cullompton, 2007).
Winstanley, R., and Nowell, D., *Soul Survivors: The Wigan Casino Story* (London, 2003).
Wolfe, T., *The Pump House Gang* (London, 1969, 1989).
Wong, M. L., *Chinese Liverpudlians: History of the Chinese Community in Liverpool* (Liverpool, 1989).
Wyman, B., *Stone Alone: The Story of a Rock 'n' Roll Band* (Harmondsworth, 1990).
Young, M., and Willmott, P., *Family and Kinship in East London* (Harmondsworth, 1986).
Young, R., *Electric Eden: Unearthing Britain's Visionary Music* (London, 2010).

7. Unpublished theses

Catterall, S., 'The Lancashire Coalfield, 1945–1972: The Politics of Industrial Change' (Unpublished DPhil thesis, University of York, 2001).
Wilson, J.P., 'Beats Apart: A Comparative History of Youth Culture and Popular Music in Liverpool and Newcastle upon Tyne, 1956–1965', (Unpublished PhD thesis, University of Northumbria, 2009).

8. Selected websites

www.rocksbackpages.com
www.modculture.co.uk
www.kindakinks.net
www.sex-pistols.net
www.5years.com
www.bowiewonderworld.com

9. Selected filmography

Rock Around the Clock (1956)
The Tommy Steele Story (1957)
The Flesh Is Weak (1957)
Violent Playground (1958)
Expresso Bongo (1959)
Peeping Tom (1960)
Saturday Night and Sunday Morning (1960)
The Wind of Change (1961)
A Taste of Honey (1961)
The Leather Boys (1963)
The Damned (1963)
This Sporting Life (1963)
That Kind of Girl (1963)
The Sorcerers (1967)
Blow Up (1967)
Privilege (1967)
Up the Junction (1967)
No Blade of Grass (1970)
Permissive (1970)
That'll Be the Day (1973)
O Lucky Man (1973)
Ziggy Stardust and the Spiders from Mars (1973)
Remember Me This Way (1974)
Flame (1974)
Tommy (1975)
Quadrophenia (1979)
Distant Voices, Still Lives (1998)
Velvet Goldmine (1998)
The Filth and the Fury (2000)
Of Time and the City (2008)

10. Selected discography

Billy Fury, The Sound of Fury (1960)
The Beatles, Please Please Me (1963)
The Beatles, With the Beatles (1963)
The Beatles, A Hard Days Night (1964)
Georgie Fame, Rhythm and Blues at the Flamingo (1964)
The Who, My Generation (1965)

The Who, The Who Sell Out (1967)
The Who, Tommy (1969)
The Who, Quadrophenia (1973)
The Kinks, Face to Face (1966)
The Kinks, Something Else (1967)
The Kinks, The Kinks Are The Village Green Preservation Society (1968)
The Kinks, Arthur (Or the Decline and Fall of the British Empire) (1969)
The Kinks, Lola Versus Power Man and the Moneygoround, Part One (1970)
The Kinks, Muswell Hillbillies (1971)
Slade, Slayed? (1972)
Slade, Slade Alive! (1972)
David Bowie, Hunky Dory (1971)
David Bowie, The Rise and Fall of Ziggy Stardust and the Spiders from Mars (1972)
David Bowie, Alladin Sane (1973)
David Bowie, Diamond Dogs (1974)
Sex Pistols, Never Mind the Bollocks Here's the Sex Pistols (1977)

Index